TO GO℠ ZAGAT® zagat.com℠ ZAGA
AT® zagat.com℠ ZAGAT TO GO℠ ZAG
.com℠ ZAGAT TO

S0-CFR-959

TO GO℠ ZAGA
AT® zagat.com℠ ZAGAT
.com℠ ZAGAT TO GO℠ ZAGAT® zaga
TO GO℠ ZAGAT® zagat.com℠ ZAGA
AT® zagat.com℠ ZAGAT TO GO℠ ZAG
.com℠ ZAGAT TO GO℠ ZAGAT® zaga
TO GO℠ ZAGAT® zagat.com℠ ZAGA
T® zagat.com℠ ZAGAT TO GO℠ ZAG

Use these handy Zagat
bookmarks to mark
your favorites and the
places you'd like to try.
Plus, we've included
re-useable blank book-
marks for you to write
on (and wipe off).
Browsing through your
Zagat guide has never
been easier!

.com℠ ZAGAT TO GO℠ ZAGAT® zaga
TO GO℠ ZAGAT® zagat.com℠ ZAGA
T® zagat.com℠ ZAGAT TO GO℠ ZAG
.com℠ ZAGAT TO GO℠ ZAGAT℠ zaga
TO GO℠ ZAGAT® zagat.com℠ ZAGA
T® zagat.com℠ ZAGAT TO GO℠ ZAG
.com℠ ZAGAT TO GO℠ ZAGAT® zaga
TO GO℠ ZAGAT® zagat.com℠ ZAGA
T® zagat.com℠ ZAGAT TO GO℠ ZAG

ZAGAT®

Paris
Restaurants
2007/08

LOCAL EDITOR
Alexander Lobrano

FRENCH EDITOR
Mary Deschamps

LOCAL COORDINATOR
Claire Fitzpatrick-Quimbrot

STAFF EDITOR
Troy Segal

Published and distributed by
Zagat Survey, LLC
4 Columbus Circle
New York, NY 10019
T: 212.977.6000
E: paris@zagat.com
www.zagat.com

ACKNOWLEDGMENTS

We thank George Balkind, Axel Baum, Sabine and Patrick Brassart, Catherine and Gilbert Brownstone, Frédéric Cassegrain, Jacques Dehornois, Elizabeth d'Hémery, Erin Emmett, Alexandra Ernst and Dean Garret Siegel, Laetitia Forget, Jack D. Gunther Jr., Anne and Gérard Mazet, Bruno Midavaine, Flore and Amaury de la Moussaye, Virginia and Jean Perrette, Denis Quimbrot, Dierdre and Alfred J. Ross, Steven Shukow, Boi Skoi, Anne and Hervé Thomas, Robert C. Treuhold, Dagmar and François de la Tour d'Auvergne, Charlotte and Franck Ullman, Martine Vermeulen, Jean-Louis Vilgrain, Denise and Alexandre Vilgrain, Jennifer and Sebastien Vilgrain and Aniela and Stanislas Vilgrain, as well as the following members of our staff: Jessica Grose (editorial assistant), Reni Chin, Larry Cohn, Jeff Freier, Caroline Hatchett, Natalie Lebert, Mike Liao, Dave Makulec, Emily Parsons, Becky Ruthenburg, Sharon Yates and Kyle Zolner.

© 2007 Zagat Survey, LLC
ISBN-13: 978-1-57006-862-1
ISBN-10: 1-57006-862-3
Printed in the
United States of America

Contents

Ratings & Symbols

Zagat Top Spot	Name	Symbols		Cuisine		Zagat Ratings			
						FOOD	DECOR	SERVICE	COST

Area, Address, Métro Stop & Contact*

🅉 **Tim & Nina's** ◕ *French/Thai* ▽ 19 | 15 | 18 | €195

6ᵉ | 604, rue de Buci (Odéon) | 01 23 45 54 32 | fax 23 44 55 66 | www.zagat.com

Review, surveyor comments in quotes

Jamais fermé, this "crowded" 6th-arrondissement cafe started the "French-Thai craze" (e.g. foie gras in pad Thai or lychee bouillabaisse); though it looks like a "garage" and T & N "never heard of credit cards or reservations" – yours in particular – the "*merveilleuse* Bangkok-Lyonnaise cuisine" draws delighted diners despite "dubious service."

Ratings   **Food, Decor** and **Service** are rated on a scale of 0 to 30.

0	– 9	poor to fair
10	– 15	fair to good
16	– 19	good to very good
20	– 25	very good to excellent
26	– 30	extraordinary to perfection
▽		low response | less reliable

Cost reflects our surveyors' average estimate of the price of a dinner with one drink and tip and is a benchmark only. Lunch is usually 25% less.

For **newcomers** or survey **write-ins** listed without ratings, the price range is indicated as follows:

I	30€ and below
M	31€ to 50€
E	51€ to 80€
VE	81€ or more

Symbols

🅉	Zagat Top Spot (highest ratings, popularity and importance)
◕	serves after 11 PM
🆂	closed on Sunday
🅼	closed on Monday
⊘	no credit cards accepted

* When calling from outside France, dial the country code +33, then omit the first zero of the number listed.

About This Survey

This **2007/08 Paris Restaurants Survey** is an update reflecting significant developments since our last Survey was published.

WHAT IT COVERS: 1,002 restaurants in Paris and its immediate suburbs, including over 50 important additions. We've also indicated new addresses, Web sites and phone numbers, management and chef changes and other major innovations.

HELPFUL LISTS: Whether you're looking for a celebratory meal or a bargain bite, our lists can help you find exactly the right place. See Most Popular (page 9), Top Ratings (pages 10–16) and Best Buys. We've also provided 44 handy indexes.

WHO PARTICIPATED: Input from over 4,800 avid diners forms the basis for the ratings and reviews in this guide (their comments are shown in quotation marks within the reviews). Collectively they bring roughly 743,000 meals worth of experience to this Survey. We sincerely thank each of these participants – this book is really "theirs."

OUR EDITORS: We are also grateful to our editors, Alexander Lobrano, European correspondent for *Gourmet* and a food and travel writer based in Paris, and Mary Deschamps, a freelance writer and translator, also based in Paris. Our thanks go as well to our coordinator, Claire Fitzpatrick-Quimbrot.

ABOUT ZAGAT: This marks our 28th year reporting on the shared experiences of consumers like you. What started in 1979 as a hobby involving 200 people rating NYC restaurants has come a long way. Today we have over 250,000 surveyors and now cover dining, entertaining, golf, hotels, movies, music, nightlife, resorts, shopping, spas, theater and tourist attractions worldwide.

MAKE YOUR OPINION COUNT: We invite you to join any of our upcoming surveys – just register at **zagat.com,** where you can rate and review establishments year-round. Each participant will receive a free copy of the resulting guide when published.

AVAILABILITY: Zagat guides are available in all major bookstores, by subscription at **zagat.com,** and for use on BlackBerry, Palm, Windows Mobile devices and mobile phones.

FEEDBACK: There is always room for improvement, thus we invite your comments and suggestions about any aspect of our performance. Just contact us at paris@zagat.com.

New York, NY
May 15, 2007

Nina and Tim Zagat

What's New

EASTERN INCLINE: With its reasonable rents and restaurant-loving population of bobos (bohemian-bourgeois couples and singles), Paris' eastern edge is emerging as the most appealing area of the city for young restaurateurs. In the 11th arrondissement, there's the lively bistro Au Petit Monsieur; Le Chateaubriand, where chef Iñaki Aizpitarte packs 'em in nightly with nervy New French menus that change monthly; and L'Unico, a hugely popular Argentine steakhouse. The neighboring 12th plays host to such hip arrivals as La Gazzetta, serving edgy Mediterranean–New French fare, and Le Tarmac, an Eclectic brasserie.

VIVE L'ANNEXE: If last year's trend was big-name Haute Cuisine toques opening easygoing bistros, the latest take is popular bistros replicating themselves. Newcomers Le Bis du Severo, Le Petit Pamphlet and Le Soleil are all *annexes*, or offshoots of, respectively, Le Severo, Le Pamphlet and the original Le Soleil. Apparently, a name that references (or even duplicates) the parent's is a prerequisite for an *annexe* – as is the same high-quality cuisine and convivial ambiance.

PLAYING THE ORGANS: Now that the mad-cow scare has faded, Parisians are mad for organ meats. Tripe and sweetbreads, calf's head and pig's feet are taking pride of place on menus all over Paris, and one novice, Le Ribouldingue, serves Classic French 'off-cuts' almost exclusively: diners might see breaded pork snout and nostrils, or even cow teats, on the menu. Boucherie Roulière proudly presents marrow bones and veal kidneys. And it's not just bistros that are getting on the offal bandwagon. Chef-owner Jean-Pierre Vigato's version of *tête de veau* is a hit at Apicius and chef Eric Frechon has been offering oxtail at Le Bristol.

(ALMOST) PRIVATE PARTY: Forsaking the formality of the traditional restaurant format, some chefs are opening places so intimate that eating there is more like attending a dinner party than a commercial venue. A single waitress serves some 16 patrons at Chicago-born chef Daniel Rose's modern bistro, Spring (sometimes he even pitches in too). Toque Alain Bourgade, ex La Poêle d'Or, invites a dozen diners literally into his home – an elegant townhouse and garden – to feast on his New French fare.

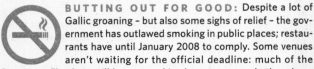

BUTTING OUT FOR GOOD: Despite a lot of Gallic groaning – but also some sighs of relief – the government has outlawed smoking in public places; restaurants have until January 2008 to comply. Some venues aren't waiting for the official deadline: much of the Brasseries Flo chain will be nonsmoking by summer, and others have already banned *le tabac* too. The clean air may make those high Parisian tabs (the average meal costs 52.41€, or $69.34) easier to swallow.

Paris
May 15, 2007

Alexander Lobrano

Key Newcomers

The dining scene never dims in the City of Light, thanks to the sparks provided by a constant flow of new places. Here is our take on some of the past year's most notable additions. (For a full list, see page TK.)

Accolade	Ozu
Alain Bourgade	Petit Pamphlet
Black Calvados	Pré Salé
Chateaubriand	Ribouldingue
Cibus	San
Ferrandaise	Sensing
First	Spring
Gazzetta	35° Ouest
Hôtel Amour	Unico
Jardinier	Versance
Mori Venice Bar	21

Other notable newcomers are actually old-timers that have been rejuvenated by fresh management or a fresh address. A dusty old Montparnasse bistro, **Caméléon,** changed its colors – to great acclaim – when new owner Jean-Paul Arabian injected some hipness into the decor and the menu of robust classics; veteran **Pétrus,** an expensive fish specialist in the 17th, underwent a sea change, transformed by a new team into a brasserie deluxe for seafood lovers and carnivores alike; and the father-son duo behind **Bath's** moved their beloved Auvergnat from the 8th to a contemporary home in the 17th, slashing menu prices and adding New French dishes along the way.

Yet to come are the results of two other takeovers, both courtesy of Alain Ducasse. Later this spring, the super-chef/restaurateur is assuming command of **Rech,** the 1925 seafood brasserie in the 17th. And in the autumn, he's slated to unveil his makeover of **Jules Verne** atop the Eiffel Tower; word is that it will include both a new look and a new menu from one of the master's lieutenant toques.

Some other high-profile openings on the horizon include a Left Bank branch of the famous **Au Pied de Cochon** brasserie, just in time to celebrate its 60th anniversary, in the space currently occupied by L'Arbuci; a second eatery in the Hôtel Le Bristol, this one a modern, luxurious grill room, also under the auspices of Le Bristol chef Eric Frechon; a new restaurant at **Fauchon,** the renowned purveyor of gourmet goodies to go in the 8th; a reincarnation of one of Paris' most famous belle epoque establishments, the **Pavillon Puebla** in the Parc Buttes-Chaumont, under the management of Vincent Cozzoli (the proprietor of the popular Chez Vincent); and a new restaurant in the 1st by Oth Sombath (ex Banyan and Blue Elephant), perhaps the highest-regarded Thai chef in France.

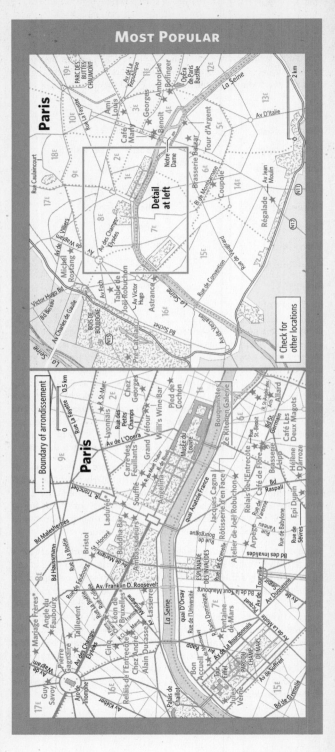

Most Popular

Each surveyor has been asked to name his or her five favorite places. This list reflects their choices.

1. Taillevent
2. Atelier/Joël Robuchon
3. Tour d'Argent
4. Guy Savoy
5. Cinq
6. Jules Verne
7. Grand Véfour
8. Alain Ducasse
9. Ladurée
10. Pierre Gagnaire
11. Bofinger
12. Arpège
13. Epi Dupin
14. Ami Louis
15. Lasserre
16. Ambassadeurs
17. Bouquinistes
18. Ambroisie
19. Café Les Deux Magots
20. Bristol
21. Relais/l'Entrecôte
22. Astrance
23. Angelina
24. Buddha Bar*
25. Brass. Lipp
26. Soufflé
27. Allard
28. Benoît
29. Ze Kitchen Galerie*
30. Lyonnais
31. Coupole
32. Chez Georges
33. Georges*
34. Table de Robuchon
35. Fontaine de Mars
36. Hélène Darroze
37. Pré Catelan*
38. Angle du Faubourg
39. Jacques Cagna*
40. Michel Rostang
41. Café de Flore
42. Mariage Frères
43. Carré des Feuillants
44. Léon/Bruxelles
45. Chez André
46. Willi's Wine Bar
47. Café Marly
48. Régalade
49. Bon Accueil
50. Brass. Balzar
51. Rôtiss. d'en Face*
52. Pied de Cochon

It's obvious that many of the restaurants on the above list are among Paris' most expensive, but if popularity were calibrated to price, we suspect that a number of other restaurants would join the above ranks. Given the fact that both our surveyors and readers love to discover dining bargains, we have added a list of 80 Best Buys on page 17. These are restaurants that give real quality at extremely reasonable prices.

* Indicates a tie with restaurant above

Top Ratings: Food

Food ratings are shown to the left of restaurant names. Excluding places with low voting.

28 | Taillevent
Pierre Gagnaire
Alain Ducasse
Cinq
Guy Savoy

27 | Grand Véfour
Hiramatsu
Ambroisie
Bristol
Astrance
Isami
Ambassadeurs
Michel Rostang
Lasserre
Atelier/Joël Robuchon

26 | Pavillon Ledoyen
Arpège
Table de Robuchon
Jacques Cagna
Trois Marches
Meurice
Caviar Kaspia
Apicius
Elysées
Pré Catelan

Relais d'Auteuil/Pignol
Ami Louis

25 | Relais Louis XIII
Tour d'Argent
Carré des Feuillants
Gérard Besson
Réminet
Kinugawa
Table du Lancaster
Marée
Stella Maris
Espadon
Avant Goût
Salon d'Hélène

24 | Duc
Céladon
Florimond*
Violon d'Ingres*
Cave Gourmande
Truffière
Ormes
Clos des Gourmets
Ostéria
Sormani
Chamarré

BY CUISINE (FRENCH)

BISTRO (CONTEMPORARY)

24 | Cave Gourmande
Mon Vieil Ami
23 | Epi Dupin
Ardoise
22 | Maison du Jardin

BISTRO (TRADITIONAL)

26 | Ami Louis
24 | Benoît
Bon Accueil
23 | Christine
Régalade

BRASSERIES

22 | Garnier
Relais Plaza
20 | Bofinger
Petit Zinc
19 | Sébillon

CLASSIC

26 | Ami Louis
25 | Gérard Besson
Stella Maris
Espadon
24 | Céladon

CONTEMPORARY

27 | Hiramatsu
Astrance
Ambassadeurs
Michel Rostang
25 | Réminet

HAUTE CUISINE

28 | Taillevent
Pierre Gagnaire
Alain Ducasse
Cinq
Guy Savoy

LYON

- 24 Benoît
- 22 Lyonnais
  - Moissonnier
- 21 Aub. Pyrénées Cévennes
  - Chez René

OTHER REGIONS

- 24 Braisière/Gascony
- 23 Troquet/Basque
  - Pamphlet/Basque
- 22 Graindorge/Northern
  - Tante Louise/Burgundy

PROVENCE

- 22 Jardin
  - Olivades
- 21 Fish La Boissonnerie
- 20 Bastide Odéon
  - Bistro de l'Olivier
  - Chez Janou*

SEAFOOD

- 25 Marée
- 24 Duc
  - Luna
  - Goumard
- 23 Divellec

SHELLFISH

- 22 Dôme
  - Garnier
- 21 Marius et Janette
  - Marée de Versailles
- 18 Bar à Huîtres

SOUTHWEST

- 25 Salon d'Hélène
- 24 Cerisaie
  - Trou Gascon
- 23 Dauphin
  - Hélène Darroze

STEAKHOUSES

- 23 Relais/l'Entrecôte
- 22 Relais de Venise
- 21 Gavroche
- 19 Gourmets des Ternes
- 17 Boeuf Couronné

WINE BARS/BISTROS

- 22 Bourguignon du Marais
  - Enoteca
- 21 Caves Pétrissans
- 20 Bistrot du Sommelier
  - Cave de l'Os à Moëlle

BY CUISINE (OTHER)

CHINESE

- 24 Chen Soleil d'Est
- 21 Tsé-Yang
- 20 Chez Vong
  - Diep
  - Tong Yen

ECLECTIC

- 23 Ze Kitchen Galerie
  - Spoon, Food & Wine
- 22 Relais Plaza
- 20 Market
- 18 Georges

GREEK/ MEDITERRANEAN

- 22 Mavrommatis
- 18 Sept Quinze
  - Délices d'Aphrodite∇
- 17 7ème Sud
- 15 Sud

ITALIAN

- 24 Ostéria
  - Sormani

- 22 Sardegna a Tavola
  - Chez Vincent
  - Grand Venise

JAPANESE

- 27 Isami
- 25 Kinugawa
- 20 Orient-Extrême
  - Azabu
- 19 Kaïten

MIDDLE EASTERN

- 24 As du Fallafel
- 22 Al Dar
- 19 Al Diwan
- 18 Noura
  - Chez Marianne

MOROCCAN

- 22 Timgad
- 21 Chez Omar
  - 404
- 20 El Mansour
- 19 Mansouria

SPANISH/PAN-LATIN

- 22 Anahï
- 21 Anahuacalli
- 20 El Palenque
- Fogón
- 19 Bellota-Bellota

THAI

- 21 Baan-Boran
- 20 Erawan

- 19 Blue Elephant
- 18 Thiou
- 17 Chieng Mai

VIETNAMESE

- 22 Tan Dinh
- 21 Kim Anh
- 19 Davé
- Lac-Hong
- 16 Coin des Gourmets

BY SPECIAL FEATURE

BRUNCH

- 21 404
- Mariage Frères
- 20 Jardin des Cygnes
- Télégraphe
- Market

HOTEL DINING

- 28 Pierre Gagnaire
  - Hôtel Balzac
- Alain Ducasse
  - Hôtel Plaza-Athénée
- Cinq
  - Four Seasons George V
- 27 Bristol
  - Hôtel Le Bristol
- Ambassadeurs
  - Hôtel de Crillon

LATE DINING

- 27 Atelier/Joël Robuchon
- 26 Caviar Kaspia
- 23 Os à Moëlle
- Chez Michel
- Christine

LIVE ENTERTAINMENT

- 27 Lasserre
- 23 Jules Verne
- 22 Jardin

- 21 Bar Vendôme
- 20 Maxim's

SUNDAY DINING

- 27 Bristol
- Atelier/Joël Robuchon
- 26 Ami Louis
- 25 Tour d'Argent
- Réminet

TEA & DESSERTS

- 24 Jean-Paul Hévin
- 23 Dalloyau
- 22 Ladurée
- Table d'Hédiard
- 22 Mariage Frères

TRENDY

- 22 144 Petrossian
- Comptoir du Relais
- 19 Cristal Room
- 18 Georges
- 17 Costes

WINNING WINE LISTS

- 28 Cinq
- 27 Michel Rostang
- 25 Tour d'Argent
- 20 Bistrot du Sommelier
- 17 Lavinia

BY ARRONDISSEMENT

1ST

- 27 Grand Véfour
- 26 Meurice
- 25 Carré des Feuillants
- Gérard Besson
- Kinugawa

2ND

- 24 Céladon
- 22 Lyonnais

- Café Moderne
- 21 Chez Georges
- Gavroche

3RD

- 26 Ami Louis
- 23 Pamphlet
- 22 Anahï
- Bascou
- 21 Chez Omar

4TH

- 27 Ambroisie
- Isami
- 24 Ostéria
- Mon Vieil Ami
- As du Fallafel

5TH

- 25 Tour d'Argent
- Réminet
- 24 Truffière
- 23 Pré Verre
- Petit Pontoise

6TH

- 26 Jacques Cagna
- 25 Relais Louis XIII
- Salon d'Hélène
- 23 Epi Dupin
- Christine

7TH

- 27 Atelier/Joël Robuchon
- 26 Arpège
- 24 Florimond
- Violon d'Ingres*
- Ormes

8TH

- 28 Taillevent
- Pierre Gagnaire
- Alain Ducasse
- Cinq
- 27 Bristol

9TH

- 23 Casa Olympe
- 22 Ladurée
- 21 Table d'Anvers
- 16 Haussmann
- 20 Petite Sirène/Copen.

10TH

- 23 Chez Michel
- 18 Chez Papa
- Deux Canards
- 17 Brass. Flo
- Brass. Julien

11TH

- 23 Villaret
- Amognes
- 22 Astier
- 21 Aub. Pyrénées Cévennes
- 20 Bistrot Paul Bert

12TH

- 24 Trou Gascon
- 22 Sardegna a Tavola
- 21 Oulette
- Biche au Bois
- 19 Train Bleu

13TH

- 25 Avant Goût
- 22 Petit Marguery
- 21 Ourcine
- 20 Aub. Etchégorry
- 17 Chez Paul

14TH

- 24 Duc
- Cerisaie
- 23 Régalade
- 22 Dôme
- 21 Cagouille

15TH

- 24 Chen Soleil d'Est
- 23 Os à Moëlle
- Troquet
- Dalloyau
- 22 Grand Venise

16TH

- 27 Hiramatsu
- Astrance
- 26 Table de Robuchon
- Pré Catelan
- Relais d'Auteuil/Pignol

17TH

- 28 Guy Savoy
- 27 Michel Rostang
- 24 Sormani
- Braisière
- 22 Graindorge

18TH, 19TH & 20TH

- 24 Cave Gourmande
- 22 Chez Vincent
- 20 Allobroges
- Boulangerie*
- 17 Boeuf Couronné

OUTSIDE PARIS

- 26 Trois Marches
- 23 Tastevin
- Dalloyau
- 22 Magnolias
- Potager du Roy

Top Ratings: Decor

Decor ratings are shown to the left of restaurant names.

29 Cinq
Ambassadeurs

28 Grand Véfour
Cristal Room
Lasserre
Meurice
Taillevent
Tour d'Argent
Alain Ducasse
Pré Catelan

27 1728
Bar Vendôme
Pavillon/Grande Cascade
Espadon
Pavillon Ledoyen
Train Bleu
Bristol
Jules Verne

26 Ambroisie
Lapérouse
Laurent
Georges
Trois Marches
Buddha Bar

25 Elysées
Table du Lancaster
Guy Savoy
Maison de l'Amér. Latine
Céladon
404
Coupe-Chou
Costes
Pierre Gagnaire

24 Apicius
Pershing
Kong
Mandala Ray
Maison Blanche
Maxim's
Bon
Bofinger
Relais Louis XIII
Grand Colbert
Blue Elephant
Chalet des Iles*
Café Marly

23 Brass. Julien
Télégraphe
Fermette Marbeuf
Bouillon Racine

OUTDOORS

Absinthe
Alain Bourgade
Bar Vendôme
Bistrot du Cap
Bristol
Café Lenôtre
Café Marly
Copenhague
Délices de Szechuen
Espadon
Georges

Jardins de Bagatelle
Laurent
Maison de l'Amér. Latine
Pavillon/Grande Cascade
Pavillon Montsouris
Petite Cour
Petit Poucet
Pré Catelan
Rest. du Palais Royal
Square
Vieux Bistro

ROMANCE

Ambassadeurs
Ambroisie
Astrance
Caviar Kaspia
Chalet des Iles
Coupe-Chou
Coupole
Dôme
First
Fontaine de Mars
Georges
Grand Véfour
Guirlande de Julie
Jules Verne
Lapérouse
Meurice
Pavillon/Grande Cascade
Pavillon Ledoyen
Pavillon Montsouris
Pré Catelan
Tour d'Argent
Train Bleu

ROOMS

Ambassadeurs
Ambroisie
Apicius
Black Calavados
Buddha Bar
Cinq
Costes
Cristal Room
1728
First
Georges
Grand Véfour
Guy Savoy
Jardinier
Kong
Lasserre
Maison Prunier
Mandala Ray
Meurice
Mori Venice Bar
Ozu
Pavillon/Grande Cascade
Pavillon Montsouris
Pétrelle
Pré Catelan
Sensing
Taillevent
Train Bleu

VIEWS

Altitude 95
Basilic
Bouquinistes
Brass. de l'Ile St. Louis
Café Beaubourg
Café Marly
Caviar Kaspia
Copenhague
Diapason
Georges
Grand Véfour
Jules Verne
Kong
Lapérouse
Lasserre
Maison Blanche
Maison de l'Amér. Latine
Ombres
Pavillon/Grande Cascade
Pavillon Ledoyen
Rest. du Palais Royal
Tour d'Argent

Top Ratings: Service

Service ratings are shown to the left of restaurant names.

28 Cinq
Taillevent
Alain Ducasse

27 Pierre Gagnaire
Guy Savoy
Ambassadeurs
Grand Véfour
Lasserre

26 Espadon
Michel Rostang
Tour d'Argent
Ambroisie
Bristol

25 Pavillon Ledoyen
Pré Catelan
Hiramatsu
Obélisque
Meurice
Arpège
Apicius

24 Caviar Kaspia
Florimond
Astrance
Elysées
Relais Louis XIII

Bar Vendôme
Jules Verne
Table de Robuchon
Trois Marches
Carré des Feuillants

23 Dominique Bouchet
Trou Gascon
Jacques Cagna
Cerisaie
Christine
Gérard Besson*
Tastevin
Truffière
P'tit Troquet
Céladon
Timbre
Pavillon/Grande Cascade
Braisière
Bistro de l'Olivier
Table du Lancaster
Laurent
Petit Prince de Paris
Relais d'Auteuil/Pignol*

22 Réminet
Duc

Best Buys

1. As du Fallafel
2. Crêperie de Josselin
3. Cosi
4. Loir dans la Théière
5. BE Boulangépicier
6. Jean-Paul Hévin
7. Lina's
8. Café Very/Dame
9. Chartier
10. Mariage Frères
11. Chez Papa
12. Andy Wahloo
13. Angelina
14. Breakfast in America
15. Ladurée
16. Boulangerie
17. Trumilou
18. Dalloyau
19. A Priori Thé
20. Languedoc
21. Chez Marianne
22. Chez Omar
23. Tav. Henri IV
24. Wadja
25. Petit Prince de Paris
26. Polidor
27. Relais/l'Entrecôte
28. Fous d'en Face
29. Maison du Jardin
30. Timbre
31. Bistrot du Peintre
32. 404
33. Perraudin
34. P'tit Troquet
35. Bistrot Baracane
36. Grille St-Germain
37. 16 Haussmann
38. Cosi (Le)
39. Cerisaie
40. Comptoir

OTHER GOOD VALUES

Ardoise
Astier
Avant Goût
Baan-Boran
Banyan
Baron Rouge
Biche au Bois
Bistro de Breteuil
Bistrot du Dôme
Bistrot Vivienne
Café Constant
Café du Commerce
Café Moderne
Chez Prune
Chez Ramulaud
Coin des Gourmets
Dix Vins
Entredgeu
Epi Dupin
Erawan
Ferrandaise
Fish La Boissonnerie
Georgette
Lao Siam
Lescure
Lozère
Maupertu
Ourcine
Papilles
Petit Pamphlet
Petit Pontoise
Petit St. Benoît
Pré Verre
Réminet
Scheffer
Severo
Temps au Temps
Temps des Cerises
Troquet
Verre Volé

ALPHABETICAL
DIRECTORY

Abadache (L') 🗷 *Bistro*

FOOD	DECOR	SERVICE	COST
-	-	-	M

17ᵉ | 89, rue Lemercier (Brochant/Pl. de Clichy) | 01 42 26 37 33 | fax 01 42 26 37 33

"The kind of informal farmhouse [place] you'd never expect to find in the streets of Paris, with unmatched chairs and tables and an open kitchen", this young bistro in the trendy Batignolles district augments its Gallic classics with an occasional English accent – haddock salad, Stilton cheese – to reflect the origins of its French chef-owner and his British girlfriend-hostess; if a few find it "overpriced for the ordinary fare" and stark stucco walls, most vaunt its "good value."

Absinthe (L') 🗷 *Bistro*

FOOD	DECOR	SERVICE	COST
19	17	17	€48

1ᵉʳ | 24, pl du Marché St-Honoré (Pyramides) | 01 49 26 90 04 | fax 01 49 26 08 64 | www.michelrostang.com

Now "under the direction of Caroline Rostang", Michel's daughter, this "stylish" place "decorated like a NYC loft" with exposed-brick walls and a big clock face overlooks "one of the trendiest addresses in Paris today" – the Marché Saint-Honoré, which makes it "a must, even if the food is mediocre", as some snap; others, however, applaud the bistro cooking for its "inventive touch"; service is "friendly", if "spotty", prices are "relatively reasonable" and there's a "great terrace" to grab early.

NEW Accolade (L') 🗷 *Bistro*

FOOD	DECOR	SERVICE	COST
-	-	-	M

17ᵉ | 23, rue Guillaume Tell (Péreire) | 01 42 67 12 67 | www.laccolade.com

The creative quality of the contemporary French bistro cooking at this cozy, colorful newcomer not far from the Porte de Champerret has quickly attracted accolades from young working couples and 17th-arrondissement locals; friendly service and an easygoing atmosphere make the sometimes stiff prices more digestible.

A et M, Restaurant 🗷 *Bistro*

FOOD	DECOR	SERVICE	COST
15	13	15	€50

16ᵉ | 136, bd Murat (Porte de St-Cloud) | 01 45 27 39 60 | fax 01 45 27 69 71

"Popular with TV and radio people from the nearby studios", this "nice little neighborhood bistro" in the Porte de Saint-Cloud area has "a talent for fish" (but then, you "can't go wrong with a classic menu"); sometimes "too fast" and other times "too slow", the "staff seems to forget what service means", unfortunately.

Affriolé (L') 🗷🅜 *Bistro*

FOOD	DECOR	SERVICE	COST
21	15	19	€44

7ᵉ | 17, rue Malar (La Tour-Maubourg/Invalides) | 01 44 18 31 33

Tucked away in a "quiet street in the 7th" arrondissement is this "small, hip" "gastronomic pearl with low prices" – that is, relative to the "excellent" bistro menu that is "modern without being too trendy" and "changes often"; "young professionals who look as good as the chef's offerings" dine in the "hip, small" surrounds, distinguished mainly by the "gorgeous mosaic-topped tables"; "service is frenetic, if affable", and overall, this "tiny little place packs a delightful punch."

	FOOD	DECOR	SERVICE	COST

Aida ☒ *Japanese*
— — — E

7ᵉ | 1, rue Pierre Leroux (Duroc/Vanneau) | 01 43 06 14 18 |
fax 01 43 06 14 18

Hidden in a hushed corner of the 7th, this tiny Nipponese is a favorite hang of fashionistas and Japanophiles alike; its dramatically Zen, minimalistic decor allows you to focus on the food, especially the specialty teppanyaki made with Chateaubriand, best eaten at one of the nine places at the bar; it's expensive, but so is any ticket to Tokyo.

Aiguière (L') ☒ *Classic French*
— — — E

11ᵉ | 37 bis, rue de Montreuil (Faidherbe-Chaligny) | 01 43 72 42 32 |
fax 01 43 72 96 36 | www.l-aiguiere.com

"A real find" is how the intrepid few who've journeyed to an off-the-beaten-track corner of the 11th describe this "remarkable" restaurant serving "excellent" Classic French food in a blue-and-yellow-painted dining room garnished with bouquets of fresh flowers; the service is "superb" in this auberge that dates back to the reign of Louis XIII.

Aimant du Sud (L') ●☒ *Classic French*
— — — M

13ᵉ | 40, bd Arago (Les Gobelins) | 01 47 07 33 57 |
fax 01 44 24 24 84

With a name that means 'lover of the south', it's no surprise there's much Midi on the menu of this Classic French, "one of the better little bistros in the 13th"; service is "friendly but irregular", and if the kitchen "occasionally misses", the "good Basque wine list" restores a sunny disposition.

NEW Alain Bourgade ☒☒⇪ *New French*
— — — VE

16ᵉ | 25, rue de Boulainvilliers (La Muette/Ranelagh) | 01 45 56 10 41

After closing La Poêle d'Or, Alain Bourgade (who has also cooked with Alain Ducasse and Alain Solivérès) invented a new concept in Parisian restaurants: once a week, he receives a dozen or so guests for dinner at his beautiful mansion in the 16th; the menu varies with the season, but runs to stylish New French dishes, and the expensive experience is akin to attending a very chic dinner party – one that extends to a gorgeous garden when weather permits; *bien sûr*, you better book well in advance.

☑ Alain Ducasse au Plaza Athénée ☒ *Haute Cuisine*
28 28 28 €184

8ᵉ | Hôtel Plaza-Athénée | 25, av Montaigne (Alma Marceau/
Franklin D. Roosevelt) | 01 53 67 65 00 | fax 01 53 67 65 12 |
www.alain-ducasse.com

"The world's superstar chef" – "if God cooked, this would be the food" – lives up to his reputation at his Plaza-Athénée home, an "opulent" "18th-century space done modern" for which "every superlative is appropriate" (i.e. "the pinnacle of Haute Cuisine"); kudos, too, for the "exemplary", "well-orchestrated" servers, even if they do "emphasize expensive wines"; the place is "prodigiously" pricey, "but who cares – everybody needs to splurge" once (and you get a free treat to take home for breakfast).

	FOOD	DECOR	SERVICE	COST

Alcazar ● New French

17 | 21 | 17 | €51

6ᵉ | 62, rue Mazarine (Odéon) | 01 53 10 19 99 | fax 01 53 10 23 23 | www.alcazar.fr

Perhaps it's "not quite as trendy as it used to be" ("what once seemed fresh and modern now seems just big and brash"), but still it's "always interesting" to "take in the scene" at Terence Conran's Saint-Germain brasserie – and what a scene it is, with seats for 200 under a skylight roof; the New French "food is not up to the panache of the place", but it's "pleasant" and "light" – and there's always the "buzzy bar", which compensates for the oft-"inattentive" service.

Al Dar ● Lebanese

22 | 14 | 19 | €48

5ᵉ | 8, rue Frédéric Sauton (Maubert-Mutualité) | 01 43 25 17 15
16ᵉ | 93, av Raymond Poincaré (Victor Hugo) | 01 45 00 96 64 | fax 01 45 01 61 67

"Excellent, authentic" – if comparatively "expensive" – Lebanese food (including "the best baklava" in Paris) is the draw at these popular twins in the 5th and 16th; the "less-than-convincing atmosphere" makes some believe it's "better to get the same dishes at the take-out counter"; still, the servers "are always smiling" and so they're assiduously frequented by expats and others ("we eat there so often the maitre d' asked if we owned a kitchen").

Al Diwan ● Lebanese

19 | 14 | 17 | €41

8ᵉ | 30, av George V (Alma Marceau/George V) | 01 47 23 45 45 | fax 01 47 23 60 98

"Another golden spot in the Golden Triangle" of the 8th, this place is perennially packed with patrons sampling "some of the tastiest Lebanese food in town", whether sandwiches, schwarma or "meze that's a feast in itself"; the chow compensates for the drab decor and service that's a tad tetchy, unless you're a "known client" (tip: "be sure to wear leather to blend in").

Alivi (L') Corsica

17 | 17 | 17 | €36

4ᵉ | 27, rue du Roi de Sicile (Hôtel-de-Ville/St-Paul) | 01 48 87 90 20 | fax 01 48 87 20 60 | www.restaurant-alivi.com

"Corsican cuisine, Corsican ambiance, Corsican waiters" characterizes the scene at this small spot "on a little lane" in the Marais; there's debate whether the fare is "original" or "uninspiring" (it may depend on whether you "skip the formula menu, strictly for tourists, and order à la carte"); but all agree the "staff's friendly" and the prices fair.

⚡ Allard Bistro

22 | 18 | 20 | €59

6ᵉ | 41, rue St-André-des-Arts (Odéon) | 01 43 26 48 23 | fax 01 46 33 04 02 | www.restaurant-allard.com

"What you think of when you think of Paris bistros", this "small" Saint-Germain spot packs 'em in for "huge" portions of "*magnifique*" Classic "comfort food" ("go for the duck with olives") served amid "vintage lacey decor"; "lots of Americans come here, for good reason", which makes it a tad "touristy", and a few carp about "tables so cheek-by-jowl you need to ask the adjoining ones for permission to leave"; but overall, it "reminds you of why you love France."

	FOOD	DECOR	SERVICE	COST

Allobroges (Les) 🚫 Ⓜ *Bistro*   20 | 15 | 18 | €46

20ᵉ | 71, rue des Grands-Champs (Maraîchers/Nation) |
01 43 73 40 00 | fax 01 40 09 23 22

Not many know this "agreeable" bistro "tucked away in the 20th near
Père Lachaise" cemetery, but those who do extol its "well-done country cooking" and "brilliantly low prices" at lunch, along with "amiable
service" and rustic decor of wood-grain wallpaper and *bibelots*.

Al Mounia *Moroccan*   16 | 17 | 16 | €51

16ᵉ | 16, rue de Magdebourg (Trocadéro) | 01 47 27 57 28 |
fax 01 45 06 18 80 | www.al-mounia.com

At this 16th-arrondissement Moroccan, the "absolutely stunning
atmosphere instantly transports you to North Africa" (as, alas, do
the "slow service" and "low seats"); though many find it "a little expensive", it's "reliable" for a "quality meal" à la Marrakech.

Alsace (L') 🕒 *Alsace*   15 | 16 | 13 | €45

8ᵉ | 39, av des Champs-Elysées (Franklin D. Roosevelt) |
01 53 93 97 00 | fax 01 53 93 97 09 | www.restaurantalsace.com

With a "great location on the Champs-Elysées", this "big", long-
running workhorse of a brasserie is "a tourist trap into which, nevertheless, you'll fall" for a "fix of Alsatian food"; the regulars (yes,
"one does see Parisians here") advise you "stay with the traditional
dishes" – "comforting quiche Lorraine", "fresh oysters" and "good
choucroute garnie"; the "slow" and "snippy" service might be ex-
plained by the fact that it stays open 24 hours a day.

Alsaco (L') 🚫 *Alsace*   18 | 12 | 14 | €35

9ᵉ | 10, rue Condorcet (Gare du Nord/Poissonnière) | 01 45 26 44 31

"Without a doubt the best *weinstube* west of Alsace", this "warm
and homey (in a Germanic sort of way)" wood-paneled den on a quiet
side street in the 9th seduces with "succulent" food, "a charming
owner" who "makes his own choucroute" and a "sumptuous" selection of schnapps, eaux de vie and regional wines – all for "wonderfully low prices"; just be aware the snug room can get smoky.

Altitude 95 *Classic French*   16 | 23 | 18 | €51

7ᵉ | Tour Eiffel | Champ-de-Mars, 1st level (Bir-Hakeim/Champ-de-Mars) |
01 45 55 20 04 | fax 01 47 05 94 40

"Staggered tables" ensure that "most seats get some of the wonderful"
panorama around this Eiffel Tower eatery, whose "trendy decor reminds you of the ironwork"; maybe it's the "sublime view" that makes
the Classic French fare seem somewhat "airplane-y", and "thus
pricey"; still, the staff keeps things "comfortable for kids", making this
one of "the best outings for families in Paris"; N.B. new management
by chef Alain Ducasse's group is planning changes for autumn 2007.

Ambassade d'Auvergne *Auvergne*   19 | 16 | 20 | €44

3ᵉ | 22, rue du Grenier St-Lazare (Rambuteau) | 01 42 72 31 22 |
www.ambassade-auvergne.com

"Come hungry" to this "cozy", country-style table in the 3rd, a "satisfying, belt-loosening experience" whose "rustic food" "at reason-

able prices" is not only "good" but offers a snapshot of the "hearty", "salty" kitchens of the Auvergne; the "friendly service borders on the paternal", urging you to finish all the signature *aligot* (potatoes whipped with cheese curds and garlic), before diving into dessert.

☑ Ambassadeurs (Les) ⌧Ⓜ *New French* 27 | 29 | 27 | €147

8ᵉ | Hôtel de Crillon | 10, pl de la Concorde (Concorde) | 01 44 71 16 16 | fax 01 44 71 15 02 | www.crillon.com

The Crillon's "incredible" New French is "fabulous in every way", especially since the arrival of chef Jean-François Piège, who's brought "fun and whimsy" to the fare; his "delectable delights" contrast with the "staggeringly grand" surrounds; "from the gilded barges for ferrying [champagne] to the tiny stools for handbags" to the "phenomenal service that's formal, but friendly (for France)", this is "the closest you'll get to living like Louis XV – and you'll wish you had his wealth, when the bill comes."

☑ Ambroisie (L') ⌧Ⓜ *Haute Cuisine* 27 | 26 | 26 | €159

4ᵉ | 9, pl des Vosges (Chemin-Vert/St-Paul) | 01 42 78 51 45

You may well feel "as if you'd drunk the nectar of the gods" after a "transporting" trip to this small site in the 4th; it's "the epitome of class from a bygone era", from the "superb", "sophisticated" Haute Cuisine to the decor that recalls the Renaissance – "inlaid stone-parquet floors and Aubusson tapestries hanging on honey-hued walls"; "beneath the Gallic bravado, the staff has hearts of gold"; naturally, this heavenly experience commands "astronomical prices."

Amici Miei ⌧Ⓜ *Italian* ▽ 19 | 13 | 15 | €36

11ᵉ | 44, rue Saint-Sabin (Bréguet-Sabin/Chemin-Vert) | 01 42 71 82 62 | fax 01 43 57 07 71 | www.amici-miei.net

Many fans of the "really good pizzas" thrown at this tiny place regret its move to larger digs in the 11th, saying the "charm got lost" – but the "high-strung service" stayed ("where's the warmth of Italy?"); still, those pining for pie pant it's a decent enough "neighborhood address."

☑ Ami Louis (L') Ⓜ *Bistro* 26 | 16 | 20 | €103

3ᵉ | 32, rue du Vertbois (Arts et Métiers/Temple) | 01 48 87 77 48

When seeking out this "superlative bistro" in the 3rd, bring an appetite, as portions of the Classic French fare ("foie gras served in actual slabs", "roast chicken as rich as a steak") are "so big that sharing is a matter of survival"; true, the room "won't win any decor awards", and some sniff the staff seems "self-important" (though the savvy smile that's just "part of the shtick"); even "*amis* of Louis" lament the tabs – "it may be cheaper to buy a ranch – but you won't leave hungry or unhappy."

Ami Marcel (L') ⌧Ⓜ *Bistro* ▽ 21 | 13 | 21 | €40

15ᵉ | 33, rue Georges Pitard (Plaisance/Convention) | 01 48 56 62 06 | fax 01 48 56 62 06

It may "look like a simple storefront, but go on in" and you'll find "refined", "creative" cooking and "professional, attentive service" at this "nice" member of "the Paris creative bistrot scene" in the 15th;

	FOOD	DECOR	SERVICE	COST

it gets "a little noisy" sometimes, but the atmosphere is "relaxed and friendly", and it's a good buy for the money too.

Ami Pierre (A l') ● ☒ Ⓜ *Southwest* ▽ 19 | 17 | 18 | €33
11ᵉ | 5, rue de la Main-d'Or (Ledru-Rollin) | 01 47 00 17 35
Not much bigger than a cork, this "small, noisy" *bistrot à vins* near the Bastille claims a devoted following of vinophiles who, in between sips, soak up the "good, simple" Southwest cooking under the watchful eye of the "charming" owner.

Amognes (Les) ☒ Ⓜ *Classic French* 23 | 15 | 19 | €44
11ᵉ | 243, rue du Faubourg St-Antoine (Faidherbe-Chaligny) | 01 43 72 73 05
A while back, "this little place near the Bastille" had a "change of ownership", chef and menu – and Survey says "it's even better" as a result, with now-"excellent" (if "less cutting-edge") French cuisine, newly "attentive" service and "improved decor"; "while perhaps not worth a trip across Paris, it's an outstanding choice in the neighborhood" "if you want an intimate meal."

Ampère (L') ☒ *Bistro/Eclectic* 15 | 13 | 15 | €46
17ᵉ | 1, rue Ampère (Wagram) | 01 47 63 72 05 | fax 01 47 63 37 33
The "cooking is simple but varied" and the "service swift" at this "neighborhood restaurant for the 17th", where former wonder-boy chef Philippe Detourbe has made a quiet comeback; while it's not a destination, locals find the "comfortable surroundings relaxing" – and the Eclectic–French bistro menu a "good deal for lunch."

Amuse Bouche (L') Ⓜ *New French* 17 | 13 | 17 | €43
14ᵉ | 186, rue du Château (Gaîté/Mouton-Duvernet) | 01 43 35 31 61 | fax 01 45 38 96 60
This "charming, small" *amuse-bouche* "off the Avenue du Maine" in the 14th may be "a little out of the way" but its "original" New French menu has many murmuring "yum, yum" within the "*très fun*" environs; prices are judged "correct" and service "considerate", and a new owner has used family photos and copper pots to create a cozier feel (post-dating the Decor score).

Anahï ● *Argentinean* 22 | 15 | 17 | €49
3ᵉ | 49, rue Volta (Arts et Métiers/Temple) | 01 48 87 88 24 | fax 01 48 87 93 04
A "South American restaurant par excellence" cries the "starry-chic" crowd that comes to this 3rd-arrondissement address for a "hip" high-protein feed of "first-rate Argentine beef", even if "certain cuts can get pricey"; while some "love the old-butcher-shop" digs, others grumble about "tangoing with the table next to you"; "but the scene's the thing" here, "and the caipirinhas make it worthwhile."

Anahuacalli *Mexican* 21 | 14 | 20 | €38
5ᵉ | 30, rue des Bernardins (Maubert-Mutualité) | 01 43 26 10 20
Adoring amigos attest that this Latin Quarter cantina – "Margaritaville in the City of Lights" – is "the only good Mexican" in Paris, with "genuine", "expertly prepared" south-of-the-border eats ("come early for

the chiles rellenos, before they run out") and "a warm welcome" from the staff; some feel "the prices are high", given the "cramped" digs, "but a pitcher or two of margaritas will help you forget" all that.

Andy Wahloo ●☑ ⊠ Moroccan

FOOD	DECOR	SERVICE	COST
12	21	15	€24

3ᵉ | 69, rue des Gravilliers (Arts et Métiers) | 01 42 71 20 38 | fax 01 42 74 03 41

"Best for a snack and drinks" – the Moroccan menu "consists mainly of meze" – this "cool bar" in the ever hipper northern Marais is "an annex of 404", the popular eatery next door; it packs 'em in nightly with "a fun, funky atmosphere", "speedy service" from "cute", "friendly bar men" and a "creative", eye-poppingly colorful decor of stools made from old paint drums and crates for tables.

☑ Angelina Tearoom

FOOD	DECOR	SERVICE	COST
20	21	15	€29

1ᵉʳ | 226, rue de Rivoli (Concorde/Tuileries) | 01 42 60 82 00 | fax 01 42 86 98 97

"The world's best hot chocolate" (aka "liquid fudge") and an "elegantly" "dilapidated faux-baroque decor" make this 1903 tearoom an ideal perch from which to "watch the snow painting the Tuileries" across the street; true, "it's riddled with tourists", the service is "harried" and the cocoa doesn't come cheap; but supporters shrug off these shortcomings in favor of the "superb pastries" ("please don't tell my cardiologist I was here"), vowing "I want to die with a mug of the *Chocolat Africain* in my hands."

☑ Angle du Faubourg (L') ⊠ New French

FOOD	DECOR	SERVICE	COST
23	20	21	€71

8ᵉ | 195, rue du Faubourg St-Honoré (Charles de Gaulle-Etoile/Ternes) | 01 40 74 20 20 | fax 01 40 74 20 21 | www.taillevent.com

"Delicious, inventive, smart" are just some of the accolades accorded this New French that "lives up to the standard of its sister, Taillevent", for those "on a relative budget"; the "innovative cooking" is proffered by "unobtrusive servers" in "sophisticated surroundings"; it's "in the heart of the business quarter" of the 8th – and indeed, some find "the menu and ambiance rather corporate" – but most maintain "it's a wonderful place" for either "your date or your client."

Angl'Opera New French

FOOD	DECOR	SERVICE	COST
▽ 21	18	16	€43

2ᵉ | Hôtel Edouard VII | 39, av de l'Opéra (Opéra/Pyramides/Quatre-Septembre) | 01 42 61 86 25 | fax 01 42 61 47 73 | www.anglopera.com

"Expect your taste buds to travel nonstop from childhood memories to the most refined preparations – candy canes meet Charolais beef – in this unique restaurant operated by young sensation Gilles Choukroun" in the Hôtel Edouard VII; but the New French fare that fans find "Franco fusion fun" antagonists attack as "absurd", and "uneven service" doesn't help; even so, if you're after "an adventurous, ultramodern culinary trip", this "trendy place" will oblige.

Annapurna ●⊠ Indian

FOOD	DECOR	SERVICE	COST
▽ 19	14	15	€48

8ᵉ | 32, rue de Berri (George V/St-Philippe-du-Roule) | 01 45 63 91 62

Although some speculate that it's "too Westernized", most applaud this "good Indian" off the Champs for its "excellent curries" "cooked

	FOOD	DECOR	SERVICE	COST

in a glass-enclosed kitchen"; for "romantic dinners, the Punjab room is worth the extra cost", as a sitar player adds ambiance to the sunken tables and chairs.

AOC (L') 🗷 Ⓜ *Bistro* ▽ 19 | 14 | 21 | €43

5ᵉ | 14, rue des Fossés St-Bernard (Cardinal Lemoine/Jussieu) | 01 43 54 22 52 | www.restoaoc.com

"One of the best buys" in the Latin Quarter, this French bistro delights with a "warm welcome" and "generous portions" of "simple, delicious foods", all bearing the AOC label (meaning it's been produced according to strict government standards); it's a "charming" place to "eat something's heart out", as the rotisseried organs and meats are especially "wonderful."

Z Apicius 🗷 *Haute Cuisine* 26 | 24 | 25 | €126

8ᵉ | 20, rue d'Artois (George V/St-Philippe-du-Roule) | 01 43 80 19 66 | fax 01 44 40 09 57 | www.relaischateaux.com

"Surrounded by gardens in the heart of [the 8th], the locale is a showstopper" swoon supporters of chef-owner Jean-Pierre Vigato's Haute Cuisine "hidden gem", which occupies a "marvelous" "mansion that dates from the 18th century"; "the food's as great as ever" – a mix of classic and "audacious dishes" (e.g. duck with chocolate) – and the "delightful staff" is "unpretentious"; of course, it's "very expensive", but habitués "haven't had a bad meal yet."

Apollo ● *Eclectic* 14 | 18 | 14 | €35

14ᵉ | 3, pl Denfert Rochereau (Denfert-Rochereau) | 01 45 38 76 77 | fax 01 43 22 02 15 | www.restaurant-apollo.com

Its "fantastic terrace" on the street-level concourse of a métro station in the 14th may be "super-nice in summer", but otherwise this "kitschy" Eclectic–New French fails to inspire: "Apollo was the god of prophesy; I wish that someone had prophesized that this place serves totally forgettable food"; N.B. a change of ownership post-Survey may outdate the above scores.

Appart' (L') ● *Classic French* 15 | 17 | 15 | €47

8ᵉ | 9, rue du Colisée (Franklin D. Roosevelt) | 01 53 75 42 00 | fax 01 53 75 42 09 | www.lappart.com

The "cozy, dark" decor of this "crowded" Classic French just off the Champs-Elysées – it's done up to resemble an apartment – doesn't quite compensate for the "pretty average" cuisine and "cute" but "slow" waitresses; "it's more of a family place" now, "good if you want to bring your brood" – especially "for Sunday brunch", when "kids bake cakes and cookies with the chefs."

A Priori Thé *Tearoom* 16 | 19 | 13 | €27

2ᵉ | 35, Galerie Vivienne (Bourse/Palais Royal-Musée du Louvre) | 01 42 97 48 75

"Deliciously fresh and creatively prepared" cakes, scones and savories (including many meat-free, "great-for-vegetarians" varieties) make this "adorable" little tearoom "under a gorgeous glass ceiling" in the "sparkling" Galerie Vivienne a perennial favorite – even, dare we say, a priority – "between two shopping sessions" in the 2nd;

"owned by a cheery American expat", Peggy Hancock, for 27 years, it also does "a nice Sunday brunch."

Arbuci (L') ● Brasserie
15 | 13 | 13 | €40

6ᵉ | 25, rue de Buci (Mabillon) | 01 44 32 16 00 | fax 01 44 32 16 09 | www.arbuci.com

"Located in the middle of the bustling Latin Quarter", this place pulls 'em in with a "nice jazz club downstairs" on weekends and "reasonable prices" for "typical" brasserie dishes; "however, the food is inconsistent – the same dish can be perfect one night, so-so two weeks later" – and the "staff unusually undertrained"; also, many moan the "modern decor" has made it "too gentrified – *quel dommage!*"; N.B. the Frères Blanc group has announced plans to transform it into a Left Bank branch of Au Pied de Cochon in summer 2007.

Ardoise (L') Ⓜ Bistro
23 | 13 | 18 | €39

1ᵉʳ | 28, rue du Mont-Thabor (Concorde/Tuileries) | 01 42 96 28 18 | www.lardoise-paris.com

"Put this little hip pocket of a place on your own slate [*ardoise*] to visit in Paris" say supporters of this "noisy" "modern bistro" "near the Place de la Concorde", where "a young, bilingual staff" serves "superb", "innovative" takes on "French standards"; drawbacks include the "spartan decor" and what's possibly "the tightest seating in town" (it's perennially "packed with tourists" and "elderly locals with dogs on their laps") – "but the food makes up for it."

NEW Arome (L') ⑤ Classic/New French
– | – | – | M

8ᵉ | 3 rue St-Philippe-du-Roule (St-Philippe-du-Roule) | 01 42 25 55 98 | fax 01 45 25 55 97

A stylish international crowd fills this low-lit dining room with Moorish arches (left over from the old tenant, a Moroccan restaurant) to dine on fine French dishes, both Classic and New (reflecting the chef's stint under Pierre Gagnaire); gracious service and well-spaced tables make it comfortable, as befits its silk-stocking location in the 8th.

ⓩ Arpège (L') ⑤ Haute Cuisine
26 | 23 | 25 | €180

7ᵉ | 84, rue de Varenne (Varenne) | 01 47 05 09 06 | fax 01 44 18 98 39 | www.alain-passard.com

"It's not your typical" Haute Cuisine haven, "but if you're looking for a simple, product-based approach to food", an "ethereal culinary experience" awaits at this address in the 7th; aided by a "symphony of service", red meat–eschewing chef Alain Passard "gets more flavor out of vegetables than you'd think possible"; a few foes find the decor and staff "kinda cold" and the "prices exorbitant", but scores side with the supporters; P.S. "don't let them stick you in the dungeon (cellar)."

As du Fallafel (L') ● Mideastern
24 | 7 | 16 | €12

4ᵉ | 34, rue des Rosiers (St-Paul) | 01 48 87 63 60

Fervent fans say it'd be a pita to miss this Marais Israeli, a kosher eatery established in 1979, since it serves "the world's best falafel sandwiches" (or at least the "best outside of Israel") at a price that has gotten it boosted to the No. 1 Best Buy in Paris; the "brisk service" "efficiently handles" the "long lines", but because the hole-in-the-wall premises are "not the prettiest", mavens "get it to go" and "eat in the street with everybody else."

	FOOD	DECOR	SERVICE	COST

Asian ● Asian
16 | 20 | 14 | €52

8ᵉ | 30, av George V (Alma Marceau/George V) | 01 56 89 11 00 | fax 01 56 89 11 01 | www.asian.fr

"Grandiose", "dark"-lit Asiatic decor remains the main, if not "the only reason to visit" this once "trendy", now "touristy" bar/restaurant that's "quite expensive, as it's in the Champs-Elysées" area; though "they try hard", the Pan-Asian cuisine – "20 percent Thai, 20 percent sushi, 20 percent Chinese and the rest, indeterminate" – "just doesn't measure up", except possibly "for Sunday brunch", and the service could "drive even the Dali Lama to drink."

Assiette (L') Ⓜ Bistro
▽ 20 | 15 | 17 | €72

14ᵉ | 181, rue du Château (Gaîté/Mouton-Duvernet) | 01 43 22 64 86 | fax 01 45 20 54 66 | www.chezlulu.fr

Established "by a pioneering female chef" in the early '80s, this traditional bistro in Montparnasse serves up "simple", solid Southwest specialties that used to delight the late President Mitterrand; but living mortals mutter that even if "the food's still good", "it's quite expensive for what you get" in your *assiette*; and while the staff's "nice, why does it take 45 minutes to get the check?"

Astier Bistro
22 | 12 | 19 | €38

11ᵉ | 44, rue J.P. Timbaud (Oberkampf/Parmentier) | 01 43 57 16 35

The crowd's "mostly locals", but it's worth the cab fare to the 11th as this "warhorse" wows with "serious", "hearty bistro classics" topped off with a "cheese tray that's not to be believed"; the scene's "completely unpretentious" ("prepare to sit elbow-to-elbow"), but a "good-natured ambiance" prevails, and overall this is a "truly Parisian experience" – and for "a great price" too; N.B. a new owner and chef have added some modern dishes – but fear not, fromage fans: the cheese tray remains.

Astor (L') Ⓩ Haute Cuisine
20 | 19 | 19 | €81

8ᵉ | Hôtel Astor | 11, rue d'Astorg (St-Augustin) | 01 53 05 05 20 | fax 01 53 05 05 30 | www.hotel-astor.net

Since a change in the chef and the maitre d', the "food and service standards have fallen somewhat" at this dining room in the 8th; nevertheless, it maintains a comfortable "cruising speed", with a "well-stocked bar" and "delightful", "traditional" Haute Cuisine "beautifully presented" and served "with casual skill" in a "sophisticated" setting (though "very hotel" some say); the "well-spaced tables encourage confidentiality" for corporate types, and "prices are fair for the quality and quantity of food."

Ⓩ Astrance (L') Ⓩ Ⓜ New French
27 | 21 | 24 | €113

16ᵉ | 4, rue Beethoven (Passy) | 01 40 50 84 40

Assuming you can snag a reservation ("it takes Houdini to get in"), "a superb eating experience" awaits at this "small hideout in the posh 16th", where "genius" chef/co-owner Pascal Barbot's New French cooking is a "gorgeous" "daily invention, based on the morning market"; there's also "super-smart service" and "sophisticated yet cozy" digs; while "no longer a great value" (in fact, it's quite expensive), it's "worth it" for "the most creative cuisine in Paris."

Atelier Berger (L') ⊠ New French   21 | 15 | 18 | €50
1er | 49, rue Berger (Louvre-Rivoli) | 01 40 28 00 00 | fax 01 40 28 10 65 | www.restaurant-atelierberger.com

The Scandinavian chef-owner comes up with some "really fascinating combinations, like tuna tartare with black squid-ink sorbet" on the New French–with–Norwegian-notes menu at this duplex on the edge of Les Halles; sometimes the service and "surrealist" cuisine are "uneven" and "the room could be freshened up" a bit, but overall, this "original" offers "good value for the money."

⊠ Atelier de Joël Robuchon (L') ● Haute Cuisine   27 | 22 | 22 | €88
7e | Hôtel Pont Royal | 5, rue de Montalembert (Rue du Bac) | 01 42 22 56 56 | fax 01 42 22 97 91 | www.hotel-pont-royal.com

"A must for any foodie", this "relaxed", "hip sushi bar–cum–upscale diner" in the 7th from "one of the great chefs of our time" has an "innovative" Haute Cuisine menu that showcases "a fusion of flavors" served small plates-style; "the waiters are a fun bunch", if "too fast" ("order a lot", "slow the kitchen down"); "while not cheap, it's a bargain" for a trip down "Robuchon memory lane"; P.S. those "perturbed by" the "long waits", rejoice: "they take reservations" for certain hours.

Atelier Maître Albert (L') ● Bistro   21 | 22 | 21 | €57
5e | 1, rue Maître-Albert (Maubert-Mutualité) | 01 56 81 30 01 | fax 01 53 10 83 23 | www.ateliermaitrealbert.com

"Redone nicely" since it became a Guy Savoy-run rotisserie a while back, this Latin Quarter site juxtaposes "traditional French" bistro cooking - it's "amazing how tasty roast chicken and mashed potatoes can be" - with an "edgy contemporary look and beautiful fireplace" to create a "dark", "smart atmosphere"; a few gripe about "the limited menu" and "painful" bill, but most appreciate the "thoughtful food and glitzy crowd" ("even the servers look hip").

Atlas (L') Ⓜ Moroccan   18 | 14 | 13 | €36
5e | 12, bd St-Germain (Maubert-Mutualité) | 01 46 33 86 98 | fax 01 40 46 06 56

"After an exhibit at the Institut du Monde Arabe nearby, prolong" your Middle Eastern meanderings at this Latin Quarter Moroccan known for "magnificent tagines" ("try the one with prunes"); true, the "rich decor" is looking a little "outmoded" nowadays, and the service is slow; but all that's "worth tolerating" for "a dose of Tangiers."

Auberge Aveyronnaise ● Auvergne   - | - | - | M
12e | 40, rue Gabriel Lamé (Cour St-Emilion) | 01 43 40 12 24 | fax 01 43 40 12 15

"Comfort food" à la the Auvergne is the draw at this relaxed, reasonably priced table in the 12th - not a destination, but "a nice place if you're in the neighborhood"; "for the optimal experience, stick to the regional wines, meat specialties" and the infamous *aligot,* a whipped potatoes and cheese curd dish that's so gloriously gloppy "you have to develop a technique for eating it."

Auberge Bressane (L') *Classic French* | 17 | 14 | 18 | €44 |

7ᵉ | 16, av de la Motte-Picquet (Ecole Militaire/La Tour-Maubourg) | 01 47 05 98 37 | fax 01 47 05 92 21 | www.auberge-bressane.com

Alas, the cuisine's "dropped in quality", "but it's still enjoyable" at this Classic French in the 7th arrondissement "with an old-fashioned look and taste"; the former's provided by the "quaint" "neo-Gothic" decor and the latter by such "comforting" dishes as chicken in cream with chanterelles and chocolate soufflé, served by "a really nice" crew; in between the "American tourists" and – later on – "lots of locals", a "vivacious" ambiance prevails.

Auberge Dab (L') ◑ *Brasserie* | 16 | 15 | 14 | €53 |

16ᵉ | 161, av de Malakoff (Porte Maillot) | 01 45 00 32 22 | fax 01 45 00 58 50 | www.rest-gj.com

Come to this "honest", "practical" "neighborhood brasserie" for a "fresh" shellfish fix or some "consistent" classic dishes, served non-stop till 2 AM; fans find the well-heeled crowd from the surrounding 16th adds to the "old-fashioned charm" of the "typical decor"; but foes fume the place is "pretentious" and "overpriced for what it is."

Auberge de la Reine Blanche *Classic/New French* | 20 | 17 | 21 | €38 |

4ᵉ | 30, rue de St-Louis-en-l'Ile (Pont-Marie/St-Paul) | 01 46 33 07 87

"Cozy and charming", just like the Ile Saint-Louis where it's located, this "warm" little bistro is perfect for a low-key lunch or "casual dinner" of carefully cooked Classic and New French fare, served by an "inviting" staff; views vary as to whether the tight tables are "romantic" or "so small you risk eating your neighbors' dish", but prices are "very reasonable", given the "generous portions."

Auberge du Champ de Mars ⊠ *Classic French* | 23 | 19 | 22 | €41 |

7ᵉ | 18, rue de l'Exposition (Ecole Militaire) | 01 45 51 78 08

For fans of Classic French cooking, this "real gem" in the 7th offers "fantastic fare" for "incredibly good prices" in an "intimate neighborhood [atmosphere] that makes you feel like a regular"; the "adorable" "husband cooks, while his wife serves and greets", assisted by "uncommonly pleasant waiters"; in short, almost nothing but praise for this place that "breathes Old Paris."

Auberge du Clou (L') *Classic French* | ▽ 13 | 16 | 18 | €49 |

9ᵉ | 30, av Trudaine (Anvers/Pigalle) | 01 48 78 22 48 | fax 01 48 78 30 08 | www.aubergeduclou.fr

The "lovely" terrace out front is a major draw at this table "tucked away" in an increasingly gentrified corner of the 9th – though inside the "atmosphere is appealing" too, with its big working fireplace; a "change in owners in 2005" has meant a "much more Classic menu", though some "original" New French touches remain, as do the "attentive staff."

Auberge Etchégorry 🅢🅜 *Southwest*   20 | 16 | 17 | €44

13ᵉ | 41, rue Croulebarbe (Corvisart/Les Gobelins) | 01 44 08 83 51 | fax 01 44 08 83 69 | www.etchegorry.com

"Really good Southwestern cooking" has this long-running table Basque-ing in attention from admirers who "like cassoulet" and other "hearty" dishes; some sniff the food and "traditional-inn decor are a little faded" ("the place seems to be crumbling under dust") but "jolly service" and an "excellent price-value ratio" ensure "happy crowds" at this 13th-arrondissement address.

Auberge Nicolas Flamel 🅢 *Bistro*   20 | 19 | 18 | €48

3ᵉ | 51, rue de Montmorency (Rambuteau/Reamur Sébastopol) | 01 42 71 77 78 | fax 01 42 77 12 78 | www.auberge-nicolas-flamel.fr

"A haven for history buffs", this Marais mansion – the oldest in Paris – was the residence of medieval alchemist Nicolas Flamel; surprisingly, given its estimable age, it "isn't touristy" but rather pulls an arty crowd of locals for classic bistro cuisine with a few "inventive" touches that is "rather good", if "a little expensive", for the quality.

Auberge Pyrénées Cévennes (L') 🅢 *Southwest*   21 | 15 | 20 | €49

11ᵉ | 106, rue de la Folie-Méricourt (République) | 01 43 57 33 78

"The cassoulet could be the best in the world – but all else is pretty good too" at this "honest neighborhood table" near the Place de la République; a "hoot of an owner" reigns amid an "atmospheric" aubergelike decor as "friendly servers" set down "generous portions" of Lyonnais and Southwest dishes; prices are rising, but most still find them "reasonable", and the overall vibe "simply marvelous."

Auguste 🅢 *Classic French*   19 | 17 | 17 | €56

7ᵉ | 54, rue de Bourgogne (Varenne) | 01 45 51 61 09 | fax 01 45 51 27 34 | www.restaurantaugust.fr

With chef Gaël Orieux (ex Le Meurice) in back and "modern, sophisticated decor" out front, this Classic French on one of the 7th's poshest side streets "promises much, but misses on some of the executions" critics cavil (and the "small portions" don't help); still, the silk-stocking clientele finds the "rich" eats "tasty" enough, and the "service discreet."

Autobus Imperial (L') 🅢 *Classic French*   - | - | - | M

1ᵉʳ | 14, rue Mondétour (Etienne Marcel/Les Halles) | 01 42 36 00 18 | fax 01 42 36 00 18 | www.autobus-imperial.fr

Those willing to climb aboard this Classic French "right in the heart of Paris" near Les Halles will find a "remarkably good", if "slightly limited" menu served in a "calm", somewhat streamlined belle epoque setting topped by a glass-tiled skylight; there's also a tea salon where you can relax with a cuppa and listen to music while playing on your laptop or reading a local paper.

	FOOD	DECOR	SERVICE	COST

Autour du Mont ⑧Ⓜ Seafood — | — | — | M

15ᵉ | 58, rue Vasco de Gama (Lourmel) | 01 42 50 55 63

This cozy seafooder near the Porte de Versailles pulls a media crowd at noon – there are several TV studios nearby – and young working couples at night with an imaginatively prepared catch-of-the-day menu and a relaxed atmosphere; the contemporary, marine-themed decor may not be a memory-maker, but the hip atmosphere and moderate prices have made it popular.

Autour du Saumon Seafood — | — | — | M
(fka Comptoir du Saumon)

4ᵉ | 60, rue François Miron (St-Paul) | 01 42 77 23 08 | fax 01 42 77 44 75

15ᵉ | 116, rue de la Convention (Boucicaut) | 01 45 54 31 16 | fax 01 45 54 49 68 ⑧

17ᵉ | 3, av de Villiers (Villiers) | 01 40 53 89 00 | fax 40 53 89 89

Upstream surveyors say this trio of smoked-fish specialists are "places where you can taste all kinds of salmon of different origin"; but on the downstream side, the "decor looks like a company cafeteria", and cynics snap the food's "too expensive for what you get."

⦿ Avant Goût (L') ⑧Ⓜ New French 25 | 15 | 19 | €41

13ᵉ | 26, rue Bobillot (Place d'Italie) | 01 53 80 24 00 | fax 01 53 80 00 77

"If you're willing to make the trip to the 13th, this bustling bistro will never disappoint – and sometimes it'll stun" say supporters; the New French cuisine is "original", even "surprising" ("where else would we have been inspired to try a pig pot-au-feu?"), and "for a heck of a price" too; while the "minimally decorated" dining room has been redone, still "the tables are mighty close together" and service swings from "smiling" to "surly."

Avenue (L') ❶ New French 18 | 19 | 15 | €56

8ᵉ | 41, av Montaigne (Franklin D. Roosevelt) | 01 40 70 14 91 | fax 01 40 70 91 97

"Extreme style" sums up this "place to see-and-be-seen in the heart of fashionland", aka the Avenue Montaigne; Jacques Garcia's "cool" baroque decor is backdrop to the "up-to-the-minute-trendy" New French menu, and while "always good" – if "sooo nouveau riche" in price – "it's secondary to the people-watching"; "if you're not famous, getting the attention of the waitresses (all apparently models waiting to be spotted) can be tedious"; P.S. try to sit in the "lovely" "sidewalk-window area."

Azabu Japanese 20 | 17 | 19 | €49

6ᵉ | 3, rue André Mazet (Odéon) | 01 46 33 72 05

"A far cry from the usual sushi-and-yakitori" joints, this teppanyaki table near the Odéon "surprises" with "somber decor" and "a live chef who juggles the Kobe beef and shiitake mushrooms in front of you"; it's "certainly not cheap, as ingredients like foie gras find their way on to the menu, but this is the place to go if you want to feel like you're having a top-drawer business dinner on the Ginza"; P.S. the Philippe Starck–designed "bathrooms are not to be missed."

	FOOD	DECOR	SERVICE	COST

Baan-Boran ●🈲 Thai
21 | 15 | 18 | €40

1er | 43, rue de Montpensier (Palais Royal-Musée du Louvre) |
01 40 15 90 45 | www.baan-boran.com

"Thai food with a delicate touch" – including "typical dishes from
different regions" – distinguishes this "authentic" Siamese standby
in the 1st; amid a "nice, bright" – some say "sterile" – setting, patrons also praise the "non-pompous" servers; pity that the "portions
seem kind of small."

Babylone (Au) 🈲🍽 Bistro
- | - | - | I

7e | 13, rue de Babylone (Sèvres-Babylone) | 01 45 48 72 13 |
fax 01 45 50 36 52

Open only for lunch, this "old favorite" bistro in Sèvres-Babylone
may be "a bit outdated, but it's always a sure thing" for a "good
value" meal if you're museum-going or shopping on the Left Bank;
the '50s decor (complete with cracked-tile floor), brisk but friendly
waitresses and hearty homestyle cooking add to the sepia-toned
feel here, but don't dawdle – they sell out quickly.

Bacchantes (Les) ●🈲 Wine Bar/Bistro
- | - | - | M

9e | 21, rue de Caumartin (Havre-Caumartin/Opéra) |
01 42 65 25 35 | fax 01 47 42 65 87

"Nearly all the diners are French" at this "terrific little" *bistrot à vins*
near the Opéra Garnier, "a good post-theater address" for "quality"
"traditional French cuisine" to supplement the ample supply of
Southeastern vintages; bacchanalians beg "don't change a thing"
about the place – except the "slow service."

Baie d'Ha Long (La) Vietnamese
- | - | - | E

16e | 164, av de Versailles (Porte de St-Cloud) | 01 45 24 60 62 |
fax 01 42 30 58 98 | www.baiedhalong.com

"Not the usual run-of-the-mill Asian", this "authentic gem" on the
outskirts of the 16th offers up the "marvelous tastes of Vietnam"
"freshly cooked" in a recently redecorated, "intimate setting" of
bamboo, carved chairs and greenery ("hokey but sweet"); and if
some cynics say pho-ey to the "somewhat steep prices", others
think the "refined cuisine" is "worth every penny."

Ballon des Ternes (Le) ● Brasserie
15 | 12 | 13 | €54

17e | 103, av des Ternes (Porte Maillot) | 01 45 74 17 98 | fax 01 45 72 18 84
Located near the Porte Maillot, this "traditional brasserie" is a "convivial", if "slightly noisy" destination for "excellent shellfish" and
other "respectable" French classics; however, most foes find the fare
"costly for what it is", the service "middling" and even the "retro"
belle epoque decor, consisting of wood paneling, glass partitions,
moleskin banquettes and bric-a-brac, "uninteresting."

Ballon et Coquillages Seafood
- | - | - | M

17e | 71, bd Gouvion-St-Cyr (Porte Maillot) | 01 45 74 17 98 |
fax 01 45 72 18 84

Believers in bivalves assert the world really will be your oyster if you
head for this "wonderful" seafooder with counter-only service near

the Porte Maillot in the 17th; "sure, there's not much space, but that's the charm of this magical place where the waiter-host in the middle of the round bar" is a huge, knowledgeable "fan of shellfish who doesn't skimp on the wine" – "and the prices aren't prohibitive", either.

Bamboche (Le) *New French* 18 | 15 | 19 | €60
7ᵉ | 15, rue de Babylone (Sèvres-Babylone) | 01 45 49 14 40 | fax 01 45 49 14 44

Its ratings may not fully reflect the changed regime that's "trying hard" at this tiny table on a street "behind the Bon Marché" department store in the 7th; fans find that "owners Serge Arce and Philippe Fabert are brilliant chefs who do inventive New French cuisine", abetted by "efficient service", while opponents feel "the current offerings are well prepared but not outstanding" – and "definitely not worth the price."

Banyan ●🅢🅩 *Thai* ▽ 25 | 18 | 19 | €39
15ᵉ | 24, pl Etienne Pernet (Félix Faure) | 01 40 60 09 31 | fax 01 40 60 09 20

"Hyper-creative" cooking ("try the chocolate nems" for dessert) encourages enthusiasts to make the trek to this Thai table in the 15th; the "dishes are as good as they are pretty", and the storefront setting is "nice and cozy" too; while lunch is "super-reasonable", dinner can be "a bit pricey", wallet-watchers warn; but most surveyors don't mind since there is "so much imagination" at work here.

Baptiste 🅢🅜 *New French* ▽ 19 | 16 | 18 | €41
17ᵉ | 51, rue Jouffroy d'Abbans (Malesherbes/Wagram) | 01 42 27 20 18 | fax 01 43 80 68 09

Few know this "sophisticated" New French near the Place Wagram but those who do recommend it for the "excellent value" of its "good eats"; the "refined", cream-and-chocolate-colored decor pulls bankers at noon and well-dressed working couples in the evening, and service is generally "efficient" if a tad on the "stiff" side.

Bar à Huîtres (Le) ● *Seafood* 18 | 15 | 17 | €41
3ᵉ | 33, bd Beaumarchais (Bastille) | 01 48 87 98 92 | fax 01 48 87 04 42
5ᵉ | 33, rue St-Jacques (Maubert-Mutualité) | 01 44 07 27 37 | fax 01 43 26 71 62
14ᵉ | 112, bd du Montparnasse (Raspail/Vavin) | 01 43 20 71 01 | fax 01 43 20 52 04
www.lebarahuitres.com

The "eponymous [oyster] is the best thing" at this trio of seafooders "with kitschy, shells-plastered-all-over-the-walls" decor by Jacques Garcia; they're a tad "touristy" and "factorylike" (while "cordial", the staff's "happy to have you finish fast"), but they're "reliable for a quick, late supper"; do stick to playing the shell game, however, as "they don't know how to cook fish."

Baratin (Le) 🅢🅜 *Wine Bar/Bistro* – | – | – | M
20ᵉ | 3, rue Jouye-Rouve (Belleville) | 01 43 49 39 70

For a bona fide taste of *la vie bohème* in Paris today, this Belleville bistro/wine bar is hard to beat; painters, dancers and other *artistes* crowd into the two small dining rooms decorated with art for sale; Argentine chef Raquel Carena keeps them satisfied with a regularly changing market menu of contemporary dishes alongside cosmopolitan recipes of her own creation (in season, the red tuna tartare with black cherries is worth checking out).

Bar des Théâtres ❶ *Bistro*   13 | 10 | 14 | €44

8ᵉ | 6, av Montaigne (Alma Marceau) | 01 47 23 34 63 | fax 01 45 62 04 93
For 50 years, this "classic" bistro "facing the Théâtre des Champs-Elysées" has been "a rendezvous before or after the theater", "a place to stop if shopping on the Avenue Montaigne" or a "great perch for people-watching" the performers who often patronize it; if the "steak tartare is *magnifique*, the rest" of the menu is barely "adequate" – as is the service – and even the aura's "not what it was" since this vet "lost most of its dining rooms" to construction.

Barlotti ❷ *Italian*   15 | 21 | 15 | €48

1ᵉʳ | 35, pl du Marché St-Honoré (Pyramides/Tuilleries) | 01 44 86 97 97 | fax 01 44 86 97 98
"It's all about the decor" at this "modern Italian" in the midst of the furiously "trendy" Place du Marché Saint-Honoré – and yes, the setting's "superb", a two-story atrium with soaring glass windows, parquet floors and jewel-toned seats; but the "disappointed" declare if you're looking for "authentic cuisine" that's not "overpriced", you should walk right on past; as for the staff, they're quite "caring . . . about their tip."

Baron Rouge (Le) Ⓜ *Wine Bar/Bistro*   ▽ 19 | 15 | 14 | €26

12ᵉ | 1, rue Théophile Roussel (Ledru-Rollin) | 01 43 43 14 32
"Just off the Marché d'Aligre", this "really pleasant" *bar à vins* – a neighborhood "institution" – is a must for "amazing oysters" (a Sunday tradition) or "good cheese and sausage plates"; but of course, "it's mostly about the wine", which you can consume "standing up" *sur place* or bring home, in "decanters filled right from the barrel."

Barrio Latino ❶ *Pan-Latin*   11 | 19 | 10 | €40

12ᵉ | 46-48, rue du Faubourg St-Antoine (Bastille) | 01 55 78 84 75 | fax 01 55 78 85 30 | www.buddhabar.com
The "Pan-Latin fare" "isn't exceptional" – comparisons to "college dorm–type food" come to mind – and the service is close to "incompetent", but those seeking a "hot scene" for dancing and drinking don't mind at this "multilevel club"/restaurant in the 12th with an "international vibe", "great music" and "super decor" dominated by a grand staircase; in short, "not a first-date place (but maybe a third)."

Barroco ❷ *Pan-Latin*   – | – | – | M

6ᵉ | 23, rue Mazarine (Odéon/St-Germain-des-Prés) | 01 43 26 40 24 | fax 01 55 04 86 19 | www.restaurant-latino.com
Off the Odéon, this Pan-Latin shines with some of the "best Brazilian food in Paris", plus "tasty" dishes from other South American countries, served by "sexy staffers" in the earth-toned, "comforting", *casa*-like premises; live music nightly adds "nice ambiance."

	FOOD	DECOR	SERVICE	COST

Bartolo ◑ Ⓜ Italian | 18 | 9 | 11 | €38

6ᵉ | 7, rue des Canettes (St-Germain-des-Prés) | 01 43 26 27 08
What's "probably the best pizza in town – the way they do it in Naples", baked in a wood-burning beehive-shaped oven – has kept 'em coming for over 50 years to this Italian in Saint-Germain; however, its notoriously "nasty" service, tacky 1950s-vintage decor (complete with Bay of Naples vistas) and "pricey" tabs which you "must pay with cash" cause many to murmur it's "for masochists" only.

☒ Bar Vendôme *Classic French* | 21 | 27 | 24 | €60

1ᵉʳ | Hôtel Ritz | 15, pl Vendôme (Concorde/Opéra) | 01 43 16 33 63 | fax 01 43 16 33 75 | www.ritzparis.com
"Cosmopolitan", "elegant and movie-star-ish" – "would you expect anything less from the Ritz?" – this "*très* chic" bar in the famed hotel is a "favorite for lunches" of "delicious", "light" Classic French fare served by "excellent", "discreet" staffers ("it's also good for tea"); of course, prices are pretty "decadent", but "treat yourself, even if just for a drink" – "it'll be the most expensive cocktail you've ever ordered, but worth every centime."

Bascou (Au) ☒ *Basque* | 22 | 13 | 20 | €39

3ᵉ | 38, rue Réaumur (Arts et Métiers) | 01 42 72 69 25 | fax 01 55 90 99 77
"A touch of French Basque country right at the center of Paris" flourishes at this cracked-tile "hole-in-the-wall" in the 3rd; with its "wonderful food" and "quality Southwestern wines", "this is the kind of place you tell no one about, so it remains uncrowded" – and its prices "fair"; N.B. the arrival of a new chef-owner post-Survey may outdate the scores.

Basilic (Le) *Basque* | 14 | 13 | 15 | €39

7ᵉ | 2, rue Casimir Périer (Invalides/Solférino) | 01 44 18 94 64 | fax 01 44 18 33 97 | www.lebasilic.fr
Possessing a "lovely terrace" "away from traffic and overlooking the park" that surrounds the Basilique Sainte-Clothilde ("hence, the play on basilica" in the name), this establishment in the silk-stocking 7th can be "charming for a Sunday evening" admirers attest; however, some sermonize that the Basque–Classic French cooking is "pleasant without prompting any gastronomic emotion" – even the signature leg of lamb is "uninteresting" – and there's almost "no service to speak of."

Bastide Odéon (La) ☒ Ⓜ *Provence* | 20 | 18 | 19 | €47

6ᵉ | 7, rue Corneille (Odéon) | 01 43 26 03 65 | fax 01 44 07 28 93 | www.bastide-odeon.com
This "contemporary" bistro in Saint-Germain is popular with Americans in-the-know – so much so, they "tend to be seated together; some say it's to ensure we have an English-speaking server, while a cynic might surmise we're being hidden from the locals"; tables aside, surveyors split over this Southern French specialist: fans find the cuisine and "pleasant atmosphere" in the red-and-yellow rooms make it "almost as good as a trip to Provence", but others shrug it's "a standby, not a destination."

	FOOD	DECOR	SERVICE	COST

Bath's 🄢 *Auvergne/New French* — — — M

17ᵉ | 25, rue Bayen (Charles de Gaulle-Etoile) | 01 45 74 74 74 |
fax 01 45 74 71 15 | www.baths.fr

Aficionados of the Auvergne, rejoice: the father/son management
team of Jean-Yves and Stéphane Bath is back, now serving up both
New French and those hearty-yet-refined Auvergnat dishes (don't
miss the stuffed cabbage, when it's available) that made their old
place in the 8th so popular with the professional crowd; however, as
befits the address in the outlying 17th, prices in their new cozy, contemporary dining room are now significantly lower.

Beato 🄢 *Italian* ▽ 18 | 16 | 18 | €59

7ᵉ | 8, rue Malar (Invalides) | 01 47 05 94 27 | fax 01 45 55 64 41

Near Les Invalides, this "tranquil" Italian with a "beautiful interior"
pulls politicians at noon and stylish neighborhood couples at night
with "food that's more than pleasurable", served by a "professional"
staff; perhaps it's "pricier than others of its ilk", but it's a "class"
operation – and "you can dine late" (until 11 PM) too.

Beaujolais d'Auteuil (Le) *Classic French* 15 | 11 | 14 | €36

16ᵉ | 99, bd de Montmorency (Porte d'Auteuil) | 01 47 43 03 56 |
fax 01 46 51 27 81

"Simple food and fair prices" – nearly every voter says it offers "good
value for the money" – explain why this Classic French has "aged
well" over the last 20 years, attracting a "lively, local crowd" from
the 16th; it's a "perfect example of the red-checkered tablecloth
genre", even if the decor "deserves a lick of paint" and the snug seating "forces you to listen to your neighbor's conversations."

BE Boulangépicier *Sandwiches* 22 | 14 | 16 | €20

8ᵉ | 73, bd de Courcelles (Courcelles/Ternes) | 01 46 22 20 20 |
fax 01 46 22 20 21
NEW **9ᵉ** | Printemps | 64, bd Hausmann, 3rd fl. (Havre-Caumartin) |
01 42 82 67 17 🄢🄜
www.boulangepicier.com

Look for "amusing, if expensive, alternatives to classic sandwiches",
"tasty salads" and "too many wonderful pastries" at this "posh" "bak-
ery/grocery store by Alain Ducasse"; it's perfect for taking "gourmet
lunches" "to the Parc Monceau" close by – perhaps a preferable option
to eating in the "Formica setting" of the "small restaurant in back";
N.B. there's now a second snacking site in the Printemps store.

Bel Canto *Italian* 15 | 15 | 20 | €54

4ᵉ | 72, quai de l'Hôtel de Ville (Hôtel-de-Ville/Pont-Marie) |
01 42 78 30 18 | fax 01 42 78 30 28
14ᵉ | 88, rue de la Tombe-Issoire (Alésia) | 01 43 22 96 15 |
fax 01 43 27 09 88 🄢🄜
Neuilly-sur-Seine | 6, rue du Commandant Pilot (Les Sablons) |
01 47 47 19 94 | fax 01 47 38 60 49 🄢🄜
www.lebelcanto.com

"An excellent idea for opera lovers", this Italian trio's staffed by students "with delicious voices" from the Opéra de Paris Conservatory

who perform when not "doing table service"; "it's a pity the food is not better" – in fact, it feels "way overpriced", despite the added live-entertainment factor; still, "the servers are singing lyrical arias, and that makes everything romantic" (or conversely, "perfect with people you have nothing to say to").

Bellini ⑤ *Italian*

| 18 | 14 | 14 | €54 |

16ᵉ | 28, rue Lesueur (Argentine) | 01 45 00 54 20 | fax 01 45 00 11 74
"With its ochre-colored walls and air-conditioning", this *raffinato* Italian in the 16th serves up "very agreeable" pastas, including "one that comes inside of a hollowed-out wheel of Parmesan cheese"; a few cast doubts on the authenticity of the kitchen, suspecting that many of "the sauces are made with crème fraîche", but the "formal service" and "peaceful atmosphere" carry the day for most.

Bellota-Bellota ⑤ Ⓜ *Spanish*

| 19 | 14 | 16 | €48 |

7ᵉ | 18, rue Jean-Nicot (La Tour-Maubourg) | 01 53 59 96 96 | fax 01 53 59 70 44
"If there were a Nobel prize for ham", they'd win it at this *jamon*-and-wine bar in the 7th, which attracts with an "awesome" array of the cured pork, plus Spanish cheeses, wines and bread from the bakery next door; "amiable service" and modest but "pretty decor" of azulejo tiles explain why the place is so "popular with the locals", though even they lament the "expensive" cost of hamming it up.

Benkay *Japanese*

| ▽ 23 | 16 | 18 | €92 |

15ᵉ | Hôtel Novotel Tour Eiffel | 61, quai de Grenelle (Bir-Hakeim/Charles Michels) | 01 40 58 21 26 | fax 01 40 58 21 30 | www.novotel.com
Perched atop a hotel in the 15th, what some call "the best Japanese in Paris" has "gorgeous views of the Seine", although you're not likely to spend a lot of time river-gazing when the sushi and teppanyaki chefs are practicing their "imaginative" art in front of you; "prices are as spectacular" as the food, but the fact that it's patronized by presidents (this is a "Chirac hangout") makes Benkay A-ok for most.

ⓩ Benoît *Lyon*

| 24 | 21 | 22 | €73 |

4ᵉ | Hôtel de Ville | 20, rue St-Martin (Châtelet-Les Halles) | 01 42 72 25 76 | fax 01 42 72 45 68 | www.alain-ducasse.com
Since this "ultimate" belle epoque–era bistro "close to Les Halles" is one of the best-loved "time capsules" in Paris, anxiety greeted the news that gastro-entrepreneurs Alain Ducasse and Thierry de la Brosse had bought it; but steady scores suggest it's "still wonderful and worth the money" – a lot of money – for "delicious", "decadent" Lyonnais "classics" ("make sure you have nap time planned"); "service is lively", but "don't cross the maitre d'", or you'll be "rushed into the side room with all of the Americans."

Berkeley (Le) ● *Eclectic*

| 12 | 15 | 12 | €53 |

8ᵉ | 7, av Matignon (Champs-Elysées-Clémenceau) | 01 42 25 72 25 | fax 01 45 63 30 06 | www.leberkeley.com
It may have "a great location" just off the Champs-Elysées, but the "indifferent", "expensive-for-what-you-get" Classic French–Eclectic

eats and "cool – make that frozen – service" at this "brasserie de luxe" leave most surveyors cold; still, some supporters smile at the striped-tented ceiling, the most noticeable feature of the decor, and "the great terrace out front", "a fantastic spot to see everyone who's anyone pass by."

Beurre Noisette (Le) 🗷 🅼 *Bistro* | 21 | 12 | 15 | €44 |

15ᵉ | 68, rue Vasco de Gama (Lourmel/Porte de Versailles) | 01 48 56 82 49 | fax 01 48 28 59 38

"Young and inventive chef"-owner Thierry Blanqui makes it "worth the trek to the remote reaches of the 15th" and this "tiny" bistro, with cooking that "creatively builds on the classics" using "lots of herbs and spices"; the Provençal-toned decor is "simple, but in good taste", and if some say the service ranks low "on the hospitality scale", the "fair prices" restore the balance ("the lunch menu for only 20 euros – how do they do it?").

Biche au Bois (A la) 🗷 *Bistro* | 21 | 12 | 20 | €36 |

12ᵉ | 45, av Ledru-Rollin (Gare de Lyon) | 01 43 43 34 38

"Not far from the Gare de Lyon", this "crowded" site has been a "reliable bistro" since 1925, offering "down-home Classic French cookin'" served by a "remarkably attentive staff"; as the name suggests (*biche* means deer), it's also "the place to go for game" in season; but they're "always busy", so book ahead.

BIOArt 🗷 *New French* | - | - | - | M |

13ᵉ | 3, quai François Mauriac (Bibliothèque François Mitterrand) | 01 45 85 66 88 | fax 01 45 85 04 24 | www.bioart.fr

Resetting the clock on 1960s hippie-ish health food, this spacious, contemporary dining room – self-styled as the largest organic restaurant in Paris – uses "excellent quality produce" to create "light and refined" New French dishes (such as guinea fowl with cabbage, chocolate-orange terrine); the naturally minded orientation extends to the environs, an ecological building with glass-wall views of the Seine and the area around the Bibliothèque François Mitterrand.

NEW Bis du Severo (Le) 🗷 🅼 *Bistro* | - | - | - | M |

14ᵉ | 16, rue des Plantes (Mouton Duvenet/Pernetty) | 01 40 44 73 09

In a quiet corner of Montparnasse, this tiny, warm-toned annex to the very popular Le Severo just down the street fills its bare-wood tables nightly with locals who love the traditional bistro cooking of Japanese chef Shigeno Makoto; his kitchen works with first-rate ingredients and dishes out generous servings, both of which make the gentle prices even more appetizing.

Bistral (Le) 🗷 🅼 *Bistro* | ▽ 23 | 14 | 18 | €44 |

17ᵉ | 80, rue Lemercier (Brochant/Pl. de Clichy) | 01 42 63 59 61 | fax 01 42 63 59 61

Led by chef-owner "Alexandre Mathieu, a protégé of François Pasteau of L'Epi Dupin fame", "the people who [run] this restaurant are passionate" and it shows in the "inspired", "uniformly innovative dishes" – "particularly the cooked-to-perfection vegetables" – produced "at fair prices"; the "staff's lovely" and the "decor attractively zany", and although you're "cramped" in the "smoky, narrow room", "it's a small amount to pay for the privilege of eating here" at this modern bistro in the 17th.

Bistro 121 *Bistro* ▽ 20 | 15 | 19 | €56

15ᵉ | 121, rue de la Convention (Boucicaut) | 01 45 57 52 90 | fax 01 45 57 14 69

The "decor's slightly faded" (as the very "bright lights" reveal) and it gets "crowded and noisy", but you can order "a good meal" of "classical cooking" at this bistro in the 15th; service is friendly and "unpretentious", so the general verdict on this veteran is "still one of my favorites."

Bistro de Breteuil (Le) *Bistro* 18 | 16 | 17 | €36

7ᵉ | 3, pl de Breteuil (Duroc) | 01 45 67 07 27 | fax 01 42 73 11 08 | www.bistro-et-cie.fr

"A real bargain of a prix fixe that includes three courses and a bottle of wine" keeps this "stuff-yourself" bistro "popular with the locals" of the 7th; admittedly, the Classic French fare "ain't no Haute Cuisine" and the pace makes for rather "mechanical service", but "there's plenty to choose from on the regularly changing menu", "tables are decently spaced" and there's a "great terrace in summer", so why carp?

Bistro de l'Olivier (Le) *Provence* 20 | 17 | 23 | €49

8ᵉ | 13, rue Quentin-Bauchart (George V) | 01 47 20 78 63 | fax 01 47 20 74 58

"Imagine you're in Nice" at this "welcoming spot" "just a few blocks off the Champs-Elysées"; in between the "quite nice" cuisine and the "hospitable staff", it offers an "authentic" "glimpse of Provence in the upscale 8th"; best of all, the "menu's a bargain" "for this expensive area of town."

Bistro des Deux Théâtres (Le) ● *Bistro* 15 | 12 | 13 | €42

9ᵉ | 18, rue Blanche (Trinité) | 01 45 26 41 43 | fax 01 48 74 08 92 | www.bistrocie.fr

Featuring "three courses and a bottle of wine", "the prix fixe is a fabulous value" at this veteran in the 9th arrondissement that's part of the "same chain as Bistro Melrose"; however, it's clearly the cheap eats that keep this production running, since most "find it average" foodwise, and the "theatrical, red-curtained" decor is "aging"; but at least the "hurried service" makes it "good for [pre- and] post-theater meals."

Bistro d'Hubert (Le) *Bistro* 20 | 16 | 18 | €48

15ᵉ | 41, bd Pasteur (Pasteur) | 01 47 34 15 50 | fax 01 45 67 03 09 | www.bistrodhubert.com

The country chic of the "original" "yellow-and-blue decor" pleases all comers at this "agreeable bistro not too far from the Gare Montparnasse", which dishes up "down-to-earth" New French food; "attentive" service gets a tip of the hat too, and overall it's "a nice little neighborhood eatery" that "isn't too expensive."

	FOOD	DECOR	SERVICE	COST

Bistro du 17ème (Le) ⑤ *Bistro* — 16 | 13 | 15 | €36
17e | 108, av de Villiers (Péreire) | 01 47 63 32 77 |
fax 01 42 27 67 66 | www.bistro-et-cie.fr
True to bargain bistrotier Willy Dorr's reputation, his outpost in the
17th offers "one of the best dinner buys you'll find in Paris" – three
courses of "solid French food and a bottle of wine", plus coffee, "at
a one-price-fits-all tab"; dissenters deride the place a "factory
bistro" – certainly the service has an "assembly-line" attitude – but
enthusiasts enjoy the "excellent value in congenial surroundings."

Bistro Melrose ❶ *Bistro* — – | – | – | I
17e | 5, pl de Clichy (Place de Clichy) | 01 42 93 61 34 |
fax 01 44 70 99 19 | www.bistrocie.fr
Whether you think this bistro on the Place de Clichy is "a tourist
trap" or "the best bang for the buck in Paris" (or both), it's clearly
"popular", thanks to its patented prix fixe formula of "three courses
with a bottle of wine" – a drill that pulls droves of denizens, as do all of
owner Willy Dorr's domains, despite "service that can be slow."

Bistro St. Ferdinand ❶ *Bistro* — 16 | 14 | 16 | €37
17e | 275, bd Péreire (Porte Maillot) | 01 45 74 33 32 |
fax 01 45 74 33 12 | www.bistro-et-cie.fr
In an expensive neck of the woods in the 17th, it's "worth hunting
down" this bistro, because "the prix fixe is really appealing" – three
courses, and "even wine's included"; true, the Classic French "food and
service are variable", but it's "always crowded" (and "too noisy") with
folks who "leave feeling they've had more than their money's worth."

Bistrot à Vins Mélac ⑤ Ⅿ *Wine Bar/Bistro* — ▽ 16 | 17 | 17 | €28
11e | 42, rue Léon Frot (Charonne) | 01 43 70 59 27 | fax 01 43 70 73 10 |
www.melac.fr
"Simple Auvergnat cuisine and potent Southern French wines are
complemented by generous and sincere service from the 'perform-
ing' barmen", which is why celebrity vinophile Jacques Mélac's "fun,
neighborhood-y *bar à vins* in the 11th has, for 40 years, offered such
a "great" time; "you only pay for what you drink [vs. the whole bot-
tle], and you always leave with a full stomach and a light heart."

Bistrot Baracane ❶❷⑤ *Southwest* — 23 | 14 | 21 | €37
4e | 38, rue des Tournelles (Chemin-Vert) | 01 42 71 43 33 |
fax 01 40 02 04 77 | www.l-oulette.com
"Fabulous" Southwest food makes this "tiny little place" in the 4th "a
favorite bistro", even if "tables are incredibly close together"; a few
fret it's "not as special now that it's been found" by the tourists, but the
cassoulet and *canard* crowd call them quacks, insisting that with a
"sweet staff", "generous servings" and "reasonable prices", "you're
never disappointed"; N.B. a recent revamp outdates the Decor score.

Bistrot Bigorneau (Le) ⑤ Ⅿ *Seafood* — 15 | 16 | 17 | €45
16e | 71, av Paul Doumer (La Muette) | 01 45 04 12 81 | fax 01 45 04 00 50
"Strategically situated" in the 16th, this seafooder's "nice red" nautical
setting provides a "young, relaxed" aura; but if the cholesterol-

conscious crow over "cuisine with little or no cream – hooray!", sharks snap "the portions are too small and the prices too big", and "service is adequate" at best; "neat but no thrills" sums up the experience.

Bistrot d'à Côté *Bistro*   20 | 17 | 16 | €46

17ᵉ | 10, rue Gustave Flaubert (Péreire/Ternes) | 01 42 67 05 81 | fax 01 47 63 82 75
17ᵉ | 16, av de Villiers (Villiers) | 01 47 63 25 61 | fax 01 48 88 92 42 🖫
Neuilly-sur-Seine | 4, rue Boutard (Pont-de-Neuilly) |
01 47 45 34 55 | fax 01 47 45 15 08 🖫
www.michelrostang.com
"Favorites with the bustling advertising and PR crowd", chef-owner Michel Rostang's "intimate" baby bistros serve "solid", "simple" Classic French cuisine that seems "always the same" – that is, "consistently delicious"; "service is variable" – "efficient" vs. "distracted" – and the fare can be "too expensive for what you get"; "but with excellent ingredients and attentive preparation", "the quality is there"; P.S. "the old-grocery decor is nice" in the 17th.

Bistrot d'André (Le) *Bistro*   – | – | – | I

15ᵉ | 232, rue St-Charles (Balard) | 01 45 57 89 14 | fax 01 45 57 97 15
Though this former factory workers' canteen (from a defunct Citroën plant across the street) is "cheap", the classic bistro cooking is "kind of ordinary" some roadsters rage; but fans find the car-making memorabilia, neighborhood groove and "trendy" vibe add up to an appealing pit stop; also, "it's open on Sunday, and that helps."

Bistrot de l'Etoile Lauriston ●🖫 *Bistro*   19 | 15 | 18 | €45

16ᵉ | 19, rue Lauriston (Kléber) | 01 40 67 11 16 | fax 01 45 00 99 87
"A great buy for the money", this bistro near the namesake Etoile is "a friendly favorite for the smart business traveler" or anyone who wants to be "away from the tourist hustle and bustle"; the menu is "reliably" "inventive but appealing" and the "service personal"; the only weak spot is "the room that aspires to minimalist elegance", but is defeated by *"Bonjour Tristesse"*-type decor.

Bistrot de l'Etoile Niel *Bistro*   19 | 13 | 16 | €47

17ᵉ | 75, av Niel (Péreire) | 01 42 27 88 44 | fax 01 42 27 32 12
In the 17th, this "cozy little bistro" by "a student of Guy Savoy" offers "spirited, creative" cooking that uses "quality produce"; however, while "friendly", the service is often "rushed, which stresses out clients", and despite the moderate tags, virtually every reviewer says it's "not such good value" for what you get; P.S. the Decor score may not fully reflect a recent, "colorful" renovation.

Bistrot de l'Université 🖫 *Bistro*   ▽ 15 | 12 | 18 | €32

7ᵉ | 40, rue de l'Université (Rue du Bac) | 01 42 61 26 64 | fax 01 42 61 26 64
The "simple" "little bistro you've been looking for" may reside in this "local spot" in the 7th; perhaps the cuisine's "nothing to write home about", but given the relatively "inexpensive" prices, patrons "have yet to find a *plat* that will not please"; if the service can be "frustratingly slow", "this place is so sincerely Parisian, you forget the clock."

	FOOD	DECOR	SERVICE	COST

Bistrot de Marius (Le) *Seafood*
17 | 13 | 16 | €53

8ᵉ | 6, av George V (Alma Marceau) | 01 40 70 11 76 | fax 01 40 70 17 08

"Functional fish" is the bait at this "reliable offshoot of Marius et Janette next door" in the "fashionable" Golden Triangle (tip: "speak French to avoid talking to the rich American women who are here because it's close to Chanel"); if the food's "unoriginal", at least it's "fresh", and the atmosphere "pleasant", especially if you "try the terrace" in summer.

Bistrot de Paris (Le) ●🗲 *Bistro*
19 | 18 | 20 | €43

7ᵉ | 33, rue de Lille (Rue du Bac/St-Germain-des-Prés) | 01 42 61 16 83 | fax 01 49 27 06 09

Its "current management has worked hard" to turn this "old bistro" (circa 1903) in the 7th around, and an across-the-board score rise confirms "they've succeeded"; "good, if not excellent" "honest French cooking" is dished up by "cheerful" servers in a "wonderful", "traditional" gas-lamp and bevel-mirror setting; if it gets "too noisy" at times, that's all part of the "classic" ambiance.

Bistrot des Dames (Le) ● *Bistro*
▽ 15 | 16 | 12 | €34

17ᵉ | Hôtel El Dorado | 18, rue des Dames (Place de Clichy) | 01 45 22 13 42 | fax 01 43 87 25 97

"You have to go in summer for the garden" and "wonderful terrace" at this edgy, stylish little bistro in the ever-trendier Batignolles neighborhood; the "menu's unchanging, but suitable", and it's a "great place for friends and drinks", especially when the prices are as easygoing as the cigarette-happy crowd.

Bistrot des Vignes (Le) *Bistro*
▽ 13 | 14 | 15 | €34

16ᵉ | 1, rue Jean-de-Bologne (La Muette/Passy) | 01 45 27 76 64 | fax 01 45 27 76 64 | www.bistrotdesvignes.fr

Habitués hail this Passy place as a "good little" bistro, with "really nice service" – "they bring the dishes on wooden trays" – and colorful, "charming decor"; if the food itself is at best "acceptable", at least "the tabs are honest."

Bistrot d'Henri (Le) ● *Bistro*
17 | 14 | 20 | €37

6ᵉ | 16, rue Princesse (Mabillon/St-Germain-des-Prés) | 01 46 33 51 12

"Tight quarters" ("it's better when the weather allows the front windows to stay open") mean "a warm and friendly atmosphere" at this "tiny, bustling bistro" "in the heart of Saint-Germain"; the Classic French cuisine is "plentiful, without being fine or light" – rather, "the accent's on good meat, hearty wine and maybe the best potato gratin in the world"; if foes insist "you can do better in this area", at least it's "a relative bargain" – with "cute waiters" too.

Bistrot du Cap (Le) *Seafood*
– | – | – | M

15ᵉ | 30, rue Peclet (Convention/Vaugirard) | 01 40 43 02 18 | fax 01 40 43 02 18

"A fine establishment", especially for fish, affirm the few who've found this teakwood-furnished, family-run bistro in a quiet spot overlooking a pedestrian-only street in the 15th; the owners, "the

	FOOD	DECOR	SERVICE	COST

Quintards, are always quite nice", and it's "great for lunch outside" on the bushy terrace.

Bistrot du Dôme (Le) *Seafood*   19 | 15 | 17 | €44
14ᵉ | 1, rue Delambre (Vavin) | 01 43 35 32 00

Dôme Bastille (Le) *Seafood*
4ᵉ | 2, rue de la Bastille (Bastille) | 01 48 04 88 44 | fax 01 48 04 00 59

"Never empty", this pair of seafood bistros, in the 14th and the 4th, form "a miraculous chain" that some think rivals the *maison mère,* Le Dôme; certainly, "it's a better deal than its parent", offering "always delicious fish" ("that's all they have") with "good-humored service."

Bistrot du Peintre (Le) ◗ *Bistro*   16 | 16 | 14 | €29
11ᵉ | 116, av Ledru-Rollin (Bastille/Ledru-Rollin) | 01 47 00 34 39

"Come to people-watch in the up-and-coming neighborhood" near the Bastille at this venue with a "great old chipped art nouveau interior" and "solid" "bistro basics" at a "good buy"; however, "the service deteriorates as the night goes on and it gets busier."

Bistrot du Sommelier ⬛ *Wine Bar/Bistro*   20 | 13 | 19 | €68
8ᵉ | 97, bd Haussmann (St-Augustin) | 01 42 65 24 85 |
fax 01 53 75 23 23 | www.bistrodusommelier.com

"A charming sommelier encourages you to guess the wine before he identifies it" at this bacchanalian bistro known for "selected pairings with each course" of "succulent", "inventive" fare; situated in a well-heeled business quarter of the 8th; it can get "very dear", but "sometimes you just have to offer yourself a good time."

Bistrot Papillon (Le) ⬛ *Bistro*   ▽ 20 | 15 | 18 | €38
9ᵉ | 6, rue Papillon (Cadet/Poissonnière) | 01 47 70 90 03 |
fax 01 48 24 05 59

"Hard to find but definitely worth the trip", this classic bistro in the 9th takes its name from the somewhat "strange" framed butterfly collections on the walls; in contrast to the fluttery ambiance, the kitchen produces "solid", "creamy" "French comfort food" from a "traditional menu that uses really good produce"; "reasonable prices" and "discreetly attentive service" make this a place to flap your wings.

Bistrot Paul Bert (Le) ⬛Ⓜ *Bistro*   20 | 12 | 17 | €38
11ᵉ | 18, rue Paul Bert (Faidherbe-Chaligny) | 01 43 72 24 01 |
fax 01 43 72 24 66

Featuring "funky decor" of flea-market finds and a "beautiful blackboard" of bistro delights, this "wonderful neighborhood standby" in the 11th conjures up *Vieux Paris* with a vengeance; "service is fast", and there's a 450-label "wine list to satisfy everyone"; only problem is, it's now "too well-known", and hence "crowded" and ringing with the din of those who've made it their "den."

Bistrot Vivienne ⬛ *Bistro*   15 | 18 | 15 | €36
2ᵉ | 4, rue des Petits-Champs (Bourse/Palais Royal-Musée du Louvre) |
01 49 27 00 50 | fax 01 49 27 00 40

"Best for a quick lunch" with friends decrees the "young crowd" that frequents this "well-located" "little bistro"; it's got "average food, but great ambiance", especially if you "obtain a table" outside "in the fabulous Galerie Vivienne."

NEW Black Calavados ●⊠ *Eclectic* | – | – | – | E |

8ᵉ | 40, av Pierre 1er de Serbie (George V) | 01 47 20 77 77 | fax 01 47 20 77 01 | www.bc-paris.fr

Named after a legendary '60s club (in turn inspired by a Serge Gainsbourg song), this newcomer is already one of the hottest hangouts for the 8th's fashion crowd, tempting its jaded palates with Eclectic dishes like peanut butter sole and caramelized quail; co-owned by rocker Chris Cornell, the black-lacquer and leather room was created by Alexandre de Betak, who's done runway shows for Christian Dior and Viktor & Rolf – so yes, that guy with the pirate mustache next to you may well be Dior designer John Galliano; N.B. the bar downstairs whirls up alcohol-laced milkshakes until 4 AM.

Blue Elephant ● *Thai* | 19 | 24 | 17 | €52 |

11ᵉ | 43-45, rue de la Roquette (Bastille/Voltaire) | 01 47 00 42 00 | fax 01 47 00 45 44 | www.blueelephant.com

While it's "more theme park than restaurant, with jungle sounds, waterfalls and bamboo thickets", the "whimsical" food is a "pleasant surprise" at what the "transported" term one of the "top Thais" in town; "service is friendly although a bit automated", and "on nights with lots of groups" the place is "like a Dantesque version of Trader Vic's" – and it's "overpriced" ("you mainly pay for the decor"); still, most esteem this "extravaganza" for offering a "Bangkok escapade" close to the Bastille.

Bocconi (Trattoria) ⊠ *Italian* | ▽ 22 | 14 | 23 | €48 |

8ᵉ | 10 bis, rue d'Artois (St-Philippe-du-Roule) | 01 53 76 44 44 | fax 01 45 61 10 08

"Worth a detour", this Italian with "a swanky setting in an upscale neighborhood" (the 8th) is "reminiscent of Tuscany"; "genius chef Ciro Polge" (ex Il Cortile) does "delicious antipasti and pastas" in a "light, modern" style, and it's brought to table by equally "authentic" service – that is, "charming" and "good-humored."

Boeuf Couronné (Au) ● *Classic French* | 17 | 12 | 15 | €49 |

19ᵉ | 188, av Jean Jaurès (Porte de Pantin) | 01 42 39 44 44 | fax 01 42 39 17 30 | www.rest-gj.com

"The French answer to American steakhouses", this "old-fashioned" carnivores' cave in a distant corner of the 19th (where the city's slaughterhouses once were) specializes in "excellent meat"; the remainder of the menu's "nothing exceptional", but patrons applaud the "patient staff", and the once-"dated" decor has recently gotten a refurb (not reflected in the Decor score).

Boeuf sur le Toit (Le) ● *Brasserie* | 16 | 19 | 15 | €50 |

8ᵉ | 34, rue du Colisée (Franklin D. Roosevelt/St-Philippe-du-Roule) | 01 53 93 65 55 | fax 01 53 96 02 32 | www.boeufsurletoit.com

Off the Champs-Elysées, this "warehouse-sized restaurant" is a "true brasserie, with all that implies": "beautifully mirrored" "art deco ambiance", "noisy rooms" and "reliable steaks" – though "you'll have no beef with" the "huge seafood platters" either; true, it's "a bit touristy" – hence "pricey" – and the service uneven ("half the staff ignored us; unfortunately that was the half we were trying to order with"); but at least, "it's great for late-night."

☒ Bofinger ◗ *Brasserie*   `20` `24` `18` `€52`
4ᵉ | 5, rue de la Bastille (Bastille) | 01 42 72 87 82 |
fax 01 42 72 97 68 | www.bofingerparis.com

"The decor is awesome" – "everyone wants to eat under the glass dome" – at this "beautiful" "time machine" ("it feels like a French movie set") "in the trendy Bastille quarter"; filled with the "constant buzz of busy *serveurs*", it's still "a must-go, as much for the crowd as the food", though the "authentic" Alsatian eats ("choucroute, etc.") are quite "enjoyable"; as with many "venerable" venues, cynics sneer it's "resting on its reputation laurels", but to most this "institution" is among "the best brasseries you'll find."

Bon ◗ *New French*   `15` `24` `14` `€63`
16ᵉ | 25, rue de la Pompe (La Muette) | 01 40 72 70 00 |
fax 01 40 72 68 30 | www.restaurantbon.fr

"You'll never eat in a more surreal environment" than at this almost "painfully hip" table in the 16th, with its "impressive" "Philippe Starck design"; stalwarts say the "creative" Contemporary French cuisine has "improved" since the team that runs Copenhague took over, and is now "pretty darned" *bon* (if still "too dear for what it is"); but the belligerent bellow the place has become "boring and dated" – oh, and "forget the food, since most of the waiters have forgotten you."

Bon Accueil (Au) ☒ *Bistro*   `24` `19` `22` `€50`
7ᵉ | 14, rue de Monttessuy (Alma Marceau/Ecole Militaire) |
01 47 05 46 11 | fax 01 45 56 15 80

What a pleasure it is "to come out of a fantastic meal and see the Eiffel Tower all lit up" profess fans of this "friendly bistro with an up-scale feel" in the 7th; "the amazing view helps the decor" inside, but the food – think "refined" and "delicious" Classic French cuisine – does quite well on its own; an "incredibly gracious staff" and "reasonable prices" make it "beloved by tourists and locals alike."

Bon Saint Pourçain (Le) ☒⇗ *Classic French*   `17` `9` `21` `€36`
6ᵉ | 10 bis, rue Servandoni (Odéon/St-Sulpice) | 01 43 54 93 63

"If French home cooking exists in public, this is where you'll find it" – "hidden on a picturesque street" in Saint-Germain, at a "hole-in-the-wall" where Papa the *patron* "rules the roost and his daughter provides smooth service"; while the "menu's limited", you get "large portions" of "real old-fashioned" classic dishes, which compensate for the "cramped" "dingy" digs.

Bons Crus (Aux) ☒ *Wine Bar/Bistro*   `–` `–` `–` `|`
1ᵉʳ | 7, rue des Petits-Champs (Bourse/Palais Royal-Musée du Louvre) |
01 42 60 06 45 | fax 01 42 33 62 83

"Go as often as you can" to one of "the best wine and charcuterie bars in Paris", "located on the backside of the Palais Royal"; "they've been serving for over 100 years", and the place is still bursting at the rafters at noon (but more "relaxed" at night).

Boucherie Roulière ⓜ *Bistro*

	FOOD	DECOR	SERVICE	COST
	-	-	-	M

6ᵉ | 24, rue des Canettes (St-Sulpice) | 01 43 26 25 70

Adorned with plain, brown-and-white decor and bare wooden tables, this narrow, traditionally brisk bistro near Saint-Sulpice attracts antiques dealers and book editors with an appealing menu that emphasizes grilled meats (well, that's what happens when the amiable owners are, respectively, a fifth-generation butcher and a native of the beef-producing Auvergne region), though there's nice tuna steak too.

Bouchons de François Clerc (Les) 🗷 *Wine Bar/Bistro*

	FOOD	DECOR	SERVICE	COST
	19	15	17	€54

8ᵉ | 7, rue du Boccador (Alma Marceau) | 01 47 23 57 80 | fax 01 47 23 74 54

Cuisine Colbert (La) *Wine Bar/Bistro*

5ᵉ | 12, rue de l'Hôtel-Colbert (Maubert-Mutualité) | 01 43 54 15 34 | fax 01 43 34 68 07

"With wines close to cost", this duo of separately owned *bistrots à vins* "titillates the tastes buds" of imbibers, but the New French "food's not bad, either" – especially the "heart-stopping (literally) cheese plate" – even if "prices have risen"; each address has a "different personality", but "the 5th-arrondissement one is especially worth the visit for its old stone vaulted cellar room"; "arrogant service" is the main downside.

Bouillon Racine *Brasserie*

	FOOD	DECOR	SERVICE	COST
	14	23	14	€39

6ᵉ | 3, rue Racine (Cluny La Sorbonne/Odéon) | 01 44 32 15 60 | fax 01 44 32 15 61 | www.bouillonracine.com

Everyone "loves the tiled and stained-glass space" of this historic Saint-Germain venue with a "fabulously restored art nouveau interior"; but longtimers lament "it's so sad to see the Belgian cuisine disappear in favor of ordinary brasserie stuff", "indifferently" served; it's "best for a quick drink" – preferably of some of the "hard-to-find beer" on tap – especially if you can snag "a window table with the sunlight pouring in."

Boulangerie (La) 🗷 *Bistro*

	FOOD	DECOR	SERVICE	COST
	20	16	19	€30

20ᵉ | 15, rue des Panoyaux (Ménilmontant) | 01 43 58 45 45 | fax 01 43 58 45 46

"The owners have lifted the level" of cooking at this "bistro with friendly service", but the prices remain "wonderfully affordable" for a "less-than-affluent younger crowd"; while it's situated in a somewhat "raunchy area" of the 20th, the ex-bakery interior is "pretty", with a mosaic-tiled floor.

Boule Rouge (La) ❶🗷 *African*

	FOOD	DECOR	SERVICE	COST
	-	-	-	M

9ᵉ | 1, rue de la Boule-Rouge (Grands Boulevards) | 01 47 70 43 90 | fax 01 42 46 99 57

Few surveyors know this large North African in the 9th, but those who do commend the couscous (especially the "excellent" Friday special with spinach); prices are as easygoing as the warm service,

and the atmos...
the Tunisian ea...

Bound *Japan...*
8ᵉ | 49-51, av C...
fax 01 53 67 8...
With a huge b...
wood, brushed...
Avenue George...
late of these p...
quality Japane...
man out front,...
to the attentive...

🗲 **Bouquinis...**
6ᵉ | 53, quai des Grands-Augustins (St-Michel) | 01 43 25 45 94 |
fax 01 43 25 23 07 | www.lesbouquinistes.com
Owned by Guy Savoy, this "upbeat" New French remains "a busy
place filled with smart foodies" who appreciate the "unusual", even
"audacious" eats served in a "streamlined" "light room" "overlooking
the Seine" in Saint-Germain; but a fair number of foes fume it "feels
like it's lost its freshness" – "they're too interested in turning the tables over" to the "tourists who overrun" it, making it "definitely
overpriced"; all agree about the "accommodating service", however.

22 | 17 | 19 | €49

Bourguignon
du Marais (Au) 🗲 *Wine Bar/Bistro*
4ᵉ | 52, rue François Miron (Pont-Marie/St-Paul) | 01 48 87 15 40 |
fax 01 48 87 17 49
"Modern but cozy, with a warm French feel", this Marais *bistrot à
vins* offers "quite good food" that "pairs really well with the wines"
("if you love Burgundies, this is the place"); though it can be "one of
the best deals in Paris", beware – "the bill has a way of zipping up-
ward" with all those "delicious" vinos by the glass.

24 | 17 | 23 | €67

Braisière (La) 🗲 *Gascony*
17ᵉ | 54, rue Cardinet (Malesherbes) | 01 47 63 40 37 | fax 01 47 63 04 76
"Family-operated at the highest level", this "hidden secret" in the
17th is "to be recommended" for "robust yet refined cuisine" that
marries New French flavors with traditional Gascony favorites (e.g.
the "best foie gras" with "duck breast with pineapple and Muscat
grapes marmalade"), plus "great personal service"; a "cozy atmosphere" ensures almost all reviewers "would return with pleasure."

18 | 19 | 18 | €42

Brasserie Balzar ◑ *Brasserie*
5ᵉ | 49, rue des Ecoles (Cluny La Sorbonne/St-Michel) |
01 43 54 13 67 | fax 01 44 07 14 91 | www.brasseriebalzar.com
"A classic on the Left Bank" just across the street from the Sorbonne
(hence, "a favorite with the university crowd"), "one of the best
smaller turn-of-the-century brasseries" "continues to deliver"
"unpretentious" "old-fashioned" dishes, "*très* typical decor" and
"well-prepared service"; of course, "they say it's not what it once

", and even if it's "more crowded
 ... e Groupe Flo takeover", "noisy" and
 ... we always go back."

... . Louis ● *Brasserie* | 16 | 16 | 18 | €38

... rbon (Cité/Pont-Marie) | 01 43 54 02 59 |

... on the Ile Saint-Louis" "facing Notre Dame", this "at-
 ... brasserie is blessed with decor of "1890s-vintage ad-
 ... posters" on dark-wood walls – a "tavernlike" setting for
 ... Alsatian" eats, served by "slightly wry waiters"; and if a Food
 ... ore drop supports skeptics who say "yes, Virginia, you can get a
bad meal in Paris", at least the place is "not part of a chain."

Brasserie du Louvre *Brasserie* | 18 | 21 | 17 | €38
1er | Hôtel du Louvre | Place André Malraux (Palais Royal-Musée du Louvre) | 01 42 96 27 98 | fax 01 44 58 38 00 | www.hoteldulouvre.com
"Just steps from the Louvre", "the location of this brasserie is so out-standing that who cares about the food – which is, in fact, pretty good" (if on the "standard" side); the recently refreshed decor "glitters", and there's nice "outdoor seating overlooking a charming square" too; "slow service" is the main drawback.

Brasserie Flo ● *Brasserie* | 17 | 21 | 18 | €48
10e | 7, cour des Petites-Ecuries (Château d'Eau) | 01 47 70 13 59 | fax 01 42 47 00 80 | www.flobrasseries.com
This patch of the 10th may be a bit "grimy", but the decor of sinuous molding and mirrors "speaks of the belle epoque" at this brasserie that's "part of the Groupe Flo"; possessing the "noisy", "fun" "feeling of a Toulouse-Lautrec painting", it's a fine place "to take tourists", but with the food no more than "acceptable", most suggest you "keep to the conservative side of the menu and chew on the ambiance."

Brasserie Julien ● *Brasserie* | 17 | 23 | 18 | €48
10e | 16, rue du Faubourg St-Denis (Strasbourg-St-Denis) | 01 47 70 12 06 | fax 01 42 47 00 65 | www.flobrasseries.com
"The decor's worth the detour" to this "art nouveau gem" of a brasserie in a "not-so-great neighborhood" in the 10th; it's "part of the Groupe Flo empire, so don't expect anything outstanding from the chef"; but the "cassoulet and foie gras are always reliable", the "staff is truly friendly" and all in all, "great fun if not great food."

Brasserie La Lorraine ● *Brasserie* | 16 | 15 | 14 | €56
8e | 2, pl des Ternes (Ternes) | 01 56 21 22 00 | fax 01 56 21 22 09 | www.brasserielalorraine.com
This "typical large brasserie" in the 8th was overhauled in 2004, but many find the "makeover disappointing": while "the place looks brighter", it's "a bit too Vegas", the formalized service "has become chilly" and though the food's "good" ("of course you must order the quiche"), "the prices, always high, have skyrocketed"; still, this "neighborhood standby" "definitely has an upbeat atmosphere"; N.B. don't ignore the *voiturier,* or you may be mysteriously towed away in the night.

	FOOD	DECOR	SERVICE	COST

Brasserie L'Européen ● *Brasserie*

| - | - | - | M |

12ᵉ | 21 bis, bd Diderot (Gare de Lyon) | 01 43 43 99 70 |
fax 01 43 07 26 51 | www.brasserie-leuropeen.fr

Travelers waiting for a train toss back a few oysters or drinks at this "classic Parisian brasserie" (one of the remaining few in the city that is not part of a chain) steps from the Gare de Lyon; after a century in business it "maintains its reputation" with "high-level" seafood platters and "defies the wear and tear of time" with a '70s decor by Slavik – a smorgasbord of mirrors, chandeliers and chesterfield banquettes.

☒ Brasserie Lipp ● *Brasserie*

| 17 | 19 | 16 | €50 |

6ᵉ | 151, bd St-Germain (St-Germain-des-Prés) | 01 45 48 53 91 |
fax 01 45 44 33 20 | www.brasserie-lipp.fr

"The old-fashioned grand brasserie charm compensates for the just-decent cooking" at this legendary "rendezvous of the Saint-Germain intelligentsia"; "reputation precedes" other practices, like putting "unknowns upstairs and celebrities in the ground-floor room" (which has the art nouveau decor); "the waiters can be utterly perfunctory or delightful"; even so, "you can't say you've visited Paris without coming here"; P.S. a "sign reads 'no salad as a meal' – Americans, that means you."

Brasserie Lutétia *Brasserie*

| 17 | 18 | 17 | €52 |

6ᵉ | Hôtel Lutétia | 23, rue de Sèvres (Sèvres-Babylone) |
01 49 54 46 76 | fax 01 49 54 46 00 | www.lutetia-paris.com

"Not bad for a hotel restaurant", this "plush and stylish" brasserie with art deco–style decor by Sonia Rykiel is "perfect" for "lunch while shopping" (though "service is slow" sometimes); it's a "lovely place for a seafood platter", but otherwise there are "no real surprises here", including the 6th-arrondissement-"expensive" bills.

Brasserie Mollard ● *Brasserie*

| 16 | 15 | 14 | €45 |

8ᵉ | 115, rue St-Lazare (Auber/St-Lazare) | 01 43 87 50 22 |
fax 01 43 87 84 17 | www.mollard.fr

It may have "fabulous art nouveau mosaics everywhere" but foes feel this long-running brasserie near the Gare Saint-Lazare is "living on its looks", as "food and service need significant work"; but boosters believe that while "basic", there's "better execution for the prices" here than at others of its ilk.

NEW Brasserie Printemps ☒ *Classic French*

| - | - | - | M |

9ᵉ | Printemps | 64, bd Haussmann (Auber/Havre-Caumartin) |
01 42 82 58 84 | fax 01 45 26 31 24 | www.printemps.com

Following a change of ownership, this brasserie "under the dome on the top floor of Printemps" has had a slick makeover by French interior designer Dider Gomez; the new look ditches the former art nouveau-inspired decor for a lounge-bar attitude created by ebonized furniture, a lit-from-within bar and rich doses of color; the menu is now Classic French, but still popular with the ladies who lunch, as dishes like calf's liver and skate grenobloise offer "enough sustenance to go out and shop some more!"

	FOOD	DECOR	SERVICE	COST

Breakfast in America *American*

	13	14	14	€21

NEW **4ᵉ** | 4, rue Mahler (St-Paul) | 01 42 72 40 21 🛇 Ⓜ
5ᵉ | 17, rue des Ecoles (Cardinal Lemoine/Jussieu) | 01 43 54 50 28
www.breakfast-in-america.com

"Sorbonne types and expat Americans alike gather at this '50s-style
diner, a reconversion of an old Latin Quarter cafe" (with a new 4th-
arrondissement branch); "it's a pity the service isn't as friendly as
you'd find in the States", though, and while technically "affordable",
many moan "if breakfast in America actually cost this much, no one
would go out anymore"; still, as a "trusted source" for "tasty treats"
and the "brunch basics", "it's as close to a Denny's in Paris as you
can get" (whether that's praise or a pan, you decide).

Ⓩ Bristol (Le) *Haute Cuisine*

	27	27	26	€132

8ᵉ | Hôtel Le Bristol | 112, rue du Faubourg St-Honoré (Miromesnil) |
01 53 43 43 40 | fax 01 53 43 43 01 | www.lebristolparis.com

"Eric Frechon is the resident culinary genius here" at the Bristol,
cooking "updated Haute Cuisine" that's "classic but creative"; while
the food "is worth the trip alone", the dining rooms – a round oak-
paneled salon in winter and a garden pavilion in summer – are both
"stunningly beautiful", and the service is "surprisingly not haughty"
for a place that offers one of the "most refined dining experiences in
the world"; even the "heavy-on-the-wallet prices" don't stop it from
being "sublime in every way."

Ⓩ Buddha Bar ⬤ *Asian*

	16	26	15	€57

8ᵉ | 8, rue Boissy-d'Anglas (Concorde) | 01 53 05 90 00 |
fax 01 53 05 90 09 | www.buddhabar.com

Its "junky but funky" decor dominated by a giant gold Buddha, this
"loud" eatery/club in the 8th may be "not as hip and hot as it was a
few years ago, but it's still packed cheek-by-jowl" (expect "outrageous delays, even with reservations"); "if you're interested in what
you eat, you're in the wrong place" – the Asian food is pretty "average", given the "heart-stoppingly expensive" tabs; so many "just go
for drinks", "fantastic music" and "sexy surroundings."

Buffalo Grill *Steak*

	9	10	11	€25

3ᵉ | 15, pl de la République (République) | 01 40 29 94 98
5ᵉ | 1, bd St-Germain (Jussieu) | 01 56 24 34 49
9ᵉ | 3, pl Blanche (Blanche) | 01 40 16 42 51
10ᵉ | 9, bd Denain (Gare du Nord) | 01 40 16 47 81
13ᵉ | 2, rue Raymond Aron (Quai de la Gare) | 01 45 86 76 71
14ᵉ | 117, av du Général Leclerc (Porte d'Orléans) | 01 45 40 09 72
15ᵉ | 154, rue St-Charles (Javel) | 01 40 60 97 48 | fax 01 40 60 17 48
17ᵉ | 6, pl du Maréchal Juin (Péreire) | 01 40 54 73 75
19ᵉ | 29, av Corentin Cariou (Porte de la Villette) | 01 40 36 21 41 |
fax 01 53 26 88 17
www.buffalo-grill.fr

Like a "surreal take on an American steakhouse", this "popular faux-
cowboy chain" serves up a mishmash of Yank eats (ribs, beef,
Buffalo wings) in an "imitation Wild West" setting, complete with
"Indian statues standing guard at the swinging saloon doors"; foes

gun it down, calling "the pictures on the menu more appetizing than the food" itself and the "cowgirl"-clad staff "disagreeable"; "the only reason to go – they're kid-friendly", and the "affordable" eats are "better than a gas station's."

Buisson Ardent (Le) 🅩 *Classic French*

▽ 20 | 14 | 20 | €42

5ᵉ | 25, rue Jussieu (Jussieu) | 01 43 54 93 02 | fax 01 46 33 34 77

In the 5th, this "informal eatery" attracts ardent admirers for its "wonderful" Classic French cooking and 1925-era "dining room, a nice setting" in which to have a bargain lunch surrounded by "researchers and the local intelligentsia from neighboring institutes and universities"; "the staff is casual and friendly", and if some say it's "too austere", most call it "a gem."

Butte Chaillot (La) *Bistro*
20 | 17 | 18 | €50

16ᵉ | 110 bis, av Kléber (Trocadéro) | 01 47 27 88 88 | fax 01 47 27 41 46 | www.guysavoy.com

"Always pleasant for a simple business lunch" or "Sunday night supper", this "modern" bistro "under the auspices of Guy Savoy" has become a "classic" by offering "dependable food at reasonable prices"; the handy location near the Trocadéro is almost as much of a crowd-pleaser as what may be "the best roast chicken and mashed potatoes in the world", "well and quickly served."

Cabane (La) 🅩 *Seafood*
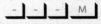
- | - | - | M

17ᵉ | 96, rue de Levis (Villiers) | 01 46 22 51 50

This "neighborhood seafooder" on a much-loved "market street" in the 17th isn't well known, but fans of "quality" shellfish love the beach-house decor, adding that "the welcome and the service are really uncommonly good"; it's a great place to go when your wallet's at low tide too, since the prices are notably easygoing for a "fresh, inventive" maritime meal.

Ca d'Oro *Italian*
- | - | - | M

1ᵉʳ | 54, rue de l'Arbre-Sec (Louvre-Rivoli) | 01 40 20 97 79

A "favorite nobody-goes-there restaurant", this little location "overlooking the Louvre" is "great for light Italian food" as well as some mighty "prime pasta"; "friendly waiters" add to the "relaxing atmosphere" of the place.

Café Beaubourg ➊ *Classic French*
15 | 20 | 14 | €34

4ᵉ | 100, rue St-Martin (Châtelet-Les Halles/Rambuteau) | 01 48 87 63 96 | fax 01 48 87 81 25

"The beautiful people are still, well, beautiful" at this "aging" but "hip cafe run by the Costes brothers" that "sits right in the face of the Centre Pompidou"; such a "great location" "makes it a good spot to meet friends" and offers some of the "best people-watching in Paris", within or without the "interesting", "plush", "podlike interior"; however, the "updated French classics menu" is typical of the *frères'* cuisine (that is, "not too creative"), and the service is "often negligent."

	FOOD	DECOR	SERVICE	COST

Café Burq ● 🚭 ⚠ *Wine Bar/Bistro*

| | - | - | - | M |

18ᵉ | 6, rue Burq (Abbesses/Blanche) | 01 42 52 81 27

Though it's little known, this trendy Montmartre *bistrot à vins* "has become a hangout for bohemian-bourgeois" types; the bistro dishes are "pretty creative" and modestly priced, which more than compensates for "rather dumpy" decor.

Café Charbon ● *Classic French*

| | 11 | 17 | 11 | €26 |

11ᵉ | 109, rue Oberkampf (Parmentier/Rue St-Maur) | 01 43 57 55 13 | fax 01 43 57 57 41

This "hipster hideaway" "with a beautifully restored, fin de siècle interior" may be a "classic" of the "trend-driven" Oberkampf quarter in the 11th; but opponents opine this "original" working-class cafe all too fittingly serves "factory"-like traditional French fare, with "attitude that can be tiresome"; in short, "better for drinks than a meal."

Café Constant *Bistro*

| | 22 | 12 | 17 | €37 |

7ᵉ | 139, rue St-Dominique (Ecole Militaire) | 01 47 53 73 34 | www.leviolondingres.com

"When you're not up to the big stars", chef-owner Christian Constant's "cozy" (or "tight") "second restaurant" makes a "nice substitute for its posh parent", Le Violon d'Ingres; "no reservations, but it's worth the wait" for "classic (if not classy) bistro food" "prepared with love" at "prices among the most reasonable in the whole 7th"; the "decor's old and tired and that rubs off on the waiters" critics carp; but converts call it "charming", as long as you "get a table on the main floor."

Café d'Angel (Le) ⚠ *Bistro*

| | 19 | 14 | 18 | €37 |

17ᵉ | 16, rue Brey (Charles de Gaulle-Etoile/Ternes) | 01 47 54 03 33 | fax 01 47 54 03 33

"A darling neighborhood" spot in the 17th, this bistro brings in "a sophisticated crowd with a creative menu" that varies monthly but always "demonstrates delicacy" (so "don't skip dessert"); "service is quite attentive", and the bill, very "accessible"; N.B. the advent of a new bordeaux-and-brown design scheme outdates the Decor score.

Café de Flore ● *Classic French*

| | 15 | 19 | 16 | €35 |

6ᵉ | 172, bd St-Germain (St-Germain-des-Prés) | 01 45 48 55 26 | fax 01 45 44 33 39 | www.cafe-de-flore.com

"Nostalgia aside, it's still worth" visiting this "platonic ideal of the Paris cafe", the Saint-Germain stomping ground of Sartre and various expat writers; true, it's "cramped and noisy" ("how did Hemingway get anything done here?"), "the staff is full of itself" and, the "passable breakfast" aside, the "basic" Classic French food is "outrageously expensive"; the trick is to get a table on the "select second floor", order drinks and enjoy "one of the best people-watching spots in Paris."

Café de la Musique ● *Classic French*

| | - | - | - | M |

19ᵉ | Cité de la Musique | 213, av Jean Jaurès (Porte de Pantin) | 01 48 03 15 91 | fax 01 48 03 15 18 | www.cite-musique.fr

"The view of the fountain and the architecture of the Cité de la Musique makes dining on the terrace worth the trip" to this Costes brothers outpost; the place misses a beat with its "pretentious" Classic French cuisine, but it's almost the only option if you're heading to a concert in the 19th.

Café de la Paix ● _Classic French_

19	23	20	€55

9ᵉ | InterContinental Le Grand Hôtel | 12, bd des Capucines (Auber/Opéra) | 01 40 07 36 36 | fax 01 40 07 36 13 | www.paris.intercontinental.com
Following a "magnificent renovation" a while back, this famous cafe across from the Opéra Garnier remains generally "touristy but reliable"; surveyors clash over the Classic French cuisine, with warriors wailing it's "mediocre and overpriced" and peacemongers positing "it's not what it was when I was younger, but then neither am I" (also, the recent arrival of chef Laurent Delarbre, who has fancified the food, outdates the score); certainly, the Napoleon III decor retains all its "past glories", and "the waiters are charming."

Café de la Poste ⊠ _Classic French_

▽ 16	13	19	€27

4ᵉ | 13, rue Castex (Bastille) | 01 42 72 95 35
With its "homey" cracked-tile floor and mirrors, this "small, personal" cafe near a historic Marais post office is "a good place" for "good traditional French dishes" and "smiling service"; a few deem it "disappointing" "since an ownership change" last year, but the majority stamps this "reasonably priced" place with their approval.

Café de l'Esplanade (Le) ● _Classic/New French_

17	21	15	€52

7ᵉ | 52, rue Fabert (Invalides/La Tour-Maubourg) | 01 47 05 38 80 | fax 01 47 05 23 75
Kitty-cornered to Les Invalides is this "trendy canteen", and "if you look at the menu and think you've seen it before, you're right – it's another one in the Costes brothers' series", a sampler of "decent" Classic and New French fare; you might also recognize the same "haughty" but "pretty waitresses and crowd wearing black and sporting sunglasses, darling", even when occupying the "ultimate-in-hip" interior.

Café de l'Industrie ● _Bistro_

13	15	13	€30

11ᵉ | 16-17, rue St-Sabin (Bastille/Bréguet-Sabin) | 01 47 00 13 53 | fax 01 47 00 92 33
"You go more for the atmosphere and to be cool than for the food" at this "buzzy" "super-crowded" "find in the 11th"; still, the bistro fare is "affordable" and "generously served" by staffers that are "polite if often overwhelmed"; many deem the "old-fashioned"-but-"updated" decor "cute."

Café de Mars ●◗⊠ _Bistro_

16	15	16	€36

7ᵉ | 11, rue Augereau (Ecole Militaire) | 01 47 05 05 91 | fax 01 47 05 05 91
Near the Rue Clerc in the 7th, this "typical little French bistro" ("it looks like where they'd shoot a scene establishing this is Paris") has a "charming decor" of tiles and mosaics; "the staff dotes on all" the "neighborhood residents" and "unobtrusive tourists" who consume the cuisine with some Eclectic "innovative" touches; "prices are very fair for this level."

	FOOD	DECOR	SERVICE	COST

Café du Commerce (Le) ● *Bistro*

	13	18	11	€31

15ᵉ | 51, rue du Commerce (Emile Zola) | 01 45 75 03 27 |
fax 01 45 75 27 40 | www.lecafeducommerce.com

"They just keep filling the hundreds of seats" at this veteran in the
15th, famed mainly for its "wonderful 1920s atrium setting" ("they
open the skylight on sunny days"); the bistro food is "solid, if not
very creative" – though the service remains rather "absent-minded";
still, it's a "remarkably good buy", "so you can't go too far wrong
with this bustling institution."

Café du Passage (Le) ● *Wine Bar/Bistro*

	–	–	–	M

11ᵉ | 12, rue de Charonne (Bastille/Ledru-Rollin) | 01 49 29 97 64 |
fax 01 49 29 97 64

With "an owner who's passionate about wine and whiskey", this *bistrot
à vins* in the 11th has "a fantastic selection, much of which is served by
the glass" and accompanied by "excellent small plates" with an Italian
edge; the "old-world" decor makes a great backdrop for good times.

Café Etienne Marcel ● *Eclectic*

	13	12	11	€35

2ᵉ | 34, rue Etienne Marcel (Etienne Marcel) | 01 45 08 01 03 |
fax 01 42 36 03 44

"Champagne McDonald's is the best way to describe" this Costes
brothers outpost on the northern edge of Les Halles that features
much of their "locked-in formula" but is still "just sort of average",
from the "passable" Eclectic eats to the "slightly kitschy" *A
Clockwork Orange*-style decor to the "wannabe-hip suburban
crowd"; "the prices are pretty high given the quality of the food and
service, but that's typical of fashion restaurants."

Café Faubourg *Classic French*

	17	20	17	€50

8ᵉ | Sofitel Le Faubourg | 11 bis, rue Boissy-d'Anglas (Concorde/
Madeleine) | 01 44 94 14 24 | fax 01 44 94 14 28 | www.sofitel.com

Overlooking a pretty little atrium garden, this "tranquil" dining room
is "very nice for a hotel restaurant", with "comforting" Classic
French–Southwestern cuisine from a student of consulting chef
Alain Dutournier and an "extremely friendly" staff (though a Service
score drop confirms complaints they could be more "consistent");
since it's just steps from the Place de la Concorde in the heart of
town, it often "caters to business travelers."

Café Fusion ● *Eclectic*

	–	–	–	M

13ᵉ | 12, rue de la Butte aux Cailles (Place d'Italie) | 01 45 80 12 02

"Well-decorated", with stainless-steel tables and colored billboards
on the walls, this "trendy" table in the 13th may not offer gourmet
revelations – the Eclectic eats are "ok but not adventurous" – but the
"service is respectable", and "there's a nice terrace" for lingering.

Café Guitry 🅂 *Classic French*

	–	–	–	M

9ᵉ | Théâtre Edouard VII | 10, pl Edouard VII (Auber/Opéra) |
01 40 07 00 77 | fax 01 47 42 77 68

Situated within the Edouard VII theater in the 9th, this Classic French
offers soigné, red-and-chestnut-toned comfort, including "soft arm

chairs and a nice terrace in good weather"; though the cooking's "not bad for cafe fare", both "the cuisine and the service could be better"; still, given the location, you can't beat it for a pre-curtain bite.

Café la Jatte *Eclectic*   14 | 18 | 16 | €48

Neuilly-sur-Seine | 60, bd Vital-Bouhot (Pont-de-Levallois) | 01 47 45 04 20 | fax 01 47 45 19 32 | www.cafelajatte.com
Its "beautiful setting on a *petite* island in the middle of the Seine" explains the ongoing popularity of this "airy", Eclectic Neuilly bistro that bags "a business clientele at noon and a hip one at night"; but reviewers rave more about "the fabulous terrace" than the "diverse menu", which carries such "standardized-chic" "dishes like sushi, curry and Italian-style grilled fish" that critics carp it "could go the route of the dinosaur" whose skeleton dominates the room.

Café Lenôtre (Le) *New French*   19 | 20 | 18 | €42

8e | Pavillon Elysée | 10, av des Champs-Elysées (Champs-Elysées-Clémenceau) | 01 42 65 85 10 | fax 01 42 65 76 23 | www.lenotre.fr
With a "charming, simply charming" setting in the Pavillon Elysée, this Italian-accented New French from the Lenôtre caterers is "great on a sunny day" when you can sit on "one of the nicest terraces in Paris"; the "finely displayed foods" are "nice", if "limited", and foes find "prices high" for what's essentially "gourmet sandwich fare"; but all ends on a sweet note, since everyone loves the "beautiful pastries."

Café Le Petit Pont ● *Classic French*   ▽ 24 | 19 | 18 | €23

5e | 1, rue du Petit Pont (St-Michel) | 01 43 54 23 81
"The view of Notre Dame is without par" ("eat on the patio") at this "quaint place" in the 5th, whose "excellent" eats go beyond basic traditional French fare; most nights there's "a jazz duo that can really swing the old American classics."

☑ Café Les Deux Magots ● *Classic French*   15 | 20 | 16 | €37

6e | 6, pl St-Germain-des-Prés (St-Germain-des-Prés) | 01 45 48 55 25 | fax 01 45 49 31 29 | www.lesdeuxmagots.fr
"Renowned, revered and steeped in pre-war history" ("imagine an espresso with Picasso"), this "landmark" Saint-Germain cafe, "though a tourist trap, never fails to delight" those to whom people-watching and "ambiance is all"; certainly, its "claim to fame is not the Classic French food" (never have "so many paid so much for so little"), and "service ranges from attentive to frosty"; "however, you just gotta do it anyway" "at least once"; "drink heavily and eat lightly" for maximum bang for the buck.

Café M *New French*   16 | 17 | 17 | €58

8e | Hôtel Hyatt | 24, bd Malesherbes (Madeleine/St-Augustin) | 01 55 27 12 34 | fax 01 55 27 12 35 | www.paris.madeleine.hyatt.com
"There's nothing grand" about this Hyatt hotel dining room in the 8th, but the "tranquil, pleasant" "postmodern" surrounds, "thoughtful service" and "fresh", "good, if unspectacular" New French cuisine ensure it's often "frequented by fortysomething executives", who don't mind how the "check has a way of taking off at the end."

	FOOD	DECOR	SERVICE	COST

Café Marly ● *Classic/New French*   `15` `24` `13` `€43`
1ᵉʳ | 93, rue de Rivoli (Palais Royal-Musée du Louvre) |
01 49 26 06 60 | fax 01 49 26 07 06

A "superb view" of the I.M. Pei glass pyramid from a "fabulous terrace" is the reason many put up with this "sumptuous" site in the Royal Musée du Louvre, because inside you'll find "the same old food you find at all the Costes venues – "so-so" Classic and New French fare at "rip-off prices" – and "disgruntled individuals who pass themselves off as waiters"; the skinny from the skinny "beautiful-people crowd" is: "request an outside table and pretend you're a guest of the king."

Café Moderne 🅩 *Bistro*   `22` `21` `21` `€42`
2ᵉ | 40, rue Notre-Dame-des-Victoires (Bourse) | 01 53 40 84 10 |
fax 01 53 40 84 11

"Overlooking a pretty courtyard" in the 2nd "with, as the name would suggest, a modern interior", this long, narrow dining room has real buzz generated by its young, stylish, international clientele; they come both for the "inventive take on traditional bistro food" and the "excellent wine list", which periodically offers *grands crus* at cost; a "gracious owner" leads a "friendly" staff.

Café Ruc ● *Bistro*   `14` `18` `15` `€43`
1ᵉʳ | 159, rue St-Honoré (Palais Royal-Musée du Louvre) |
01 42 60 97 54 | fax 01 42 60 94 81

"Yet another Costes" address, this bistro in "a critical tourist location" "close to the Louvre" works "for a quick bite with style" – but only if "you're hip and French" opponents opine; otherwise, the "beautiful" but "moody staff" "often seems preoccupied elsewhere", and when they "finally get around to your order, you'll receive" "standard fare" that's "a pretty bad buy for the buck"; but for "excellent views of Paris' human delicacies" amid a "Robert Palmer video" ambiance, it's "unbeatable."

Café Terminus *Classic French*   `–` `–` `–` `E`
8ᵉ | Hôtel Concorde St-Lazare | 108, rue St-Lazare (St-Lazare) |
01 40 08 43 30 | fax 01 42 93 01 20 | www.concordestlazare-paris.com

Though little-known – perhaps due to its locale in an "uninteresting part of town" near the Gare Saint-Lazare – this hotel Classic French features "intelligent, savory" cooking (though no longer "at a reasonable price"); the belle epoque interior designed by Sonia Rykiel fits right in with the "beautiful hotel lobby" that dates from 1889.

Café Very ● *Sandwiches*   `13` `18` `14` `€21`
1ᵉʳ | Jardin des Tuileries (Concorde/Tuileries) | 01 47 03 94 84 |
fax 01 47 03 94 84

Dame Tartine *Sandwiches*
4ᵉ | 2, rue Brisemiche (Hôtel-de-Ville) | 01 42 77 32 22 |
fax 01 42 77 32 22

"Reliable for light meals from lunch into the evening", this pair of sandwich purveyors provides perfect perches to "watch Paris go by" – whether it's the "magical Tuileries" address or the one just opposite "the colorful, modern-art-laden fountain" near the Pompidou Center; *tartines* on the terrace are "tasty", even if "service is slow" sometimes.

Caffé Minotti 🅢 🅜 *Italian*   ▽ 23 | 17 | 19 | €59

7e | 33, rue de Verneuil (Rue du Bac) | 01 42 60 04 04 | fax 01 42 60 04 05 | www.caffeminotti.fr

"Risotto to kill for" is only one reason to discover this "classy", "chic Italian" near the Musée d'Orsay; "sexy service" and "inventive cooking that's a reflection of the decor" – think Milano minimalism spiked by lollipop-red Murano chandeliers – pull a soigné crowd of book editors, fashion folks, gallery owners and aristos; the "price-value ratio isn't so excellent", but "consider the neighborhood" (the well-heeled 7th).

Caffé Toscano 🅢 *Italian* – | – | – | M

7e | 34, rue des Sts-Pères (St-Germain-des-Prés) | 01 42 84 28 95 | fax 01 42 84 26 36

This "great small spot for a quick plate of pasta" and Sicilian vino in the 7th is "often crowded" with a stylish group of Left Bank "regulars" – fashion designers, editors, professors and antique dealers – who like the modest prices; an airy, Tuscan-style decor adds to the appeal.

Cagouille (La) *Seafood* 21 | 13 | 16 | €51

14e | 10, pl Constantin Brancusi (Gaîté/Montparnasse-Bienvenüe) | 01 43 22 09 01 | fax 01 45 38 57 29 | www.la-cagouille.fr

It's always high tide at this Montparnasse table, which specializes in – and only in – "unbelievable seafood" (so "meat lovers abstain"), "irreproachably fresh" and "simply prepared"; the "stark" "interior is a little cold" – though "the terrace is a treat in the summer" – and while the service can be "a little clumsy", the place is still "popular with journalists and politicians" who proclaim it "hard to find but tough to beat"; P.S. don't overlook the "ultimate cognac list."

Cailloux (Les) 🅢 🅜 *Italian*   ▽ 16 | 15 | 15 | €31

13e | 58, rue des Cinq-Diamants (Corvisart/Place d'Italie) | 01 45 80 15 08 | fax 01 45 65 67 09

"Worth a trip" "as much for the ambiance as for the pasta" attest advocates of this intimate Italian in the tranquil Buttes-aux-Cailles *quartier*; though humble, the woody decor is "pleasant", and it's "a good buy" to boot – if "not as economical" since it's been discovered by a "young, attractive crowd."

Caïus 🅢 *New French* ▽ 18 | 16 | 16 | €51

17e | 6, rue d'Armaillé (Charles de Gaulle-Etoile) | 01 42 27 19 20 | fax 01 40 55 00 93

Opinions vary on this New French in the 17th; while positives profess it's "perfect for an innovative take on the classics", doubters deem the "dishes inconsistent – the chef likes his spices but they don't belong everywhere"; likewise, some appreciate that the staff isn't "interfering when you don't want" 'em, but others proclaim them "pretentious"; at least the revamped decor has brightened up the once-"somber" dining room.

| | FOOD | DECOR | SERVICE | COST |

Caméléon (Le) ⓩ *Bistro* — — — M
6ᵉ | 6, rue de Chevreuse (Vavin) | 01 43 27 43 27 | fax 43 27 97 91
Translating as 'the chameleon', the name of this vintage bistro is especially appropriate nowadays since, after over 30 years on a "nice cozy" Montparnasse street, it's been bought and revamped by veteran restaurateur Jean-Paul Arabian; expect an old-meets-new decor (zinc bar and plasma TV) and hearty classic dishes made from market-fresh fare.

Camélia (Le) ⓩ *New French* — — — M
Bougival | 7, quai Georges Clémenceau (RER La Défense) | 01 39 18 36 06 | fax 01 39 18 00 25 | www.lecamelia.com
The "best in the west" – the western suburb of Bougival, that is – exclaim enthusiasts of this "excellent" New French in an old stone-walled 19th-century inn; "a dedicated staff" serves the "perfectly executed" dishes in a "nice room", whose butter-yellow walls, red printed-cloth banquettes and caned chairs create a "calm ambiance."

Camille ❶ *Bistro* ▽ 20 19 19 €41
3ᵉ | 24, rue des Francs-Bourgeois (St-Paul) | 01 42 72 20 50 | fax 01 40 27 07 99
All lace curtains and retro bric-a-brac, the traditional "romantic atmosphere perfectly complements the well-prepared French classics" at this bistro on an "oh-so-chic" Marais street; they're "open all day, seven days a week", and if the "menu rarely changes", it "never disappoints", either; be aware that despite "efficient service", "in summer there can be a long wait for the cramped sidewalk tables."

NEW Cantine de Quentin (La) Ⓜ *Wine Bar/Bistro* — — — M
10ᵉ | 52, rue Bichat (Jacques Bonsergent/République) | 01 42 02 40 32
With wine displayed in open-stock mahogany-stained wood shelves, this new *bistrot à vins* in the trendy 10th is pulling an equally trendy young crowd that likes its easygoing atmosphere – bare wood tables set with red napkins and serve-yourself bottles of vino; the kitchen is directed by a former assistant of Guy Savoy, and the modestly priced menu runs to comfort food in a traditional French register.

Cap Seguin (Le) ⓩ *Classic French* — — — M
Boulogne-Billancourt | Face au 27, quai le Gallo (Pont-de-Sèvres) | 01 46 05 06 07 | fax 01 46 05 06 88 | www.lecapseguin.com
Boasting "a great setting" on a barge moored in Boulogne, this Classic French is most popular during the summer months, although it does a busy trade with advertising and TV types at lunch; the cuisine's "good", if "unimaginative", but be forewarned that "service can be unbelievably inefficient."

Cap Vernet (Le) ⓩ *New French* 18 15 17 €63
8ᵉ | 82, av Marceau (Charles de Gaulle-Etoile) | 01 47 20 20 40 | fax 01 47 20 95 36
Tucked away at the top of the Champs, this fashionable fish house "has recently renovated decor" that conjures up a chic, sandy-colored

beach house; even "in the winter", it's "a wonderful place for oysters" – "but little else" snap those who find the rest of the New French "food disappointing"; still, "it's good for business meals" or at teatime.

	FOOD	DECOR	SERVICE	COST

NEW Carmine *Italian*
- - - M

7ᵉ | 81, ave Bosquet (Ecole Militaire) | 01 47 05 36 15 | fax 01 47 53 88 13 | www.restaurant-carmine.com

Not far from the Ecole Militaire in the 7th, this new warm-toned trattoria is pasta perfect, thanks to a young chef who knows his noodles inside and out (along with other Italian classics); a mix of locals, diplomats – UNESCO isn't far away – and travelers populates an animated dining room with smart and supervising service.

Carpaccio (Le) *Italian*
▽ **22 21 21 €88**

8ᵉ | Hôtel Royal Monceau | 37, av Hoche (Charles de Gaulle-Etoile/ Ternes) | 01 42 99 98 90 | fax 01 42 99 89 94 | www.royalmonceau.com

"In a most un-Italian setting" (it's by designer Jacques Garcia), this cosseted Italian in the 8th has been "rejuvenated" , which is why the usual clientele – "businessmen at noon" – is evolving in favor of well-dressed shoppers and curious locals; the digs are "luxurious", the "service excellent" and the "food refined", even if some jest "the portions are suited to a slenderizing diet."

☒ Carré des Feuillants ☒ *Haute Cuisine*
25 21 24 €122

1ᵉʳ | 14, rue de Castiglione (Concorde/Tuileries) | 01 42 86 82 82 | fax 01 42 86 07 71 | www.carredesfeuillants.fr

"Since everything is fabulous, order with confidence" at this "super-chic" Haute Cuisine table in the 1st, where "chef-owner Alain Dutournier's Southwest-inspired cuisine" "enthralls" with its "innovative", "subtle" flavors; surveyors also smile on the staff – "formal, but not at all snobby", and if the "modern decor" that mixes "splendid Venetian chandeliers" with exposed-steel beams leaves some "indifferent", most deem dinner here well "worth all those euros."

Carr's *Irish*
▽ **12 13 12 €29**

1ᵉʳ | 1, rue du Mont-Thabor (Tuileries) | 01 42 60 60 26 | fax 01 42 60 33 32 | www.carrsparis.com

Though "Irish food is not an obvious choice" in Paris, they give "great brunch" on weekends at this bit o' "the Emerald Isle" near the Tuileries; it's "friendly", with "cordial hosts that look like they stepped out of Dickens", and has gotten to be quite a singles venue with the Anglophile-meets-French crowd, even if some of them "go for the beer" (Guinness, of course) rather than the eats.

Carte Blanche ☒ *Bistro*
- - - M

9ᵉ | 6, rue Lamartine (Cadet) | 01 48 78 12 20 | fax 01 48 78 12 21

Exposed-stone walls and wooden beams add warmth to the small simple dining room of this bistro, an instant hit with the *bobo* (bohemian-bourgeois) double-income couples who've gentrified this area of the 9th; they're charmed by the reasonable prices for the Classic French fare packed with unusual flavors (e.g. cod with a red-pepper marmalade, or basil ice cream).

	FOOD	DECOR	SERVICE	COST

Cartes Postales (Les) ⑤ *New French*

▽ 19 | 12 | 14 | €55

1er | 7, rue Gomboust (Opéra/Pyramides) | 01 42 61 02 93 |
fax 01 42 61 02 93

"French cuisine with Japanese touches", reflecting the chef-owner's
"dual culinary heritage", makes for "inspired and rather innovative"
eating at this "cozy" place near the Place du Marché Saint-Honoré;
the dishes come in full and half portions – "what a good idea!" –
though it "can be very pricey if you don't stick to the set menu"; "pity
that the decor" (basically, "scores of postcards adorning the beige-
and-white walls") "doesn't live up to" the food.

Casa Alcalde *Basque/Spanish*

▽ 15 | 14 | 14 | €43

15^e | 117, bd de Grenelle (La Motte-Picquet-Grenelle) |
01 47 83 39 71 | fax 01 45 66 49 01 | www.casaalcade.fr

It's "almost impossible to get a table if you're not a regular – and difficult even if you are" at this "bustling" bastion for Basque bites in
the 15th; although cynics snap this is "Spain for Parisians who've
never crossed the Pyrénées", most maintain it's "worth going to";
P.S. if you can't score a seat in the "cramped" surrounds, you can get
the paella to go.

Casa Bini *Italian*

20 | 13 | 15 | €47

6^e | 36, rue Grégoire de Tours (Odéon) | 01 46 34 05 60 | fax 01 40 46 09 71

"This is the place" for a "real Italian" experience, "from the chef to
the staff" say surveyors of this "recently remodeled" address "in the
heart of the 6th"; "service and food can be erratic", leading to a
"was-it-worth-that-price feeling", but most are delighted with the
"delicious" dishes and wines from the northern part of The Boot;
P.S. one sometimes "sees French stars dining here."

Casa Olympe (La) ⑤ *Corsica/Provence*

23 | 13 | 17 | €53

9^e | 48, rue St-Georges (St-Georges) | 01 42 85 26 01 | fax 01 45 26 49 33

Perhaps "the best-kept secret of the 9th", this "small space" showcases the "consistently delicious" "Corsican and Provençal-accented"
cooking of Olympe Versini, one of the best-known female chefs in
Paris; service is "attentive", if "not always welcoming when they don't
know you", and the vanilla-colored dining room "can be crowded" –
but what do you expect when the cooking is so "remarkable"?

Casa Tina ① *Spanish*

12 | 12 | 12 | €35

16^e | 18, rue Lauriston (Charles de Gaulle-Etoile/Kléber) |
01 40 67 19 24 | fax 01 41 44 73 63 | www.casa-tina.net

A "lively atmosphere" attracts aficionados of Spain to this "Latino"-
decorated address in the 16th that's "open late"; but while amigos
acclaim the "fun tapas" and "convivial" service, malcontents mutter
this place "is proof that the Rue Lauriston is very far from Madrid."

Caveau du Palais (Le) *Classic French*

21 | 17 | 18 | €45

1er | 17-19, pl Dauphine (Cité/Pont-Neuf) | 01 43 26 04 28 |
fax 01 43 26 81 84

On the "tranquil" place Dauphine, in a "quiet 17th-century courtyard", this "lovely secret spot" is "definitely worth the visit" for its

"consistent, delicious food" in the Classic French vein; at lunch the service tends to be "rushed" due to "all the lawyers and judges" from the Palais de Justice nearby, but "on a summer evening, it makes you forget you're in the heart of Paris", especially since your "romantic dinner will not break the bank."

Cave de l'Os à Moëlle *Bistro*

| 20 | 15 | 15 | €35 |

15ᵉ | 181, rue de Lourmel (Lourmel) | 01 45 57 28 28 | fax 01 45 57 28 00

Those with "adventurous tastes" enjoy the "amusing" "concept of shared tables and all-you-can-eat buffet" ("you serve yourself from the stove or oven") at this "tiny joint" in the 15th; it's "great for a group", since the "good and agreeable" bistro food and "nice wines" come at "unbelievable prices", and the whole ambiance is "no-stress, like eating at a friend's home."

Cave Gourmande (La) - le Restaurant de Mark Singer ⑤ *Bistro*

| 24 | 15 | 22 | €44 |

19ᵉ | 10, rue du Général Brunet (Botzaris/Danube) | 01 40 40 03 30 | fax 01 40 40 03 30

"Maybe it's a bit out of the way for the average tourist", but gourmands gush it's "well worth the Homeric effort to find" this bistro in the far reaches of the 19th, thanks to the "splendid market-driven", "inventive" cuisine concocted "with much thought to taste, texture and presentation" by chef-owner Mark Singer, an "American in Paris"; "efficient service" and an "affordable, sharp wine list" make up for the "modest setting."

Caves Pétrissans ⑤ *Wine Bar/Bistro*

| 21 | 19 | 15 | €48 |

17ᵉ | 30 bis, av Niel (Péreire/Ternes) | 01 42 27 52 03 | fax 01 40 54 87 56

"It's always a pleasure to come back" to this "old-style" "bustling" *bistrot à vins* in the residential 17th, where the Classic French food is "tasty and the courses generous" (they've got "probably one of the best *tête de veau* in town"); although the staff can be "brusque", the "lively" ambiance, the rooms with "polished dark wood and sparkling mirrors" and the "great wine list" draw an "interesting local crowd."

☑ Caviar Kaspia ●⑤ *Russian*

| 26 | 21 | 24 | €110 |

8ᵉ | 17, pl de la Madeleine (Madeleine) | 01 42 65 33 32 | fax 01 42 65 66 26 | www.kaspia.fr

"Unchanged, and even better than 50 years ago", the "best address in Paris for caviar" "with a gorgeous view on the side" caters to a "*très* trendy clientele" with "over-the-top" Russian decor and cuisine – though the formula that most follow is "fish eggs, spoon, mouth, vodka, repeat (maybe smoked salmon for variety)"; the "exceptional service" and "romantic" Place de la Madeleine ambiance ensure a "delightful" time, even if you must "sell your Fabergé eggs to come here."

Cazaudehore La Forestière Ⓜ *Haute Cuisine*

| 20 | 19 | 17 | €76 |

Saint-Germain-en-Laye | 1, av Kennedy (RER St-Germain-en-Laye) | 01 30 61 64 64 | fax 01 39 73 73 88 | www.cazaudehore.fr

Enveloped by a garden, this "lovely house in Saint-Germain-en-Laye" is "pleasant for a family lunch on the weekend or an intimate dinner"; "though it's rather expensive, you won't be disappointed" in the "refined", "abundant" Haute Cuisine – "classic, but rejuvenated" with some New French "creativity"; perhaps the service "could be improved", but a trip here is always an "agreeable escapade."

Céladon (Le) 🅱 *Classic French* | 24 | 25 | 23 | €75 |

2ᵉ | Hôtel Westminster | 15, rue Daunou (Opéra) | 01 47 03 40 42 | fax 01 42 61 33 78 | www.leceladon.com

Near the ritzy Place Vendôme, the plush dining room of the Hôtel Westminster "serenely" serves up "superb" Classic French fare in an "elegant", "classical setting"; since the "excellent prix fixe" is a "relative bargain given the quality of the food and service", executives find it "fantastic for a business lunch", but it's also a good "stop for an after-dinner drink and chat with the wonderful master bartender."

144 Petrossian (Le) 🅱🅼 *Seafood* | 22 | 20 | 21 | €113 |

7ᵉ | 18, bd de La Tour-Maubourg (La Tour-Maubourg/Invalides) | 01 44 11 32 32 | fax 01 44 11 32 35

"Noted of course for the caviar" – it's situated above the famed boutique, near Les Invalides – this peach and gray-toned table "prettily presents" "Classic French seafood overlaid with a hint of Mother Russia"; it's "great for a celebratory meal", and "luxury lies within reach" on the reasonable (35-euro) lunch menu – "perfect for making an impression without going broke"; N.B. the Food score may not fully reflect the advent of chef Rougui Dia.

182 Rive Droite *New French* | ▽ 12 | 15 | 14 | €42 |

16ᵉ | 182, quai Louis Bleriot (Porte de St-Cloud/Exelmans) | 01 42 88 44 63 | fax 01 42 88 79 17 | www.182rivedroite.com

"Very hip for the neighborhood" – a riverside patch of the 16th – this site combines an "old-time bistro air" with a mod, loft-style setting, recently redone in bordeaux and khaki colors; many say it's "pleasant enough", with its New French–Provençal menu and "nice" terrace; but pessimists puff this "pretentious" place "could do better."

Cerisaie (La) 🅱 *Southwest* | 24 | 14 | 23 | €39 |

14ᵉ | 70, bd Edgar-Quinet (Edgar Quinet/Montparnasse) | 01 43 20 98 98 | fax 01 43 20 98 98

In Montparnasse, this "popular" "miniature bistro" is an "absolute gem", serving up "genuine", "excellent" dishes from the Southwest at "reasonable prices"; though it's "very crowded" ("you eat on your neighbor's lap"), "the smiling hostess" and the "convivial" atmosphere make it "definitely worth the detour."

Chai 33 ⬤ *Wine Bar/Bistro* | 12 | 16 | 13 | €44 |

12ᵉ | 33, Cour St-Emilion (Cour St-Emilion) | 01 53 44 01 01 | fax 01 53 44 01 02 | www.chai33.com

"Located in one of the old warehouses in Bercy village", a rapidly renovating district, this "à la mode" wine bar/eatery offers "a great place to try some different varietals by the glass" (you can "choose it directly from the *cave*"); but the Classic French fare fares less well ("mediocre"), and the "service borders on the nonexistent"; so some titter that only "the trendy setting" "can explain its success."

	FOOD	DECOR	SERVICE	COST

Chalet de Neuilly (Le) *Alpine/Classic French*   – | – | – | M

Neuilly-sur-Seine | 14, rue du Commandant Pilot (Les Sablons/Porte Maillot) | 01 46 24 03 11 | fax 01 46 37 18 80 | www.lechaletdeneuilly.com
"It's just like being in a mountain resort" claim "cheese connoisseurs" who happily head to this "joyful, noisy" outpost in suburban Neuilly with wood-paneled decor of old skis and sleds; "the cuisine also conjures up a winter vacation", with hearty alpine specialties (raclette and fondue) complementing the Classic French fare; but if the food is rich, the prices are not.

Chalet des Iles (Le) *Classic French*   15 | 24 | 17 | €52

16e | Lac Inférieur du Bois de Boulogne (La Pompe/La Muette) | 01 42 88 04 69 | fax 01 42 88 84 09 | www.chaletdesiles.net
"You take a little ferry boat" to reach this Classic French with "a knockout setting in the Bois de Boulogne" – and indeed, that's what "makes this place", since "the food is fine but nothing exceptional" (especially for the "expensive" tabs) and "service could be more professional"; but given it's got one of "Paris' most romantic decors", it "remains a favorite", especially for those "from out of town."

Chamarré (Le) ⊠ *New French*   24 | 17 | 19 | €80

7e | 13, bd de la Tour-Maubourg (Invalides/La Tour-Maubourg) | 01 47 05 50 18 | fax 01 47 05 91 21 | www.lechamarre.com
"Forget all you've ever tasted and dare to explore the unique New French cuisine with a Mauritian accent" at this "exotic" address in the 7th, where two chefs team up to produce "original" "high-end" dishes; surveyors split on the service – "knowledgeable" vs. "nonchalant", but all agree about the "astronomical prices" that leave them "always happy to go here, happier if invited."

Chantairelle ⊠ *Auvergne*   – | – | – | E

5e | 17, rue Laplace (Maubert-Mutualité) | 01 46 33 18 59 | fax 01 46 33 18 59 | www.chantairelle.com
"Tucked behind the Panthéon, this wonderful little regional bistro" uses Auvergnat cuisine to appeal to bucolics; the "country-style cooking" comes "with "charming country ambiance" – specifically, "a mechanical mooing cow, a clock that croaks like a frog" and a little inside well; N.B. get it to go at the adjacent grocery outlet.

Chapeau Melon ⊠ Ⓜ *Classic French/Eclectic*   – | – | – | M

19e | 92, rue Rébeval (Belleville/Pyrénées) | 01 42 02 68 60
Deep in the 19th, this dinner-only wine bistro with warm decor of red walls and varnished wood has become a word-of-mouth hit with the young couples who are settling this off-the-beaten-track *quartier*; its single menu changes weekly but might include such traditional French favorites as oysters Saint-Jacques.

Chardenoux *Bistro*   15 | 20 | 15 | €50

11e | 1, rue Jules Vallès (Charonne/Faidherbe-Chaligny) | 01 43 71 49 52 | fax 01 43 71 80 89
In the remote 11th ("a little out of the way but worth it"), this "small", "über-typical" "bistro brings back prewar days", with its "cleaned-

up art nouveau setting", "hearty" "classic fare" and "friendly waiters", friends feel; however, foes find that "it was better in the past" – now "the food is only so-so and the service average."

Charlot - Roi des Coquillages ❶ Brasserie
▽ 15 | - | 16 | €54

9ᵉ | 12, pl Clichy (Place de Clichy) | 01 53 20 48 00 | fax 01 53 20 48 09 | www.charlot-paris.com

Reflecting the improving demographics of the once "dodgy" Place de Clichy neighborhood, sleek new decor has replaced the kitschy look of this veteran brasserie; menuwise, you can still "always count on the fresh shellfish", and if some find it "hard on the wallet", "order a *plateau* for a group, and it's surprisingly reasonable."

Charpentiers (Aux) ❶ Bistro
18 | 16. | 19 | €41

6ᵉ | 10, rue Mabillon (Mabillon/St-Germain-des-Prés) | 01 43 26 30 05 | fax 01 46 33 07 98

"Linked to the Carpenter's Guild, this solid landmark of French culinary history" – established 1856 – still serves "no-frills bistro" comestibles in a "comfortable", collegial setting ("your new best friend is at the next table"); the "unmovable menu" and "oh-so typical *garçons*" suggest that "it's never changed and, we suspect, never will."

Chartier Classic French
13 | 21 | 14 | €23

9ᵉ | 7, rue Faubourg Montmartre (Grands Boulevards) | 01 47 70 86 29 | fax 01 48 24 14 68 | www.restaurant.chartier.com

"Tucked away off the Grands Boulevards", "one of the last classic dining halls" of Paris makes you "feel like you're stepping back in time" to an era of "no-frills" Classic French food, "rushed waiters" and communal tables in a "barn"-sized "beautiful building"; the food is "incredibly cheap" – but most jeer you get "the quality you pay for", plus often you "have to wait next to the garbage cans"; but that doesn't stop "both natives and tourists" lining up for the "lively" ambiance.

NEW Chateaubriand (Le) 🚫 Ⓜ New French
- | - | - | M

11ᵉ | 129, av Parmentier (Goncourt/Parmentier) | 01 43 57 45 95 | fax 01 43 57 45 95

To sample the Asian-accented, produce-driven New French cooking that's all the rage right now, hoof it over to this funky, hugely popular bistro in the Oberkampf quarter, where a vintage grocery store-turned-dining room is the newest setting for rising-star chef Iñaki Aizpitarte; a native of the Basque country, he describes his cooking style as "*cuisine de vagabonde*", a reference to his international travels, and it results in dishes with clean but unexpected combinations of flavors – e.g. asparagus with tahini foam and sesame-seed brittle.

Chaumière en l'Ile (La) ❶ Classic French
▽ 22 | 19 | 23 | €47

4ᵉ | 4, rue Jean du Bellay (Pont Marie) | 01 43 54 27 34

Considered "a charmer" near the Hôtel de Ville, "this small bistro with a lot of flair" serves Classic French fare that's "always fresh and inventive"; advocates also appreciate the "traditional", "lovely ambiance" and the "good prices."

	FOOD	DECOR	SERVICE	COST

Chen Soleil d'Est ☒ Chinese
24 | 12 | 17 | €84

15ᵉ | 15, rue du Théâtre (Charles Michels) | 01 45 79 34 34 |
fax 01 45 79 07 53

Maybe it's "the most expensive Chinese in Paris, but it's also the best" swear Sinophiles of this table in the 15th; even fans of the "refined dishes" and "good wines", however, dis the "dreary environment" in a modern complex.

Cherche Midi (Le) ◑ Italian
18 | 13 | 18 | €40

6ᵉ | 22, rue du Cherche-Midi (Sèvres-Babylone/St-Sulpice) |
01 45 48 27 44

"On a lovely quiet street near Saint-Sulpice" in the 6th, this "hole-in-the-wall is an insider's favorite" for "reliably good Italian cuisine" that's often served with "tongue-in-cheek commentary from the waiter"; "ideal for celebrity-spotting", it's usually "crowded and noisy", due to the "elbow-to-elbow seating", so you "better reserve or be a habitué" (who heads straight for the coveted "seats on the sidewalk terrace").

Chez André ◑ Bistro
20 | 15 | 18 | €51

8ᵉ | 12, rue Marbeuf (Franklin D. Roosevelt) | 01 47 20 59 57 |
fax 01 47 20 18 82

"Just a block from the hustle and bustle" of the Champs sits this "epitome of bistros", complete with "oyster shucker outside"; seems as if "nothing here has changed since before World War II", when it opened: neither the "simple and oh-so-good" cuisine (their "coq au vin is the stuff of legend") nor the "classic environment" nor the "matronly" waitresses, "all dressed in black with white nurse caps"; however, "if you don't like [sitting] close to strangers, this is not the place for you."

Chez Catherine ☒ New French
23 | 18 | 22 | €63

8ᵉ | 3, rue Berryer (George V/St-Philippe du Roule) | 01 40 76 01 40 |
fax 01 40 76 03 96

While its side-street address in the 8th is "a tad off the beaten track for most tourists", it's worth "studying your map" to find this New French, with "pricey" but "interesting" and "inventive" cuisine offered amid "lovely", gray-toned decor; the "warm, welcoming service" is led by chef Catherine Guerraz, who "takes the time to talk to every table and is adorable."

NEW Chez Cécile ☒ Classic French
– | – | – | M

8ᵉ | La Ferme des Mathurins | 17, rue Vignon (Madeleine) |
01 42 66 46 39 | www.chezcecile.com

Formerly known as La Ferme des Mathurins (and famously frequented by the mystery writer Simenon), this venue near La Madeleine in the 8th has been transformed by a new owner – the eponymous Cécile Desimpel – and a young chef, who trained at the Ritz Hotel in London; they've brightened up the decor and freshened up the menu; which now offers intriguingly spiced Classic French fare; live jazz on Thursday nights adds a swinging ambiance.

	FOOD	DECOR	SERVICE	COST

Chez Clément ◐ *Classic French*   12 | 15 | 14 | €31

2ᵉ | 17, bd des Capucines (Opéra) | 01 53 43 52 00 | fax 01 53 43 82 09
4ᵉ | 21, bd Beaumarchais (Bastille/Chemin-Vert) | 01 40 29 17 00 |
fax 01 40 29 17 09
6ᵉ | 9, pl St-André-des-Arts (St-Michel) | 01 56 81 32 00 |
fax 01 56 81 32 09
8ᵉ | 123, av des Champs-Elysées (Charles de Gaulle-Etoile) |
01 40 73 87 00 | fax 01 40 73 87 09
8ᵉ | 19, rue Marbeuf (Franklin D. Roosevelt/George V) |
01 53 23 90 00 | fax 01 53 23 90 09
14ᵉ | 106, bd du Montparnasse (Vavin) | 01 44 10 54 00 |
fax 01 44 10 54 09
15ᵉ | 407, rue de Vaugirard (Porte de Versailles) | 01 53 68 94 00 |
fax 01 53 68 94 09
17ᵉ | 47, av de Wagram (Charles de Gaulle-Etoile/Ternes) |
01 53 81 97 00 | fax 01 53 81 97 09
17ᵉ | 99, bd Gouvion-St-Cyr (Porte Maillot) | 01 45 72 93 00 |
fax 01 45 72 93 09
Boulogne-Billancourt | 98, av Edouard Vaillant (Marcel Sembat) |
01 41 22 90 00 | fax 01 41 22 90 09
www.chezclement.com

"Everything is average" at this "country-style chain with lots of copper decor" ("kitschy, but not bad") and "standard" Classic French cuisine; still, it's a "popular spot for tour groups", "cheap reunions" or "a quick meal before or after a movie."

Chez Denise - La Tour   23 | 17 | 19 | €44
de Montlhéry ◐ 🄑 *Bistro*

1ᵉʳ | 5, rue des Prouvaires (Châtelet-Les Halles) | 01 42 36 21 82 |
fax 01 45 08 81 99

"Every night's a party" (one that runs all night) at this "wonderful old-style bistro that has survived for years" in the old Les Halles ("you'll expect Hemingway to be seated next to you any minute"); cuisine "doesn't come more traditionally Parisian" than the "delicious", "hearty portions" of "traditional French rustic food", including "many animal parts that may seem strange to city folk", "served with humor that takes your mind off the noise level" and the fact "you're sitting in your neighbor's lap."

Chez Francis ◐ *Brasserie*   14 | 16 | 15 | €50

8ᵉ | 7, pl de l'Alma (Alma Marceau) | 01 47 20 86 83 | fax 01 47 20 43 26
Blessed with "the best terrace in Paris for viewing the Eiffel Tower", this brasserie in the 8th is a "major mecca for the business crowd at lunch" and "ideal after the theater"; but if the locale "can't be beat for the price", the "predictable" food and "hardworking, but insufficient service" easily can be; still, it's "a true treat" for "lots of people-watching."

Chez Françoise ◐ *Classic French*   15 | 13 | 17 | €46

7ᵉ | Aérogare des Invalides (Invalides) | 01 47 05 49 03 |
fax 01 45 51 96 20 | www.chezfrancoise.com
Located inside the Invalides *aérogare*, this is a "favorite place for French politicians" who ignore the "air-terminal ambiance" and con-

centrate on the "quite acceptable" Classic French cuisine; it's ideal for a business meal, especially as the staff is "efficient and diplomatic."

Chez Fred ◪ *Lyon* | - | - | - | M |

17ᵉ | 190 bis, bd Péreire (Péreire/Porte Maillot) | 01 45 74 20 48
"Tasty" Lyonnais dishes (each day has its specialty) dominate the menu at this neighborhood bistro "on a busy street" in the 17th, whose "classic surroundings" include tiled floors inside and "tables on the sidewalk" in summer; the impressive cellar of Bordeaux and Beaujolais helps wash down the sometimes "heavy food."

Chez Gégène ◪ *Classic French* | - | - | - | M |

Joinville-le-Pont | 162 bis, quai de Polangis (RER Joinville-le-Pont) | 01 48 83 29 43 | fax 01 48 83 72 62 | www.chez-gegene.fr
"On the banks of the Marne" in suburban Joinville, this *guinguette* is a throwback to the '20s with "an amazing dance hall and decor right out of a Toulouse-Lautrec painting"; so come out for Classic French treats, including "some of the world's best french fries and respectable basics like roast chicken" and mussels at affordable prices.

◪ Chez Georges ◪ *Bistro* | 21 | 18 | 20 | €54 |

2ᵉ | 1, rue du Mail (Bourse) | 01 42 60 07 11
"In the less-touristy 2nd", this "quintessential bistro", "run by the same family for decades", "generously delivers" "dishes that are so dated they're fashionable again" ("it was love at first bite"); "a subtle look suffices to get the attention of the remarkably competent staff"; "seating is tight, but that just adds to the ambiance" that says "this is the real thing" – as does "their method of putting a wine bottle on your table and then only charging you for what you drink."

Chez Georges-Porte Maillot ● *Brasserie* | 15 | 12 | 15 | €55 |

17ᵉ | 273, bd Péreire (Porte Maillot) | 01 45 74 31 00 | fax 01 45 74 02 56 | www.chez-georges.com
Near Porte Maillot lies this "pretty decent brasserie with a good wine selection" and "a roast lamb that's the best in Paris"; though the decor is a little "slick" for some, the "service is professional"; pity that, "like most restaurants in the area, it's a bit overpriced."

Chez Gérard ◪ *Auvergne* | ∇ 19 | 15 | 14 | €34 |

Neuilly-sur-Seine | 10, rue Montrosier (Porte Maillot) | 01 46 24 86 37 | fax 01 46 37 21 72
"The owner greets clients as friends", serving them "fresh, authentic" bistro dishes with "lots of Auvergnat specialties" at this "excellent Neuilly refuge" (despite staff and "decor that could use some updating"); since the "room is a little small, it's better to reserve."

Chez Grisette ◪ *Wine Bar/Bistro* | - | - | - | I |

18ᵉ | 14, rue Houdon (Abessess/Pigalle) | 01 42 62 04 80 | fax 01 42 62 04 80 | www.chez-grisette.fr
Now, "this is what an evening in Montmartre should be" declare devotees of this wine bistro: "a pleasant owner's" welcome, a "nice" if tiny room with bottles adorning the walls, "good, sound" Classic French cuisine and "friendly service"; in short, "Brava Grisette!"

	FOOD	DECOR	SERVICE	COST

Chez Janou ● *Provence* | 20 | 17 | 18 | €36 |

3ᵉ | 2, rue Roger Verlomme (Bastille/Chemin-Vert) | 01 42 72 28 41
"Hidden on a quiet Marais street", this "eclectic eatery" "is jumping" with a "diverse crowd ranging from arty chain-smoking students to American tourists"; if a few feel the "food ranges from amazingly innovative to disappointingly bland", most support the "superior" Southern French fare, including an "amazing chocolate mousse" served in "unlimited" quantities; P.S. "don't forget to order one of the many varieties of pastis."

Chez Jenny ● *Alsace* | 17 | 16 | 16 | €47 |

3ᵉ | 39, bd du Temple (République) | 01 44 54 39 00 | fax 01 44 54 39 09 | www.chezjenny.com
"The choucroute is worth the trek" to this big "traditional brasserie" in the 3rd, a "regional Alsatian at its rustic best" fans find; the more critical call the 500-seat premises a "food factory" and deem the *winstub* decor a little "hokey"; but the "mounds" of food make it a "great value", and it's "tourist- and kid-friendly" too.

Chez L'Ami Jean ●ⓈⓂ *Basque/Bistro* | 22 | 12 | 16 | €42 |

7ᵉ | 27, rue Malar (Invalides/La Tour-Maubourg) | 01 47 05 86 89 | www.amijean.com
"If you find yourself between the Invalides and the Eiffel Tower, it's more than worth a stop" at this "always packed" "rustic" place; the chef-owner, an "alum of La Régalade", "knows how to marry modern bistro and regional Basque cuisines" into "succulent, flavorful" dishes; the staff operates on a "principle of informality" and "tables are quite tight" ("you think you've seen crowded? try this"), "but it's all part of a convivial evening."

Chez la Vieille Ⓢ *Bistro* | ∇ 22 | 14 | 19 | €45 |

1ᵉʳ | 1, rue Bailleul (Louvre-Rivoli) | 01 42 60 15 78 | fax 01 42 33 85 71 | www.gerardbesson.com
Near Les Halles, this "tiny" bistro with an "old-time working-class ambiance" serves "wonderful", "authentic home cooking" in "generous portions"; the "crusty old decor" is seemingly untouched since the '50s, but few care because the place is "perfect for a weekday lunch on a cold day, provided you can sleep it off" afterwards; N.B. dinner served Thursdays only.

Chez Léna et Mimile ⓈⓂ *Bistro* | – | – | – | M |

5ᵉ | 32, rue Tournefort (Censier-Daubenton/Place Monge) | 01 47 07 72 47 | fax 01 45 35 41 94
With "a bottle of adequate wine included in the price of the prix fixe", "pleasant meals" can be had at this '30s bistro blessed with a "charming location" that "overlooks a quiet square with a fountain" in the 5th; the Classic French "food is ok, but sitting on the terrace is delightful."

Chez Léon Ⓢ *Bistro* | 17 | 12 | 13 | €30 |

17ᵉ | 32, rue Legendre (Villiers) | 01 42 27 06 82 | fax 01 46 22 63 67
On a busy street in the popular 17th, this "good value neighborhood bistro" with a 1930s decor caters to locals and the occasional tourist

en route to the Parc Monceau; "the wide selection of typical dishes", including Burgundy snails, *tête de veau* and chocolate profiteroles, is "well prepared" and served by "a helpful staff of one."

Chez Les Anges 🅂 *Brasserie*

| - | - | - | E |

7ᵉ | 54, bd de la Tour Maubourg (La Tour Maubourg) | 01 47 05 89 86 | www.chezlesanges.com

In the residential 7th, the ex-owner of Le Bon Accueil has redesigned this old-timer, giving it a minimalist "Zen decor of immaculate whiteness" (with some subsequent warm-toned touches); though a little "pricey", the contemporary brasserie cuisine is "original", and there's "a good selection of Burgundy wines."

Chez Livio *Italian*

| 13 | 12 | 12 | €41 |

Neuilly-sur-Seine | 6, rue de Longchamp (Pont-de-Neuilly) | 01 46 24 81 32 | fax 01 47 38 20 72

A family-run "institution" for 50 years, Neuilly's "popular" trattoria serves up a wide array of Italian eats; detractors dis the "mediocre" "small portions" and "interminable waits", "particularly on the weekends"; but it's "an excellent choice for families with kids", especially "when they open up the roof on a hot summer day."

Chez Ly ➋ *Chinese/Thai*

| - | - | - | M |

17ᵉ | 95, av Niel (Péreire) | 01 40 53 88 38 | fax 01 40 53 88 36

Just off the Place Péreire in the 17th, this elegant Asian casts a spell with its soigné decor of flowers, Oriental-style furniture and porcelain and low lighting that's animated by the charming maitresse d'; an imaginative and authentic Chinese-Thai menu uses only the best quality French ingredients in innovative ways (don't miss their version of foie gras, stuffed with lotus seeds and marinated in sake).

Chez Maître Paul *Alsace*

| 20 | 16 | 20 | €48 |

6ᵉ | 12, rue Monsieur-le-Prince (Odéon) | 01 43 54 74 59 | fax 01 43 54 43 74 | www.chezmaitrepaul.com

"Every foodie loves coming to this bistro" for an insider's take on "utterly delicious", "reliable" regional "cuisine from the Jura" mountains (their signature "chicken in yellow wine with morels is heavenly"); it's served "with a welcoming smile" in a "small, cozy and classy" space near Odéon.

Chez Marcel 🅂 *Lyon*

| ▽ 21 | 16 | 20 | €40 |

6ᵉ | 7, rue Stanislas (Notre-Dame-des-Champs) | 01 45 48 29 94

For "a vision of Paris past", hop over to this "authentic bistro", "tucked away in a touristy neighborhood" of the 6th ("may it remain pure!"); even if the decor is old-fashioned ("lace curtains on the door"), surveyors insist it's "one of the must-eats" of the capital, serving Lyonnais fare that's "incredible" given the relatively "low prices."

Chez Marianne *Mideastern*

| 18 | 12 | 13 | €25 |

4ᵉ | 2, rue des Hospitalières St-Gervais (St-Paul) | 01 42 72 18 86 | fax 01 42 78 75 26

"Even if you're broke" you can come to this haven in the historical "heart of the Marais" for a "great variety" of "tasty", "solid Middle

Eastern" and Eastern European food; but service is "irregular" and "getting a table in the dining room can be a struggle, especially on weekends", as it's "very crowded even by Paris standards"; hence, "if it's nice weather, eating outside is recommended."

	FOOD	DECOR	SERVICE	COST

Chez Michel ●⊠ *New French* | 23 | 13 | 18 | €42

10ᵉ | 10, rue de Belzunce (Gare du Nord/Poissonnière) | 01 44 53 06 20 | fax 01 44 53 61 31

"A few blocks from the Gare du Nord, but otherwise in the middle of nowhere" ("take a taxi at night"), this New French "filled with both locals and tourists" serves "creative, delicious dishes from chef-owner Thierry Breton's native Brittany", including lots of "squeaky-fresh fish"; "prices are terrific" and the "atmosphere pleasant" – the "service is not nearly as surly as everyone says" – so never mind the "crammed tables", but do "avoid the dreary, barrackslike basement if you can."

Chez Nénesse ⊠ *Classic French* | ▽ 19 | 12 | 20 | €53

3ᵉ | 17, rue de Saintonge (Filles-du-Calvaire/République) | 01 42 78 46 49 | fax 01 42 78 45 51

This "tiny" family-run "favorite" in the Marais is "like eating at home", with its "reassuring" Classic French fare and "personable staff"; converts call it "a cozy retreat in winter (ask for a table near the stove)."

Chez Omar ●⇎ *Moroccan* | 21 | 16 | 19 | €32

3ᵉ | 47, rue de Bretagne (République/Temple) | 01 42 72 36 26

For "couscous at its most trendy", check out this "casual" "fashion-industry favorite" in the 3rd, where plates are "piled high" with "pleasant" Moroccan morsels, the "jovial" owner makes "you feel like a local on your first" visit and the "waiters never stop joking around"; the place is usually "packed" and they "don't take reservations", but "don't be turned off by the line that often extends out the door" – it's "worth the wait."

Chez Papa ● *Southwest* | 18 | 12 | 16 | €23

8ᵉ | 29, rue de l'Arcade (Madeleine/St-Lazare) | 01 42 65 43 68
10ᵉ | 206, rue la Fayette (Louis Blanc) | 01 42 09 53 87
14ᵉ | 6, rue Gassendi (Denfert-Rochereau/Raspail) | 01 43 22 41 19 | fax 01 40 47 55 73
15ᵉ | 101, rue de la Croix-Nivert (Commerce/Félix Faure) | 01 48 28 31 88

"Cheap and nourishing", this chain is "aimed toward students" and "young, underpaid office workers" with its "huge portions" of "typically Southwestern fare" ("meaning heavy and full of fat"); "the food is not tops", "the decor's pretty lowbrow" and the servers are geared toward turning over tables; but "if you're hungry, this is the place to go"; P.S. the "salade Boyarde with fried potatoes, Cantal and blue cheese, ham and lettuce is by far the best choice on the menu."

Chez Papinou ●Ⓜ *Bistro* | - | - | - | M

Neuilly-sur-Seine | 26, rue du Château (Pont-de-Neuilly) | 01 55 24 90 40

Wannabe wine stewards get their kicks at this "nice casual place" in Neuilly, where "you go down to get your own bottle of wine from the cellar"; the classic bistro cooking is "not bad" and the service is "nice" under the "young owners", but nostalgists attest "the ambiance is missing" now that "the old Papinou is definitely gone."

Chez Paul ❶ *Bistro*   20 | 16 | 16 | €34

11ᵉ | 13, rue de Charonne (Bastille/Ledru-Rollin) | 01 47 00 34 57 | fax 01 48 07 02 00

"It's worth the wait" (if you "arrive without reservations") at this "old classic" bistro in the 11th known for "generous, rustic" dishes; even though the "tables are tucked in tightly" ("you never know if you will be sitting next to a designer, a lawyer or a family birthday party") and "the service can be slow", this is the kind of place "that, while it never surprises, also never disappoints"; N.B. the recent addition of an extra room may ease the squeeze.

Chez Paul ❶ *Bistro*   17 | 14 | 16 | €33

13ᵉ | 22, rue de la Butte-aux-Cailles (Corvisart/Place d'Italie) | 01 45 89 22 11 | fax 01 45 80 26 53

"Eat like a Parisian" on grandmotherly dishes ("the baked figs in autumn are the stuff dreams are made of") at this bistro "off the tourist beat" in the 13th; the decor's "not very original" and the service is "up and down", but overall "the energy level is high", fueled by the "affordable prices."

Chez Pauline ☒ *Bistro*   21 | 17 | 20 | €58

1ᵉʳ | 5, rue Villedo (Pyramides/Palais Royal) | 01 42 96 20 70 | fax 01 49 27 99 89 | www.chezpauline.com

Near the Palais Royal, here is "another classic bistro that hasn't lost its skill or charm" with its French "comfort food" ("good game in season"); while it "could use an update, decorwise", the "attentive, though not hovering, service" compensates; it's a bit "expensive" alas.

Chez Prune *Eclectic*   12 | 17 | 13 | €27

10ᵉ | 36, rue Beaurepaire (Jacques Bonsergent/République) | 01 42 41 30 47 | fax 01 42 00 32 28

"Frequented by hipsters" "and their offspring", this Eclectic is *the* place to be in the Canal Saint-Martin area" ("you have to fight to get a seat in the sun on the terrace"); while "nice for a nibble and beer", however, most say it's "more for people-watching than eating."

Chez Ramona Ⓜ *Spanish*   – | – | – | M

20ᵉ | 17, rue Ramponneau (Belleville-Coronne) | 01 46 36 83 55

A warm Iberian welcome from chef-owner Ramona and her daughter, Cucu, plus their excellent tapas and other Spanish dishes, have trendy young types charging for this affordable bodega in bohemian Belleville; the simple, charming decor re-creates an old-fashioned grocery store, and prices are as friendly as the atmosphere.

Chez Ramulaud ❶☒ *Bistro*   ▽ 22 | 15 | 21 | €37

11ᵉ | 269, rue du Faubourg St-Antoine (Faidherbe-Chaligny/Nation) | 01 43 72 23 29 | fax 01 43 72 57 03

"This is just the kind of local restaurant everyone wishes he had" smile supporters of this bistro where "the food is refreshingly creative without losing its power to satisfy the palate and warm the heart"; the "friendly staff will make you feel at home" and some nights there's even a "guitar player who amuses with his French oldies but goodies"; "it's worth traveling to" and even "makes moving to the 11th something to consider."

Chez René ⑤ Lyon
FOOD	DECOR	SERVICE	COST
21	14	21	€48

5e | 14, bd St-Germain (Maubert-Mutualité) | 01 43 54 30 23
At the beginning of the Boulevard Saint-Germain, this "old favorite" with "decades of delicious delights" behind it is "the type of place that gives French bistros their reputation"; patrons praise the Lyonnais-accented cuisine, starring "perhaps the best boeuf bourguignon in the world", that's "served by an experienced staff in a comfortable", albeit slightly "uninspired", setting.

Chez Savy ⑤ Aveyron
FOOD	DECOR	SERVICE	COST
▽ 21	14	18	€50

8e | 23, rue Bayard (Franklin D. Roosevelt) | 01 47 23 46 98
In a "good location" off the chic Avenue Montaigne, this "old-school mirrored bistro" "buzzes with atmosphere" and "traditional" Aveyron dishes "expertly prepared"; signature dishes featuring Aubrac meats make it a "hidden treasure" "for beef lovers."

Chez Vincent ⑤ Italian
FOOD	DECOR	SERVICE	COST
22	11	17	€56

19e | 5, rue du Tunnel (Botzaris/Buttes-Chaumont) | 01 42 02 22 45 | fax 01 40 18 95 83
One of "the best Italians in town" proclaim pasta people of this *piccolo* place – consume even "a simple dish like spaghetti Bolognese and it feels like you're eating it for the first time"; it's "expensive", even "if you don't count the long taxi ride" to the 19th, and as for the service – led by chef-owner Vincent Cozzoli, "a show in himself" – "you either love it or hate it"; judging by its popularity, though, love wins, especially among celebs ("don't tell anyone, but it's Scorcese's and De Niro's favorite in Paris").

Chez Vong ●⑤ Chinese
FOOD	DECOR	SERVICE	COST
20	19	20	€55

1er | 10, rue de la Grande Truanderie (Etienne Marcel) | 01 40 26 09 36 | fax 01 42 33 38 15 | www.chez-vong.com
"Chef Vong Vai Kaun came to Paris over 25 years ago", and what he cooks is "as close to Haute Chinese cuisine as you can get" converts claim – though purists pout that the "overpriced", "Frenchified cooking lacks authenticity"; still, in a shabby part of Les Halles, the decor of this "upscale" Asian offers a "mysterious atmosphere with its old stone dining rooms dotted with Buddhas, parasols and bamboo", and the "service is adorable."

Chiberta (Le) ⑤ New French
FOOD	DECOR	SERVICE	COST
23	21	22	€105

8e | 3, rue Arsène Houssaye (Charles de Gaulle-Etoile) | 01 53 53 42 00 | fax 01 45 62 85 08 | www.lechiberta.com
Now "one of Guy Savoy's stable", this "renewed" site in the 8th gets mixed responses: scores side with those who find the "inventive" New French fare "wonderful", the "modern decor" "elegant" and the "service fine"; but dissenters deem the digs "dark" ("wear a miner's helmet in the restrooms if you want to see") and the "rather simple"

cuisine "much too dear for what it is", making this site do-able "only for business lunches."

Chieng Mai ● *Thai*

	FOOD	DECOR	SERVICE	COST
	17	12	15	€37

5ᵉ | 12, rue Frédéric Sauton (Maubert-Mutualité) | 01 43 25 45 45

"Run in an old-fashioned way", this "authentic Thai" in the 5th "near Notre Dame" "is like taking a mini-vacation from Paris"; but while the "multicourse meals are an adventure, it's too bad the rooms are so plain"; luckily service is *un peu* more "pleasant", as are the prices.

Chien qui Fume (Au) ● *Brasserie*

	17	18	16	€44

1ᵉʳ | 33, rue du Pont-Neuf (Châtelet-Les Halles) | 01 42 36 07 42 | fax 42 36 36 85 | www.au-chien-qui-fume.com

At "the edge of the Les Halles garden", this "standard brasserie" with "original" images of "dogs smoking" offers "a good deal for what you get" – namely, Classic French dishes; some growl that it's "living off its history and its name" – in particular, the staff, "although witty, is ineffective" – but you gotta "keep it in perspective: it's about fun, not Haute Cuisine" or service here.

China Club ● *Chinese*

	16	21	15	€47

12ᵉ | 50, rue de Charenton (Bastille/Ledru-Rollin) | 01 43 43 82 02 | fax 01 43 43 79 85 | www.chinaclub.cc

Near Bastille, this "chic" salon draws devotees with a "dark, smoky" "1930s-Shanghai decor" to "listen to live music in the jazz cellar downstairs" or consume cocktails in the "cozy bar" upstairs; "you definitely go more for the [digs] than for the food", but the Chinese fare "is more than passable", making this "the best place to enjoy glancing at your future mistress in a candlelit setting."

Christine (Le) ● *Bistro*

	23	21	23	€51

6ᵉ | 1, rue Christine (Odéon/St-Michel) | 01 40 51 71 64 | fax 01 43 26 15 63

"Off the beaten path" and "oozing charm" near the Odéon, this bistro is considered by many to be a "little gem" with its "warm, inviting room" in "an old Parisian house", "delightful service" and "uncomplicated, but perfectly executed" French classics; however, to avoid all those "loud tourists", "ask to be seated in the "'non-English-speaking' back room."

NEW Cibus ⊠ *Italian*

	–	–	–	E

1ᵉʳ | 5, rue Molière (Pyramides/Palais-Royale) | 01 42 61 50 19

It may not be promising at first glance – the drab facade hasn't changed since its long-gone crêperie days – but the creative cooking at this Italian in the 2nd has supporters singing 'O Sole Mio'; the organically based cuisine is backed up by Italian vinos, including a housemade variety, the service is friendly and the tiny digs have the buzz that comes from being a rather confidential foodie address.

Cigale Recamier (La) ⊠ *Classic French*

	22	19	20	€55

7ᵉ | 4, rue Recamier (Sèvres-Babylone) | 01 45 48 86 58

"Lots of neighborhood regulars" gather at this Classic French in a cul-de-sac near the Bon Marché store (it's "lovely dining outside without cars buzzing in your face"); "they really know how to make soufflés", which are "varied and wonderful" – though critics caution "choosing anything else will leave you deflated"; even though "the staff is sometimes overwhelmed", it's "still nice."

☑ Cinq (Le) *Haute Cuisine*  28 | 29 | 28 | €171

8e | Four Seasons George V | 31, av George V (Alma Marceau/George V) | 01 49 52 71 54 | fax 01 49 52 71 81 | www.fourseasons.com/paris

"For an incredible experience – what royalty must feel like every day" – surveyors tout this "temple of Haute Cuisine" in the George V, rated "Le Top" in Paris in Decor and Service; with its "oasis of flowers", the setting is "enchanting", while the staff is so "faultless" it's like "items appear at the table as though your server never left", and the dishes are "the stuff culinary dreams are made of"; true, it's a "traditional" place, and "you might be left a peasant" by the prices – but dining's "as good as it gets" here.

Cinq Mars ☑ Ⓜ *Bistro* – | – | – | M

7e | 51, rue de Verneuil (Rue du Bac/Solférino) | 01 45 44 69 13

In the chic part of the 7th, this "pretty little place" with "charming" decor runs the gamut of familial, classic bistro cuisine, in "well-executed, generous" portions that are served, well, family-style; service is *"sympathique"*, as the French say, leaving advocates to advise "go soon, it can only go down from here."

Citrus Etoile ☑ *Classic/New French* – | – | – | E

8e | 6, rue Arsène Houssaye (Etoile) | 01 42 89 15 51 | fax 01 42 89 28 67 | www.citrusetoile.com

After a long stint at Los Angeles' L'Orangerie, chef-owner Gilles Epié has opened his own table just off the Champs; a Malibu-esque modern orange-and-white room, overseen by his American wife, provides the bright backdrop for his nervy, Californian-influenced menu that combines New French flavors (like rotisseried cod) with Gallic classics (chocolate soufflé).

Cloche des Halles (La) ☑ Ⓓ *Wine Bar/Bistro* ▽ 16 | 12 | 12 | €31

1er | 28, rue Coquillière (Les Halles/Louvre-Rivoli) | 01 42 36 93 89

Named after the bell that used to ring the opening and closing hours of the old Les Halles market, this "typical" wine bar is "one of the affordable treats in Paris", serving a "spectacular quiche" and other pub grub with a wide selection of Beaujolais on "Formica-like tables"; service is "rushed but efficient", so you can "go at midday" and "look at the beautiful people."

Clos des Gourmets (Le) ☑ Ⓜ *New French* 24 | 20 | 22 | €49

7e | 16, av Rapp (Alma Marceau/Ecole Militaire) | 01 45 51 75 61 | fax 01 47 05 74 20 | www.leclosdesgourmets.com

"It's really worth the trip" to the quiet residential 7th in order to sit down in this "lovely room (even if the tables are really close together)"; run by a "husband-and-wife team that keeps clients coming back", it serves "exquisite, refined" New French dishes, especially on the "inventive prix fixe" whose "supplements are worth the splurge"; all this "in a price range" that'll make you "spoiled forever."

	FOOD	DECOR	SERVICE	COST

Closeries des Lilas (La) ● *Classic French*
16 | 22 | 17 | €56

6e | 171, bd du Montparnasse (Port Royal/Vavin) | 01 40 51 34 50 | fax 01 43 29 99 94 | www.closeriedeslilas.fr

This Montparnasse "mythical place" "has a great reputation to live up to" and how well it succeeds depends on which part you patronize; "the brasserie is an experience" – "even though Hemingway is long gone, the oysters and drinks are still fine", and in the "charming bar" the piano-playing and "people-watching are divine"; but "the restaurant is formal and stuffy" with merely "reliable" Classic French cuisine that "can get very expensive"; "all in all, this historical landmark is worth a visit", though.

Clos Morillons (Le) ⓈⓂ *New French*
– | – | – | M

15e | 50, rue des Morillons (Porte de Vanves) | 01 48 28 04 37 | fax 01 48 28 70 77

Another team's taken over this New French in the 15th, and not surprisingly, nostalgists gripe it's "not as good as when the former owner was there"; but others find the "cuisine ingenious", and say the "tiny" room's renovated, candlelit decor makes it "a good neighborhood place."

Clou (Le) Ⓢ *Bistro*
– | – | – | M

17e | 132, rue Cardinet (Malesherbes) | 01 42 27 36 78 | fax 01 42 27 89 96 | www.restaurant-leclou.fr

In the residential 17th, this cozy little bistro has become a standby for locals and those willing to stray off the beaten track for traditional, refined fare from chef-owner Christian Leclou (ex Ledoyen); the earth-toned room is adorned mostly with crisp white linen tablecloths, vintage posters and the proverbial blackboard listing the specials – though guests can usually count on a slow-cooked shoulder of lamb, along with a good selection of Loire Valley wines.

Clovis (Le) Ⓢ *New French*
19 | 21 | 19 | €86

8e | Sofitel Arc de Triomphe | 14, rue Beaujon (Charles de Gaulle-Etoile) | 01 53 89 50 53 | fax 01 53 89 50 51 | www.accorhotels.com

Near the Etoile, this New French boasts subdued but "sumptuous decor", and a "reliable" menu that makes it a good "place to have business lunches"; however, its Haute Cuisine aspirations result in it seeming a little "too expensive for what is served on the plate", and "service is a bit stuffy", as well.

Clown Bar ●⇗ *Wine Bar/Bistro*
∇ 19 | 22 | 16 | €33

11e | 114, rue Amelot (Filles-du-Calvaire) | 01 43 55 87 35 | www.clown-bar.fr

Near the Cirque d'Hiver in a remote part of the 11th, this "small" but "very pretty" *bar à vins* boasts "original" art nouveau decor with landmarked, circus-themed tiles; "delicious" nibbles accompanying the "interesting wines" make it an "ideal" hangout, though some could do without the clownish "attitude of the servers."

Coco de Mer ●◪ *Seychelles* ▽ 22 | 18 | 17 | €37

5ᵉ | 34, bd St-Marcel (Les Gobelins/St-Marcel) | 01 47 07 06 64

In the 5th, this "second embassy of the Seychelles" serves "very good cuisine that allows you to travel with your feet in the sand" sprinkled across the entrance; in particular, the prix fixe offers "excellent fish" at "reasonable prices"; don't be surprised if "coming out, you'll feel like taking off for Mahé, La Digue or another of the archipelago's islands."

Coffee Parisien ● *American* 15 | 12 | 12 | €27

6ᵉ | 4, rue Princesse (Mabillon) | 01 43 54 18 18 | fax 01 43 54 94 96
16ᵉ | 7, rue Gustave Courbet (Trocadéro/Victor Hugo) |
01 45 53 17 17 | fax 01 45 53 48 33
Neuilly-sur-Seine | 46, rue de Sablonville (Les Sablons) |
01 46 37 13 13 | fax 01 46 37 55 15

"Surprisingly filled with" "trendy Gallic teens", this trio of "crammed" Yankee-style coffee shops offers a "French take on diner food" ("real pancakes, eggs Benedict, club sandwiches, hamburgers, etc."); critics claim that though it's among "the best American fare" in town, it's still "not great", and abhor the "amateurish service"; but "excited expats" aver "if you've the patience to wait a long time" ("particularly on weekends"), you'll feel "just like back home."

Coin des Gourmets (Au) *Cambodian/Vietnamese* 16 | 9 | 18 | €36

5ᵉ | 5, rue Dante (Cluny La Sorbonne/Maubert-Mutualité) |
01 43 26 12 92

Indochine ◪Ⓜ *Cambodian/Vietnamese*

1ᵉʳ | 38, rue du Mont Thabor (Concorde) | 01 42 60 79 79

"Loaded with regulars", this Latin Quarter Southeast Asian (with a new corner near Concorde) offers Vietnamese and Cambodian "delicacies" that are "well prepared" and proffered by an "extremely friendly staff" find friends who are "undisturbed" by the "barebones simplicity" of the setting; but the "disappointed" declare the fare "used to be fabulous", now it "seems ordinary."

Comédiens (Les) ●◪ *Classic French* - | - | - | M

9ᵉ | 7, rue Blanche (Trinité) | 01 40 82 95 95 | fax 01 40 82 96 95

Two steps from the Trinité church in the 9th, showbiz denizens and theatergoers congregate at this Classic French with exposed-brick walls, a zinc bar and posters galore; amid the boisterous ambiance, it's "fun to watch everything going on in the open kitchen"; the "superb" service is swift, and the specials on the chalkboard menu are "always different."

Comptoir (Le) *Moroccan* 16 | 19 | 17 | €34

1ᵉʳ | 37, rue Berger (Les Halles/Louvre-Rivoli) | 01 40 26 26 66 |
fax 01 42 21 44 24

"It feels like a Moroccan souk" (though you're actually in Les Halles) at this "cozy" North African serving "ample amounts of food, deliciously prepared" ("especially the tagine") in a characteristic copper-platter-and-leather-pouf decor; "the place is always packed" and "tables are a little tight", but the "ambiance compensates", and it's especially "pleasant in summer when the doors are open."

Comptoir du Relais (Le) *Bistro* | 22 | 15 | 16 | €44 |
6e | Relais St. Germain Hôtel | 9, carrefour de l'Odéon (Odeon) | 01 44 27 07 97 | fax 01 46 33 45 30 | www.hotelrsg.com

"Ex-Monsieur La Régalade" chef Yves Camdeborde is back at his own "true" bistro in the 6th – and it's "as hard to get your kids into Eton as to get a table" for dinner, "a no-choice, prix fixe showcase" for his "luscious classics"; critics carp the "seating is cramped" and a meal "takes far too long", but when there's such "high-quality cuisine at bistro prices", who cares?; N.B. weeknights require reservations three months in advance; lunch and weekends are first come, first served.

Comte de Gascogne (Au) Ⓩ *Gascony* | ▽ 25 | 20 | 20 | €101 |
Boulogne-Billancourt | 89, av Jean-Baptiste Clément (Pont-de-St-Cloud) | 01 46 03 47 27 | fax 01 46 04 55 70 | www.aucomtedegascogne.com

"Furnished like a tropical paradise", with palm fronds and cascading fountains, this elegant Boulogne suburbanite serves "superb" Gascon food, with "many manifestations" of "foie gras in the spotlight"; diners are "helped by witty, charming staffers, including a sommelier who guides you to perfect matches at good prices."

Congrès Maillot (Le) ◗ *Brasserie* | 14 | 13 | 14 | €53 |
17e | 80, av de la Grande-Armée (Porte Maillot) | 01 45 74 17 24 | fax 01 45 72 39 80

This "unpretentious traditional brasserie" has "improved since a recent renovation" in the "classic" style; some detractors still find the "service a little too rushed", and tabs a little "expensive" for such "standard" fare; but positives proclaim the prices, while pushed up by its "proximity to the Palais des Congrès' expense-account clientele", still "match the quality of the food", especially the "wonderful seafood platters."

Contre-Allée (La) Ⓩ *Bistro* | ▽ 24 | 20 | 21 | €48 |
14e | 83, av Denfert Rochereau (Denfert-Rochereau) | 01 43 54 99 86 | www.contre-allee.com

"Busy but charming, this delightful place on a typical Paris street" in the 14th offers a "lovely" array of contemporary bistro dishes, brought to table by "with-it but warm" servers; though it was recently "refurbished" in beige and caramel hues, it's "nice in summer when you can eat outside."

Cook Book Ⓩ *Eclectic* | - | - | - | M |
7e | 9, rue Surcouf (Invalides) | 01 45 51 92 82

Near Les Invalides, this Eclectic with simple but colorful decor (bare wood floors, red and yellow chairs) draws mixed reviews: readers ravenous for "world food" praise the "interesting" eats ranging from Argentine steak to kangaroo to curried fruit, while malcontents mutter about a "mediocre" menu and an "intrusive" staff; still, it can be "nice for lunch if you happen to be in the neighborhood."

	FOOD	DECOR	SERVICE	COST

Copenhague 🅂 *Danish*
20 | 18 | 19 | €72

8ᵉ | 142, av des Champs-Elysées (Charles de Gaulle-Etoile/George V) | 01 44 13 86 26 | fax 01 44 13 89 44 | www.restaurantfloradanica.com

"A few paces from the craziness of the Champs", this "hidden gem" is "fine if you're craving Scandinavian-inspired food" and "aquavit by the centiliter"; while some enjoy the "quiet" atmosphere ("ideal for business meals"), foes find the "typically Danish decor is cold" – "you better like eating under the eye of the Queen of Denmark", whose portrait graces the premises; damn if it hasn't "gotten expensive" too.

Cordonnerie (La) 🅂 *Classic French*
– | – | – | M

1ᵉʳ | 20, rue St-Roch (Pyramides/Tuileries) | 01 42 60 17 42 | fax 01 40 15 97 21 | www.restaurantlacordonnerie.com

Always "welcoming", "chef-owner Hugo Wolfer and his wife are the entire staff" of this "tiny" but "precious" place in the 1st; what was once a 17th-century cobbler's shop (*cordonnerie*) now houses an open kitchen producing seasonal Classic French food that makes "inventive" use of the market's bounty; the final tab is "quite reasonable."

Cosi *Sandwiches*
19 | 9 | 13 | €16

6ᵉ | 54, rue de Seine (Mabillon/Odéon) | 01 46 33 35 36

"You like sandwiches and music?" they come together in this eat-in or take-out "trendy" Saint-Germain shop, a "student hangout gone yuppie" with "delicious combinations of meats, cheese and veggies" on "fresh-from-the-oven breads" as well as "real salads"; a "cool staff and laid-back atmosphere, with Vivaldi playing, complete the experience."

Cosi (Le) 🅂 *Corsica*
17 | 13 | 16 | €29

5ᵉ | 9, rue Cujas (Cluny La Sorbonne/Luxembourg) | 01 43 29 20 20 | fax 01 43 29 26 40 | www.le-cosi.com

In the 5th near the Sorbonne, this sunny table offers "original, inventive Corsican cuisine that features traditional ingredients" like bruschetta, cheese and roast lamb, flown in from the island itself; large windows, handsome bookcases and a "convivial atmosphere greet the guests" who appreciate the "reasonable" prices.

Costes ● *Eclectic*
17 | 25 | 15 | €66

1ᵉʳ | Hôtel Costes | 239, rue St-Honoré (Concorde/Tuileries) | 01 42 44 50 25

"It's all about the scene" at this "trendy" Hôtel Costes brasserie with "good music" and "great" crowd-watching ("where do they find so many beautiful people?"); foes fume over the "snobby staffers who try to be hipper than the hipsters that dine here" and the "generally good" but "expensive" Eclectic eats – "even the lettuce has an attitude"; still, many are mollified by the "sumptuous" setting – the "richly decorated rooms" or the "delightful" courtyard with a "palatial tent in winter."

Cottage Marcadet (Le) 🅂 *New French*
▽ 21 | 17 | 22 | €51

18ᵉ | 151 bis, rue Marcadet (Lamarck-Caulaincourt) | 01 42 57 71 22 | fax 01 42 57 71 22 | www.cottagemarcadet.com

"While this cottage is not in the countryside, it is an oasis of calm on the backside of Montmartre" – a "charming seven-table hideaway that makes the trek well worth the hassle"; the "adventuresome" New French specialties "meet expectations" "for a romantic evening", especially when they're "personally served by the owner"; N.B. the Decor score may not reflect a new chef-owner's redo – Louis XVI style with contemporary art.

Coude Fou (Le) ● *Wine Bar/Bistro* — 16 | 13 | 18 | €36

4ᵉ | 12, rue du Bourg-Tibourg (Hôtel-de-Ville) | 01 42 77 15 16 | fax 01 48 04 08 98

Oenophiles opine this is "the most pleasant wine bar in the neighborhood" behind the Hôtel de Ville; even if the small room offers "not much in terms of decor" (despite native frescoes and tile floors), it's a "good basic place for a nice bite" of "comforting" bistro dishes; "tables are tight, so if you tend to get hot, you won't have a good time", but the staff "is fine with Americans, of which there are multitudes."

NEW Cou de la Girafe (Le) ⊠ *New French* — | – | – | M

8ᵉ | 7, rue Paul Baudry (Franklin D. Roosevelt/St-Philippe-du-Roule) | 01 56 88 29 55 | fax 01 42 25 28 82

With a sleek bronze, steel-gray and prune decor by fashionable interior designer Jean-Yves Rochon, this stylish New French off the Champs-Elysées has an animated atmosphere and great-looking crowd, many of whom are dressed for a night on the town; the easygoing young staff is attentive, and prices are gentler than they are at similarly modish tables in this very trendy corner of Paris.

Couleurs de Vigne ⊠ *Wine Bar/Bistro* — | – | – | I

15ᵉ | 2, rue Marmontel (Convention/Vaugirard) | 01 45 33 32 96 | fax 01 45 33 32 96 | www.lecoudefou.com

This "sweet" "intimate *bar à vins* is worth seeking out" in a remote part of the 15th, with "wines that are well chosen" and wrapped up in a "typically French ambiance"; the food is "not bad, but not special – best bet is the quite good charcuterie" – but your accompanying bottle can be "taken home" if you don't finish it at table.

Coupe-Chou (Le) ● *Classic French* — 20 | 25 | 20 | €52

5ᵉ | 9-11, rue de Lanneau (Maubert-Mutualité) | 01 46 33 68 69 | fax 01 46 33 71 96 | www.lecoupechou.com

"On a quiet street near the Panthéon", "you feel transported back in time" at this Classic French, a "charming low-ceilinged, medieval space with big fireplaces and a warm atmosphere year-round"; if most find the "staff gracious" and the "refined cuisine" "well prepared", critics complain the place "has a little too much of a tour-bus mentality" ("predominantly English-speaking patrons"); even so, "if you can't be romantic here, get thee to a nunnery."

Coupe Gorge (Le) ● *Bistro* — | – | – | I

4ᵉ | 2, rue de la Coutellerie (Hôtel-de-Ville) | 01 48 04 79 24 | fax 01 42 46 11 72 | www.coupegorge.com

"It's always a pleasure to dine in this cute, eccentric spot" "hidden away on a side street" in the 4th, where "customers choose their own wine from a well-stocked cellar"; the bistro "food is always good" ("insist on the minced beef tartare"), and the "staff is droll."

	FOOD	DECOR	SERVICE	COST

Z Coupole (La) ◐ *Brasserie* `18` `23` `17` €50

14ᵉ | 102, bd du Montparnasse (Vavin) | 01 43 20 14 20 |
fax 01 43 35 46 14 | www.flobrasseries.com

The "mythical place of Montparnasse" is "packed" with "more tourists than natives" now, but "it still has the charm of '20s Paris", with
a "stunningly preserved" art deco decor of "columns painted by the
likes of Chagall, Picasso, etc."; while the brasserie fare's "predictable", the "seafood platter's an adventure", and despite some "glar-
ing errors", the "army of waiters in black-and-white" is
"professional"; so maybe she's "a shadow of her former self", but
this grande dame remains "a must-see."

Crêperie de Josselin (La) ◐Ⓜ� *Brittany* `21` `13` `18` €19

14ᵉ | 67, rue du Montparnasse (Edgar Quinet/Montparnasse-Bienvenüe) |
01 43 20 93 50

On a "street filled with 'em in Montparnasse", what's "maybe the
most famous crêperie in Paris" wins praise for a pancake filled with
"both novel combinations and traditional flavors" that's "so enormous the plate's incapable of containing it"; given the "snug" surrounds, "you'll get to know your neighbors even if you don't want
to", but rest assured, this Breton's "crêpes are worth the crowding"
(and "service is fast" too).

Z Cristal Room Ⓢ *New French* `19` `28` `19` €84

16ᵉ | Baccarat | 11, pl des Etats-Unis (Boissière/Iéna) |
01 40 22 11 10 | fax 01 40 22 11 99 | www.baccarat.fr

In the Baccarat HQ in the 16th, what really sparkles is designer
Philippe Starck's "superb decor", which imparts an "exquisite look"
of oversized plaster medallions, exposed-brick walls and "lots of
marble and crystal" (of course) to an old townhouse; if the New
French "food doesn't hold up to the fantastic" setting – maybe "the
chef tries too hard" – it's still "inventive and served with a flourish";
so most raise a glass to this glittery and "expensive" experience.

Crus de Bourgogne (Aux) Ⓢ *Bistro* `–` `–` `–` M

2ᵉ | 3, rue Bachaumont (Les Halles/Sentier) | 01 42 33 48 24 |
fax 01 40 28 66 41

"If nothing else, go for the lobster" (served with "homemade may-
onnaise" "every Thursday") at this "bona fide Parisian bistro", a real
"institution" replete with red-checkered tablecloths in Les Halles; regulars rave "it's the perfect place to take tourists – or yourself", but
foes fret it's fatigued: "it'd be better if everything were sharper."

Cuisine (La) *New French* ▽ `21` `19` `23` €65

7ᵉ | 14, bd de la Tour-Maubourg (Invalides/La Tour-Maubourg) |
01 44 18 36 32 | fax 01 44 18 30 42 | www.lacuisine.lesrestos.com

"A pleasant atmosphere" awaits at this dressy New French in the
7th; the "modern", "elegant dining room", a study in beige with flat-
tering low lighting, well-spaced tables and "Modigliani reproductions to add an artistic touch", puts the "chic" clientele at ease, as
does the highly "friendly welcome" and service; the cooking
is equally "refined."

	FOOD	DECOR	SERVICE	COST

Curieux Spaghetti Bar (Le) ● *Italian* — — — M

4ᵉ | 14, rue St-Merri (St-Paul/Châtelet) | 01 42 72 75 97 |
fax 01 40 13 87 58 | www.curieuxspag.com

"Young people" in the market for "a fun place" with "cheap, good
food" strike it rich at this self-styled spaghetti bar, a "busy, noisy"
spot behind the Pompidou Center; it provides pastas, of course, plus
Italian antipasti, a house limoncello and a pop baroque design of
long red bar, chandeliers and an ever-changing display of wallpaper.

Dalloyau *Dessert/Tearoom* 23 | 18 | 17 | €32

4ᵉ | 5, bd Beaumarchais (Bastille) | 01 48 87 89 88 |
fax 01 48 87 73 70
6ᵉ | 2, pl Edmond Rostand (Cluny La Sorbonne/Odéon) |
01 43 29 31 10 | fax 01 43 26 25 72
8ᵉ | 101, rue du Faubourg St-Honoré (Miromesnil/St-Philippe-du-Roule) |
01 42 99 90 00 | fax 01 45 63 82 92
15ᵉ | 69, rue de la Convention (Boucicaut) | 01 45 77 84 27 |
fax 01 45 75 27 99
Boulogne-Billancourt | 65-67, av J.B. Clément (Boulogne-Jean Jaurès) |
01 46 05 06 78 | fax 01 46 03 90 30
www.dalloyau.fr

"Magnificent éclairs, stupendous tarts and fabulous macaroons"
are among the "sweet-tooth satisfiers" offered at these "calm",
"high-class" *salons de thé* "all over Paris" – you could "have breakfast
at the one on Faubourg Saint-Honoré, then afternoon tea on the terrace across from the Luxembourg Gardens" and finally "before the
Opéra Bastille", a light dinner on "something savory to justify a few
desserts"; they're also "wonderful" for takeout – in fact, even "flight
attendants get their picnics for the plane, and eat better than anyone!"

Da Mimmo ● 🖹 Ⓜ *Italian* 15 | 9 | 12 | €40

10ᵉ | 39, bd de Magenta (Gare de l'Est/Jacques Bonsergent) |
01 42 06 44 47 | fax 01 42 06 31 35

The unlovely location in the 10th and "no-frills" decor don't deter
disciples of this Italian, a sort of "celebrity's darling" for its "classics", including "some of the best pizza in Paris"; the famed are also
unfazed by the "mediocre service", but a real debate develops over
the tabs – "correct" vs. "too expensive", with some cautioning
"don't let the owner chose the antipasti for you, unless you've
brought your American Express black card" along.

Da Rosa *Classic French* ▽ 19 | 14 | 15 | €31

6ᵉ | 62, rue de Seine (Mabillon/Odéon) | 01 40 51 00 09 |
fax 01 40 51 04 59

"Perfect for watching the shoppers" in Saint-Germain, "this small
restaurant" in a "gourmet grocery store" serves up "delicious"
Classic French light bites made with "Spanish Bellota ham, cheeses"
and other nonpareil products – plus some "wines of the same
caliber" – that owner José Da Rosa seeks out and supplies to many
chefs around town; some sniff there's "no real cuisine" here, but
since they serve continuously from 11 AM to 10 PM, it's "good
when everything else is closed."

	FOOD	DECOR	SERVICE	COST

Daru ☒ *Russian*
–	–	–	M

8ᵉ | 19, rue Daru (Courcelles/Ternes) | 01 42 27 23 60 |
fax 01 47 54 08 14 | www.daru.fr

This candlelit, dachalike Russian in the 8th has been in business ever since Paris became the preferred exile of those fleeing the Bolsheviks; expect a "warm welcome" and "exotic" atmosphere, along with "simple, good-quality" food like smoked salmon, caviar with blini and beef stroganoff.

Dauphin (Le) *Southwest*
23	18	21	€42

1ᵉʳ | 167, rue St-Honoré (Palais Royal-Musée du Louvre) |
01 42 60 40 11 | fax 01 42 60 01 18

"See the 'Mona Lisa', then enjoy a perfect lunch" or dinner here at this "genuine bistro located two blocks from the Louvre in the heart of a touristy area"; the "consistently fine" menu contains "true Southwestern and Classic French staples" that are often "a piece of art" themselves; led by the team behind Biarritz's esteemed Cafe de Paris, the staff is "very attentive and polite", as well.

Davé *Chinese/Vietnamese*
19	14	19	€48

1ᵉʳ | 12, rue de Richelieu (Palais Royal-Musée du Louvre) |
01 42 61 49 48 | fax 01 42 60 96 18

"An institution for fashion-world [types] when they're in Paris" ("Marc Jacobs has parties here"), this "cool", compact Chinese-Vietnamese in the 1st arrondissement "boasts images of the celebrities who've dined" and been doted on by the namesake owner, who is something of "a legend" himself; lesser mortals call the place "overrated, overpriced, just plain over" – but they're over-ridden by devotees who declare "eccentric service is what makes this place charming."

D'Chez Eux ☒ *Southwest*
22	16	22	€60

7ᵉ | 2, av Lowendal (Ecole Militaire) | 01 47 05 52 55 |
fax 01 45 55 60 74 | www.chezeux.com

Since "Chirac brought Putin here", this venue in the 7th must be the "quintessential Paris bistro, right down to the red-checkered window treatments and tablecloths"; "the traditional Southwestern country cooking" means you should "go with a large appetite" – or else "skip the main course and just gorge on hot and cold appetizers" like the serve-yourself charcuterie; add in an "accommodating staff that's generous with the portions", and there's "nowhere better to warm your stomach and soul."

Delicabar ☒ *New French*
15	17	12	€36

7ᵉ | Bon Marché | 26-38, rue de Sèvres (Sèvres-Babylone) |
01 42 22 10 12 | fax 01 42 22 08 60 | www.delicabar.fr

"While taking a break from *le shopping* at the Bon Marché" department store, "you can always count on" this "amusing" in-store eatery, filled "with hip attitude and furniture" (undulating, lollipop-colored chairs amid a "pleasant" white circular room and terrace); an ex-pastry chef from Fauchon furnishes a "limited menu" of "trendy" New French nibbles.

FOOD | DECOR | SERVICE | COST

Délices d'Aphrodite (Les) *Greek* ▽ 18 | 12 | 14 | €40

5ᵉ | 4, rue de Candolle (Censier-Daubenton) | 01 43 31 40 39 | fax 01 43 36 13 08 | www.mavrommatis.fr

As long as you're not bothered by the "busy", "noisy" dining room, you too may want to worship at this "amazing Greek" in the Latin Quarter, the "less pretentious" sibling to Mavrommatis; supporters laud the "low-fat" cuisine ("special mention: the grilled meats") that, along with the taverna setting, "could almost have you thinking you're in Piraeus"; "copious" portions make it "good value for the money" too.

Délices de Szechuen 🅼 *Chinese* 16 | 13 | 16 | €38

7ᵉ | 40, av Duquesne (St-François-Xavier) | 01 43 06 22 55

"You may meet movie and TV people" at this "old reliable Chinese" in a swanky section of the 7th; the savvy say the "spicy" "specialties are the best", "even though they're tamed for European" taste buds; some grouse about the high price of the rice (due to the "upscale crowd") especially since "the decor is nothing special"; "outside is nice on a summer evening", however.

Dell Orto ●🅼🅼 *Italian* – | – | – | E

9ᵉ | 45, rue St-Georges (St-Georges) | 01 48 78 40 30

Just off of the stylish Place Saint-Georges, this clubby Italian serves some "remarkable, inventive" dishes like a "delectable salad of octopus and fennel bulb", plus a "hallucinogenic selection of pastas"; but critics carp that "in light of the prices, you'd expect the ambiance to be a notch better" and to get more "attention" from the staff.

Dessirier *Seafood* ▽ 21 | 17 | 20 | €81

17ᵉ | 9, pl du Maréchal Juin (Péreire) | 01 42 27 82 14 | fax 01 47 66 82 07 | www.michelrostang.com

Near the Place Péreire, this "well-mannered" Michel Rostang–run "grand fish specialist" serves "delicious seafood", which makes it a bull's-eye for business dining – though even the executive clientele goes ballistic over the "breathtaking prices"; malcontents are mollified, however, by the "pleasant service" and an "excellent wine list."

Deux Abeilles (Les) 🅼 *Dessert/Tearoom* ▽ 18 | 15 | 16 | €30

7ᵉ | 189, rue de l'Université (Alma Marceau) | 01 45 55 64 04 | fax 01 45 55 64 04

"Young and not-so-young ladies of the 7th" converge at this "consistent, charismatic tearoom" that serves "a variety of salads" and "lovely cakes"; though they "removed the chintz" a while ago, the salon still has "a homey feel" that's "great for a break."

Deux Canards (Aux) 🅼 *Classic French* 18 | 14 | 18 | €41

10ᵉ | 8, rue du Faubourg Poissonnière (Bonne Nouvelle) | 01 47 70 03 23 | fax 01 47 70 18 85 | www.lesdeuxcanards.com

Fans say you'd have to be a quack not to love this rather offbeat Classic French in the 10th, where "chatty" owner Gérard Faesch "makes you feel like part of his family"; "his narration of the chalkboard menu is priceless" too, and "obviously the duck is a must"; some find the decor, adorned with "jars of oranges in various states of fermentation", "a little overwrought" but most say it's "warm" and "rustic" – and "nicely nonsmoking."

2 Pieces Cuisine 🆉 *Bistro*   — | — | — | M

18ᵉ | 65, rue du Ruisseau (Jules Joffrin) | 01 42 23 31 23 |
www.2pieces-cuisine.com

Tucked away in a gentrifying corner of Montmartre, this casual Classic French bistro has won an arty young clientele with a good-value prix fixe that changes every few months; the decor highlights the old bar, left over from its days as a corner cafe, while warm tones and modern lighting fixtures add a little style.

Devèz (Le) ◑ *Steak*   ▽ 14 | 13 | 12 | €47

8ᵉ | 5, pl de l'Alma (Alma Marceau) | 01 53 67 97 53 |
fax 01 47 23 09 48 | www.devezparis.com

Malcontents moo that this "stylish" steakhouse just off the Place de l'Alma "should be better, considering the prices"; still, others herd in for the Aubrac beef, prepared a variety of different ways – including "the best cheeseburger in the neighborhood", punningly named the 'Mac' Aubrac, and cellar of Languedoc-Roussillon and Rhône Valley wines.

Diamantaires (Les) ◑ *Armenian/Greek*   — | — | — | M

9ᵉ | 60, rue La Fayette (Cadet/Le Peletier) | 01 47 70 78 14 |
fax 01 44 83 02 73 | www.lesdiamantaires.com

New black-and-red decor provides backdrop for "the irreplaceable taste of homemade Greek and Armenian cooking" at this "simple place" in the 9th; if you need "proof it's the real thing, check out the place on Saturday nights, when tables are packed with Mediterranean families gathering to eat, drink and party as if they were back home."

Diapason (Le) 🆉 *Southwest*   ▽ 16 | 24 | 18 | €63

18ᵉ | Terrass Hotel | 12-14, rue Joseph de Maistre (Abbesses/Place de Clichy) | 01 44 92 34 00 | fax 01 42 52 29 11 | www.terrass-hotel.com

"Seeing Paris from the seventh floor of this hotel is the beginning of a romantic evening" sigh the sentimental about this "comfortable" Montmartre "retreat" in cool, modern gray and beige tones; how-ever, since the "somewhat limited" Southwestern menu is at best just "reasonably good" ("try to ignore the prices"), "the real point of interest is the [tree-lined] terrace" open June–September.

Diep ◑ *Asian*   20 | 15 | 17 | €56

8ᵉ | 55, rue Pierre Charron (Franklin D. Roosevelt) | 01 45 63 52 76 |
fax 01 42 56 46 56 | www.diep.fr

"Good but expensive" – the latter "due to the location" in a pricey part of the 8th – is the majority read on this "jet-setty" Asian; "it's not a place to recommend for a romantic dinner", given the gallop-ing service of "waiters who are in a hurry for you to leave, bringing the check before you ask" and the "ok, not extraordinary" Oriental decor; on the other hand, the victuals are "among the best Chinese-Thai-Vietnamese in Paris" and – for those who care about such things – it's "an indispensable [site] for seeing and being seen."

	FOOD	DECOR	SERVICE	COST

Divellec (Le) ☒ Seafood
23 | 19 | 21 | €131

7ᵉ | 107, rue de l'Université (Invalides) | 01 45 51 91 96 |
fax 01 45 51 31 75 | www.ledivellec.com

"Conservative but sound" sums up this "traditional French seafooder" on the Esplanade des Invalides that nets "local bigwigs"
with "excellent" fish (including the "legendary pressed lobster") and
"attentive but unintrusive service"; while the recently redone decor's now "handsome", some still sniff over the "stiff atmosphere" –
folks "speaking softly as if in church" – and the "sky-high prices" are
"not for everyday"; "but from time to time, it's worth it" to splurge.

☒ 1728 ☒ New French
16 | 27 | 15 | €70

8ᵉ | 8, rue d'Anjou (Concorde/Madeleine) | 01 40 17 04 77 |
fax 01 42 65 53 87 | www.restaurant-1728.com

"Once the home of General Lafayette", this "candlelit" mansion in
the 8th "is a fabulous step away from the 21st century", with "parquet floors, wood paneling, art" and antiques that make you feel like
you're "in a Fragonard or Watteau painting"; after "the decor's wow
factor", however, the New French fare with "Asian incursions"
"somehow falls flat", as does the service; still, for locale alone, most
enthuse it's "enchantment"; P.S. one "option to avoid the eye-
popping check is the equally amazing afternoon tea."

Dix Vins (Le) ☒ Bistro/Wine Bar
▽ 16 | 11 | 19 | €31

15ᵉ | 57, rue Falguière (Pasteur) | 01 43 20 91 77 | fax 01 43 20 91 77 |
www.le-dix-vins.com

Maybe "one of the best buys for the money in Paris", this "narrow" but
"charming, charming, charming" *bistrot à vins* in the 15th delights
with "delicious bistro cooking" and "interesting wines" ("unsurpris-
ingly, given the name") in a "candlelit" dining room with "fresh flowers"; "patient servers" and "cheerful, youthful patrons give it a
friendly countercultural feel", so "what more could you want?"

Djakarta Bali ☒ Indonesian
▽ 19 | 19 | 21 | €33

1ᵉʳ | 9, rue Vauvilliers (Châtelet/Louvre-Rivoli) | 01 45 08 83 11 |
fax 01 45 08 17 81 | www.djakart-bali.com

If everyone admires the "unbelievably nice" brother-and-sister team
behind this Java joint in Les Halles, Djakarta devotees diverge as to
whether the Indonesian eats are "incredibly authentic" and "excellent" or "irregular in quality"; still, the "warm welcome", traditional
decor and extras such as native dancing on Fridays ensure "a trip to
Bali in the heart of Paris."

Domaine de Lintillac ☒ Southwest
– | – | – | –

2ᵉ | 10, rue St-Augustin (Quatre Septembre) | 01 40 20 96 27
7ᵉ | 20, rue Rousselet (Duroc) | 01 45 66 88 23 ☒
9ᵉ | 54, rue Blanche (Blanche/Trinité) | 01 48 74 84 36
www.lintillac-paris.com

"Duck, duck, goose – and not much more" is on the menu at this
small string of Southwesterners owned by Lintillac, a gourmet-food
company; but if the cuisine's "based on canned goods, they're good
canned goods" (there are hot plates as well); it's "perhaps the best

place in Paris to make a meal of foie gras", and "toasters are set at each table, so you have hot bread" to consume with your *confit* or pâté.

Dôme (Le) ● *Seafood*

	FOOD	DECOR	SERVICE	COST
	22	21	19	€63

14ᵉ | 108, bd du Montparnasse (Vavin) | 01 43 35 25 81 | fax 01 42 79 01 19

This "lovely, luxurious" seafooder with "a rich literary" heritage has a "traditional atmosphere with overstuffed booths and large floral arrangements filling nooks and crannies"; "you can spend an afternoon just sampling the oyster selection" and "the best bouillabaisse" ("we so obviously enjoyed it, they offered us seconds"); "service is precise", if "in a hurry", and while the "expensive" prices make some mourn its bohemian brasserie past, for most it's "worth a visit to Montparnasse."

Dôme du Marais (Le) 🅢 Ⓜ *New French*

	18	21	16	€44

4ᵉ | 53 bis, rue des Francs-Bourgeois (Hôtel-de-Ville/Rambuteau) | 01 42 74 54 17 | fax 01 42 77 78 17

Situated in an old chapel "with a high ceiling", "the decor is the thing" at this address "in the heart of the Marais"; however, it also offers "nice fusionesque French cooking", "inventive under its traditional air", "at affordable prices"; "bordering on surly", "the service is in decline", but still "you can't beat the historic setting" ("make sure you get seated in the main room, the one with the dome").

Dominique Bouchet 🅢 *Haute Cuisine*

	24	19	23	€74

8ᵉ | 11, rue Treilhard (Miromesnil) | 01 45 61 09 46 | fax 01 42 89 11 14 | www.dominique-bouchet.com

"Dominique Bouchet's deconstructed takes on French classics are welcome" cheer converts of the chef-owner's "cozy" Haute Cuisine haven in   only is the food "impeccably prepared", it's served   ed" (and "oh-so-cute") staff in "sophisticated,   with pale stone walls, black tables and modern crystal"; a few miss they "had higher expectations" for an ex–Les Ambassadeurs toque, but scores side with those who deem his solo endeavor "excellent."

Don Juans (Les) 🅢 *New French*

	–	–	–	M

3ᵉ | 19, rue de Picardie (Filles-du-Calvaire/Temple) | 01 42 71 31 71

The vaguely industrial decor of this duplex space in a super-trendy part of the 3rd conveys the unconventional personality of this young New French, whose "fine cuisine revolves around all the Mediterranean lands"; "convivial and affordable", it pulls a hip young crowd that likes the "nice atmosphere."

Doobie's Ⓜ *Eclectic/New French*

	▽ 12	9	11	€40

8ᵉ | 2, rue Robert Estienne (Franklin D. Roosevelt) | 01 53 76 10 76 | fax 01 42 25 21 71 | www.doobies.net

"They check you out through a small window before allowing you to enter" this site off the Champs-Elysées, "a curious place that serves as an inter-company cafeteria at lunch and turns into a trendy bar/restaurant at night"; but many say go "only for" the "wonderful

	FOOD	DECOR	SERVICE	COST

Sunday brunch"; the rest of the time, it's "noisy and smoky", with "lame decor" and "unexceptional" Eclectic–New French fare.

Dos de la Baleine (Le) 🔏 Ⓜ *Bistro*   16 | 13 | 15 | €43
4ᵉ | 40, rue des Blancs-Manteaux (Hôtel-de-Ville/Rambuteau) | 01 42 72 38 98 | fax 01 43 45 43 34 | www.ledosdelabaleine.com
Expect a "warm welcome" at this low-lit, stone-walled "traditional bistro with a nontraditional clientele" "in the Marais' gay quarter" ("but heteros are equally comfortable" here); the "cooking shows creativity" and the service is "efficient", but it's the "relaxed and re-laxing ambiance" that keeps it "often crowded."

Drouant ● *Classic French*   – | – | – | VE
2ᵉ | 16-18, pl Gaillon (Opéra/Quatre-Septembre) | 01 42 65 15 16 | fax 01 49 24 02 15 | www.drouant.com
One of the most "classic of classic" Paris places in the 2nd has been reborn since it was acquired by chef Antoine Westermann post-Survey; architect Pascal Desprez's hip decor respects the space's good bones – the Ruhlmann wrought-iron stairway, the sea-themed ceiling painting and the 18th-century paneling in the salon Goncourt (site of the literary prize) – while framing them in ivory-and-beige hues; the traditional French fare is brought by well-drilled servers.

Duc (Le) 🔏 Ⓜ *Seafood*   24 | 16 | 22 | €82
14ᵉ | 243, bd Raspail (Raspail) | 01 43 20 96 30 | fax 01 43 20 46 73
Ah, but life is good when you're seated in front of "a buttery *sole meunière* served in a room resembling a ship of the French line" – as you are at this "sedate" but "sublime" seafooder in Montparnasse; after nigh on 40 years, perhaps the "tired" hull needs overhauling, but "watching waiters fillet the fish is great fun", so plenty are pleased to put into port at "one of the top" *poisson* palaces in Paris.

Duc de Richelieu (Le) ●🔏 *Lyon*   – | – | – | M
12ᵉ | 5, rue Parrot (Gare de Lyon) | 01 43 43 05 64 | fax 01 40 19 08 70
In their race to catch trains at "the Gare de Lyon nearby", many sur-veyors may have missed this carnivores' cave of a Lyonnais bistro (complete 1930s decor) in the 12th; those who have say it's "excel-lent", with a "great atmosphere and fine choice of Beaujolais", not surprising when you know that the owner used to run Le Gavroche.

Durand Dupont Drugstore ● *Eclectic*   ▽ 9 | 14 | 10 | €48
Neuilly-sur-Seine | 14, pl du Marché (Les Sablons) | 01 41 92 93 00 | fax 01 46 37 56 79
It may be "trendy, but don't expect more" of this Eclectic "frequented by families in Neuilly" (especially for brunch on the "agreeable ter-race"); the "disappointingly inconsistent menu and service make every visit hit-or-miss", and given that risk-reward ratio, it's "too expensive."

Ebauchoir (L') 🔏 *Bistro*   – | – | – | M
12ᵉ | 43-45, rue de Citeaux (Faidherbe-Chaligny) | 01 43 42 49 31 | www.lebauchoir.com
It's "out of the way" in the 12th, "but the food and prices are good enough to be worth investigating" at this "cute" corner, "one of the

first 'new' Paris bistros" back in the '90s; if "a bit tired" now, it's still "interesting", and hence "always bustling" (read: "noisy"), with young yuppies enjoying "a relaxing evening."

Ecaille de la Fontaine (L') 🗷 *Shellfish* ▭ ▭ ▭ M

2e | 15, rue Gaillon (Opéra) | 01 47 42 02 99 | fax 01 47 42 82 84 | www.la-fontaine-gaillon.com

The bright red facade and star power of owner-actor Gérard Depardieu hasn't yet attracted the notice of many surveyors when it comes to this raw bar not far from the Opéra Garnier, but the few who've found their way here laud the super-fresh trays of shellfish, the friendly service and the fact that you don't have to shell out too much to get the best of French bivalves.

Ecailler du Bistrot (L') 🗷 M *Seafood* ▭ ▭ ▭ M

11e | 20-22, rue Paul Bert (Faidherbe-Chaligny) | 01 43 72 76 77 | fax 01 43 72 24 66

This popular site in the 11th has "a limited selection, but what they offer is impeccable", especially the "excellent oysters and cheese"; so "run here" to the old-style woody digs for a laid-back good time.

Ecluse (L') 🌑 *Wine Bar/Bistro* 14 14 15 €35

1er | 34, pl du Marché St-Honoré (Pyramides/Tuileries) | 01 42 96 10 18 | fax 01 42 96 10 17
6e | 15, quai des Grands-Augustins (St-Michel) | 01 46 33 58 74 | fax 01 44 07 18 76
8e | 15, pl de la Madeleine (Madeleine) | 01 42 65 34 69 | fax 01 44 71 01 26
8e | 64, rue François 1er (George V) | 01 47 20 77 09 | fax 01 40 70 03 33
11e | 13, rue de la Roquette (Bastille) | 01 48 05 19 12 | fax 01 48 05 04 88
17e | 1, rue d'Armaillé (Charles de Gaulle-Etoile) | 01 47 63 88 29 | fax 01 44 40 41 91
www.leclusebaravin.com

Tipplers toast this bevy of *bistrots à vins* for being so handy for "a quick snack" "while shopping", "a reliable lunch", "a late dinner" "post-Opéra Bastille" or "on Sunday night", when "all [else] is closed"; they specialize in "Bordeaux by the glass or bottle", and while the Classic French food's "patchy", the "rustic" decor of dark-wood paneling and old posters is "charming" – "you'd never think it's a chain" – and the ambiance convivial ("look at the cutie-packed bar and you'll know why").

Editeurs (Les) 🌑 *Brasserie* 15 21 17 €37

6e | 4, Carrefour de l'Odéon (Odéon) | 01 43 26 67 76 | fax 01 46 34 58 30 | www.lesediteurs.fr

Rapidly becoming the "cornerstone of the square" around the Odéon, this "sophisticated rendezvous" is renowned for its "conge-nial" "library decor", with "comfortable chairs and shelves filled with books you can take down and actually read"; it's the "great setting that makes it a busy place all day – you don't come here for the food" ("solid but overpriced" brasserie eats) or the somewhat "slow service"; indeed, the bookish believe it's "best just for drinks and snacks."

	FOOD	DECOR	SERVICE	COST

El Mansour ⓩ *Moroccan*   20 | 17 | 19 | €49

8ᵉ | 7, rue de La Trémoille (Alma Marceau) | 01 47 23 88 18 |
fax 01 40 70 13 53

A "wonderful display of Moroccan" "meat stews and mounds of couscous" "warm the stomach" at this upmarket address off the Avenue George V patronized by Parisians and expats alike; add in "hospitable service" and a "refined" dining room filled with "North African furbelows", carved wood paneling and comfortably spaced tables, and you see why surveyors say it's "high-priced, but worth it."

El Palenque ⓩⒹ *Argentinean*   20 | 10 | 13 | €36

5ᵉ | 5, rue de la Montagne Ste-Geneviève (Maubert-Mutualité) |
01 43 54 08 99

"Heaven for homesick Argentines", this pint-sized patch of the pampas in the Latin Quarter is a "*bueno, bueno, bueno*" address for "delicious meat", along with "typical dishes, including *dulce de leche* and wonderful wines"; "a student-y atmosphere" and "friendly service from the Latin American waiters" ensure it's "excellent value for the money", but "be sure to ask for a nonsmoking table, unless you like smoked beef."

⒵ Elysées (Les) ⓩ *Haute Cuisine*   26 | 25 | 24 | €127

8ᵉ | Hôtel Vernet | 25, rue Vernet (Charles de Gaulle-Etoile/George V) |
01 44 31 98 98 | fax 01 44 31 85 69 | www.hotelvernet.com

The "phenomenal service" and glass-domed "ceiling designed by Gustave Eiffel" – yes, of Tower fame – create a genteel atmosphere at this "delightful" Haute Cuisine table in the 8th; unlike some celebrity chefs, toque Eric Briffard (ex Plaza Athénée) "is actually in the kitchen cooking and checking on his diners", which is why his contemporary dishes are so "refined" and full of "wonderful flavors"; in short, this is one to add "to your little black book" even if "it's a bit expensive."

Elysées Hong Kong *Chinese*   - | - | - | M

16ᵉ | 80, rue Michel-Ange (Exelmans) | 01 46 51 60 99

In the silk-stocking 16th, this well-mannered Chinese with "interesting" if slightly somber decor of Asian antiques pulls a soigné crowd of regulars, including French show biz types, with "consistently excellent" classics; the authentic-minded attack the food as "Westernized"; but most find it suits them to a tea, especially since prices are moderate.

Emporio Armani Caffé ◗ⓩ *Italian*   18 | 17 | 15 | €49

6ᵉ | 149, bd St-Germain (St-Germain-des-Prés) | 01 45 48 62 15 |
fax 01 45 48 53 17

"As you would expect", "a fab fashion attitude – dramatic decor, beautiful people galore and a staff straight off a catwalk" – dominates this "sooo chic" cafe "on the second floor of the Emporio Armani"; but "surprisingly, there's actually decent food to go with the design", a "light" but "true taste of Northern Italy", "nicely presented"; yes, those pretty servers can be "haughty", and many moan the "model-sized portions for exorbitant prices" appeal to "Armani, not the appetite"; most, though, are "impressed."

	FOOD	DECOR	SERVICE	COST

Enoteca (L') ● *Italian*
`22` `17` `18` `€48`

4ᵉ | 25, rue Charles V (St-Paul/Sully Morland) | 01 42 78 91 44 |
fax 01 44 59 31 72

"In pasta e vino veritas" declare devotees of this "intimate" Italian vino
bar in a centuries-old Marais house; massive beams overhead create a
"romantic" but "low-key" setting in which to sample possibly the
"best list of wines from The Boot" (with the "good by-the-glass selection changing weekly") and "unfussy", "well-cooked" *cucina*; surveyors also salute "the staff that knows its stuff", even though some
warn they grow "distant if you refuse their expensive suggestions."

Entoto 🖂 *Ethiopian*
`-` `-` `-` `M`

13ᵉ | 143-145, rue L.M. Nordmann (Glacière) | 01 45 87 08 51

Though few know this "charming little corner of Ethiopia" in the
13th, those who do say it's "a great find", with "amiable owners" and
a "convivial", even "romantic" atmosphere; the place pleases all palates with "perfect tasting dishes – from vegetarian to meat, spicy to
sweet, they've got it all, and for a reasonable price" as well.

Entracte (L')
(Chez Sonia et Carlos) 🅼 *Bistro*
`-` `-` `-` `M`

18ᵉ | 44, rue d'Orsel (Abbesses/Anvers) | 01 46 06 93 41

"Tucked away on the hill leading up to Montmartre and Sacré Coeur",
this traditional bistro is "a real treasure"; "there are only 20 covers,
so reservations are a must" if you want a table in this cozy room
where "exquisite flowers set the mood" and "the owner is also the
greeter, the bartender, the chef and the dishwasher"; "it's hard to
believe that such spectacular fare could come from the tiny kitchen
out back, but it does"; no surprise that it's "always filled with locals."

Entredgeu (L') 🖂🅼 *Bistro*
`21` `12` `13` `€43`

17ᵉ | 83, rue Laugier (Porte de Champerret) | 01 40 54 97 24 |
fax 01 40 54 96 62

Perpetually "packed to the gills" ("don't go there for a relaxing
evening"), this "great little bistro" on the outer fringes of the 17th
serves "straight-ahead" food "in a small, noisy space" – expect to
dine "cheek by jowl with your neighbors"; and even if the "rushed
service" is sometimes "sharp", the "French country cooking" is a
"very good buy."

Enzo 🖂 *Italian*
`-` `-` `-` `I`

14ᵉ | 72, rue Daguerre (Denfert-Rochereau/Gaîté) | 01 43 21 66 66 |
fax 01 43 21 80 83 | www.pizzaenzo.fr

In the 14th, near the bustling Aligre market, this "cozy Italian bistro"
serves "some of the best pizzas in Paris" at a "fast" pace; there are
"long lines on the weekend" but the "neighborhood atmosphere"
and the low prices make it "worth the wait."

Epicure 108 🖂 *Alsace/Asian*
`-` `-` `-` `M`

17ᵉ | 108, rue Cardinet (Malesherbes) | 01 47 63 50 91

Expect a "consistently good experience" at this "original" in the
17th, where a "Japanese chef allies Asian flavors and cooking styles

with Alsatian cuisine"; maybe it's "not the most beautiful spot" in Paris – the dining room's rather plain – but "warm service" makes up for it, and modest prices help too.

Epi d'Or (L') 🏠 *Bistro*

1er | 25, rue Jean-Jacques Rousseau (Louvre-Rivoli) | 01 42 36 38 12 | fax 01 42 36 46 25 | www.epidor.fr

FOOD	DECOR	SERVICE	COST
21	15	17	€50

Tucked away on a quiet side street near Les Halles, this "charming bistro" is, some say, "what a French restaurant should look like" – think checkered tablecloths, copper pans on the walls and sprung-bottom leatherette banquettes; "always busy and full of life", it's just the place to come for "hearty", "true country cuisine"; "if your high-school *français* has gotten rusty, the owner will be more than glad to help out."

☑ Epi Dupin (L') 🏠 *Bistro*

FOOD	DECOR	SERVICE	COST
23	14	18	€47

6e | 11, rue Dupin (Sèvres-Babylone) | 01 42 22 64 56 | fax 01 42 22 30 42

Now starting on its second "decadent decade of outrageous value", this "favorite" "near the Bon Marché" store is "everything you expect a bistro to be – but [still] surprises with every course" of market-fresh "creative fare"; it's true some get "tourist-induced claustrophobia" in the "crowded" digs, and the "staff ranges from friendly to undisguisedly impatient", but even though "you may be cramped and may not get any service, you'll always get great food"; P.S. "being American is not a crime" here.

Erawan 🏠 *Thai*

FOOD	DECOR	SERVICE	COST
20	16	18	€35

15e | 76, rue de la Fédération (La Motte-Picquet-Grenelle) | 01 47 83 55 67 | fax 01 47 34 85 98

"Some of the best, most authentic Thai cuisine in Paris" can be found at this "great secret" Siamese, with plant-filled decor in a quiet corner of the residential 15th; it's "especially good at lunch, given the value" and "rapid" service by "staffers in costume, which is quite pleasant."

Escale du Liban (L') 🌙 Ⓜ *Lebanese*

FOOD	DECOR	SERVICE	COST
–	–	–	M

4e | 1, rue Ferdinand Duval (St-Paul) | 01 42 74 55 70 | fax 01 42 74 55 27

"Excellent mezes and adorable service" sum up the scene at this Lebanese in a historic Marais building; don't be discouraged by the downstairs at this duplex, a take-out section swarming with staffers from the nearby Hôtel de Ville – just head upstairs to the dining room for a quieter meal of Middle Eastern specialties and wines.

Escargot Montorgueil (L') 🌙 *Bistro*

FOOD	DECOR	SERVICE	COST
18	21	18	€54

1er | 38, rue Montorgueil (Les Halles) | 01 42 36 83 51 | fax 01 42 36 35 05 | www.escargot-montorgueil.com

After some 170 years, this bistro "in charming Montorgueil" is "still around – I should look so good at that age!" – and still serving up its namesake "in pretty much everything" ("who knew snails could be cooked in so many different ways?"); cynics may sniff it's "last epoch's news", but most just "enjoy the romantic, dogmatically Parisian atmosphere" even if it has gotten a "little bit pricey", reflecting the gentrification efforts of owner Laurent Couegnas.

Espadon (L') *Classic French*

	FOOD	DECOR	SERVICE	COST
	25	27	26	€148

1er | Hôtel Ritz | 15, pl Vendôme (Concorde/Opéra) | 01 43 16 30 80 |
fax 01 43 16 33 75 | www.ritz.com

"Forget harsh reality just outside the walls of this prestigious palace" – aka the Hôtel Ritz's dining room – "a bastion of tradition where all is abundant silver, crystal and fresh flowers"; chef Michel Roth's Classic French cuisine is the "pinnacle of refinement", its "delectable" dishes doled out by "doting and experienced waiters"; "it may not be cutting-edge, it might be a bit stuffy and it [definitely] will empty your wallet – but it won't be anything less than excellent."

Espadon Bleu (L') *Seafood*

19 | 16 | 19 | €49

6e | 25, rue des Grands-Augustins (Odéon/St-Michel) |
01 46 33 00 85 | fax 01 43 54 54 48 | www.jacques-cagna.com

The eateries of chef-restaurateur Jacques Cagna "at the least are always really good" and that's the case with his cheerful, colorful seafooder in the 6th – "a real find" for its "extremely fresh *fruits de mer*" and "very friendly service"; "the setting is perhaps too nautical" (even the chalkboard menu is shaped like a fish), but that doesn't deter the "noisy young crowd" fueling the "thriving bar scene."

Etoile (L') ● *Classic French*

18 | 19 | 16 | €63

16e | 12, rue de Presbourg (Charles de Gaulle-Etoile) | 01 45 00 78 70 |
fax 01 45 00 78 71 | www.letoileparis.com

With a "nice location" just on the edge of l'Etoile, you "can't beat the view" from the dining room of this "fashionable" Classic French with a "disco lounge downstairs"; though it's filled with "cool, pretty people" who "don't eat", "the food is decent for a club/restaurant"; of course, the "best ending to the night is to go below and dance the night away" – though the drinks there are "ridiculously priced."

Etoile Marocaine (L') *Moroccan*

∇ 18 | 17 | 18 | €36

8e | 56, rue Galilée (George V) | 01 47 20 44 43 | fax 01 47 23 53 75

"It's not fancy and the service can be slow", but this place serves some of "the most delicious and authentic Moroccan food in town"; intricately painted and glazed "tiled walls and small fountains" create "nice ambiance", and prices are "reasonable" for the pricey 8th.

Eugène *Eclectic*

- | - | - | M

8e | 166, bd Haussmann (St-Phillipe-du-Roule) | 01 42 89 00 13 |
fax 01 42 89 01 14

Named after Baron Eugène Haussmann, who rebuilt much of Paris in the late 1800s, this venue in the 8th has reconfigured its historic building with swank decor that features chandeliers, a long pewter bar and, in back, a landmarked window pane by another architectural giant, Gustave Eiffel; the Eclectic menu swings from seasonal French favorites like lamb with *fleur de sel* to such exotica as tikka masala.

Fables de La Fontaine (Les) *Seafood*

21 | 14 | 18 | €45

7e | 131, rue St-Dominique (Ecole Militaire) | 01 44 18 37 55

"Here's a little place with Constant quality" – Christian Constant, that is – pun pleased patrons about the chef-owner's "truly intimate" seafooder in the 7th; served by a "competent, multilingual" team, the fare's always "honest", even "amazing"; the "blue-and-white ceramic-tiled decor" is "cute" but many "wish they could push back the walls to accommodate more folks (and give me a seat more often)."

Fakhr el Dine ● _Lebanese_   17 | 13 | 16 | €50

8ᵉ | 3, rue Quentin-Bauchart (George V) | 01 47 23 44 42
16ᵉ | 30, rue de Longchamp (Trocadéro) | 01 47 27 90 00 |
fax 01 53 70 01 81 🖾
www.fakhreldine.com

"Rich", "hearty" Lebanese cuisine is the lure at this pair, "well-situated" in well-heeled parts of the 8th and the 16th; service is "convivial" – "especially if you go with Middle Easterners" some add; and if both the decor and prices seem "_un peu_ too much", most think it's "worth it" for the "subtly spiced fare."

Famille (La) 🖾 Ⓜ _New French_   ▽ 16 | 13 | 14 | €39

18ᵉ | 41, rue des Trois-Frères (Abbesses/Anvers) | 01 42 52 11 12 |
fax 01 42 52 11 12

Even though founding chef Iñaki Aizpitarte has moved on, you can continue to expect "shockingly creative food" at this edgy, "funky" New French "scene" on a steep, cobbled street in Montmartre; however, a less-than-familial feeling infuses foes who deem the cuisine "unsubstantial and excessively precious", adding "the only remaining sign that this place was so hot last year is the staff's snotty attitude."

Fellini _Italian_   19 | 15 | 20 | €47

1ᵉʳ | 47, rue de l'Arbre-Sec (Louvre-Rivoli) | 01 42 60 90 66 |
fax 01 42 60 18 04
15ᵉ | 58, rue de la Croix-Nivert (Commerce/Emile Zola) |
01 45 77 40 77 | fax 01 45 77 22 54 🖾

Spearheaded by "good-humored", "personable service", a "warmly welcoming atmosphere" pervades this pair of pasta purveyors in the 1st (with "mellow stone walls" and a Sardinian slant) and 15th (with Neopolitan cuisine); patrons also are "pleased" by the "appetizing _plats_" and the "well-selected list of wines"; some say it seems "a little expensive" for spaghetti, but most shrug "that's the price you pay" for "a trip to Italy in the course of an evening."

Ferme (La) _Sandwiches_   - | - | - | I

1ᵉʳ | 55-57, rue St-Roch (Opéra/Pyramides) | 01 40 20 12 12 |
fax 01 40 20 06 06

"One of the pioneers of the organic-food movement" in Paris, this rustic in the 1st sells "delicious, healthy fare in a cute", woodsy setting; fresh-food fiends can "choose from a diverse array of pre-packaged sandwiches, wraps and salads or try one of their hot dishes"; "they also have a smoothie bar and feature a great brunch on weekends."

Ferme St-Simon (La) 🖾 _Classic French_   22 | 20 | 21 | €57

7ᵉ | 6, rue de St-Simon (Rue du Bac/Solférino) | 01 45 48 35 74 |
fax 01 40 49 07 31 | www.fermestsimon.com

"Everything you like about a traditional French place, without many of the things you don't" exists at this "elegant", "adult restaurant" in the

7th whose "fine, fussy food", "gracious staff" and "charming" "country-style decor" attract "France's movers and shakers" ("a lot of deals going on at the tables"); the young and the restless find it "uninspired" – "for friends who want Dining 101" – but most feel "the atmosphere's warm, the waiters hover" and this "standby still pleases."

Fermette Marbeuf 1900 (La) ● *Classic French*   18 | 23 | 19 | €59

8ᵉ | 5, rue Marbeuf (Alma Marceau/Franklin D. Roosevelt) | 01 53 23 08 00 | fax 01 53 23 08 09 | www.fermettemarbeuf.com

Highlighted by an "exquisite" stained-glass ceiling and an "extraordinary ladies' room", "the decor's the thing" at this belle epoque beauty in the 8th; but while fans find that's "worth the price of the meal", others growl the "gorgeous art nouveau" setting's "not going to fill your stomach" – and neither will the "uneven" Classic French food ("from good to passable") and service (it's "friendly", but it could be "more professional").

NEW Ferrandaise (La) 🏠 Ⓜ *Classic French*   - | - | - | M

6ᵉ | 8, rue de Vaugirard (Odéon/Cluny) | 01 43 26 36 36 | fax 01 43 26 90 91 | www.laferrandaise.com

Named after a breed of Auvergnat cows whose pictures dot the walls, this brightly lit, red-and-cream-colored Classic French in the 6th is popular with boutique owners and politicians at noon and bobo couples at night; what herds them here is the great value prix fixe that features items like chestnut-and-mushroom soup and chocolate-and-hazelnut fondant.

Filo Delle Stagioni (AL) ● *Italian*   - | - | - | M

3ᵉ | 8, rue de Beauce (Temple/République) | 01 48 04 52 24 | fax 01 48 04 52 24

Not many have yet sussed out the "savory, inventive" flavors of this small Italian in the ever-trendier northern Marais, but those who have say it's "a real discovery", not only for its "excellent" *cucina* with "numerous original touches" but also for its "agreeable" decor of stone tables and "pretty, modern tableware"; it recently added a chill-out area in the basement, complete with pool and all-you-can-eat buffet to maintain the pleasure of its penny-wise, arty clientele.

Findi ● *Italian*   17 | 18 | 16 | €48

8ᵉ | 24, av George V (Alma Marceau/George V) | 01 47 20 14 78 | fax 01 47 20 10 08 | www.findi.net

"You'd think you were in a smart home" – provided home was an "à la mode" "Italian palazzo" – at this "upscale date place"; the food is almost as "smart", especially the "good, fresh homemade pastas", and "the waiters really try to please"; costs seem "reasonable, given the prestigious location" on the swank Avenue George V.

Fins Gourmets (Aux) 🏠 Ⓜ ⇥ *Southwest*   21 | 16 | 17 | €45

7ᵉ | 213, bd St-Germain (Rue du Bac) | 01 42 22 06 57

Breathe "the atmosphere of eternal Paris" at "one of the last of the old bistros" in Saint-Germain, where "pleasant personnel" serve

	FOOD	DECOR	SERVICE	COST

"carefully prepared" Southwestern specialties in a "typical, traditional" room; true, the setting seems "tired" at times, but "you eat well and you don't pay too much", so if it "hasn't changed" since 1959, many "hope it never does."

Finzi *Italian*

▽ 20 | 10 | 15 | €41

8ᵉ | 182, bd Haussmann (St-Philippe-du-Roule) | 01 45 62 88 68 | fax 01 45 61 41 05 | www.finzi.com

In a corporate corner of the 8th, this "neighborhood Italian" is "good for business lunches" by day and by night "a place to go with the kids, since they'll accommodate all your needs" (they're a "little light on desserts", though); whatever the hour, you get "delicious" fare "at a reasonable price."

NEW First (Le) *New French*

– | – | – | E

1ᵉʳ | Westin Hotel | 234, rue de Rivoli (Concorde) | 01 44 77 10 40

This new venue in the Westin offers a plush, plum-toned setting by designer Jacques Garcia – a cross between a softly lit boudoir and a Manhattan supper club circa 1945 with mauve cut-velvet arm chairs, curtains, mirrored walls and a leaf-patterned floor in homage to the Tuileries across the street; a self-styled update on brasserie classics, chef Patrick Juhel's New French menu ranges from chicken nuggets to lobster pot-au-feu; oh, and don't miss 'Le First Baiser' (The First Kiss), a cake commissioned from Ladurée.

Fish La Boissonnerie Ⓜ *Provence*

21 | 15 | 18 | €40

6ᵉ | 69, rue de Seine (Odéon) | 01 43 54 34 69 | fax 01 43 54 33 47

"In overpriced, touristy Saint-Germain", this "hectic but friendly" old *poissonnerie* serves "remarkably good" food – dishes prepared with "a taste of Southern France", with "fish the obvious specialty", plus "exceptional wines supplied by co-owner Juan Sanchez, who has a shop around the corner"; at times service seems "overburdened and untrained", and as a virtual "home for the American expat", the room rings with "noisy" English-speaking voices.

Flandrin (Le) ◐ *Brasserie*

13 | 14 | 12 | €56

16ᵉ | 80, av Henri Martin (Rue de la Pompe) | 01 45 04 34 69 | fax 01 45 04 67 41

"A golden girl/boy staple", "this old train station–turned-brasserie" is "the place to be seen in the posh" 16th, particularly the "sunny patio"; but "unless you want to show off your Ferrari" (the car-watching is as big as the people-watching here), many moan it's "not worth going", since it's "expensive for no real reason" – certainly not the "mediocre dishes" or the servers "only interested in the regulars."

Fleurs de Thym Ⓩ *Lebanese*

– | – | – | M

4ᵉ | 19, rue François Miron (Hôtel-de-Ville/St-Paul) | 01 48 87 01 02 | fax 01 48 87 01 02

Though few know this "tiny Lebanese" in the Marais, those who do vow "I'd move here if I could" for the "incredibly fresh" fare, cozy dining room and friendly service; yellow stone walls hung with photos of Beirut and Baalbek strike a nostalgic note.

	FOOD	DECOR	SERVICE	COST

Flora Danica *Danish* — 18 | 15 | 13 | €55

8ᵉ | 142, av des Champs-Elysées (Charles de Gaulle-Etoile/George V) | 01 44 13 86 26 | fax 01 44 13 89 44 | www.restaurantfloradanica.com

"A taste of Scandinavia" on the Champs-Elysées, this "classic" is "a true revelation for those who never thought Danish food could be interesting" – and for "cheaper [tabs] than its sister, Copenhague"; there's also "an always reliable lineup of greatest hits" from France; it's too bad that the staff is as "cold" as the ice used to chill the "sumptuous fish"; N.B. scores don't reflect its recent purchase by the Frères Blanc group.

Flore en l'Ile (Le) ● *Classic French* — 16 | 19 | 16 | €38

4ᵉ | 42, quai d'Orléans (Hôtel-de-Ville/Pont-Marie) | 01 43 29 88 27 | fax 01 43 29 73 54

Boasting a "strategic location on the tip of the Ile Saint-Louis", this busy "neighborhood place" has "great views" of Notre Dame to enhance its "consistent and appealing" Classic French meals, including "brunch, lunch, tea" and "late-night Berthillion" ice cream; if several find it "overpriced", most say "it's worth whatever they charge" for that "movie-set" setting, despite "impersonal" service.

Florimond (Le) ⊠ *Classic French* — 24 | 18 | 24 | €44

7ᵉ | 19, av de la Motte-Picquet (Ecole Militaire) | 01 45 55 40 38 | fax 01 45 55 40 38

Surveyors just "can't say enough about this wonderful restaurant, which serves sublime, non-fussy Classic French fare with genuine affection not only for the food, but for its patrons"; reviewers revisit the "cozy" digs in the 7th for the "luscious stuffed cabbage", along with "attentive service even when it's crowded"; "entirely nonsmoking", it's especially a "great option for Saturday night, when many of the good places in Paris are closed."

Fogón ● Ⓜ *Spanish* — 20 | – | 14 | E

6ᵉ | 45, quai des Grands-Augustins (Maubert-Mutualité/St-Michel) | 01 43 54 31 33 | fax 01 43 54 07 00

The table reputed to be "the best Spanish place in Paris" "has changed its location" from a snug setting in the Latin Quarter to spacious and rather slick quarters in Saint-Germain; if the hip, white-and-purple decor will surprise fans of the "authentic tapas and paellas", most would agree that the kitchen remains "remarkable", especially for its "*arroz* [rice] dishes", and the service is still happily "*olé!*"

⦾ Fontaine de Mars (La) *Southwest* — 21 | 20 | 21 | €48

7ᵉ | 129, rue St-Dominique (Ecole Militaire) | 01 47 05 46 44 | fax 01 47 05 11 13

"With tables surrounding the namesake fountain" in the 7th, this "old bistro" offers an increasingly "rare" "slice of *Vieux Paris*", from its location "in the shadow of the Eiffel Tower" outside to the checkered tablecloths and moleskin banquettes inside; the cuisine is equally "classic", with "copious servings" of "fine Southwestern" eats ("foie gras as large as my fists"); "the waiters are professional", and while "prices may strike you as steep" for "the food of *grand-mère*", "you'll feel like family" here.

Fontaine Gaillon (La) ◐🅕 *Classic French* 19 | 20 | 17 | €67

2ᵉ | 1, pl Gaillon (Opéra/Quatre-Septembre) | 01 42 65 87 04 | fax 01 47 42 82 84 | www.la-fontaine-gaillon.com

With "cool modern" "decor that cries tasteful", Gérard Depardieu's Classic French enjoys a "nifty location" in the 2nd, with a fountain-side "terrace that's so lovely"; but while positives praise the "fabulous" fish dishes and "gracious staff", cynics sniff the food's just "above average" and the service "snooty"; perhaps, in this place "frequented by the well-known", your experience "depends on whether you yourself are 'known' or not."

Fontaines (Les) 🅕 *Bistro* 18 | 11 | 16 | €34

5ᵉ | 9, rue Soufflot (Cluny La Sorbonne/Luxembourg) | 01 43 26 42 80 | fax 01 93 54 44 57

"A lively choice by the Panthéon" ("the sidewalk tables offer great views"), "this bistro has all the typical" dishes in such "huge portions" that one "serving is enough for a family"; the "decor's pretty pitiful", and the "staff is available, without much else", but overall, the place is "tasty, unpretentious" and relatively "cheap."

Fontanarosa *Italian* ▽ 19 | 14 | 17 | €50

15ᵉ | 28, bd Garibaldi (Cambronne/Ségur) | 01 45 66 97 84 | fax 01 47 83 96 30 | www.fontanarosa-ristorante.com

"Owner Flavio Mascia takes you on a trip to his native Sardinia" at his intimate Italian in the 15th, where dishes are served at a "civilized pace" amid "widely spaced tables" – though regulars race for the "romantic" "little terrace bordered by olive trees"; they also suggest you "go for the tasting menu", otherwise it's a little "overpriced."

Foujita *Japanese* 14 | 6 | 12 | €34

1ᵉʳ | 41, rue St-Roch (Pyramides) | 01 42 61 42 93
1ᵉʳ | 7, rue 29 Juillet (Tuileries) | 01 49 26 07 70 | fax 01 49 26 07 60

Its fans may find "the sushi and Japanese fare fresh and refreshing" – "but the bar is really low" in Paris snap cynics who feel the food at these establishments in the 1st is no more than "acceptable"; service scores even less well (though "if you're a regular, you're treated special" some note), and "as for the decor, it hasn't really changed since the '80s"; maybe the best idea is to see the place as "not a culinary experience, but a good value for what it is."

Fouquet's (Le) ◐ *Classic French* 17 | 20 | 17 | €63

8ᵉ | 99, av des Champs-Elysées (George V) | 01 47 23 60 50 | fax 01 47 23 60 02 | www.lucienbarriere.com

"It's all about the view and the history" at this "Parisian landmark" on the Champs-Elysées, with its "tourist magnet" of a terrace without and a "charming boudoir atmosphere" (all "old-line red velvet") within; be prepared to spend "*beaucoup d' euros*" for what most call "distinctly average" Classic French fare, and be aware that "ego has crept into" the staff attitude; still, you too can "feel like someone famous here" – and that makes it "worth sampling, at least once."

Fous d'en Face (Les) ◑☒ *Bistro*
18 | 16 | 18 | €32

4ᵉ | 3, rue du Bourg-Tibourg (Hôtel-de-Ville) | 01 48 87 03 75 |
fax 01 42 78 38 03

"In a charming square near the Hôtel de Ville" ("perfect for people-watching"), this "crowded" bistro is the place to go "to find the traditional French meal you've been so desperately searching for in Paris"; with its "simple but varied menu" and "friendly servers", it's "super for a dinner with friends", and given the "great wine" and liqueurs list, a "place to linger afterwards for drinks."

Frégate (La) ☒ *Seafood*
‒ | ‒ | ‒ | M

12ᵉ | 30, av Ledru Rollin (Gare de Lyon/Quai de la Rapée) |
01 43 43 90 32 | fax 01 43 43 90 32

Located "right on the *quai*" in the 12th (its name means 'frigate'), this "elegant" seafooder is "an enchanted island", offering "never-less-than-respectable fare" in "a nice, quiet" setting for the last 30-odd years; "the clientele tends to be businesspeople and/or the middle-aged" who appreciate the courtly service and cuisine that combines classics like bouillabaisse with inventive preparations such as a cod steak with Szechuan pepper.

Frugier ☒Ⓜ *Bistro*
‒ | ‒ | ‒ | I

16ᵉ | 137, av de Versailles (Mirabeau/Exelmans) | 01 46 47 72 00 |
fax 01 46 47 72 00

This "lively" bistro in the 16th on the way to Versailles offers "traditional fare (e.g. roasted marrow bones) done to perfection"; expect a warm welcome from co-owner Caroline Frugier, while chef-husband Eric busies himself in the kitchen with the latest additions to the regularly changing prix fixe menu; though "small, it's well laid-out", with low-lighting, dark-wood tables and a long banquette running along one wall to create a cozy atmosphere.

Fumoir (Le) ◑ *Eclectic*
15 | 20 | 15 | €39

1ᵉʳ | 6, rue de l'Amiral de Coligny (Louvre-Rivoli) | 01 42 92 00 24 |
fax 01 42 92 05 05 | www.lefumoir.com

"Still a hot spot for the hip and the haute" after nine years, this Eclectic "enclave" "across the street from the Louvre" offers a "good mix of NYC-style bar and trendy Paris" eatery, with regulars heading for "the haven of tranquility of the library room" in back (the air's less of a "smoke bomb" there too); though "nice for brunch" on Sunday, it's the kind of place that's "more for the atmosphere than the food", so the savvy stick to "smart cocktails" and snacks.

Gallopin ◑ *Brasserie*
15 | 21 | 18 | €47

2ᵉ | 40, rue Notre-Dame-des-Victoires (Bourse/Grands Boulevards) | 01 42 36 45 38 | fax 01 42 36 10 32 |
www.brasseriegallopin.com

"Big, busy and [blessed] with belle epoque decor" sums up this "classic brasserie" with an "inviting bar" behind the Bourse in the 2nd; "it's a pity that the cuisine isn't up to" the environs, and that the gallopin' waiters, "garbed in long aprons", tend to be "impersonal"; still, this veteran works as "a really reliable standby."

	FOOD	DECOR	SERVICE	COST

Gamin de Paris (Au) ● *Southwest* — 18 | 16 | 15 | €34

4ᵉ | 51, rue Vieille-du-Temple (Hôtel-de-Ville/St-Paul) | 01 42 78 97 24
"With white lights twinkling through the foliage of many large plants and small trees", this mainstay in the Marais is the "favorite" of many for its "mostly meat" menu of Southwestern specialties ("don't expect to go home hungry") and "bustling-with-energy" ambiance; but while scores have held steady, detractors declare the fare's "dropped a notch" and deplore the "cramped seating and bucketfuls of attitude" from the "quirky" staff.

Gare (La) ● *Classic French* — 14 | 18 | 14 | €44

16ᵉ | 19, Chaussée de la Muette (La Muette) | 01 42 15 15 31 | fax 01 42 15 15 23 | www.restaurantlagare.com
If you're one of the 16th's "golden youth" (entry "forbidden to those over 18" some jest) you go to this "chic and *cher*" Classic French in the 16th "for the setting" – "a great renovation of an old railway station" – and "for the really pleasant terrace" in the summer; otherwise, opinion on the cooking ranges from "culinary disaster" to "very ordinary", while the staff is a bit too "casual" for comfort.

Garnier ● *Brasserie* — 22 | 20 | 21 | €72

8ᵉ | 111, rue St-Lazare (St-Lazare) | 01 43 87 50 40 | fax 01 40 08 06 93
Things go swimmingly at this brasserie just across the street from the Gare Saint-Lazare, "an area with few good restaurants"; not only does it serve some of the "best seafood in Paris" – "there's shellfish, and then there's Garnier's shellfish" – it also offers "chic" decor that somewhat "surrealistically" blends aquariums with Lalique lamps and mirrors, and an "attentive staff"; small wonder fin fans are willing to shell out for this specialist: "the tabs are high, but it's a sure value."

Gauloise (La) *Bistro* — 16 | 14 | 14 | €45

15ᵉ | 59, av de la Motte-Picquet (La Motte-Picquet-Grenelle) | 01 47 34 11 64 | fax 01 40 61 09 70
Those in search of some "reasonably priced class" find this traditional bistro in the 15th fills the bill with "jovial atmosphere" and "quite adequate cooking"; however, the circa-1900 "decor's aging" a bit, and the "service is "accommodating – for locals."

Gavroche (Le) ●🗷 *Bistro* — 21 | 15 | 20 | €48

2ᵉ | 19, rue St-Marc (Bourse/Richelieu-Drouot) | 01 42 96 89 70
It's "not recommended for those who want a place that looks pretty", "but you need only to see them bring out one of their prime ribs for two and you'll be sold" on this "low-key", "classic street bistro" in the 2nd that caters to carnivores; you might also see some of "the rough side of Paris" – "weird drunk people dwell here" some say – but the "jolly service and hearty, smoky atmosphere is an experience you cannot miss."

Gaya 🗷 *Seafood* — 22 | 17 | 19 | €61

7ᵉ | 44, rue du Bac (Rue du Bac) | 01 45 44 73 73 | fax 01 45 44 73 73
"Even more chic" since baroque toque Pierre Gagnaire acquired it (which scores don't fully reflect), this vintage Left Bank fish house is

now a cutting-edge catch-of-the-day place; his "alchemic concoc-tions" (tandoori-style monkfish, a whipped cream and arugula des-sert) are served in "hard-edged" decor of stainless steel and Corian tables with seaweed motifs; "it was always excellent and pricey; since the takeover, it's excellent, pricey – and hard to get a reservation."

NEW Gazzetta

`-` | `-` | `-` | M

(La) 🅂🅜 *Mediterranean/New French*

12ᵉ | 29, rue de Cotte (Ledru-Rollin) | 01 43 47 47 05 | fax 01 43 47 47 17 | www.lagazzetta.fr

Up-and-coming young Swedish chef Petter Nilsson (ex Troisgros, in the Rhône Valley) is attracting gourmets from all over town to this trendy trattoria not far from Bastille; his nervy New French-Med menu (example: a starter of caramelized endive with horse-radish and fresh almond purée) unfolds in a low-lit loftlike space with parquet floors, framed posters and a vibe that's hip but relaxed, like the service.

☒ Georges ● *Eclectic*

18 | 26 | 16 | €58

4ᵉ | Centre Georges Pompidou | 19, rue Beaubourg (Hôtel-de-Ville/Rambuteau) | 01 44 78 47 99 | fax 01 44 78 48 93

"The fabulous panoramic views of Paris" "from the top of the Pompidou Center" perpetually pack 'em into this high-design, high-attitude "house of glitz"; the Eclectic cuisine fails to "reach a compara-ble altitude", but it's "pretty good" – unlike the "gorgeous" servers, who often "act [like they're] more important than those they're serving"; still, the sculpture-filled, "sleek steel-and-glass room is worth the ascent" "for people-watchers" (but "definitely not for people pinching pennies").

Georgette 🅂🅜 *Bistro*

▽ 20 | 9 | 19 | €43

9ᵉ | 29, rue Saint-Georges (Notre-Dame-de-Lorette) | 01 42 80 39 13

"This is exactly the kind of place that makes eating out in Paris so charming" confide converts to this contemporary bistro in the 9th; the chef-owner "is both delightful and delighted to explain" the New French menu of "simple" foods "fresh from the market" that "mix well with the homestyle service and dinerlike decor"; admittedly, the latter's "a bit '50s, with brightly colored Formica tables", but the overall experience is "an entire pleasure."

☒ Gérard Besson 🅂 *Classic French*

25 | 21 | 23 | €109

1ᵉʳ | 5, rue du Coq-Héron (Louvre-Rivoli/Palais Royal-Musée du Louvre) | 01 42 33 14 74 | fax 01 42 33 85 71 | www.gerardbesson.com

"Gérard Besson is one of the great underrated talents cooking to-day", perhaps because "polished classicism, not innovation" is his culinary style; but most "have no complaints" about his Classic French in the 1st, even those who've "been going here for 20 years"; supporters swoon over his "wonderful" dishes and "delicious des-serts that have to be consumed, despite you're being full to burst-ing", served by a "sublime" staff in "warm surroundings"; it's "expensive but worth every euro cent."

	FOOD	DECOR	SERVICE	COST

Gitane (La) 🈯 *Southwest* — ▽ 14 | 15 | 13 | €44

15ᵉ | 53 bis, av de la Motte-Picquet (La Motte-Picquet-Grenelle) | 01 47 34 62 92 | fax 01 40 65 94 01 | www.la-gitane.com

"This modest place is perfect for a dinner with friends after a day's hard labor" say habitués happy to set up camp with this gypsy (*gitane*) in the 15th; the "food's mainly traditional" Southwest French, served by an "easygoing staff" to a "varied clientele" that includes everyone from old ladies with their dogs to dating couples.

Giulio Rebellato *Italian* — 20 | 16 | 20 | €54

16ᵉ | 136, rue de la Pompe (Victor Hugo) | 01 47 27 50 26

"In a *quartier* that's frequented by the chic clique" of the 16th, this "small", "low-key" Italian offers Venetian victuals that are "very good" but "very dear" as well; a "nice welcome" accompanies the "well-prepared" fare, though a few fear it's somewhat Frenchified.

Gli Angeli 🌓 *Italian* — 19 | 11 | 13 | €40

3ᵉ | 5, rue St-Gilles (Chemin-Vert/St-Paul) | 01 42 71 05 80

"When you need a little Italian in Paris", this site "right next to the Place des Vosges" is the place to go for "simple, savory" *cucina*, including "the best fried artichokes in town"; it's "incredibly popular" with a stylish young crowd, despite service that ranges from "adorably crabby" to downright "rude."

Gorille Blanc (Le) 🈯 *Bistro* — - | - | - | E

7ᵉ | 11 bis, rue Chomel (Sèvres-Babylone/St-Sulpice) | 01 45 49 04 54 | fax 01 45 49 04 54

Just across the street from the Bon Marché department store, this cozy little bistro cops a perfect Left Bank attitude, which explains why it's been packed with svelte, worldly well-heeled locals since it opened; the kitchen does a mix of traditional French comfort food and dishes with a more cosmopolitan inspiration, and service is correct if a little cool; prices reflect the deep pockets of this part of Paris.

Goumard *Seafood* — 24 | 20 | 20 | €91

1ᵉʳ | 9, rue Duphot (Madeleine) | 01 42 60 36 07 | fax 01 42 60 04 54 | www.goumard.fr

"The fattest sole, the sweetest lobsters, the briniest sea bass" – "everything is fresh and splendidly prepared" "in both traditional and creative ways" at this "unhurried" fish specialist in the 1st; the "now-modernized decor" strikes a few as "too formal" (though everyone loves the "amazing Lalique" wall inserts and "beautiful" Majorelle toilets), and the staff can range from "attentive" to "absent"; overall, though, this "workhorse" (or should we say 'seahorse'?) offers a "lovely, quality meal."

Gourmand (Le) 🈯 *New French* — 23 | 19 | 22 | €55

6ᵉ | 22, rue de Vaugirard (Odéon/RER Luxembourg) | 01 43 26 26 45 | fax 01 43 26 26 45

"Prepare to be pleasantly surprised" at this "little jewel" facing the Jardin de Luxembourg, where "there's a warm welcome at the door and a deft hand in the kitchen", turning out "imaginative" New French

fare; if the "narrow" room reminds some of "eating in a railway car",
to most the "cramped quarters" just mean "reserve in advance."

Gourmets des Ternes (Les) ⌧ *Bistro* 19 | 10 | 11 | €46

8ᵉ | 87, bd de Courcelles (Ternes) | 01 42 27 43 04
"Politically incorrect and unabashedly so", this "down-and-dirty
meat-and-potatoes" bistro near the Place des Ternes is "cramped
and loud – but hey, it's been like that for decades" shrug supporters
who still line up for the "steak lover's dream" of a menu; however,
the "snide, short" "attitude from the waiters if they don't know you" (or
even if they do) has several saying "you can do better elsewhere."

Graindorge ⌧ *Belgian/Northern France* 22 | 17 | 21 | €55

17ᵉ | 15, rue de l'Arc-de-Triomphe (Charles de Gaulle-Etoile) |
01 47 54 00 28
"Notoriously great for beers", this north star near the Arc de
Triomphe is also renowned for its "fine Belgian and Northern French
food", "original", "meticulously prepared" and presented by "immaculate servers" within a "homey atmosphere."

Grand Café (Le) ◑ *Brasserie* 15 | 19 | 14 | €55

9ᵉ | 4, bd des Capucines (Opéra) | 01 43 12 19 00 |
fax 01 43 12 19 09 | www.legrandcafe.com
It may have a "convenient location" near the Opéra Garnier and
"glitzy" belle epoque decor, but when it comes to cuisine, most say
that this Frères Blanc brasserie is "nothing special" ("unless you
crave a fresh seafood platter", perhaps); "service is inattentive –
you end up pouring your own wine because the waiter never
returns"; "still, it works when nothing else is open", since the
kitchen never closes.

Grand Colbert (Le) ◑ *Brasserie* 18 | 24 | 19 | €51

2ᵉ | 2, rue Vivienne (Bourse/Palais Royal-Musée du Louvre) |
01 42 86 87 88 | fax 01 42 86 82 65 | www.legrandcolbert.com
The place "where Jack Nicholson and Diane Keaton dined in
Something's Got to Give" (hence, now "discovered by Americans"),
this "grand, traditional Parisian brasserie" "within the Passage
Vivienne" is a veritable "*ville* of lights", mirrors, "ornate plaster-
work" and other elements of "old-world glamour"; while "the ambiance beats the food", the "typical" dishes "do not disappoint" and
service is "smiling and swift"; so, come here and "you'll know what
the Belle Epoque was all about."

Grande Armée (La) ◑ *Classic French* 12 | 17 | 12 | €46

16ᵉ | 3, av de la Grande-Armée (Charles de Gaulle-Etoile) |
01 45 00 24 77 | fax 01 45 00 95 50
Yet "another Costes" brothers eatery, this one is "close to the Arc de
Triomphe" with "chic" Jacques Garcia–designed striped-canvas of-
ficer's tent decor; "you can go there to mix with clubbers, and no
doubt you'll be sitting next to sexy" types; but antagonists attack
this Classic French as "a lot of noise for nothing" – or more specifically, for those "who don't care for food."

	FOOD	DECOR	SERVICE	COST

Grand Louvre (Le)   *Classic French* | 18 | 19 | 16 | €41

1er | Musée du Louvre | below the Pyramid (Palais Royal-Musée du Louvre) | 01 40 20 53 41 | fax 01 42 86 04 63

"A huge flower arrangement greets you at the entrance" to this Classic French with "a wonderful location on the courtyard of the Louvre" ("under the I.M. Pei glass pyramid") and "sleek and sophisticated" decor by Jean-Michel Wilmotte; ok, "so it's not great cuisine", but it's "not bad for a museum restaurant", either, "with varied choices"; besides, it's "a boon for tired feet" and is "perfect for a quick bite" "while the gargoyles stare down at you"; N.B. dinner Wednesday and Friday only.

☑ Grand Véfour (Le)   ⑤ *Haute Cuisine* | 27 | 28 | 27 | €147

1er | Palais Royal | 17, rue de Beaujolais (Palais Royal-Musée du Louvre) | 01 42 96 56 27 | fax 01 42 86 80 71 | www.grand-vefour.com

This "historic" Haute Cuisine "heaven" in the Palais Royal gardens is "a glittering jewel box" that offers a "culinary experience beyond compare"; chef Guy Martin's cooking is "awesome in every way", and as you wait for each "divine" course, you can gaze at brass plaques with the names of famous patrons past, like Colette and Victor Hugo; you too "are treated like royalty" "upon entering this bastion of epicurean bliss", so, even if it costs a fortune, "for a few hours, it's good to be the king."

Grand Venise (Le)   ⑤Ⓜ *Italian* | 22 | 15 | 19 | €81

15^e | 171, rue de la Convention (Convention) | 01 45 32 49 71 | fax 01 45 32 07 49

"An astonishing assortment of antipasti" leads off the "fiesta Italiana" at this pasta palazzo, decorated Venetian-style, in the 15th; "the presentation is amazing" and "the portions are extraordinary", "so don't eat for a week before coming here"; it's "too expensive", but still "wonderful."

Grange Batelière (La)   *Classic French* | - | - | - | E

9^e | 16, rue de la Grange Batelière (Richelieu-Drouot) | 01 47 70 85 15

Comedienne Mimie Mathy and her chef-husband, Gérard Benoist, recently purchased this venerable, traditional bistro in the 9th, preserving much of its fly-in-amber-19th-century decor, including the original marble-topped bar and napkin holders; it gets animated with auctioneers from Drouot nearby, as well as fans of Mimie's; happily, the elegant Classic French cuisine compensates for the crowds, and makes the sturdy prices here a little more digestible; N.B. open for lunch only aside from two Wednesdays a month.

Grille (La)   ⑤ *Bistro* | - | - | - | E

10^e | 80, rue du Faubourg Poissonnière (Poissonnière) | 01 47 70 89 73

For "a true glimpse of yesteryear", the non-timorous "trek to a less-than-charming neighborhood" in the 10th and this "family-run", "very French" "old, old-fashioned bistro" with "maybe 10 tables" and plenty of convivial spirit; couples should check out "great turbot for two", "with beurre blanc sauce so good that I would take it straight and pretty much douse everything with it."

Grille St-Germain (La) ● *Bistro*

FOOD	DECOR	SERVICE	COST
17	16	17	€32

6ᵉ | 14, rue Mabillon (Mabillon) | 01 43 54 16 87 | fax 01 43 54 52 88

With "Bordeaux-colored velvet curtains at the door and beautiful [black-and-white] celebrity photos on the wall", "a pleasant atmosphere" prevails at this "comfy neighborhood joint" in Saint-Germain; the "solid bistro food" makes most happy, since "the kitchen works with good quality produce", and if "service can be a little slow", few mind when "it's such a good buy for the money."

Guinguette de Neuilly (La) *Classic French*

FOOD	DECOR	SERVICE	COST
15	16	14	€43

Neuilly-sur-Seine | 12, bd Georges Seurat (Pont-de-Levallois) | 01 46 24 25 04 | fax 01 47 38 20 49 | www.laguinguette.net

This "old-fashioned *guinguette*" on the Ile de la Jatte is a "wonderful" spot to paddle down memory lane, since it serves up the same relaxed, blowsy atmosphere that made these waterside cafes/dance halls so popular with Parisians a century ago; as for this specimen, "you could say it's living off its reputation and Seine-side setting", but many find the Classic French fare "reliable" and even "agreeable in summer"; the servers, however, seem ready for "a career change."

Guirlande de Julie (La) ⊠ *Classic French*

FOOD	DECOR	SERVICE	COST
–	–	–	E

3ᵉ | 25, pl des Vosges (Bastille/St-Paul) | 01 48 87 94 07 | fax 48 87 01 22 | www.latourdargent.com

Tucked away under the arches of the arcade that runs around the Place des Vosges, this veteran romantic venue (owned by the Terrail family of La Tour d'Argent) recently reopened after being completely redecorated in various shades of pink, with ladder-backed, green-cushioned wooden chairs to give it the atmosphere of a country auberge; the kitchen has a festive touch with Classic French fare, the service is refined and the wine list was assembled by La Tour's sommelier.

☒ Guy Savoy, Restaurant ⊠ *Haute Cuisine*

FOOD	DECOR	SERVICE	COST
28	25	27	€168

17ᵉ | 18, rue Troyon (Etoile) | 01 43 80 40 61 | fax 01 46 22 43 09 | www.guysavoy.com

He may be "locating in Las Vegas", but chef-owner Guy Savoy's table in the 17th is "reason alone to go to Paris", because this "spectacular" Haute Cuisine site has it all: "original" dishes in which "every flavor sings", staffers who are "trained observers, or perhaps mind-readers", and attractive "minimalist" decor dominated by modern art; "bring an armored car full of money" because the tabs are "over the top", but then, this is "one of the best restaurants in Paris" – even, "arguably, the world."

Hangar (Le) ●⊠Ⓜ⇄ *Classic French*

FOOD	DECOR	SERVICE	COST
▽ 20	8	18	€40

3ᵉ | 12, impasse Berthaud (Rambuteau) | 01 42 74 55 44

"Hidden away but well worth seeking out", this "nice bistro around the corner from the Pompidou Museum" offers "surprisingly good" Classic French fare ("fans of foie gras will love their sautéed version"); regulars recommend "don't expect much from the decor" and "do remember to get cash before going" – "annoying", yes, but it ensures the "*plats* are not too pricey."

	FOOD	DECOR	SERVICE	COST

Harold *Classic/New French* — | — | — | M

17ᵉ | 48, rue de Prony (Monceau/Wagram) | 01 47 63 96 96 |
fax 01 47 63 96 97

Surveyors herald this young site in the 17th, a plush dining room decorated in black and Pompeian-red just steps from the Parc Monceau; the "exceptional food" is a combination of Classic and New French dishes ("heavenly lobster Caesar salad"), often with an Asian twist, as in the green-tea sorbet served alongside molten chocolate cake; popular with a business crowd at noon, it's much quieter at night, but whatever the time of day, "a delightful time is had" by all.

Harumi Ⓜ *New French* — | — | — | M

15ᵉ | 99, rue Blomet (Vaugirard) | 01 42 50 22 27 |
fax 01 42 50 22 27 | www.harumi.fr

A suave and savvy East-meets-West adventure awaits those willing to venture to this far corner of the 15th; the intrepid will find the cooking – New French, done with a Japanese chef's touch – "excellent", attentively served in a cosseted, modern, white-on-white room.

Ⓩ Hélène 23 | 21 | 20 | €111
Darroze Ⓢ Ⓜ *New French/Southwest*

6ᵉ | 4, rue d'Assas (Rennes/Sèvres-Babylone) | 01 42 22 00 11 |
fax 01 42 22 25 40 | www.helenedarroze.com

Though she's "a woman who knows what she's doing", reviewers report "diametrically different experiences" at Hélène Darroze's "expensive" New French–Southwestern in the 6th; supporters swear by her "exquisitely daring preparations", "beautiful, deep-toned" room and "service up to standards", while foes find the "food overcomplicated" and scold the "supercilious" staff; overall, scores "give it the benefit of the doubt" – tipped by universal acclaim for the foie gras, a slice of "sautéed heaven"; N.B. there's a new adjacent annex, Le Boudoir, serving finger foods.

NEW Hier & Aujourd'hui Ⓢ *New French* — | — | — | M

17ᵉ | 145, rue de Saussure (Péreire) | 01 42 27 35 55 |
fax 01 47 64 30 85 | resto.hieraujourdhui.free.fr

Near the Porte d'Asnières, this good-value bistro has become a local sensation for the chalkboard menus of chef Franck Dervin, who previously cooked with Alain Dutournier and Guy Savoy; his New French cuisine is creative and precise, and his co-owner wife, Karin, animates the dining room with its modern, gray-toned decor, including a kitchen window that allows the young clientele to watch the chef at work.

Higuma *Japanese* ▽ 18 | 1 | 6 | €28

1ᵉʳ | 163, rue St-Hororé (Palais-Royale) | 01 58 62 49 22 |
fax 01 58 62 49 27
1ᵉʳ | 32 bis, rue Ste-Anne (Pyramides) | 01 47 03 38 59 |
fax 01 47 03 38 52

"Satisfying, quick, authentic Japanese cuisine" is the lure at these "budget canteens" in the 1st; "decor and service are basically nonexistent", but no one really minds when gobbling the "good, basic noodle soups" or "killer gyoza."

	FOOD	DECOR	SERVICE	COST

Hippopotamus ● *Steak*   10 | 10 | 12 | €27

1er | 29, rue Berger (Les Halles) | 01 45 08 00 29
2e | 1, bd des Capucines (Opéra) | 01 47 42 75 70 | fax 01 42 65 23 08
4e | 1, bd Beaumarchais (Bastille) | 01 44 61 90 40 | fax 01 44 61 90 46
5e | 9, rue Lagrange (Maubert-Mutualité) | 01 43 54 13 99
6e | 119, bd du Montparnasse (Vavin) | 01 43 20 37 04 |
fax 01 43 22 68 95
8e | 20, rue Quentin-Bauchart (George V) | 01 47 20 30 14 |
fax 01 47 20 95 31
10e | 8, bd St-Denis (Strasbourg-St-Denis) | 01 53 38 80 28 |
fax 01 53 38 80 26
14e | 68, bd du Montparnasse (Montparnasse-Bienvenüe) |
01 40 64 14 97 | fax 01 43 21 46 10
15e | 12, av du Maine (Duroc/Montparnasse-Bienvenüe) |
01 42 22 36 75
Puteaux | CNIT | 2, pl de la Défense (La Défense-La Grande Arche) |
01 46 92 13 75 | fax 01 46 92 13 69
www.hippopotamus.fr

"Curiously, the quality and the service vary from one restaurant to another" at this "factory chain" – sort of a "TGI Fridays of France" – "catering to conventioneers, students and tourists" with steak "filets and frites"; but overall, the bar's pretty low ("who says you can't get a bad meal in Paris?") – even though parents proclaim "if you're traveling with kids, the place will save your sanity."

☑ Hiramatsu ☒ *Haute Cuisine*   27 | 22 | 25 | €127

16e | 52, rue de Longchamp (Trocadéro/Boissière) | 01 56 81 08 80 |
fax 01 56 81 08 81 | www.hiramatsu.co.jp

"Almost perfection" pant proponents of this Haute Cuisine table in the 16th that, despite the Japanese name, carries "creative and conceptually fascinating" New French dishes; "light, delicate and often transparent", they're "beautifully presented by a lovely staff"; although some "preferred the old address on the Ile Saint-Louis", the current "elegant, minimalist" "digs are beautiful and offer more tables" too.

NEW Hôtel Amour ● *New French*   - | - | - | M

9e | Hôtel Amour | 8, rue Navarin (St-Georges) | fax 01 48 74 14 09 |
www.hotelamour.com

Co-owned by Thierry Costes, this late-night newcomer in the funky Hôtel Amour is one of the hottest young spots in town; inside, there's an eye-catching collection of flea-market Danish Modern tables and chairs mixed with collector's pieces by esteemed designers Charlotte Perriand and Jean Prouvé; outside, there's a fountain splattering in the back garden; all around are easygoing, moderately priced New French eats.

Huîtrerie Régis ●☒ *Shellfish*   - | - | - | M

6e | 3, rue de Montfaucon (Mabillon) | 01 44 41 10 07

To make the world your oyster, head for this snug, stylish shellfish bar in the heart of Saint-Germain-des-Près; they shuck a variety of different bivalves in the Breton sea-shack-like surrounds, and since the prices aren't princely for this part of town, it's proving to be popular with publishers and politicos.

	FOOD	DECOR	SERVICE	COST

Huîtrier (L') 🅜 *Classic French*

	–	–	–	E

17ᵉ | 16, rue Saussier-Leroy (Ternes) | 01 40 54 83 44 | fax 01 40 54 83 86
Named 'the oysterman', this "pleasant, neighborly" Classic French in the 17th is, "as one might guess", all about "excellent" oysters from all over the country; but if many say that the big trays of bivalves are "among the best in Paris", they're "super-expensive" too, and the dining room's as "cramped" as a crustacean's shell.

I Golosi 🆉 *Italian*

	20	12	16	€41

9ᵉ | 6, rue de la Grange-Batelière (Richelieu-Drouot/Grand Boulevards) | 01 48 24 18 63 | fax 01 45 23 18 96
"The name of this gem means 'the gluttons', and you certainly will be one when you try the delicious and unusual Italian menu" ("finally, risotto worthy of the name!"), which "changes every week", and "wines by the glass that are real finds"; it's popular with bankers and the antiques crowd of the 9th, who forgive the "tacky decor."

Il Barone ◑🆉 *Italian*

	–	–	–	M

14ᵉ | 5, rue Léopold Robert (Raspail/Vavin) | 01 43 20 87 14 | fax 01 43 20 87 14
"Don't sweat the lack of decor" at this "real trattoria" in Montparnasse, since a "charming experience" awaits in "the back room" (the front dining room is only for uninitiated tourists); the robustly flavored "fresh pasta you dream about is made here and cooked al dente, like in Italy"; the "personal service" is *molto authentico* too.

Il Cortile 🆉 *Italian*

	21	18	20	€80

1ᵉʳ | Hôtel Castille Paris | 37, rue Cambon (Concorde/Madeleine) | 01 44 58 45 67 | fax 01 44 58 44 00
Chef Vittorio Beltramelli, a lieutenant of renowned Milanese toque Gualtiero Marchesi, has taken over this hotel dining room in the 1st, and fans applaud his "well-proportioned, delectable" dishes, an "inventive" version of Lombardian cuisine; in summer, "try for the outside courtyard and view the lovely fountain" – it'll distract from the "spotty service", which swings from "sublime" to "exasperatingly slow."

Ile (L') ◑ *Classic/New French*

	16	20	14	€55

Issy-les-Moulineaux | Parc de l'Ile St-Germain | 170, quai de Stalingrad (RER Issy-Val de Seine) | 01 41 09 99 99 | fax 01 41 09 99 19 | www.restaurant-lile.com
Prices are "high, but justified" by the "leafy", "exceptionally agreeable" waterside setting on the Ile Saint-Germain that's won this "stylish site" a loyal following, despite the "undistinguished", if "decent" Classic–New French cuisine; one tip is to "go early – afterwards, it's a factory" with correspondingly "industrialized service."

Il Etait une Oie dans le Sud-Ouest 🆉🅜 *Southwest*

	▽ 17	7	9	€38

17ᵉ | 8, rue Gustave Flaubert (Ternes/Courcelles) | 01 43 80 18 30 | fax 01 43 80 99 50
"If you crave foie gras, this is the place to go" grin goose lovers of this Southwestern with a ducky reputation; new, cozier prune-colored

decor has made it "a pleasant little place", and it's "less expensive than some of its neighbors" in the 17th.

Ilot Vache (L') *Classic French*

21	20	18	€46

4e | 35, rue St-Louis-en-l'Ile (Pont-Marie) | 01 46 33 55 16

With a "lovely spot on the Ile Saint-Louis", this Classic French delights with "charming, whimsical decor" "reminiscent of a cute farmhouse" (quite a bit of bric-a-brac) and "food to match" (they do much with meat, so it's "not for vegans"); if the "friendly service" is a little "slow", just bask in the "quintessentially romantic" atmosphere.

Il Viccolo 🗷 *Italian*

▽ 17	14	17	€50

6e | 34, rue Mazarine (Odéon) | 01 43 25 01 11

A chic crowd of pasta lovers, including the occasional well-known face, camps out at this "genuinely Italian" spot in Saint-Germain; the "food is good, if not high-end", the "service almost shockingly friendly" and, with a glassed-in sidewalk space, it "feels cozy, despite its modern-leaning decor"; however, "prices are a bit high" for what's essentially a "neighborhood" place.

Inagiku 🗷 *Japanese*

–	–	–	E

5e | 14, rue de Pontoise (Maubert-Mutualité) | 01 43 54 70 07 | fax 01 40 51 74 44

"Authentic Japanese" eats await at this teppanyaki table in the Latin Quarter; beyond that, "there's nothing to reproach, but there's not much reason to be enthusiastic" about the place – unless the sight of "sizzling plaques with dancing scallops, squid and Kobe beef" excites your senses.

Indiana Café ❶ *Tex-Mex*

8	8	11	€24

3e | 1, pl de la République (République) | 01 48 87 82 35 | fax 01 48 87 82 35
6e | 130, bd St-Germain (Odéon) | 01 46 34 66 31 | fax 01 46 34 66 31
8e | 235-237, rue du Faubourg St-Honoré (Ternes) | 01 44 09 80 00 | fax 01 44 09 80 00
9e | 79, bd de Clichy (Place de Clichy) | 01 48 74 42 61 | fax 01 48 74 42 61
11e | 14, pl de la Bastille (Bastille) | 01 44 75 79 80 | fax 01 44 75 79 80
14e | 1, av du Général Leclerc (Denfert-Rochereau) | 01 40 47 60 41
14e | 72, bd du Montparnasse (Montparnasse-Bienvenüe) | 01 43 35 36 28 | fax 01 43 35 07 25
www.indiana-cafe.fr

"So touristy you'd think you actually were in Indiana", this "noisy" "mass-market version of a French idea of a Western-themed restaurant" serves a "tired attempt at Tex-Mex" food (when the "forgetful waitresses" remember how, that is); it'll do "when you're craving a greasy burger and beer" perhaps – "the happy-hour prices are a good deal" – otherwise, leave it "for your concierge's kids."

Indigo Square 🗷 *Eclectic*

–	–	–	M

Bagnolet | 7, rue Marceau (Gallieni) | 01 43 63 26 95

One of several eateries springing up in the northeastern suburbs of Paris, this Bagnolet-based site is worth the trip for its edgy Eclectic cuisine; its turquoise walls house funky decor of tables recycled from sewing machines and lamp fixtures made from colanders – ideal for the arty crowd settling the area; the victuals from *la vie bohème* don't come cheap, but they are "some of the best in the neighborhood."

Indra ⑤ *Indian* ▽ 18 | 19 | 15 | €47

8ᵉ | 10, rue du Commandant Rivière (St-Philippe-du-Roule) | 01 43 59 46 40 | fax 01 42 25 00 32 | www.restaurant-indra.com

"Fine Indian cooking" is the draw at this fortysomething subcontinental in the 8th; though the heat may have been turned down in deference to timid French palates, most find the cuisine "very good" indeed, especially for vegetarians (who can partake of the meat-free prix fixe, served on a silver tray), and the slightly campy, warm-colored, native decor and smiling service contribute to a "wonderful experience"; it's not cheap, but neither's the neighborhood.

☑ Isami ⑤ Ⓜ *Japanese* 27 | 10 | 16 | €52

4ᵉ | 4, quai d'Orléans (Pont-Marie) | 01 40 46 06 97

Despite the "dull decor" and "indifferent service", no surveyor seems to be able to resist "the best sushi in Paris" ("melts in your mouth, not in your hand"), which "means reservations are essential" if you want a place at this Ile Saint-Louis "jewel box–sized" Japanese that charges "jewelry prices for each bite"; however, "once you are in, you will feel as if you are in Tokyo" – especially if you go for the "chef-recommended plate"; P.S. sit at the counter, which "lets you contemplate the maestro" chef at work.

Issé ⑤ *Japanese* 18 | 13 | 17 | €47

1ᵉʳ | 45, rue de Richelieu (Pyramides/Palais Royal-Musée du Louvre) | 01 42 96 26 60

Exhibiting "a simple environment" in the 1st, this diminutive but venerable Japanese establishment offers a unique small-plates style of serving – call it "tempura tapas", along with many "other delicious things to try", such as sushi; critics cavil the prices may seem "high" for what you get, but few argue with the "authentic" cuisine.

☑ Jacques Cagna ⑤ *Haute Cuisine* 26 | 23 | 23 | €97

6ᵉ | 14, rue des Grands-Augustins (Odéon/St-Michel) | 01 43 26 49 39 | fax 01 43 54 54 48 | www.jacquescagna.com

"Housed in an attractive old beamed building in Saint-Germain", for some 40 years this vet has seduced those in search of a "romantic" experience with "elegantly hearty" Haute Cuisine, served "with Parisian flair" by a staff that's "attentive, but doesn't crowd you"; modernist mavens may find its "classical" approach "a little outdated" – and there's nothing nostalgic about the prices – but the majority is "moved", especially since chef-owner "Jacques Cagna himself speaks to every table", "a welcome touch."

Jardin (Le) ⑤ *New French/Provence* 22 | 21 | 21 | €91

8ᵉ | Hôtel Royal Monceau | 37, av Hoche (Charles de Gaulle-Etoile) | 01 42 99 98 70 | fax 01 42 99 89 94 | www.royalmonceau.com

"A lovely space in a glass dome, with gardens all around", this quarter-century-old pavilion provides a "veritable oasis" in the 8th;

it's a "power-lunch favorite" for chef Christophe Pelé's Provençal-New French cuisine, which some surveyors say echoes that of the "unbridled Pierre Gagnaire" (with whom he trained); "classy service" navigates the tented Empire-style Jacques Garcia setting that can seem "extremely kitschy – there's even a harpist" at night.

Jardin des Cygnes *Classic French* 20 | 23 | 20 | €76

8ᵉ | Hôtel Prince de Galles | 33, av George V (George V) | 01 53 23 78 50 | fax 01 53 23 78 78 | www.luxurycollection.com
"A classic in a tranquil setting" – a courtyard overlooking a "delightful garden" in the 8th – this hotel restaurant is "perfect for that romantic date"; while "the food simply doesn't match" the ambiance, it's still "very good traditional French cuisine" and supplied by a "gracious staff"; prices are somewhat "pretentious", however.

NEW **Jardinier (Le)** Ⓩ *Classic French* - | - | - | M

9ᵉ | 5, rue Richer (Bonne Nouvelle) | 01 48 24 79 79 | fax 01 47 70 95 79
The menu may be market-fresh, but the setting is lavishly belle epoque at this bistro near the Folies Bergère, with wedding-cake moldings and a chandelier overhead; as the name ('the gardener') indicates, the chef likes his legumes, which appear often in the Classic French dishes; service is on the ball, given that it's always busy with bargain-loving businesspeople at noon and theatergoers at night.

Jardins de Bagatelle (Les) *Classic French* ▽ 17 | 23 | 15 | €74

16ᵉ | Parc de Bagatelle | Route de Sèvres (Pont-de-Neuilly) | 01 40 67 98 29 | fax 01 40 67 93 04 | www.restaurantbagatelle.com
"Wander the rose gardens and then have a leisurely lunch [or dinner] under the trees": small wonder that "in spring and summer, this is one of the most charming and romantic places in Paris" say believers in this Bois de Boulogne site; given the "wonderful venue", it's understandable the Classic French "food and service are disappointing" in comparison; but you'll hear few complaints from the cosmopolitan "clientele craving greenery"; better "bring your bank book", though; N.B. renovations were slated for early 2007.

Jarrasse, l'Ecuiller de Paris *Seafood* - | - | - | E

Neuilly-sur-Seine | 4, av de Madrid (Pont-de-Neuilly) | 01 46 24 07 56 | fax 01 40 88 35 60 | www.michelrostang.com
Although it joined the fleet of chef-restaurateur Michel Rostang early in 2006, this Neuilly neighborhood fixture still seems a "fine old traditional fish house" to fans who fawn over signatures like the "excellent" sea bass with fennel and the "always superb millefeuille" for dessert; with its East-meets-West decor (think fabric lanterns and red/beige velvet banquettes), it's a "favorite for serious working meals, if a somewhat expensive one."

Jean Ⓩ *New French* 19 | 17 | 19 | €50

9ᵉ | 8, rue St-Lazare (Notre-Dame-de-Lorette) | 01 48 78 62 73 | fax 01 48 78 66 04 | www.restaurantjean.fr
Surveyors are split when they come to this "ambitious" New French in the "not-too-glamorous 9th" ("pay attention so you can find your way

back to the métro"); while dissenters are "disappointed that two Taillevent alumni couldn't come up with better food", friends find it "truly fine", and the "prices modest" for a "memorable" experience.

Jean-Paul Hévin ☒ *Dessert/Tearoom*   24 | 17 | 17 | €27

1er | 231, rue St-Honoré (Madeleine/Tuileries) | 01 55 35 35 96 | fax 01 55 35 35 97 | www.jphevin.com

Upstairs from *"chocolatier extraordinaire"* Jean-Paul Hévin's shop in the 1st is this "lovely tearoom", aka "hot chocolate heaven"; it's "enough to make you rethink any diet", since "you'll want to have all of the desserts", maybe preceded by a "quick [bite of] traditional French fare"; there's some grousing about "inconsistent service" and "faded decor", but for most this is "perfect for a pick-me-up after a morning of shopping" – and, of course, "a must for any chocoholic."

Je Thé . . . Me ☒ *Classic French*   ▽ 22 | 18 | 22 | €41

15e | 4, rue d'Alleray (Convention/Vaugirard) | 01 48 42 48 30 | fax 01 48 42 70 66 | www.jetheme.net

"Probably one of the quaintest restaurants in Paris", this "cozy" (ok, maybe "a little cramped") venue attracts 15th-arrondissement locals with its landmarked locale in an old grocery store full of mirrors, earthenware jugs and bric-a-brac; the "charming" chef-owner provides "true Classic French fare" that's "well up to standard – but it's the overall ambiance that's so good" here.

J'Go ⬤ ☒ *Southwest*   ▽ 18 | 12 | 18 | €36

9e | 4, rue Drouot (Richelieu-Drouot) | 01 40 22 09 09 | fax 01 40 22 07 15 | www.lejgo.com

Convenient for bankers and Grands Boulevards moviegoers, this 9th-arrondissement branch of a Toulouse chain dishes up "robust cooking and wines from the Southwest, with very good roast meats" – including an "excellent namesake leg of lamb" or *gigot* (pronounced roughly like 'j'go'); "friendly service" adds to the "relaxed atmosphere", which – thanks to "very reasonable prices" – remains unruffled to the end.

Joe Allen ⬤ *American*   14 | 15 | 16 | €37

1er | 30, rue Pierre Lescot (Etienne Marcel) | 01 42 36 70 13 | fax 01 42 36 90 80 | www.joeallenparis.com

With "a somber red-brick interior lined with classic [star's] Hollywood photos", it "feels like NYC's theater district" at this "casual" Les Halles veteran, a virtual "American pied-à-terre in Paris" in terms of clientele and cuisine; it's "best to stick with the basic burgers" and brunches, ignoring the servers who often seem to be "having a bad day"; critics claim the whole place "needs to be refreshed", but why change a formula that's worked for so long?"

Joséphine "Chez Dumonet" ☒ *Bistro*   23 | 17 | 19 | €57

6e | 117, rue du Cherche-Midi (Duroc/Falguière) | 01 45 48 52 40 | fax 01 42 84 06 83

Most folks "love every minute of a visit to this authentic bistro" in the 6th, famed for its "large helpings of traditional French favorites" – oh, and "don't miss the wonderful collection of Bordeaux liquors" and wines – served by a "staff that's generous with its time and assistance"; the "old-style Rive Gauche" look adds to the "casual charm"; P.S. be advised, "a clash of civilizations is in the making if you dare ask for a doggy bag", but even the half-portions are big enough to share.

Z Jules Verne (Le) *Classic French* — 23 | 27 | 24 | €108

7ᵉ | Tour Eiffel | Champ-de-Mars, 2nd level (Bir-Hakeim) | 01 45 55 61 44 | fax 01 47 05 29 41

Since it's in the Eiffel Tower, "some fear this is a tourist trap" – but you can expect "first-class everything" at this Classic French, offering "one of the most romantic" views in the world ("propose here"), plus "much-better-than-expected" meals and an "incredibly polite staff" (though folks who show "in shorts and sneakers get a well-deserved short end of the stick"); some dis the black "'70s-inspired decor" and a "bill as high as the room", but "spectacular" sums it up for most; N.B. chef Alain Ducasse's group, which assumed command in early 2007, plans to unveil a new look and menu in autumn.

Jumeaux (Les) Z *New French* — - | - | - | M

11ᵉ | 73, rue Amelot (Chemin-Vert) | 01 43 14 27 00 | fax 01 43 14 27 00

Although its namesake twins are gone, this New French in the 11th still offers "an exquisite and serene setting for simple but creative dishes" profess the few that know it; the "superb" food is served by a "friendly staff" in a long dining room with "contemporary but polished decor" adorned with modern sculpture.

Juvéniles Z *Wine Bar/Bistro* — 17 | 13 | 18 | €36

1ᵉʳ | 47, rue de Richelieu (Bourse/Palais Royal-Musée du Louvre) | 01 42 97 46 49 | fax 01 42 60 31 52

"The food is fine, and the wine's divine" at this "scruffy but atmospheric" *bar à vins* in the 1st, where there are just enough Eclectic eats to provide ballast for the "beautiful selection of bottles from all over the world"; all unfolds under the "watchful eye of the owner", a "quick-quipping" Scot, who supplies samples for all you "sherry aficionados."

Kai M *Japanese* — - | - | - | E

1ᵉʳ | 18, rue du Louvre (Rivoli/Louvre) | 01 40 15 01 99

Near the Louvre, this Japanese is a perfect example of the increasing sophistication of Paris' Asian eateries, since it goes beyond the usual sushi-sashimi-tempura trio with modern takes on authentic comfort food, including breaded pork cutlet with red miso sauce and steamed foie gras with beaten egg – plus desserts from *pâtissier* Pierre Hermé; the taupe walls and potted orchids on the big blond-oak communal table appeal to the chic clientele.

Kaïten ◖ Z *Japanese* — 19 | 12 | 17 | €50

8ᵉ | 63, rue Pierre Charron (Franklin D. Roosevelt) | 01 43 59 78 78 | fax 01 43 59 71 51

Despite the conveyor belt that parades the chefs' efforts under your nose, this Japanese does "some of the best sushi in Paris" and is "great for a quick, chic lunch" or late-night bite in an Asian "ambiance of red, white and black" decor; perhaps because it's essentially "self-service", the size of the tabs seems a little fishy to foes, but fans say "the prices are normal for the quality" and the locale off the Champs.

Kambodgia ⓈⒶ SE Asian
▽ 18 | 20 | 16 | €45

16ᵉ | 15, rue de Bassano (Charles de Gaulle-Etoile/George V) | 01 47 23 31 80 | fax 01 47 20 41 22 | www.kambodgia.com

"Reminiscent of an opium den" in its vaguely louche, "dark" decor, this "beautiful" basement offers a chance to sample some of "Southeast Asia's best" cuisines, mainly Cambodian and Vietnamese, with touches of Thai and Laotian; some find the prices for the "highbrow" cooking higher than usual, but most just enjoy the "romantic venue."

Khun Akorn Ⓜ Thai
▽ 19 | 16 | 12 | €39

11ᵉ | 8, av de Taillebourg (Nation) | 01 43 56 20 03 | fax 01 40 09 18 44

"On the edge of the 11th, Bangkok opens its arms to you" at this "authentic" Thai with "pretty", "exotic decor" (regulars "try for the rooftop terrace in summer"); but even those who deem the cuisine "delicious" for its "truly spicy" flavors castigate the servers, who seem so "indifferent" "that we laughed out loud in disbelief."

Kifune Ⓢ Japanese
- | - | - | E

17ᵉ | 44, rue St-Ferdinand (Porte Maillot) | 01 45 72 11 19

So "understated" that surveyors often overlook it, this Japanese in the 17th offers "really good family-style cooking" and sushi amid Asian ambiance; however, it's a real insider's address – which implies "if they don't know you, the welcome can be gruff."

Kim Anh Ⓜ Vietnamese
21 | 16 | 19 | €51

15ᵉ | 51, av Emile Zola (Charles Michels) | 01 45 79 40 96 | fax 01 40 59 49 78

"The menu doesn't change", but since they serve "some of the best Vietnamese cuisine in the city, year in and year out", positives "have no problem" with the "refined food" at this 15th-arrondissement "Zen setting for a romantic date"; "however, it is more expensive than expected", and while "the owners are nice", some dissenters are left "disappointed."

☒ Kinugawa Ⓢ Japanese
25 | 14 | 18 | €73

1ᵉʳ | 9, rue du Mont-Thabor (Tuileries) | 01 42 60 65 07 | fax 01 42 60 45 21

8ᵉ | 4, rue St-Philippe-du-Roule (St-Philippe-du-Roule) | 01 45 63 08 07

www.kinugawa.fr

A sizable Asian clientele persuades many surveyors that this pair of sushi slingers, which also delivers delicate dishes from Kyoto and Tokyo, is "almost as good as what you'll find in Japan" – and certainly among "the best in Paris"; both the "sublime" sashimi and the "excellent" cooked fare are "charmingly served"; "but the prices cut like a samurai's sword", and the "traditional" digs "feel kind of musty."

Kiosque (Le) *Classic French*

14 | 11 | 12 | €43

16ᵉ | 1, pl de Mexico (Trocadéro) | 01 47 27 96 98 | fax 01 45 53 89 79
Despite an original "journalistic" theme – they "offer a daily newspaper with your meal, and the menu simulates a paper as well" – a drop in scores suggests this site is becoming old news; while it's "constantly evolving" with different regional dishes each week, the Classic French menu seems "mundane" and "the sexy servers don't know how to explain the *plats*"; still, "it's always packed in the evening", perhaps because it's "one of the only places in the 16th [that serves] as late as 11 PM."

Kodo ℳ *Japanese/New French*

- | - | - | E

4ᵉ | 29, rue du Bourg-Thibourg (Hôtel-de-Ville) | 01 42 74 45 25
The refined Japanese–New French fusion fare (think lamb maki) served at this stylish table in the Marais may come at a steep price, but that doesn't deter its growing following of regulars, many of whom work in the fashion business; studiously polite service and a handsome brown and brick-toned setting featuring Asian art create a subdued mood.

Kong ● *Eclectic*

14 | 24 | 14 | €49

1ᵉʳ | Pont Neuf Bldg. | 1, rue du Pont-Neuf (Pont-Neuf) |
01 40 39 09 00 | fax 01 40 39 09 10 | www.kong.fr
With an "aquariumlike glass room" boasting "beautiful top-floor views of the Seine" and "high-tech decor", it's definitely all about the eye-candy setting at this Eclectic in the 1st – especially since the "food's uninspired" and it's served by "a young staff with not much experience but a lot of attitude"; it's "a must-go for people under 40" but to fully enjoy, "you better be dressed to the nines, be paper-thin and have the fattest wallet around."

Lac-Hong ⊠ *Vietnamese*

19 | 9 | 13 | €44

16ᵉ | 67, rue Lauriston (Boissière/Victor Hugo) | 01 47 55 87 17
Its service may be "mediocre" and the Asian decor's "getting old", but this "calm" Vietnamese in the 16th still offers "some very flavorsome dishes, such as the steamed fishes"; the savvy "stick to the lunch menu", since going à la carte can be "expensive."

ℤ Ladurée *Classic French/Tearoom*

22 | 23 | 17 | €33

6ᵉ | 21, rue Bonaparte (St-Sulpice) | 01 44 07 64 87 | fax 01 44 07 64 93
8ᵉ | 16, rue Royale (Concorde/Madeleine) | 01 42 60 21 79 |
fax 01 49 27 01 95
8ᵉ | 75, av des Champs-Elysées (George V) | 01 40 75 08 75 |
fax 01 40 75 06 75 ●
9ᵉ | Printemps | 52, bd Haussmann (Havre-Caumartin) |
01 42 82 40 10 | fax 01 42 82 62 00 ⊠
www.laduree.fr
"Exquisite places for both the palate and the eyes", these "upscale tearooms" "provide the most charming break in the day", be it for breakfast, lunch, tea or an early dinner; from "heaven in your mouth" to "devilishly wonderful", the desserts "are individual works of art", but all the Classic French fare is "quite good"; service can get

"Waspish" as the "classically elegant" rooms grow "packed", but one taste of the "truly sinful" *macarons,* and you too will wonder "what's not to love?"

Languedoc (Le) *Southwest* | 19 | 14 | 21 | €30 |

5ᵉ | 64, bd de Port-Royal (Les Gobelins/Glacieres) | 01 47 07 24 47
Apparently "unchanged for 30 years", this "mom-and-pop operation" in the 5th still delights with "dependable" dishes of "authentic Southwestern food", particularly from the namesake region; while the digs are "small enough to have the owner's dog under your legs", the "portions are generous" and the "staff good-humored"; best of all, it's as "reasonable" as it is "reliable."

Lao Siam ● *Thai* | ▽ 23 | 10 | 14 | €28 |

19ᵉ | 49, rue de Belleville (Belleville/Pyrénées) | 01 40 40 09 68 | fax 01 42 03 14 26
"The atmosphere leaves something to be desired" and the "service is so-so", but this Belleville address is still "the place to go for Thai fare", plus some "splendid" Laotian dishes; "get there early or be prepared to wait for a table" – the "cheap" quality eats ensure "it's crowded."

Lao Tseu *Chinese* | 18 | 10 | 18 | €40 |

7ᵉ | 209, bd St-Germain (Rue du Bac) | 01 45 48 30 06 | fax 01 40 59 91 21
"Catering to a posh neighborhood on the maid's night out", this "solid Chinese" in the 7th offers "nicely prepared dishes and friendly, solicitous service"; critics carp about the "Communist Era decor", but "the price is right", making this a Sinophile "standby" for over 20 years.

☑ Lapérouse ⓢ *Haute Cuisine* | 21 | 26 | 21 | €90 |

6ᵉ | 51, quai des Grands-Augustins (Pont-Neuf/St-Michel) | 01 43 26 90 14 | fax 01 43 26 99 39 | www.restaurantlaperouse.com
"In a setting along the Seine", lovers laud this 18th-century 6th-arrondissement address as "one of the most romantic places in the most romantic city in the world", due to its salons "with chaise longues and gilt mirrors" "where you can enjoy a meal in almost full privacy"; the Haute Cuisine "and service do not quite come up to the surroundings", but the former is "quite good", "if unoriginal", and the latter "exceedingly flexible and discreet"; and "if John Galliano likes it, what's not to like?"

☑ Lasserre ⓢ *Haute Cuisine* | 27 | 28 | 27 | €137 |

8ᵉ | 17, av Franklin D. Roosevelt (Franklin D. Roosevelt) | 01 43 59 02 13 | fax 01 45 63 72 23 | www.restaurant-lasserre.com
"Very, very civilized", this bastion of "traditional French Haute Cuisine" in the 8th is still a crowd-pleaser, mainly because it makes a meal a "magical experience"; chef Jean-Louis Nomicos' food is "exquisite (if also exquisitely priced)", the "service hums like a finely tuned engine" and when the "gorgeous" "dining room ceiling is opened to the star-lit sky, it just doesn't get any more romantic"; P.S. "gentlemen, don't forget your jackets."

	FOOD	DECOR	SERVICE	COST

Laurent ☒ *Haute Cuisine* — 24 | 26 | 23 | €125

8e | 41, av Gabriel (Champs-Elysées-Clémenceau) | 01 42 25 00 39 |
fax 01 45 62 45 21 | www.le-laurent.com

"In a magnificent garden right next to the Champs", this "elegant"
Haute Cuisine establishment holds sway; while "preferable in summer for its outdoor terrace", it's always "exceptional", with its "excellent" if "traditional" fare and "discreet, well-behaved" (though
slightly "stuffy") staff; it's "worth the cost" even if "you may have to
sell off a few T-bonds to pay the bill – or else you can do as many of
the other high-powered patrons do and order the prix fixe menu,
available at both lunch and dinner."

Lavinia ☒ *Classic French* — 17 | 14 | 17 | €41

1er | 3-5, bd de la Madeleine (Madeleine) | 01 42 97 20 20 |
fax 01 42 97 54 50 | www.lavinia.fr

"Just steps from the Madeleine", "plunge into a universe of wine" at
this "impressive" store – 6,500 labels, baby – with an "open" eatery
on its mezzanine (redone recently in varietal reds); while "good",
the Classic French fare is "a little pricey for what it is, considering
the wait time before getting served", but "who cares about the food
or service – what you care about here is the vino"; best of all, "any
bottle in the shop is available in the restaurant at the retail price";
P.S. "lunch only" (sandwiches until 8 PM).

Legrand Filles et Fils ☒ *Wine Bar/Bistro* — - | - | - | M

2e | Galerie Vivienne | 1, rue de la Banque (Bourse/Palais Royal) |
01 42 60 07 12 | fax 01 42 61 25 51 | www.caves-legrand.com

"Don't tell everyone – this is still a reasonably well-kept secret"
plead patrons of this *bar à vins*, "a great little place for a quick snack
and a glass of one of the truly outstanding wines served by the legendary shop" Caves Legrand; "sitting at this casual spot, you know
you are in Paris", since it's located "in one of the city's most beautiful" arcades, the glass-roofed Galerie Vivienne.

Lei Ⓜ *Italian* — 18 | 17 | 18 | €47

7e | 17, av de la Motte-Picquet (Ecole Militaire/La Tour-Maubourg) |
01 47 05 07 37

"The 7th arrondissement meets Milan" at this stripped-down "modern space" near Ecole Militaire; this is "not your average Italian
eatery – the dramatic decor is as posh as the clientele, investment
bankers with their diamond-studded wives or mistresses" or
"young" show biz types; the "simple cooking is tasty" and the "service is professional", but views vary on the prices: some moan about
the "*mezzo forte* check" and others applaud the "affordable" tab.

Léon de Bruxelles *Belgian* — 15 | 11 | 14 | €26

1er | 120, rue Rambuteau (Les Halles) | 01 42 36 18 50 | fax 01 42 36 27 50
4e | 3, bd Beaumarchais (Bastille) | 01 42 71 70 55 | fax 01 42 71 75 56 ☽
6e | 131, bd St-Germain (Mabillon/Odéon) | 01 43 26 45 95 |
fax 01 43 26 47 02 ☽
8e | 63, av des Champs-Elysées (Franklin D. Roosevelt/George V) |
01 42 25 96 16 | fax 01 42 25 95 42 ☽

(continued)

Léon de Bruxelles

9e | 1-3, pl Pigalle (Pigalle) | 01 42 80 28 33 | fax 01 42 80 27 72 ◑
9e | 8, pl de Clichy (Pl de Clichy) | 01 48 74 00 43
11e | 8, pl de la République (République) | 01 43 38 28 69 |
fax 01 43 38 33 41 ◑
13e | 64, av des Gobelins (Les Gobelins/Place d'Italie) |
01 47 07 51 07 | fax 01 47 07 89 04
14e | 82 bis, bd du Montparnasse (Edgar Quinet/Montparnasse-
Bienvenüe) | 01 43 21 66 62 | fax 01 43 21 66 76 ◑
17e | 95, bd Gouvion-St-Cyr (Porte Maillot) | 01 55 37 95 30 |
fax 01 55 37 95 35 ◑
www.leon-de-bruxelles.fr

"All mussels, all the time" is the mantra at this "bright, bustling" bevy
of Belgians that bring out bucketfuls of bivalves, "lots of beer" and "all-
you-can-eat frites"; "the service is indifferent and the decor far from
inspiring" (unless you like that "plastic-y" "family restaurant look"),
but "for what it is, a cheap chain with a theme, it's not bad at all."

Lescure ⊠ *Bistro*   16 | 13 | 16 | €32

1er | 7, rue de Mondovi (Concorde) | 01 42 60 18 91
Unless "you're shy, it's impossible not to enjoy yourself with a variety
of strangers, both local and tourist, when you're packed in family-
style" at this 1st-arrondissement "hole-in-the-wall" with rustic decor (is that "garlic and onions hanging from the ceiling"?); it's been
serving the same "tried-and-trusted French bistro fare" since 1919
at a "remarkable value"; yes, it's "too small, too loud and the food's
average – but it's absolutely charming" anyway.

Les Saveurs de Flora ⊠ *New French*   22 | 18 | 20 | €76

8e | 36, av George V (George V) | 01 40 70 10 49 | fax 01 47 20 52 87 |
www.lessaveursdeflora.com

"Wallpapered and cozy, like the house of somebody" with "simple
but sophisticated" taste, this "outpost of über-creative chef-owner
Flora Mikula" is "always a pleasure" for its "delightful" New French
cuisine, "efficient servers" and "model-filled" clientele (it's "the
perfect place for eavesdropping on discussions of the relative merits
of Cartier over Rolex"); not cheap, but the "prix fixe is a bargain for
the gourmet fare and upscale location" in the 8th.

Libre Sens ◑ *New French*   ▽ 16 | 19 | 12 | €54

8e | 33, rue Marbeuf (Franklin D. Roosevelt) | 01 53 96 00 72 |
fax 01 53 96 00 84

Divided into distinct spaces, including a psychedelic-'70s cognac bar
and a room with a white bed for elongated dining, this aspiringly
trendy lounge/eatery just off the Champs doesn't lack for "original" atmosphere; but if fans find the New French food "unexpectedly good",
detractors deplore the "dreadful service" when "it's crowded."

Lina's ⊠ *Sandwiches*   15 | 9 | 12 | €16

2e | 50, rue Etienne Marcel (Bourse/Etienne Marcel) |
01 42 21 16 14 | fax 01 42 33 78 03

(continued)

(continued)

Lina's

7ᵉ | 22, rue des Sts-Pères (St-Germain-des-Prés) | 01 40 20 42 78 | fax 01 40 20 42 79
8ᵉ | 61, rue Charon (Franklin D. Roosevelt/George V) | 01 42 25 34 24 | fax 01 42 25 34 25
8ᵉ | 8, rue Marbeuf (Alma Marceau) | 01 46 23 04 63 | fax 01 47 23 93 09
9ᵉ | 30, bd des Italiens (Opéra/Richelieu-Drouot) | 01 42 46 02 06 | fax 01 42 46 02 40
12ᵉ | 102, rue de Bercy (Bercy) | 01 43 40 42 42 | fax 01 43 40 65 11
17ᵉ | 23, av de Wagram (Charles de Gaulle-Etoile/Ternes) | 01 45 74 76 76 | fax 01 45 74 76 77
Neuilly-sur-Seine | 156, av Charles de Gaulle (Pont-de-Neuilly) | 01 47 45 60 60 | fax 01 47 45 34 68
www.linascafe.fr

"While shopping and schlepping", this string of "American-style sandwich/salad shops" makes a "good pit stop", offering "simple, dependable" "fast food with a human face"; but cynics say it's "not super-exciting" and warn "watch out – all of the extras add up", so that a seemingly "affordable" meal can turn "surprisingly expensive."

Liza *Lebanese* — | — | — | M

2ᵉ | 14, rue de la Banque (Bourse) | 01 55 35 00 66 | fax 01 40 15 04 60 | www.restaurant-liza.com

"Sweet service" and "Lebanese food from the heart prevent this trendy spot from being snobbish" say surveyors of this site in the 2nd; its "innovative" cuisine that's "a long way from the usual meze" and its "refined, pretty decor" and tableware cause converts to cry "be sure to check it out – before the word is out."

Loir dans la Théière (Le) *Dessert/Tearoom* 18 | 18 | 16 | €21

4ᵉ | 3, rue des Rosiers (St-Paul) | 01 42 72 90 61

"The most relaxed tea salon in Paris" is "a favorite for tête-à-têtes and tasting treats" in a "comfortable, funky" "shabby-chic" atmosphere that epitomizes the Marais' "bohemian ambiance"; it's a "sure value", and if the "friendly service" can get "lazy", that only makes it "perfect for long conversation with friends."

Lô Sushi ● *Japanese* 14 | 16 | 13 | €38

8ᵉ | 8, rue de Berri (Franklin D. Roosevelt/George V) | 01 45 62 01 00 | fax 01 45 62 01 10 | www.losushi.com

Fans of "sushi on the fly" can "watch the chefs preparing dishes and sending them down the conveyor belt along the edge of the counter-top seating" at this "temple of techno-Zen" in the 8th, which boasts "TVs to keep you entertained"; while "inventive", the rolls are only "remotely Japanese", and "expensive", given they're "not the best"; still, they're "quite popular, especially with the lunch crowd."

Louchebem (Le) ●Ⓢ *Steak*  ▽ 14 | 14 | 9 | €31

1ᵉʳ | 31, rue Berger (Châtelet) | 01 42 33 12 99 | fax 01 40 28 45 50 | www.le-louchebem.fr

With "a pretty view of the church of Saint-Eustache" (focus on that, because "the interior is design-challenged"), this "butcher's shop-turned-restaurant" "is a place to go for grills and [old] Les Halles ambiance"; "fine dining it ain't, but if you're not too proud to queue for a table, there's nothing pretentious about the excellent-value steaks."

Louis Vin (Le) ⇄ Wine Bar/Bistro
-	-	-	M

5ᵉ | 9, rue de la Montagne Ste-Genevieve (Maubert-Mutualité) | 01 43 29 12 12 | fax 01 43 29 12 20 | www.fifi.fr

A "detailed wine list complements the *plats*" at this "roomy" *bistrot à vins* in the Latin Quarter; the "basic" but "well-prepared" food (clearly there's "someone with pride in the kitchen"), "surprisingly attentive attendants" and "reasonable prices" ensure "this secret won't be kept for long."

Lozère (La) Auvergne
18	13	17	€38

6ᵉ | 4, rue Hautefeuille (St-Michel) | 01 43 54 26 64 | fax 01 43 54 55 66 | www.lozere-a-paris.com

"Simple", "delicious cuisine from a lesser-known region" – Lozère in the south – delights reviewers who are into "robust" eats and "rustic" scenes; "now that everyone knows about it", its "narrow" quarters get "crowded" ("reservations are a must") but it's "in a convenient location" in the 6th, and "what's more, it's not expensive"; P.S. "the Thursday night special is a great treat" – a creamy, cheesy mashed potato dish, *aligot*.

Luna (La) ✆ Seafood
24	17	18	€63

8ᵉ | 69, rue du Rocher (Villiers/Europe) | 01 42 93 77 61 | fax 01 40 08 02 44

Seafood-loving surveyors proclaim this small site behind the Gare Saint-Lazare "one of the best for fish in Paris" – plus a "*baba au rhum* that can't be beat"; all's "expertly prepared" and served, but wallet-watchers wail "for these prices, they can afford to improve the decor" a bit – though others find the gray-and-red-toned digs "pretty enough."

⌾ Lyonnais (Aux) ✆ Lyon
22	20	20	€53

2ᵉ | 32, rue St-Marc (Bourse/Richelieu-Drouot) | 01 42 96 65 04 | fax 01 42 97 42 95 | www.alain-ducasse.com

With its 1900 "classic white-tile interior" intact, this "amazing old bistro" in the 2nd is "like going to Lyon and never leaving Paris", as the "hearty" "food reflects the spirit" of that Rhône Valley *ville*; since it was "refreshed by Alain Ducasse" and Thierry de la Brosse a while back, "you'll be lucky to get a table here, and the staff will remind you of that" cavil critics who also snap it's "too cramped for what they charge"; but to most, the "noisy, crowded conditions" just contribute to the charm.

Ma Bourgogne ◐⇄ Burgundy
17	16	14	€40

4ᵉ | 19, pl des Vosges (Bastille/St-Paul) | 01 42 78 44 64 | fax 01 42 78 19 37

"Even by Paris standards, the setting under the arches of the Place des Vosges is unique", which is why this "bistro is a must" "on beautiful days"; be advised, though, that the "service is brusque" and the "simply good, not exceptional" Burgundian–Classic French "food is

| | FOOD | DECOR | SERVICE | COST |

heavy in the warmer months" (the key time to go); so some say it's "best for a coffee and croissant" before "the crowds make it crazy."

Macéo ⧄ Classic/New French
21 | 19 | 20 | €52

1er | 15, rue des Petits-Champs (Bourse/Palais Royal-Musée du Louvre) | 01 42 97 53 85 | fax 01 47 03 36 93 | www.maceorestaurant.com

"Run by Mark Williamson of Willi's Wine Bar", this more formal eatery behind the Palais Royal offers an "agreeable", "interesting" combination of Classic and New French flavors, plus a "good vegetarian menu for those looking" and, of course, a "handpicked wine list that can't be beat"; "happy, helpful waiters" wander the wood-paneled, "bright, spacious" setting, with "tables set apart enough for real conversation."

Magnolias (Les) ⧄ Ⓜ New French
22 | 17 | 21 | €68

Perreux-sur-Marne | 48, av de Bry (RER Nogent-le-Perreux, Ligne E) | 01 48 72 47 43 | fax 01 48 72 22 28 | www.lesmagnolias.com

"If you want to see the future of *la cuisine française*", "it's worth taking the RER train" to suburban Perreux-sur-Marne to sample the "creative", "original, even experimental" cooking of chef Jean Chauvel, who runs this "chic, somber" New French with his wife and an "attentive, if slightly mannered" staff; foes carp the fare's now too "complicated" and the place isn't cheap, but supporters sigh "when you're in love, you don't count" the cost.

Maharajah (Le) ● Indian
▽ 16 | 15 | 16 | €30

5e | 72, bd St-Germain (Maubert-Mutualité/St-Michel) | 01 43 54 26 07 | fax 01 40 46 08 18 | www.maharajah.fr

After 40 years, this "French-style (i.e. mild)" subcontinental is still a Saint-Germain stalwart for Northern Indian fare that, although "less spicy than you'd find in the U.S.", remains reasonably "authentic" and "a good value"; the dining room looks a bit "cheesy", but "friendly English-speaking waiters" curry favor with the crowd, and it's a better option than the "touristy joints and teenager-filled Internet cafes" that dominate the Latin Quarter.

Main d'Or (La) ● Corsica
▽ 21 | 14 | 18 | €39

11e | 133, rue du Faubourg St-Antoine (Ledru-Rollin) | 01 44 68 04 68 | fax 01 44 68 04 68

"A pleasant surprise in an out-of-the-way spot" sums up this "spicily marvelous", "authentic Corsican" near the Bastille; the personnel's "very solicititous" too, so that even if this millstone-and-wrought-iron dining room is a little spartan, a meal here is a guaranteed good time, especially given the easygoing prices.

Maison Blanche Haute Cuisine
19 | 24 | 17 | €92

8e | 15, av Montaigne (Alma Marceau) | 01 47 23 55 99 | fax 01 47 20 09 56 | www.maison-blanche.fr

To fit in with "the 'in' people", "wear black" at this "very white and chrome" Haute Cuisine "hot spot" "atop the Théâtre des Champs-Elysées"; all adore the "killer view" of Les Invalides, the Eiffel Tower and "the shimmering Seine"; but many maintain "the room promises so much more than the food and the service actually offer" – though clients are expected to deliver big when the bill comes.

Maison Courtine (La) ▣ *Southwest*

| 21 | 15 | 17 | €57 |

14ᵉ | 157, av du Maine (Mouton-Duvernet) | 01 45 43 08 04 |
fax 01 45 45 91 35

Putting an "inventive" spin on Southwestern classics, this "small, chef-owned establishment" in Montparnasse has "an interesting variety of offerings" ("if duck is your thing, you can't go wrong here"), served in a dining room dominated by decorative birds; but service ranges from "soigné" to "somewhat cursory", and it's "a bit pricey" too.

Maison de l'Amérique Latine ▣ *Classic French*

| 17 | 25 | 17 | €57 |

7ᵉ | 217, bd St-Germain (Solférino) | 01 49 54 75 10 | fax 01 40 49 03 94 | www.mal217.org

"The most beautiful place you can bring a date in Paris, period" reveal romancers about this "surprise in the 7th", a cultural center with an "idyllic" outdoor terrace; "but don't bother if the garden out back is closed", because the interior "room's a little sad", and the Classic French fare a bit "banal"; P.S. to get at the greenery you should "book a week in advance" at least.

Maison du Caviar (La) ● *Russian*

| 21 | 13 | 19 | €87 |

8ᵉ | 21, rue Quentin-Bauchart (George V) | 01 47 23 53 43 |
fax 01 47 20 87 26 | www.caviar-volga.com

"Good caviar and even better vodka" make an unbeatable combination at this luxurious Russian in the silk-stocking 8th arrondissement; it's a "bustling scene with global socialites" dining on "decadent meals" that include Soviet specialties and an "excellent crab salad"; perhaps the vaguely art deco decor could use "rethinking", but ambiance enough is provided by all the beautiful "people putting on a show"; as to price – well, that depends "on how much caviar you consume."

Maison du Jardin (La) ▣ *Bistro*

| 22 | 18 | 21 | €39 |

6ᵉ | 27, rue de Vaugirard (Rennes/St-Placide) | 01 45 48 22 31 |
fax 01 45 48 22 31

"A hidden treasure" "snuggled into a side street" "near the Luxembourg Gardens", this "understatedly elegant" bistro by the owners of La Ferme St-Simon sports "warm colors", a look that flatters the "imaginative" New French food (i.e. cod with cardamom-flavored sauce, blueberry crème brûlée); "amiable service" ensures it's a "real charmer", frequented mainly by the local bourgeoisie who know an "unbeatable" value when they eat one.

Maison Prunier ▣ *Seafood*

| 22 | 23 | 21 | €90 |

16ᵉ | 16, av Victor Hugo (Charles de Gaulle-Etoile) | 01 44 17 35 85 | fax 01 44 17 90 10 | www.prunier.com

With an art deco "cruise liner–like" look in one room and a gilded Czarist setting an another, "the decor is a national treasure", literally, at this veteran den of "decadence" in the 16th known for "positively sublime" smoked salmon and caviar, plus "fish dishes, both traditional and new"; the service is "deft and helpful" too; some wonder "if it's worth the price", but most are delighted by this remnant of "dazzling" days gone by.

Mandala Ray ◐ Ø *Eclectic*

	FOOD	DECOR	SERVICE	COST
	15	24	14	€59

8ᵉ | 34, rue Marbeuf (Franklin D. Roosevelt) | 01 56 88 36 36 |
fax 01 42 25 36 36 | www.mandalaray.com

"Hypnotic techno music" is "spun by the DJ upstairs, the dining's downstairs" and the crowd, "comprised of fabulous 18-to-22-year-olds and the men who love them", rocks on at this movie star-backed, "Franco-Asian chic" club in the 8th; the "dark, cool" decor still delights, but most say "don't waste money on the Eclectic food" – "this is for liquids only", preferably the "happy-hour delicious cocktails"; as per "lounge expectations", the "staff is too cool to be friendly."

Mandalay (Le) Ø *Eclectic*

FOOD	DECOR	SERVICE	COST
-	-	-	M

Levallois-Perret | 35, rue Carnot (Anatole France/Louise Michel) |
01 47 57 68 69 | fax 01 40 89 05 76

Chef-owner Guy Guenego's Eclectic "exotic cuisine, full of flavors and fragrances" from around the world, makes this modest place worth the trek to quiet suburban Levallois-Perret; the tables are a tad "tight" in the colorful dining room with "ethnic decor", but the "welcome is warm" and the prices are reasonable.

Mandarin de Neuilly Ø *Chinese*

FOOD	DECOR	SERVICE	COST
-	-	-	M

Neuilly-sur-Seine | 148, av Charles de Gaulle (Pont-de-Neuilly) |
01 46 24 11 80

This "nice neighborhood place" in Neuilly gets nods for "traditional" Chinese cooking that's generally "well executed" (sometimes "the deep-frying is a little too deep"); local mandarins also appreciate the "prompt service" and "constantly cordial owner", but remain mysteriously mum on the decor.

Mansouria Ø *Moroccan*

FOOD	DECOR	SERVICE	COST
19	17	15	€43

11ᵉ | 11, rue Faidherbe (Faidherbe-Chaligny) | 01 43 71 00 16 |
fax 01 40 24 21 97

"Authentic" is the name of the game at this "well-known classic" for Moroccan food in the 11th, run by the formidable Fatéma Hal, a passionate ambassador of her native country's cuisine; sitting on "comfortable cushions", clients get "carried away" to the Maghreb with such specialties as "varied, fragrant couscous" and a 12th-century lamb dish with 27 spices called *mourouzia*.

Marc Annibal de Coconnas M *Classic French*

FOOD	DECOR	SERVICE	COST
17	16	17	€56

4ᵉ | 2 bis, pl des Vosges (Bastille/St-Paul) | 01 42 78 58 16 |
fax 01 42 78 16 28 | www.tourdargent.fr

The King's three musketeers still haunt this "romantic restaurant on the Place des Vosges", which is "putting more effort into" the fancier Classic French specialties; critics carp about the "tight quarters" and "boring decor" and say it's gotten "too expensive for the mediocre food"; but swashbucklers swear by the "remarkable environment", "especially in summer on the terrace."

		FOOD	DECOR	SERVICE	COST

☑ Marée (La) 🅱 *Seafood*   25 | 17 | 21 | €102

8ᵉ | 1, rue Daru (Ternes/Courcelles) | 01 43 80 20 00 |
fax 01 48 88 04 04 | www.lamaree.fr

For more than 40 years this "haute" seafooder in the 8th has hooked
politicians and other big *poissons* with "fish of the highest quality",
prepared in both classic and "inventive" ways, "and incredible desserts"; with "professional service" and an "elegant" setting of
Flemish paintings and stained-glass windows, it is "expensive – and
worth it"; N.B. its recent acquisition by the Frères Blanc group may
outdate the scores.

Marée de Versailles (La) 🅱Ⓜ *Seafood*   21 | 20 | 19 | €41

Versailles | 22, rue au Pain (RER Versailles-Rive Droite) | 01 30 21 73 73 |
fax 01 39 49 98 29 | wwww.restaurantlamaree.com

Designed to look like a wood-paneled yacht moored in tony Versailles,
this "delightful spot" facing the town market specializes in "fresh",
luxury-level seafood (notably lobster), served by an "attentive
staff"; there's also "nice outdoor eating on the square", free from
the "mobs of tourists" storming the château.

Mariage Frères *Dessert/Tearoom*   21 | 22 | 20 | €30

4ᵉ | 30, rue du Bourg-Tibourg (Hôtel-de-Ville) | 01 42 72 28 11 |
fax 01 42 74 51 68
6ᵉ | 13, rue des Grands-Augustins (St-Michel) | 01 40 51 82 50 |
fax 01 44 07 07 52
8ᵉ | 260, rue du Faubourg St-Honoré (Ternes) | 01 46 22 18 54 |
fax 01 42 67 18 54
www.mariagefreres.com

A "temple of tea" with three "shrines" in the city, this "divine time
warp" has a "colonial ambiance" "straight out of the movie *Indochine*" –
right down to the "solicitous" waiters "in spotless white jackets";
even the "couture prices" don't deter the lines at the door for "refined" lunches and brunch, "heavenly" cakes and an "extraordinary
selection" of brews "from the far reaches of the world" with "heady
aromas" and "names that make you dream."

Marius 🅱 *Seafood*   20 | 14 | 17 | €66

16ᵉ | 82, bd Murat (Porte de St-Cloud) | 01 46 51 67 80 |
fax 01 40 71 83 75

Its "regular" clientele of "locals" from the 16th ensures this "classic"
seafooder is "always almost full"; for nigh on 18 years it's reeled 'em
in with "delicious" shellfish of "exceptional freshness" and a whale
of a bouillabaisse; customers also commend the "affordable" prices
and "agreeable terrace in summer."

Marius et Janette ◑ *Seafood*   21 | 15 | 16 | €80

8ᵉ | 4, av George V (Alma Marceau) | 01 47 23 84 36 | fax 01 47 23 07 19

"Those who want to breathe salty ocean air just have to board at the
Port d'Alma", where *le tout Paris* comes for "seafood so fresh it almost swims on your plate", "executed beautifully" in "elaborate" or
"simple preparations"; giving the "impression that you're on a boat",
the "decor is either classic or tired, depending on your point of

view" – though the "crowded tables" and "noisy, smoky" ambiance make some wish for fewer seafarers ("the busy staff is not always able to cope").

Market ◐ *Eclectic* | 20 | 22 | 16 | €70 |
8ᵉ | 15, av Matignon (Champs-Elysées-Clémenceau) | 01 56 43 40 90 | fax 01 43 59 10 87 | www.jean-georges.com

"Paris' Golden Triangle meets New York" at celebrity chef-restaurateur Jean-Georges Vongerichten's venture in the 8th, a "sleek and chic" destination; while a few snap it's "more of a status restaurant than the real thing", most savor the "sophisticated" Eclectic eats (truffle pizza, crème fraîche cheesecake) that "taste as exciting as they look"; "the only thing to distract you from the food is the clientele", since "all the lovely young things" come here "to be seen" – unlike the staff, which is "often MIA."

Marlotte (La) ⊠ *Classic French* | 20 | 16 | 17 | €46 |
6ᵉ | 55, rue du Cherche-Midi (Sèvres-Babylone/St-Placide) | 01 45 48 86 79 | fax 01 45 44 34 80 | www.lamarlotte.com

Literati, politicos, humorists and tourists from the area around the Bon Marché store "really like" this "neighborhood place" with its rustic country-inn decor; it's partly the "very Classic French" "family-style cooking" at "reasonable" prices, but also because they "don't feel like visitors" here – "each diner is treated as special."

Martel (Le) ◐⊠ *Classic French/Moroccan* ∇ | 16 | 15 | 14 | €42 |
10ᵉ | 3, rue Martel (Château d'Eau) | 01 47 70 67 56

"Hang with the fashionistas" at the "hippest couscous joint in the city", where owner Mehdi Gana, formerly a waiter at Chez Omar, has created a "great" hideaway "for non-dieting Parisians with a sense of style" in the shabby-chic 10th; the menu includes both Moroccan mainstays and simple Classic French fare, and the "cool" 1900 bistro decor has soft lighting to flatter all the beautiful people.

Marty *Brasserie* | 17 | 18 | 17 | €50 |
5ᵉ | 20, av des Gobelins (Les Gobelins) | 01 43 31 39 51 | fax 01 43 37 63 70 | www.marty-restaurant.com

"Finally, a brasserie that's a little different" say patrons of this "jo-vial" family business, opened in the 5th in 1913 and now run by the founders' granddaughter; she's created a "chic" art deco setting where reproductions of paintings by Picasso and Erté hang on the walls, while her chef creates "flavorful" dishes to accompany the enticing seafood; however, hostiles hiss at the "highish prices" for "smallish portions."

Mascotte (La) ◐ *Auvergne* | – | – | – | M |
18ᵉ | 52, rue des Abbesses (Abbesses/Blanche) | 01 46 06 28 15 | fax 01 42 23 93 83 | www.la-mascotte-montmartre.com

Those in search of a "typical Montmartre place" find it at this "old Rue des Abbesses institution", an art deco–style brasserie where lo-cals dig into "superlative oysters" and "fine" Auvergnat fare "with appropriate accompanying alcohols"; "ambiance is guaranteed on

Sundays", especially when a local accordionist gets things swinging in the bar.

Mathusalem (Le) 🗷 *Bistro* ▽ 14 | 11 | 14 | €35

16ᵉ | 5 bis, bd Exelmans (Exelmans) | 01 42 88 10 73 |
fax 01 42 88 42 43 | www.restaurant-mathusalem.com

Habitués raise their glass to this "casual", "unpretentious" neighborhood bistro whose name refers to a six-liter champagne bottle; located in a "slightly orphaned" part of the 16th, at lunch it's "packed with media people" from nearby France Télévision, who say this is "one of the best buys in the area" for "typical" "filling" Classic French fare and ever-"smiley service."

Matsuri *Japanese* 12 | 13 | 13 | €34

1ᵉʳ | 36, rue de Richelieu (Pyramides) | 01 42 61 05 73 |
fax 01 42 96 60 64 🗷
16ᵉ | 2-4, rue de Passy (Passy) | 01 42 24 96 85 | fax 01 42 24 14 54
Neuilly-sur-Seine | Tour Coeur Défense | 70, Esplanade Charles de Gaulle (La Défense) | 01 49 01 27 09
www.matsuri.fr

"Instant sushi gratification" is on offer 365 days a year at this "convivial" chain where the Japanese specialties constantly circle "on a conveyor belt"; it's "practical at lunch", given the guarantee of "extremely fast service from the parading plates"; but skeptics sneer at the "worn-out gimmick", saying the morsels taste "machine-made."

Maupertu (Le) 🗷 *Classic French* 20 | 17 | 21 | €40

7ᵉ | 94, bd de la Tour-Maubourg (Ecole Militaire/La Tour-Maubourg) |
01 45 51 37 96 | fax 01 53 59 94 83 | www.restaurant-maupertu-paris.com

It may be surprising to find this "little charmer" in such an aristocratic area of town "opposite Napoleon's tomb", but those in-the-know say it's a "never-miss" both for its "pleasant" Provence-inspired Classic French food (a "fantastic value") and its "warm", "bilingual" proprietors; there's a new raspberry-hued and Wenge wood decor (unreflected in the score), but it's hard to compete with the "superb" view of the "lighted Invalides dome", especially when out on the "wonderful terrace."

Mauzac (Le) 🗷 *Wine Bar/Bistro* - | - | - | E

5ᵉ | 7, rue de l'Abbé de l'Epée (Luxembourg) | 01 46 33 75 22 |
fax 01 46 33 25 46 | www.lemauzac.com

A zinc bar sculpted with bunches of grapes signals that this inviting spot near the Luxembourg Gardens is serious about wine, with a "very fine list" from independent French producers and 30 vintages by the glass; the kitchen turns out a "limited menu" of traditional bistro food too, though curmudgeons complain the eats are simply "adequate."

Mavrommatis 🗷 *Greek* 22 | 15 | 17 | €50

5ᵉ | 42, rue Daubenton (Censier-Daubenton) | 01 43 31 17 17 |
fax 01 43 36 13 08 | www.mavrommatis.fr

"Best food this side of Athens" say surveyors who sail into this "grand Greek" in the Latin Quarter for "novel" dishes from the archipelago, along with "warm" service and a lovely "flowered terrace";

it's "not cheap but the price is justified" for a feast that could launch a thousand ships; N.B. the same Cypriot owners operate the more casual Les Délices d'Aphrodite nearby.

	FOOD	DECOR	SERVICE	COST

Maxan (Le) 🛇 *Haute Cuisine* | - | - | - | E |

8ᵉ | 37, rue de Miromesnil (Miromesnil) | 01 42 65 78 60 | fax 01 49 24 96 17 | www.rest-maxan.com

Young chef Laurent Zajac, who sharpened his skills with Alain Dutournier (Carré des Feuillants) and Gérard Vié (Les Trois Marches), goes it alone with this small but "chic" table "in a ritzy neighborhood" near the Faubourg Saint-Honoré; the elegant, ultra-minimalist setting allows foodies to concentrate on the inventive Haute Cuisine, and already admirers affirm this address is "expensive, but a treat."

Maxim's 🛇 🅼 *Classic French* | 20 | 24 | 20 | €94 |

8ᵉ | 3, rue Royale (Concorde/Madeleine) | 01 42 65 27 94 | fax 01 42 65 30 26 | www.maxims-de-paris.com

"It would be a shame not to go at least once" to this "bygone restaurant of a bygone era" in the 8th that lives on under the ownership of another "monument", designer Pierre Cardin; "it's worth the trip just to see the sumptuous belle epoque decor", and though the Classic French "food does not hit the top notes", it's "decent", even "delicious"; so maybe "the crowds and the elegance are gone", but where else would you ever get the "surreal experience of dining in an empty room with an entire brigade to serve you."

Meating *Steak* | ▽ 19 | 17 | 19 | €68 |

17ᵉ | 122, av de Villiers (Péreire) | 01 43 80 10 10 | fax 01 43 80 31 42

Taking up residence in Apicius' old digs in the 17th, this posh meating and meeting house offers Black Angus beef that, most say, is "masterfully cooked" in an "American broiler-oven"; but other aspects of its "New York style" draw scorn – specifically, the fact that "side dishes cost extra", "elevating" the tabs.

Méditerranée (La) *Classic French* | 19 | 19 | 18 | €56 |

6ᵉ | 2, pl de l'Odéon (Odéon) | 01 43 26 02 30 | fax 01 43 26 18 44 | www.la-mediterranee.com

"The Mediterranean exists in Paris, virtually at least", on the Place de l'Odéon where this Classic French, opened in 1944, has long netted a "superb clientele" for "fine" *cuisine de la mer*, such as "bouillabaisse that sets the standard"; "at lunch hour the sunlight adds to the charm" of the "delightful setting" that features "Cocteau designs and mermaid lamps", which compensates for the "erratic service."

Mesturet (Le) 🛇 *Southwest* | - | - | - | M |

2ᵉ | 77, rue de Richelieu (Bourse) | 01 42 97 40 68 | fax 01 42 97 40 68 | www.lemesturet.com

Steps from the old Paris stock exchange, this classic cafe offers "very good" value for any portfolio, its Southwestern dishes made with high-quality regional products sourced by the owner; it gets "noisy" at noon, but the service remains "affable" through bull market and bear, and the modest prices boast a strong buy recommendation.

	FOOD	DECOR	SERVICE	COST

Z Meurice (Le) *S* *Haute Cuisine* 26 28 25 €141

1er | Hôtel Meurice | 228, rue de Rivoli (Concorde/Tuileries) | 01 44 58 10 55 | fax 01 44 58 10 76 | www.meuricehotel.com

In the 1st, "one of the most beautiful dining rooms in Paris" is the setting for one of the "best meals in town" fawn fans of the "remark-able" Yannick Alléno's "highly inventive" Haute Cuisine, delivered by waiters who treat patrons "like royalty" amid the "gorgeous" marbled, mirrored and mosaic room that "screams opulence"; "considering the decor, food and service, this is a bargain", but "if you're on a budget", "the terrific lounge is half the price for the same chef's" cuisine.

Z Michel Rostang *S* *New French* 27 23 26 €141

17e | 20, rue Rennequin (Péreire/Ternes) | 01 47 63 40 77 | fax 01 47 63 82 75 | www.michelrostang.com

Surveyors "swoon" over "dishes that sparkle with taste" by this "grand chef"-owner whose New French in the 17th is "one of the best in Paris" (especially in winter, when it becomes "a truffle lover's paradise"), enhanced by a "serious wine list" and "superb somme-lier"; the wood-paneled, "rich setting" seems "grandmotherly" to some, but others feel "right at home", thanks to "flawlessly graceful service", and devotees declare that "coming back each time is like putting on a warm glove."

Mirama *Chinese* 16 6 10 €26

5e | 17, rue St-Jacques (Maubert-Mutualité/St-Michel) | 01 43 54 71 77 | fax 01 43 25 37 63

The "long lines of people waiting to get in" are a guarantee of "authenticity" at this Latin Quarter Chinese where a faithful follow-ing is hooked on "basic" but "delicious" dishes; nevertheless, nay-sayers are not sure whether it's worth the "unfriendly service" and "super-cramped" digs.

Moissonnier *S* *M* *Lyon* 22 12 20 €52

5e | 28, rue des Fossés St-Bernard (Cardinal Lemoine/Jussieu) | 01 43 29 87 65 | fax 01 43 29 87 65

This "longstanding" Latin Quarter Lyonnais is so "reliable" "there's doubt you'd find any better in Lyon" itself – or so believe boosters of this bistro and its "efficient but discreet servers"; the "unpreten-tious" "decor doesn't detract" from the "impeccably prepared tradi-tional cuisine", some of whose specialties (such as tripe) are admittedly "an acquired taste – but worth acquiring."

Monsieur Lapin *M* *Classic French* 20 18 20 €48

14e | 11, rue Raymond Losserand (Gaîté/Pernety) | 01 43 20 21 39 | fax 01 43 21 84 86 | www.mousier-lapin.fr

"You've got to like rabbit" if you're going to eat at this Montparnasse mainstay whose menu has a fair share of hare; *lapin* lovers say it's "worth hopping across town" for the "lovely" Classic French food and the staff's "gentle *politesse*", even if the "bunny decor" is a bit "over the top" for some tastes; N.B. it changed owners recently, but the theme remains the same.

	FOOD	DECOR	SERVICE	COST

Montalembert (Le) *New French*
17 | 20 | 19 | €62

7ᵉ | Hôtel Montalembert | 3, rue de Montalembert (Rue du Bac) | 01 45 49 68 03 | fax 01 45 49 69 49 | www.montalembert.com

"The crowd is as chic as it gets" in this "cool" eatery with an "elegant and modern" "minimalist environment" in a Left Bank boutique hotel; the New French cuisine's also "a little chichi" for critics, but others insist its "tableau of colors, shapes and textures" is "better than you'd expect", and the service is "quite receptive" – especially if you're "young, thin and dress in black"; N.B. the advent of a new management team post-Survey may outdate the scores.

Mont Liban (Le) *Lebanese*
– | – | – | M

17ᵉ | 42, bd des Batignolles (Rome) | 01 45 22 35 01 | fax 01 43 87 04 59

Meze maniacs find "delicious" morsels "at bargain prices" in this casual, modern Lebanese on a busy boulevard near the Place de Clichy; a "nice kofta kebab or chiche taouk sandwich" can be washed down with a shot of anise-flavored arak; N.B. takeout also available.

Montparnasse 25 (Le) ⓈHaute Cuisine
▽ 24 | 21 | 21 | €89

14ᵉ | Le Méridien Montparnasse | 19, rue du Commandant René Mouchotte (Montparnasse-Bienvenüe) | 01 44 36 44 25 | fax 01 44 36 49 03 | www.m25.fr

"Go back to 1925" Montparnasse at this "elegant" hotel restaurant with its "art deco ambiance" (complete with Modigliani and Van Dongen reproductions); the Haute Cuisine is near-"faultless", especially the "out-of-this-world" cheese trolley; fans advise "let the knowledgeable master guide your selection", for "he knows his 200 to 300 [varieties] as well as any good sommelier knows his stock."

Mon Vieil Ami Ⓜ *Bistro*
24 | 20 | 21 | €52

4ᵉ | 69, rue St-Louis-en-l'Ile (Pont-Marie) | 01 40 46 01 35 | fax 01 40 46 01 36 | www.mon-vieil-ami.com

Strasbourg star chef-owner Antoine Westermann offers his "divine food" at this "lively" bistro where patrons sit "elbow to elbow" – either at a communal or a regular table – and dig into fare full of "unusual flavors and lots of vegetables", served by staffers who are "neither too familiar nor too stiff"; the "fabulous bargain" prix fixe and Ile Saint-Louis location mean you'll be "surrounded by tourists", but the "informal" ambiance will bring back "memories of Sunday lunch in Alsace" anyway.

NEW Mori Venice Bar *Italian*
– | – | – | VE

2ᵉ | 2, rue du Quatre Septembre (Bourse) | 01 44 55 51 55 | fax 01 44 55 00 77 | www.mori-venicebar.com

Fit for a Doge, and with regal prices to match, this year-old see and-beseen site near the old Bourse packs in the power brokers and show-biz types; owner Massimo Mori formerly ran the Emporio Armani Caffè, and this table is similarly ambitious in terms of serving authentic, high-quality Venetian fare within its sleek Philippe Starck decor of rich wood paneling, Baccarat chandeliers and Murano mirrors; it's packed at every service, so reservations are essential.

	FOOD	DECOR	SERVICE	COST

Moulin à Vent (Au) *Bistro*
| 22 | 17 | 20 | €61 |

5ᵉ | 20, rue des Fossés St-Bernard (Cardinal Lemoine/Jussieu) |
01 43 54 99 37 | fax 01 40 46 92 23 | www.au-moulinavent.com
Nostalgists looking for that "old-time feeling" say this "cozy",
"quintessential bistro" in the 5th serves it up in spades, along with
"overly generous" portions of "fabulous steaks" and "delicious
frogs' legs"; it's "the type of meal that one takes home as a memory
of the classic Paris dinner", right down to the "friendly, communal
atmosphere", in which even the occasional "late-night singing by
customers is tolerated with a smile."

Moulin de la Galette (Le) *Classic French*
| ▽ – | 16 | 14 | €38 |

18ᵉ | 83, rue Lepic (Abbesses/Lamarck-Caulaincourt) |
01 46 06 84 77 | fax 01 46 06 84 78
With a "mythical" name referring to a 19th-century dance hall, this
restaurant has a "glorious location at the top of Montmartre" and a
"beautiful little garden" underneath a historical windmill where "you
can feel like you're posing for Renoir"; however, it's become a
"pricey option" since its recent acquisition by the talented team of
Le Chamarré, who have installed a new Classic French–Mauritian
menu and larger wine list.

Mousson (La) *Cambodian*
| – | – | – | M |

1ᵉʳ | 9, rue Therese (Pyramides) | 01 42 60 59 46
Connoisseurs of Khmer cuisine head to this "delightful Cambodian"
near the Palais-Royal for classic dishes from the Mekong Delta, del-
icately flavored specialties such as beef with lemongrass or fish
cooked in banana leaves; the price is right and the room is tiny, so
"patrons are kindly asked not to smoke."

Murano (Le) *New French*
| 17 | 23 | 16 | €66 |

3ᵉ | Murano Urban Resort | 13, bd du Temple (Les Filles-du-Calvaire/
République) | 01 42 71 20 00 | fax 01 42 71 21 01 |
www.muranoresort.com
"Hip" habitués and hotel guests frequent this "fabulous" watering
hole in the northern Marais, where the mega-white, "magnificent
contemporary" decor is accented with "spectacular" colored lighting; trendoids tuck into "inventive" New French food that's "minimalist" in style (and content), then head to the bar for "very good
cocktails" and 164 brands of vodka; P.S. "the inner courtyard is
lovely in summer."

Murat (Le) *Classic French*
| 15 | 17 | 13 | €57 |

16ᵉ | 1, bd Murat (Porte d'Auteuil) | 01 46 51 33 17 |
fax 01 46 51 88 54
A restaurant that "hides its name" at the entrance may seem just "so
snobbish", but the "jet-set people" who come to "show off" at this
place near the Porte d'Auteuil say they "adore" the "original" Russo-
Napoleonic decor by Jacques Garcia and the "varied" take on Classic
French cuisine that's "not bad, if predictable"; but grousers gripe the
whole scene is "too trendy for regular eaters", especially the "fashion model" "servers who think they're superior" to the clientele.

	FOOD	DECOR	SERVICE	COST

Muscade 🅼 *Bistro/Tearoom*
— — — M

1er | 36, rue Montpensier (Palais Royal-Musée du Louvre/
Pyramides) | 01 42 97 51 36 | fax 01 42 97 51 36

The exceptional location in a wing of the Palais Royal is the biggest
draw at this "nice little lunch spot" offering simple bistro meals,
pastries and afternoon tea; dinner is also served – in summer, tables
overlooking the historical gardens are prime real estate – but do reserve in winter, to ensure they'll be open.

Muses (Les) 🆉 *Haute Cuisine*
— — — VE

9e | Hôtel Scribe | 1, rue Scribe (Opéra) | 01 44 71 24 26 |
fax 01 44 71 24 64 | www.sofitel.com

"If you have an expense account, don't miss this one" say fans of this
intimate Haute Cuisine hotel table near the Opéra Garnier; despite
its "low ceilings" and slightly "sterile", traditional decor, the staff is
"attentive", and the "great food" has gotten a more modern spin under chef Franck Charpentier (ex Restaurant W).

Musichall ◕ *New French*
▽ 15 | 18 | 14 | €61

8e | 63, av Franklin D. Roosevelt (St-Philippe-du-Roule) |
01 45 61 03 63 | fax 01 45 61 03 88 | www.music-hallparis.com

It's a never-ending spectacle at this "lively" club/eatery off the
Champs that keeps jumping until 4 AM on weekends; the decor is
"as kitsch as it could be", with "all-white" walls bathed by "continu-
ally changing" colored lights and "tight tables" so low they're "practically on the floor"; cynics sneer "the action's all on the walls, not
on the plates", but defenders declare the New French cuisine is "better than you would expect" for such a "trendy" spot, with special
mention for the "remarkable" desserts.

Natacha ◑🆉 *Classic French*
21 | 18 | 17 | €43

14e | 17 bis, rue Campagne-Première (Raspail) | 01 43 20 79 27 |
fax 01 43 22 00 90

In 2003, the "highly talented" Alain Cirelli took over this veteran for
celebrity-spotting in Montparnasse, and supporters say the "good
food is back" – Classic French fare that's both "flavorful and visually
appealing" – and welcome "the warm colors and high ceilings of the
lovely room"; some sense the staff "attitude has improved", as well.

Nemrod (Le) 🆉 *Auvergne*
15 | 12 | 14 | €28

6e | 51, rue du Cherche-Midi (Sèvres-Babylone/St-Placide) |
01 45 48 17 05 | fax 01 45 48 17 83

Shoppers "take a break from the Bon Marché" and other boutiques
for the "hustle and bustle" of this "hopping" Auvergnat cafe, serving
"hearty portions" of "authentic cooking", plus "huge salads";
it's "old-fashioned fun" with "good terrace seating" and "people-
watching", despite the "pure craziness" of lunch hour.

New Jawad ◕ *Indian/Pakistani*
16 | 13 | 19 | €36

7e | 12, av Rapp (Alma Marceau) | 01 47 05 91 37 | fax 01 45 50 31 27

When struck by sudden Sunday night subcontinental cravings, residents of the posh 7th head to this Indo-Pakistani, a "good standby

when you're not wanting to leave the neighborhood for 'ethnic' food"; "kind" servers await in "a spacious room", and the "moderate prices" ensure "you'll [depart] satisfied."

New Nioullaville ● *Chinese*

11e | 32-34, rue de l'Orillon (Belleville) | 01 40 21 96 18 | fax 01 41 58 55 14

As "bustling" as a Beijing train station, this "immense" "temple of Chinese food" may be in Belleville, but "the carts of fresh dim sum are just like you'd find in Hong Kong" and the menu offers a "vast repertory" representing "several different Asian cuisines"; it's "exotic enough" to please, even if "the decor's nonexistent" and the service "impersonal" (but "immediate", thanks to those carts).

Noces de Jeannette (Les) *Bistro*

2e | 14, rue Favart (Richelieu-Drouot) | 01 42 96 36 89 | fax 01 47 03 97 31 | www.lesnocesdejeannette.com

With its central location off the Grands Boulevards and five salons decorated in a range of styles, this "tourist-group destination" for traditional bistro fare is often "crowded" with foreigners, who find the food of "uneven quality" though generally "not bad" (some sightseers suspect the caliber "depends on the price of your tour"); "the staff allows plenty of time for people-watching."

Nos Ancêtres les Gaulois, A ● *Classic French*

4e | 39, rue St-Louis-en-l'Ile (Pont Marie) | 01 46 33 66 07 | fax 01 43 25 28 64 | www.nosancetreslesgaulois.com

"Those who like noisy conviviality" say the "ribald" "feast" at this Ile Saint-Louis ancient Gaul-themed eatery is like a "frat party" à la Asterix; the "stone-walled dining room" with a "roving musician" "packs itself nightly with hundreds of tourists" who crowd around "big wooden tables" and dig into a "rustic" prix fixe of Classic French charcuterie and grilled meats; "the food is bad, and the wine is worse, but there's lots" of both, so while the "hokey" quotient is high, it can be "fun" to "do it once."

No Stress Café ● 🅜 *Eclectic*

9e | 2, pl Gustave Toudouze (St-Georges) | 01 48 78 00 27 | fax 01 42 81 36 03

"In a quiet part of the 9th", touchy-feely types come to this "fun place" for its "cool laid-back atmosphere", Med-inspired setting and hands-on service, including the option of a "massage before, during or after your meal"; the ever-changing Eclectic menu runs the gamut from wok-fried dishes to tapas, and while surveyors stress that the cuisine is only "average", there's a "great terrace" for hanging loose on the square Gustave Toudouze; N.B. there's no stress – and no phone or reservations either.

Noura *Lebanese*

2e | 29, bd des Italiens (Chaussée d'Antin/Opéra) | 01 53 43 00 53 | fax 01 53 43 83 53 ●
6e | 121, bd du Montparnasse (Vavin) | 01 43 20 19 19 | fax 01 43 20 05 40 ●

(continued)

(continued)

Noura

16ᵉ | 21, av Marceau (Alma Marceau/George V) | 01 47 20 33 33 | fax 01 47 20 60 31 ☾
16ᵉ | 27, av Marceau (Alma Marceau/George V) | 01 47 03 02 20 | fax 01 47 23 99 80
www.noura.fr

There's almost always a Noura nearby when a hankering for hummus hits; true, "the decor is plain" and the staff "could try harder", but it's "a safe choice for Lebanese fare" – hence, this "high-quality chain" is "constantly crowded"; P.S. "for more chic quarters and refined service, choose the Pavilion" at 21 Avenue Marceau.

Nouveau Village Tao-Tao ☾ *Chinese/Thai*

▽ 14 | 13 | 14 | €31

13ᵉ | 159, bd Vincent Auriol (Nationale) | 01 45 86 40 08 | fax 01 45 86 46 21

Though this Asian a few blocks from Place d'Italie is big enough to feed a village, its popularity means reservations are required if you want to taste traditional dishes from China and Thailand; the experience can be akin to eating at a "large factory" foes find; yet advocates argue it's "always a sure value" for the "real" thing, including an "especially good" Peking duck.

O à la Bouche (L') ✍ *Bistro*

▽ 17 | 14 | 19 | €42

14ᵉ | 124, bd du Montparnasse (Vavin) | 01 56 54 01 55 | fax 01 43 21 07 87

Montparnasse denizens depend on the "quite good" New French food at this neighborhood bistro, which is "neither cozy nor trendy but just fine for dining with family, friends or on a date"; "service is pleasant", but opinions vary on the Mediterranean-like decor: "pretty" vs. "less-than-inviting."

☑ Obélisque (L') *Classic French*

23 | 22 | 25 | €87

8ᵉ | Hôtel de Crillon | 10, pl de la Concorde (Concorde) | 01 44 71 15 15 | fax 01 44 71 15 02 | www.crillon.com

Connoisseurs confide that the "Crillon coffee shop" (as they call the palatial hotel's more "casual" restaurant) is a "fantastic alternative" to "Les Ambassadeurs next door", with "pleasurable" Classic French cuisine that "comes from the same kitchen", served in "portions fit for an (American) king"; though "less refined", the decor's still pretty "lavish", and that, plus the "outstanding service", makes it "perfect for business lunches" or "when shopping the Rue du Faubourg Saint-Honoré."

Oeillade (L') *Bistro*

15 | 11 | 14 | €41

7ᵉ | 10, rue de St-Simon (Rue du Bac/Solférino) | 01 42 22 01 60

"Tucked away" in the posh 7th arrondissement, this bistro for the bourgeoisie serves up a "true Gallic meal" from a "limited menu" that is "good if uninspired" fans find; but the less-forgiving declare it downright "lackluster", adding that this restaurant's decor "needs a redo" too.

| | FOOD | DECOR | SERVICE | COST |

Oenothèque (L') *Wine Bar/Bistro*

| – | – | – | M |

9e | 20, rue St-Lazare (Notre-Dame-de-Lorette) | 01 48 78 08 76 | fax 01 40 16 10 27

Diners looking to drink in a "good wine education" raise a glass to this welcoming, red-hued *cave* "with a lovely owner" near the Gare Saint-Lazare; it offers a "great cellar" of "well-priced" bottles to accompany a daily changing chalkboard of Classic French dishes and game in season.

Olivades (Les) 🗷 *Provence*

| 22 | 15 | 18 | €51 |

(aka Bruno Deligne-Les Olivades)

7e | 41, av de Ségur (Ségur/St-François-Xavier) | 01 47 83 70 09 | fax 01 42 73 04 75 | www.deligne-lesolivades.fr.tc

"You feel like you've been invited to the parlor of a long-lost friend" posit pleased patrons of this "cozy", "upscale local bistro" near the Ecole Militaire, featuring the "sunny", "artfully prepared" cooking of Provence; but while the menu is from the south, some pout the prices have gone north and become "*un peu cher*" ("but then, what hasn't in Paris?").

NEW Ombres (Les) *New French*

| – | – | – | VE |

7e | Musée du Quai Branly | 27, quai Branly, Portail Debilly (Alma Marceau) | 01 47 53 68 00 | fax 01 47 53 68 18 | www.elior.com

Located on the fifth floor of the Musée du Quai Branly (a showcase for Asian, African and North and South American art), this New French is the most glamorous debutante to have opened in Paris for some time; architect Jean Nouvel, who designed the museum, also created the sleek look of the dining room and its terrace, right down to the streamlined stainless-steel cutlery and curvy rattan chairs; the happy surprise is that young chef Arno Busquet's menu lives up to the setting's magical city views.

Opportun (L') 🌑🗷 *Lyon*

| – | – | – | E |

14e | 64, bd Edgar Quinet (Edgar Quinet) | 01 43 20 26 89 | fax 01 43 21 61 88

"A place that takes the joy of food seriously" opine the opportunists about this small bistro near Montparnasse, whose "colorful chef-owner" serves "solid Lyonnaise home cooking" in "Pantagruelesque portions" "for big appetites"; solitary business travelers find they "feel welcome" here, given the "friendly" staff and dine-in bar.

Orangerie (L') 🌑 *Classic French*

| – | – | – | VE |

4e | 28, rue St-Louis-en-l'Ile (Pont-Marie) | 01 46 33 93 98 | fax 01 43 29 25 52

With new, contemporary taupe decor, this long-running *beau monde* address on the Ile Saint-Louis is the new perch of peripatetic chef Michel Del Burgo (ex Bristol and Taillevent); he's serving up Classic French cuisine with a Haute Cuisine flourish, served by a professional, if slightly distant, staff to a crowd that's worldly, well-heeled and well-dressed – if not the famous faces who frequented the place when it was owned by actor Jean-Claude Brialy.

vote at zagat.com   135

	FOOD	DECOR	SERVICE	COST

Orénoc (L') ⓈⓂ *Asian/Classic French* — — — E

17ᵉ | Le Méridien Etoile | 81, bd Gouvion-St-Cyr (Porte Maillot) |
01 40 68 30 40 | fax 01 40 68 30 81 | www.lemeridien-etoile.com
A "delightful surprise for dining" lies at the Méridien Etoile, where
the "extremely original" Classic French–"Asian fusion" menu "adds
spices to noble dishes", "generally with good results"; but critics
complain that despite the "Oriental-inspired decor" of exotic woods
and ochre shades, it still "feels like a hotel resto"; N.B. fans of chef
Claude Colliot, ex Le Bamboche, will be glad to hear he's just taken
over the kitchen.

Orient-Extrême ●Ⓢ *Japanese* 20 15 14 €54

6ᵉ | 4, rue Bernard Palissy (St-Germain-des-Prés) | 01 45 48 92 27 |
fax 01 45 48 20 94
Sashimi-philes would swim miles to get to this "fashionable" spot in
Saint-Germain serving "among the best in Paris" with a "wider selection than the run-of-the-mill" Japanese joints; it's also "the place
to go if you want celebrity with your sushi" – so while the "service is
spotty" and it might be "a little expensive", you could never call it
a raw deal.

Ormes (Les) ⓈⓂ *Haute Cuisine* 24 17 21 €64

7ᵉ | 22, rue Surcouf (Invalides/La Tour-Maubourg) | 01 45 51 46 93 |
fax 01 45 50 30 11 | www.restaurant-les-ormes.com
Faithful foodies have followed their "favorite" toque, Stéphane
Molé, from the fringes of the 16th to these digs "near the Eiffel
Tower", trumpeting his "thoughtful, delicious" Haute Cuisine and a
prix fixe menu that's a "great bargain"; still, some nostalgists are
"not sure he should have moved", saying the fancy address has
made the place "a little starchy" ("service hasn't quite caught up to
the chef, but it's improving").

Os à Moëlle (L') ●ⓈⓂ *Classic French* 23 14 18 €47

15ᵉ | 3, rue Vasco de Gama (Lourmel) | 01 45 57 27 27 |
fax 01 45 57 28 00
This "little" address is "always jam-packed" with locals and "lots of
Americans" who say it's "worth the extra schlep" "way into the
15th" for the "outstanding" Classic French dishes, "convivial atmosphere" and "remarkable wines" at "unbeatable prices"; some coun-
sel you "choose the second seating" to avoid "being rushed out the
door", and "call to see what they're serving that night", since the six-
course prix fixe "doesn't offer many choices."

Ostéria (L') Ⓢ *Italian* 24 11 15 €51

4ᵉ | 10, rue de Sévigné (St-Paul) | 01 42 71 37 08 | fax 01 48 06 27 71
It's "missing a sign on the door" (the better to "keep out the vulgar
crowds"), but those in-the-know make tracks to this "masterful"
Marais site for "perhaps the best Italian food in Paris" including
"clouds masquerading as gnocchi" and "sublime" risotto; regretta-
bly, it's "deliriously expensive" ("food as rich as the clientele"), "service can be hectic and the room is small"; N.B. scores don't reflect
an ownership change post-Survey.

	FOOD	DECOR	SERVICE	COST

Osteria Ascolani ●⊘⇆ *Italian*   — | — | — | M

18ᵉ | 98, rue des Martyrs (Abbesses/Pigalle) | 01 42 62 43 94 |
www.osteria-ascolani.com

A "friendly staff" serves "homemade, uncomplicated Italian food",
mostly from the mountainous Abruzzo region, on the Parisian hill of
Montmartre at this "perfect neighborhood place"; the "casually elegant", "no-choice" menu of antipasti, pasta and dessert "changes
every day", and a hip young clientele appreciates the dolce prices
and la dolce vita hours, daily until 2 AM.

Oudino (L') ⊠ *Bistro*   — | — | — | M

7ᵉ | 17, rue Oudinot (Duroc) | 01 45 66 05 09 | fax 01 45 66 53 35 |
www.oudino.com

Tucked away on a short, pretty street in the 7th, this laid-back, '30s-
style French bistro attracts well-heeled locals with an eclectic menu
that ranges from slow-cooked shoulder of lamb to Caesar salad to
citrus fruit tart; prices are moderate for this pricey part of town, and
service is well-intentioned if occasionally forgetful.

Oulette (L') ⊠ *Southwest*   21 | 17 | 20 | €56

12ᵉ | 15, pl Lachambeaudie (Cour St-Emilion/Dugommier) |
01 40 02 02 12 | fax 01 40 02 04 77 | www.l-oulette.com

"It's the duck" stupid, exclaim enthusiasts explaining why they return to this "sleeper" that is "worth the ride to the Bercy" area for
"reliably delicious" Southwestern cuisine; the southern warmth extends to the "pampering" service, adding up to a "good-value-for-
money" experience – even if the decor seems "mundane" (there is a
"nice terrace" for those balmy evenings, though).

Oum el Banine ⊠ *Moroccan*   — | — | — | E

16ᵉ | 16 bis, rue Dufrenoy (Porte Dauphine/Rue de la Pompe) |
01 45 04 91 22 | fax 01 45 03 46 26 | www.oumelbanine.com

"Watch your waistline" at this "wonderful neighborhood Moroccan"
in the 16th, where the "authentic" tagines and couscous cause
"gourmets to cross town for the pure delight"; "meticulous" service
is guaranteed because the *patronne* keeps an eye" on everything.

Ourcine (L') ⊠Ⓜ *Classic/New French*   21 | 10 | 20 | €37

13ᵉ | 92, rue Broca (Les Gobelins/Glacière) | 01 47 07 13 65 |
fax 01 47 07 18 48

"From one of the sous-chefs of La Régalade", Sylvain Danière, comes
this "great addition to the bistro scene" of the 13th; it lives up to its
owner's pedigree with "divine", "inventive" Classic and Contemporary
French cuisine, an "enthusiastic staff" and the comparatively "dirt-
cheap" prices; the only drawback is the "bland and minimal" setting,
but hey – "don't judge a restaurant by its decor."

NEW Ozu *Japanese*   — | — | — | E

16ᵉ | 2, av des Nations-Unies (Trocadéro) | 01 40 69 23 90 |
fax 01 40 69 23 96

Built into the side of a hill in the 16th, this dramatic new Japanese
doesn't need to fish for compliments, since the dining room is dom-

inated by a huge aquarium (in fact, this was once the site of the Paris Aquarium); the menu includes 25 sorts of sake, sushi and sophisticated, contemporary riffs on traditional dishes, including white miso-marinated swordfish and green-tea crème brûlée; a well-drilled team provides courteous service, but you better be a big tuna to handle the high tabs.

Palanquin (Le) 🖪 *Vietnamese* ▽ 18 | 12 | 13 | €40
6ᵉ | 12, rue Princesse (Mabillon/St-Germain-des-Prés) | 01 43 29 77 66 | www.lepalanquin.com

Those looking for "a break from standard French" cooking can savor a soupçon of Saigon in Saint-Germain at this Vietnamese, which features "authentic, fresh" favorites like pho soup, Banh cuon (steamed ravioli) and ginger duck; the "cozy setting" displays the exposed beams and stones of its 18th-century building.

Pamphlet (Le) *Basque/Southwest* 23 | 19 | 20 | €42
3ᵉ | 38, rue Debelleyme (Filles-du-Calvaire) | 01 42 72 39 24

"Gather a group of real eaters" and herd them to this "delightful" "Marais gem" of a bistro for "loads of" "earthy" dishes from Basque-Southwest country; chowhounds cheer that "the kitchen just keeps improving", while the menu remains "affordable" and the staff so "cordial" that clients joke they should "change the name to Le Pampered"; N.B. closed at press time due to water damage, it's slated to reopen in April 2007 with new cool, contemporary decor.

Paolo Petrini 🖪 *Italian* ▽ 21 | 13 | 18 | €60
17ᵉ | 6, rue du Débarcadère (Argentine/Porte-Maillot) | 01 45 74 25 95 | fax 01 45 74 12 95 | www.paolo-petrini.fr

Spiffy signori and signoras frequent this Italian near Porte Maillot, where the alliterative chef-owner whips up "tasty" "traditional" Tuscan treats with "top-level ingredients"; a recent "successful" face-lift mixes cool shades of beige and gray with modern paintings and leather chairs.

Papilles (Les) 🖪 *Classic French* 22 | 16 | 18 | €38
5ᵉ | 30, rue Gay-Lussac (RER Luxembourg) | 01 43 25 20 79 | fax 01 43 25 24 35

Patrons' *papilles* (taste buds) are tantalized at this "adorable little address, something between a gourmet grocery and gastronomic port of call" near the Panthéon, where "superb wines" "shown, store-style, on the walls" complement a "one-choice menu" of "consistently flavorful" Classic French food; it's "bright and lively" (some say "noisy"), so "go with a group, but not on a first date" – especially since "you'll need a nap after" all that well-priced vino.

Paradis du Fruit (Le) ☻ *Eclectic* 13 | 12 | 10 | €25
1ᵉʳ | 4, rue St-Honoré (Les Halles) | 01 40 39 93 99
2ᵉ | 23, bd des Italiens (Opéra) | 01 44 94 08 48
5ᵉ | 1, rue des Tournelles (Bastille) | 01 40 27 94 79
6ᵉ | 29, quai des Grands-Augustins (St-Michel) | 01 43 54 51 42
8ᵉ | 35, rue Marbeuf (Alma Marceau) | 01 45 62 47 22
8ᵉ | 47, av George V (George V) | 01 47 20 74 00

(continued)

Paradis du Fruit (Le)

11ᵉ | 12, pl de la Bastille (Bastille) | 01 43 07 82 25
14ᵉ | 21, bd Edgar Quinet (Edgar Quinet) | 01 40 47 53 44
17ᵉ | 32, av de Wagram (Ternes) | 01 44 09 02 02
Neuilly-sur-Seine | 205, av Charles de Gaulle (Pont de Neuilly) |
01 46 24 66 15

Students sick of spaghetti swarm to this Eclectic chain for a "natural, fresh" fix from the "fruit-based menu", including "copious" salads and "delicious", "healthy" smoothies served amid "kitschy" "coconut tree–style" decor; "it's a nice place to refuel", but certainly "not refined", and the "young" servers are often "overwhelmed" by the crowds; in short, while cheaper than spring break in the Caribbean, it's "a bit expensive for the quality."

Paradis Thai ● *Thai* ▽ 18 | 19 | 16 | €28

13ᵉ | 132, rue de Tolbiac (Tolbiac) | 01 45 83 22 26 |
fax 01 45 83 22 26 | www.paradisthai.com

With an entrance like a Buddhist temple and live fish swimming under a glass floor, the decor makes the biggest splash at this Siamese in the 13th, "a nice surprise in this neighborhood full of greasy spoons"; while the food is definitely "decent", purists proclaim it "more bohemian-bourgeois touristy than true Thai."

Parc aux Cerfs (Le) *Classic French* 17 | 17 | 18 | €45

6ᵉ | 50, rue Vavin (Notre-Dame-des-Champs/Vavin) |
01 43 54 87 83 | fax 01 43 26 42 86

"Vintage Montparnasse" maintain mavens about this place in the 6th with "patient, sweet service" and a "quaint" setting (when warm weather arrives, the "small terrace in the back is best" regulars recommend); while the "idiosyncratic" cuisine – sometimes "imaginative", sometimes "real traditional French" – "doesn't always soar", at least you can always count on "a perfectly correct meal" that's "good value for the money."

Paris (Le) 🅰 *Haute Cuisine* ▽ 19 | 20 | 20 | €93

6ᵉ | Hôtel Lutétia | 45, bd Raspail (Sèvres-Babylone) |
01 49 54 46 90 | fax 01 49 54 46 00 | www.lutetia-paris.com

"You don't often hear about" this upscale eatery in the luxurious Hôtel Lutétia (maybe because it's "closed on weekends"), but those who do say it's a "find" for power breakfasts and leisurely dinners, with "high-quality" service and "quite good, if not remarkable" Haute Cuisine, served in a "lovely" art deco interior – "it looks like an ocean liner" – designed by Sonia Rykiel.

Paris Seize (Le) 🅰 *Italian* 14 | 10 | 11 | €37

16ᵉ | 18, rue des Belles-Feuilles (Trocadéro) | 01 47 04 56 33

"Noisy" and "crowded" with a "clientele of regulars" from the upper-crust 16th, this "neighborhood" Italian doles out "generous servings" of "correct" *cucina* at "reasonable" prices; but while some cherish the "convivial ambiance", others are irate that it's "invaded with trendy rich kids."

	FOOD	DECOR	SERVICE	COST

Pasco Ⓜ *Mediteranean/Southwest* — | - | - | M

7ᵉ | 74, bd de la Tour Maubourg (La Tour Maubourg) |
01 44 18 33 26 | fax 01 44 18 34 06 | www.restaurantpasco.com
"Locals adore it, tourists rave about it, what's not to love?" extol enthusiasts of this venue, owned by a couple of buddies named Pascal mere steps from Les Invalides; in this chichi *quartier*, its "bang-for-your-buck" Med menu is a standout, featuring "inventive, delicious cuisine" from the sunny Southwest in a "pleasant setting" – "brick arches, lots of windows and an open, spacious feeling."

Passage des Carmagnoles (Le) ◑ 🅑 *Wine Bar/Bistro* — | - | - | M

11ᵉ | 18, Passage de la Bonne Graine (Ledru-Rollin) | 01 47 00 73 30
| fax 01 47 00 65 68
"The attraction of this charming place is actually the host, Antoine Toubia", whose popular wine bar in a passage near Bastille proposes a "superb selection" of bottles and a menu of meaty Classic French dishes such as andouillette or steak tartare with mint; food for thought as well as stomach is provided by well-lubricated philosophical debates held on the first Thursday of every month.

Passiflore 🅑 *Asian/Classic French* — 23 | 18 | 21 | €70

16ᵉ | 33, rue de Longchamp (Boissière/Trocadéro) | 01 47 04 96 81
| fax 01 47 04 32 27 | www.restaurantpassiflore.com
Fusion fans find nirvana near Trocadéro thanks to the "superb" "cross-cultural" cuisine of chef Roland Durand, whose "innovative" Classic "French food with an Asian touch" is served in "serene" East-meets-West surrounds; though service can range from "immaculate" to "cavalier", it's "an ideal place for a business lunch", especially with a menu that's "easy on the pocket" (as opposed to the "astronomical" prices after dark).

Passy Mandarin *Asian* — 16 | 14 | 13 | €45

16ᵉ | 6, rue Bois-le-Vent (La Muette) | 01 42 88 12 18 |
fax 01 45 24 58 54

Passy Mandarin Opéra ◑ *Asian*

2ᵉ | 6, rue d'Antin (Opéra) | 01 42 61 25 52 | fax 01 42 60 33 92
Reportedly, "this is where Joël Robuchon comes for Peking duck – enough said" proclaim converts who crowd this Asian with two addresses, one out in the 16th with "wonderful" authentic Chinese decor, and the other near the Opéra Garnier with a more "rudimentary" setting; but while the *canard*'s "always good", critics carp the rest of the menu is "not so exciting" and the "service is quite informal", though "prompt."

Patrick Goldenberg *Eastern European* — 15 | 12 | 15 | €57

17ᵉ | 69, av de Wagram (Ternes) | 01 42 27 34 79 | fax 01 42 27 98 85
Kosher noshing is a no-brainer, thanks to this "picturesque" deli serving up "relatively good Eastern European Jewish food", plus pastrami and pickles; skeptics kvetch there's "nothing to die for" here, but c'mon – near the Place des Ternes, you were "expecting New York City"?

	FOOD	DECOR	SERVICE	COST

Paul Chêne ☒ *Classic French* — 22 | 14 | 19 | €57

16ᵉ | 123, rue Lauriston (Trocadéro/Victor Hugo) | 01 47 27 63 17 | fax 01 47 27 53 18

"One of the 16th's treasures", this "standby" near Trocadéro may be "stuck in a time warp" but that's exactly what its regulars have come to expect: "exquisitely prepared" "French comfort food" in an "intimate dining room" with a "relaxed atmosphere" where "old-line elegance and service" are assured; *bien sûr*, it's "not inexpensive, but it's a wonderful place for a special meal."

Paul, Restaurant Ⓜ *Bistro* — 19 | 17 | 19 | €37

1ᵉʳ | 15, pl Dauphine (Pont-Neuf) | 01 43 54 21 48 | fax 01 56 24 94 09

"Pretend you are in 1940s Paris" at this "quiet oasis" "on a lovely square on the Ile de la Cité", a "landmark setting" where former neighbors Yves Montand and Simone Signoret used to dine on Classic French fare; it's still served today, from "sublime breakfasts" to dinners in the traditional, mirrored bistro setting or under the stars – "an outdoor table and almost anything grilled will never disappoint" you here.

Ⓩ Pavillon de la Grande Cascade *Haute Cuisine* — 22 | 27 | 23 | €111

16ᵉ | Bois de Boulogne | Allée de Longchamp (Porte Maillot) | 01 45 27 33 51 | fax 01 42 88 99 06 | www.lagrandecascade.fr

A "beautiful setting" in an "elegant" Second Empire pavilion on the edge of the Bois de Boulogne makes this Haute Cuisine table a preferred address for the amorous ("a gorgeous glass ceiling allows the setting sun to light up the irises of your beloved"); "gracious" service makes it "great for celebrations", even if some sigh "oh, that the food matched the decor" – though with the fall 2006 arrival of chef Frédéric Robert (ex the old Lucas Carton), it soon just might.

Ⓩ Pavillon Ledoyen ☒ *Haute Cuisine* — 26 | 27 | 25 | €136

8ᵉ | 8, av Dutuit (Champs-Elysées-Clémenceau/Concorde) | 01 53 05 10 00 | fax 01 47 42 55 01

In a "parklike setting, with lush verdant views from its sumptuous dining room", this pavilion off the Champs is a "temple of good food and refinement" – not to mention "romantic as hell"; the Napoleon III-style decor is "dripping with elegance", the Haute Cuisine is "fit for the gods" and the staff "makes you feel like royalty"; "sometimes it's overrun with special events", but it's "a must" if you're going to propose – just be warned "dinner will be as expensive as the engagement ring."

Pavillon Montsouris *Classic French* — 18 | 22 | 18 | €66

14ᵉ | 20, rue Gazan (Porte d'Orléans) | 01 43 13 29 00 | fax 01 43 12 29 02 | www.pavillon-montsouris.fr

With an "enchanting", glass-roofed dining room and "exceptional terrace", it's "like eating in the middle of the park" at this Classic French that in fact overlooks the Parc Montsouris; the "refined dishes", well-"spaced" tables and "discreet, attentive" waiters make this perpetual garden party "perfect" for "grand occasions"; it's technically "expensive, but good value for the money."

	FOOD	DECOR	SERVICE	COST

Pearl *Classic French/Eclectic* — | — | — | M

13ᵉ | 53 bis, bd Arago (Les Gobelins/Glacière) | 01 47 07 58 57 | fax 01 08 73 63 93 57 | www.pearlparis.com

This unconventional venue in the residential 13th is "a little off the tourist beat, but worth the trip" for an Eclectic take on traditional French fare and dramatic neoclassical decor in alabaster tones; chef Jean-Baptiste Legros creates surprising and sophisticated dishes such as a duo of roasted duck and duck confit, or a trio prepared Saint-Jacques–style; but the menu also includes – it goes without saying – oysters.

Père Claude (Le) *Classic French* — 18 | 11 | 17 | €44

15ᵉ | 51, av de la Motte-Picquet (La Motte-Picquet-Grenelle) | 01 47 34 03 05 | fax 01 40 56 97 84

At this "institution for those meat-craving moments", this "casual, friendly" rotisserie is where "regulars from the neighborhood" around the Ecole Militaire come to chow on "serious" Classic French grilled goodies; first-timers are struck by the "bustling" "'60s-chic" ambiance – "I felt like I was in a movie by Roger Vadim" (who peddled flesh of a different sort).

Pères et Filles *Bistro* ▽ 12 | 13 | 13 | €36

6ᵉ | 81, rue de Seine (Mabillon/Odéon) | 01 43 25 00 28

A "young crowd" appreciates this "convenient" Saint-Germain address whose "cool atmosphere" is replete with all the classic bistro trimmings (zinc bar included); still, several surveyors scoff that, when it comes to the Classic French fare augmented with "light" dishes, "the food is better at home"; as for the welcome, it's less preferable to be a *père* than a *fille* – you can count on "better service if you are skinny, pretty and 25."

Perraudin (Le) 🇿 *Bistro* — 16 | 17 | 18 | €33

5ᵉ | 157, rue St-Jacques (Cluny La Sorbonne/Luxembourg) | 01 46 33 15 75 | fax 01 46 33 52 75 | www.restaurant-perraudin.com

Straight "out of the movies, with checkered tablecloths and aged decor", this century-old "classic" bistro "near the Sorbonne" is a "cheap, cheerful" hangout for students and "many Americans" looking for "a breath of old Paris" along with "excellent value" on boeuf bourguignon, tarte Tatin and other homey French standbys; "arrive early or be sure to reserve" or "you'll join the long line" waiting for a seat in the "cramped quarters."

Perron (Le) 🇿 *Italian* — 22 | 14 | 19 | €46

7ᵉ | 6, rue Perronet (St-Germain-des-Prés) | 01 45 44 71 51 | fax 01 45 44 71 51

This "friendly" "family-run" Italian located in Saint-Germain "fills up every night" with local literati and the occasional star who know you "absolutely need reservations" for a coveted table in the "rustic setting" of stone walls and wood beams; the kitchen turns out "authentic" cuisine from The Boot, with a "knack for seafood" and veal dishes that "will melt in your mouth."

	FOOD	DECOR	SERVICE	COST

Pershing, Restaurant ● *Eclectic/New French* — 15 | 24 | 14 | €69

8ᵉ | Hôtel Pershing Hall | 49, rue Pierre Charron (George V) |
01 58 36 58 36 | fax 01 58 36 58 01 | www.pershinghall.com
"Tremendous decor", with an "amazing [inside] garden wall",
makes this hotel eatery in the 8th "rather 'in'"; but critics would
"rather stay out" – while the Eclectic–New French "food is improving",
it's still "a rip-off", and if the "pretty waitresses make you forget the
uninteresting dishes and overpriced wines", they "must be grabbed
to speed along the meal"; so unless you like "paying for the scene",
maybe "it's most enjoyable just for drinks"; P.S. "don't touch anything in the garden, or you'll get yelled at."

Petit Bofinger *Brasserie* — 16 | 15 | 17 | €35

4ᵉ | 6, rue de la Bastille (Bastille) | 01 42 72 05 23 |
fax 01 42 72 04 94 ●
17ᵉ | 10, pl du Maréchal Juin (Péreire) | 01 56 79 56 20 |
fax 01 56 79 56 21 ●
La Défense | 1, pl du Dôme (La Grande Arche) | 01 46 92 46 46 |
fax 01 46 92 46 47
Vincennes | 2, av de Paris (Château de Vincennes) | 01 43 28 25 76
| fax 01 49 57 02 79
These "offshoots" of the original, historic Bofinger are "typical brasseries" serving up "classic" "if unsurprising" fare – including oysters
that are "some of the freshest in town" – "without chichi"; operated
by Groupe Flo, there's no surprise it has "a bit of a chain restaurant"
feeling; the Bastille branch is voted "the best" with "food nearly as
good as its mother's across the street", "but cheaper."

Petit Châtelet (Le) ⊠ Ⓜ *Classic French* — ▽ 19 | 22 | 20 | €39

5ᵉ | 39, rue de la Bûcherie (St-Michel) | 01 46 33 53 40
"Wedged amongst a bevy of cafes capitalizing on their proximity
to Notre Dame", this "cute spot" is a "haven of good Classic
French cuisine" "in the midst of a touristy area"; "the food is pleasantly straightforward", the service is so "welcoming" it's "endear-
ing" and if you "eat outside" facing the cathedral "you won't soon
forget the view."

Petit Colombier (Le) ⊠ *Classic French* — 17 | 13 | 15 | €63

17ᵉ | 42, rue des Acacias (Argentine/Charles de Gaulle-Etoile) |
01 43 80 28 54 | fax 01 44 40 04 29
Customers coo over the "very French" experience at this "small"
Classic table near the Etoile, where the "quality" "old-style cooking"
fits the decor *à l'ancienne*; "go in winter" to fill up on "heavy"
dishes and game in season.

Petite Chaise (A la) *Classic French* — 19 | 16 | 21 | €40

7ᵉ | 36, rue de Grenelle (Rue du Bac) | 01 42 22 13 35 |
fax 01 42 22 33 84 | www.alapetitechaise.fr
This "1600s Classic French" in the 7th claims to be the "oldest restaurant in Paris", which makes it a big draw for foreigners and an
"eccentric university clientele" seduced by the "charming" "retro"
ambiance and a "good-value", "old-fashioned" menu of "depend-

able comfort food" "served with attention"; "try to sit downstairs" since the "top floor is frequently filled with American tour groups."

Petite Cour (La) *New French*
18 | 20 | 17 | €46

6ᵉ | 8, rue Mabillon (Mabillon/St-Germain-des-Prés) | 01 43 26 52 26 | fax 01 44 07 11 53 | www.la-petitecour.com

The name says it all at this "sunken" "secluded courtyard" "right in the heart of Saint-Germain", where "old stone steps" lead to a "land-scaped terrace" with "lots of flowers" "and a fountain"; acolytes applaud the "tasty" "semi-modern French food" and "reasonable prix fixe menus", but admit it's tough to avoid the "waves of tourists" "especially in summer."

Petite Sirène de Copenhague (La) ⑤ Ⓜ *Danish*
20 | 13 | 19 | €49

9ᵉ | 47, rue Notre-Dame-de-Lorette (St-Georges) | 01 45 26 66 66

Aptly situated in the northern 9th, this bit of "Copenhagen in Paris" is "worth the detour" for "Continental food with a Scandinavian flair" courtesy of its "charming" Danish chef-owner; his siren song is "remarkable fish", along with "warm" service in a "sober" yet "light-filled" setting.

Petites Sorcières (Les) ⑤ *Bistro*
- | - | - | M

14ᵉ | 12, rue Liancourt (Denfert-Rochereau) | 01 43 21 95 68 | fax 01 43 21 95 68 | wwww.lespetitessorcieres.com

Its name means 'little witches', a reference to the girls of the "nice husband-and-wife team" behind this place in the 14th; it offers "eclectic" bistro cooking that's a "cut above" the norm and a "cozy" room that's "a perfect spot for an intimate dinner with a date or a best friend"; with tiny sorceresses hanging from the ceiling and peeking out from behind the curtains, this is a truly "enchanting" address.

Petite Tour (La) ⑤ *Classic French*
▽ 16 | 13 | 18 | €53

16ᵉ | 11, rue de la Tour (Passy) | 01 45 20 09 31 | fax 01 45 20 09 31

From its preppy setting in Passy, this "popular local" site supplies the bourgeoisie with Classic French cuisine and a "genuine welcome", even for patrons "dining alone"; while some wail it's "over-priced", the savvy submit it's a "perfect value, as long as you stick to the generous prix fixe."

Petit Lutétia (Le) *Brasserie*
16 | 16 | 17 | €44

6ᵉ | 107, rue de Sèvres (Vaneau) | 01 45 48 33 53 | fax 01 45 48 74 59

"Only in Paris can you find this retro a place", an "intimate" (by brasserie standards) space in the shopping area around Sèvres-Babylone; the "better-than-average food" is served amid "lovely", "old decor (it goes with the clientele)"; some sniff that "you clearly pay for" the "beautiful surroundings" but it's "fun for the belle epoque ambiance."

Petit Marché (Le) ● *New French*
▽ 22 | 17 | 19 | €32

3ᵉ | 9, rue de Béarn (Bastille/Chemin-Vert) | 01 42 72 06 67 | fax 01 42 76 00 03

Near the Place des Vosges, this "neighborhood joint" is "jumping with a younger crowd" that comes for "fantastic" New French cuisine with "an Asian twist" at "reasonable" prices; with an open kitchen that keeps humming till 12 AM and "frenetic but effective" service, it's "perfect for a late-night bite on a hot summer night", especially if you can snag a table on the tiny terrace.

Petit Marguery (Le) 🅂🅜 *Bistro* | 22 | 16 | 21 | €49 |

13ᵉ | 9, bd de Port-Royal (Les Gobelins) | 01 43 31 58 59 | fax 01 43 36 73 34 | www.petitmarguery.fr

This "eternal" bistro has got game, and "outstanding game" at that, along with "good old-fashioned French cuisine that practically doesn't exist anymore" (e.g. a Grand Marnier soufflé that's "out of this world"); boasting "crisp service", a "fine wine list" and "impeccably traditional ambiance", the place in the 13th is "not elegant, not fancy" but quite simply "the real thing."

NEW Petit Monsieur (Au) 🅂🅜 *New French* | - | - | - | M |

11ᵉ | 50, rue Amelot (Chemin-Vert) | 01 43 55 54 04 | fax 01 43 14 77 03

Occupying the old C'Amelot premises, this lively new *bistrot à vins* has retained the decor of exposed-stone walls, but added some comfort to the snug dining room by removing a table or two; the hearty New French dishes on the short, moderately priced menu come with a few creative flourishes, and service is alert and friendly for the bobo regulars who live in this gentrifying section of the 11th.

Petit Niçois (Le) *Provence* | 19 | 13 | 19 | €40 |

7ᵉ | 10, rue Amélie (La Tour-Maubourg) | 01 45 51 83 65 | fax 01 47 05 77 46 | www.lepetitnicois.com

"Hidden on a side street" in the 7th, this "delightful little" venue brings a "warm" breath of Mediterranean air to the metropolis, in the shape of "good, honest" Provençal cuisine, "cordial" staffers and "light-colored" decor; its "low-key environment" is particularly "popular with locals."

NEW Petit Pamphlet (Le) 🅂 *Bistro* | - | - | - | M |

3ᵉ | 15, rue St-Gilles (Chemin-Vert) | 01 42 71 22 21

In the Marais, this newborn offshoot of nearby Le Pamphlet spreads a little sunshine with a Southern French–Spanish-influenced bistro menu, a Languedoc-Roussillon–heavy wine list and prices that are as appetizing as the food; the parquet-floored dining room has a warm feel too, with apricot-hued upholstered chairs, biscuit-colored walls and smiling servers throughout.

Petit Pascal (Le) 🅂 *Bistro* | - | - | - | M |

13ᵉ | 33, rue Pascal (Les Gobelins) | 01 45 35 33 87 | fax 01 45 35 33 87

This *petit* but busy bistro is always packed with picky penny-pinchers who appreciate the excellent quality and generous portions of the Classic French cooking; quick service and a warm atmosphere explain why it grabs the Gobelins neighborhood set.

	FOOD	DECOR	SERVICE	COST

Petit Pergolèse (Le) 🔅 *Bistro* ▽ 15 | 13 | 14 | €53

16e | 38, rue Pergolèse (Argentine/Porte-Maillot) | 01 45 00 23 66 | fax 01 45 00 44 03

Owner Albert Corre has sold Le Pergolèse next door in the 16th arrondissement, but held onto its "little brother", a "more casual" bistro where he cooks up a "new version of traditional" French dishes; some say it's "just as satisfying" as its former sibling, but "cheaper, younger and very noisy" because the "slightly funky" room is "usually buzzing with people."

Petit Pontoise (Le) *Bistro* 23 | 15 | 19 | €44

5e | 9, rue de Pontoise (Maubert-Mutualité) | 01 43 29 25 20 | fax 01 43 25 09 43

"Wow" exclaim enthusiasts of this "wonderful, unspoiled Parisian bistro" in the Latin Quarter serving up "classic homestyle comfort food" "at great prices"; a "deserved favorite with Americans" along with professors and students from the Sorbonne, this "small venue with big flavors" is "noisy" and "always full", which can "overburden" the "pleasant staff."

Petit Poucet (Le) *New French* ▽ 16 | 19 | 15 | €45

Levallois-Perret | 4, rd-pt Claude Monet (Pont-de-Levallois) | 01 47 38 61 81 | fax 01 47 38 20 49 | www.le-petitpoucet.net

"See and be seen" "on the banks of the Seine" at this "trendy", spacious Ile de la Jatte New French that caters to "bourgeois Neuilly families in the evening and advertising types at noon"; wet blankets bark the eats are rather "industrial" but all concur that the "agreeable terrace" is "unbeatable in summer."

Petit Prince de Paris (Le) ◑ *Bistro* 21 | 18 | 23 | €37

5e | 12, rue de Lanneau (Maubert-Mutualité) | 01 43 54 77 26

"You'll feel like you're on another planet" at this "terrific" table "in an old townhouse by the Sorbonne", "tightly packed" with a "mixed gay-straight crowd", a "funky", "vibrant atmosphere" and the "sassiest" waiters in town; open late, it's perfect either "for couples en tête-à-tête or a group of friends", and the bistro menu, "an amazing deal", is as "adventuresome" as the Little Prince himself.

Petit Rétro (Le) 🔅 *Bistro* 20 | 18 | 18 | €42

16e | 5, rue Mesnil (Victor Hugo) | 01 44 05 06 05 | fax 01 47 55 00 48 | www.petitretro.fr

"So Paris" rave retro-verts of this "quaint belle epoque"–decorated site, "the epitome of a good bistro" "just off the Place Victor Hugo" with "well-prepared" Classic French cuisine at "reasonable prices"; the only drawback is that it's "a little *trop petit*" for its popularity – "you're almost seated on your neighbor's knees!"

Petit Riche (Au) ◑🔅 *Bistro* 16 | 21 | 14 | €51

9e | 25, rue le Peletier (Le Peletier/Richelieu-Drouot) | 01 47 70 68 68 | fax 01 48 24 10 79 | www.aupetitriche.com

Traditional French bistros are going, going, "mostly gone", but steps from the Drouot auction house in the 9th is this "survivor from the

19th century" serving *"très riche"* "old-fashioned classics" that inspire a mixed lot of views, from "so-so" to "excellent"; but in any case, "you go here for the ambiance", to sit on red velvet banquettes amid the "authentic" 1880s decor – ideal for a business lunch, entertaining "out-of-town guests" or "after the theater."

Petit St. Benoît (Le) 🗷🍽 *Classic French* | 15 | 14 | 17 | €33

6ᵉ | 4, rue St-Benoît (St-Germain-des-Prés) | 01 42 60 27 92 | www.petit-st-benoit.fr

"Shoehorn yourself into a table, steel yourself for curt service" and tuck in for a "noisy dinner with the locals" at this Saint-Germain "canteen" that's "been here forever" (or at least 1901); you'll find the same "good old family cooking *à la française* (not that we always liked what *maman* served)", the same setting, which "hasn't been redecorated since about 1929", and almost the same prices, making this one of "the cheapest eats in Paris."

Petit Victor
Hugo (Le) 🌓🗷 *Classic French* | 14 | 12 | 12 | €44

16ᵉ | 143, av Victor Hugo (Victor Hugo/Rue de la Pompe) | 01 45 53 02 68 | fax 01 44 05 13 46 | www.petitvictorhugo.com

This Classic French near the Place Victor Hugo remains a "local institution" to its loyal clientele of "neighborhood bourgeoisie" and "lots of pretty girls" despite grumbling that the food is merely "serviceable" and the "service positively disagreeable"; "while the terrace is nice in summer, it might be time to change the '70s decor" too.

Petit Zinc (Le) 🌓 *Brasserie* | 20 | 21 | 19 | €53

6ᵉ | 11, rue St-Benoît (St-Germain-des-Prés/Mabillon) | 01 42 86 61 00 | fax 01 42 86 61 09 | www.petitzinc.com

"Named for its zinc bar that's been around forever", this "art nouveau-style gem" in Saint-Germain serves brasserie fare ("seafood is the specialty") that's "surprisingly good for such a touristy" area; but nostalgists mutter it was "more fun before it became part of a big French chain", finding the "decor more interesting than the formulaic food" and service that swings from "absent-minded" to "attentive."

Pétrelle (Le) 🗷Ⓜ *New French* | – | – | – | M

9ᵉ | 34, rue Pétrelle (Anvers) | 01 42 82 11 02 | fax 01 40 23 05 69

In the 9th, this small, beautifully baroque dining room pulls a beau-monde crowd and a few famous faces with its refined antiques-furnished atmosphere and the elegant, very personal New French cuisine of chef-owner Jean-Luc André; his chalkboard menu changes regularly, following the seasons and making imaginative use of fresh herbs; service is soigné but friendly.

Pétrus 🗷 *Classic French* | – | – | – | E

17ᵉ | 12, pl du Maréchal Juin (Péreire) | 01 43 80 15 95 | fax 01 47 66 49 86

Formerly an expensive seafood house, this dining room in the 17th has been reinvented by new owners as a brasserie deluxe with modern, earth-toned decor; the Classic French menu still features a lot of fish, but carnivores are catered for too; service is swift and well mannered, smoothly shifting gears from the gray flannel crowd at lunch to a cashmere clientele at dinner.

Pharamond *Classic French* ▽ 18 | 21 | 19 | €61

1ᵉʳ | 24, rue de la Grande Truanderie (Etienne Marcel/ Les Halles) | 01 40 28 45 18 | fax 01 40 28 45 87 | www.le-pharamond.com

Nobody's talking tripe when they say this "noisy, crowded, simple place" near Les Halles is "as much a taste of Old France as you can find today" – and by old, we mean dating back to 1832, when the Pharamond family began serving tripe à la mode de Caën; it's still on the menu and still "superb", along with the other classics proffered by "friendly" servers amid the landmarked, "genuine" belle epoque decor.

Pichet de Paris (Le) 🅩 *Seafood* 20 | 13 | 16 | €73

8ᵉ | 68, rue Pierre Charron (Franklin D. Roosevelt) | 01 43 59 50 34 | fax 01 42 89 68 91

"Local businesspeople" and politicians are hooked on this "unpretentious address" just steps from the Champs, where the "seriously good fish" and the "freshest oysters" are as "solid as they've been for 30 years"; it remains "a Paris institution" with the "nostalgic air of a place that served a former president" (Mitterrand), even if agitators argue "prices are a little excessive" given the "unoriginal" decor and "service that should be better" to non-regulars.

Pied de Chameau (Au)/ - | - | - | M
Al Nour ● *Moroccan*

3ᵉ | 173, rue St. Martin (Chatelet/Rambuteau) | 01 42 78 35 00 | fax 01 42 78 00 50 | www.alnour.fr

Those "longing for a vacation in the Maghreb" get their fix of couscous and tagines at this Moroccan with a "trendy reputation", recently relocated to the 3rd; "low lighting" and "exotic" decor "make this a perfect romantic evening in Casablanca", but if you're on a first date, "beware: the belly dancer makes you dance!"

Pied de Cochon (Au) ● *Brasserie* 18 | 18 | 16 | €46

1ᵉʳ | 6, rue Coquillière (Châtelet-Les Halles) | 01 40 13 77 00 | fax 01 40 13 77 09 | www.pieddecochon.com

"Call me Miss Piggy" squeal supporters of this "lively" "remnant of the old Les Halles", who pork out on "abundant" portions of traditional brasserie fare – onion soup, "large platters of fresh seafood" and "the pig's feet that give the restaurant its name"; "open nonstop", it can feel rather "factory"-like, but for foreign visitors, its "archetypal Parisian waiters" and "kitschy" (even "gaudy") decor make it "a must, at least – but probably only – once."

Pierre au Palais Royal 🅩 *Classic French* 16 | 14 | 15 | €49

1ᵉʳ | 10, rue Richelieu (Palais Royal-Musée du Louvre) | 01 42 96 09 17 | fax 01 42 96 26 40

Loyalists deem this a "delightful little" site "near the Palais Royal", for "Classic French fare with a tad of modernity"; while the hoi polloi might hesitate at the prices, the "bar allows for drinking and dining without spending a fortune."

	FOOD	DECOR	SERVICE	COST

⊡ Pierre Gagnaire *Haute Cuisine*   28 | 25 | 27 | €183

8ᵉ | Hôtel Balzac | 6, rue Balzac (Charles de Gaulle-Etoile/George V) | 01 58 36 12 50 | fax 01 58 36 12 51 | www.pierre-gagnaire.com

"Before you die, go" to this Haute Cuisine table in the 8th, "a place to push your palate and explore new sensations" with a chef-owner who, "mad scientist–like", combines "tastes that blow your mind away"; within a "chic" "Scandi-Asian decor of blond woods and gray" tones, near-"faultless service" presents a "dizzying" number of dishes "almost too overwhelming to comprehend"; alas, the "huge" bill registers all too well, "but the price is justified", because "Pierre is still without peer."

Pinxo *New French*   20 | 19 | 20 | €57

1ᵉʳ | Renaissance Paris Vendôme | 9, rue d'Alger (Tuileries) | 01 40 20 72 00 | fax 01 40 20 72 02

Owned by "star-studded chef" Alain Dutournier, this "stylish spot" in the 1st "combines aspects of a traditional tapas bar with those of a contemporary French restaurant" where "two or three people can share dishes" of "exotic Basque-influenced cuisine" that are "not copious, but flavorful"; perhaps the best seats in the "sleek minimalist room" are "at the bar with a view of the open kitchen", but the "noise level is low" throughout, providing a "Zen-chic" experience.

Pitchi Poï *Eastern European*   – | – | – | M

4ᵉ | 7, rue Caron (St-Paul) | 01 42 77 46 15 | fax 01 42 77 75 49 | www.pitchipoi.com

"Discover Jewish cuisine" with a Polish twist at this Eastern European eatery, known for its blini washed down with a large selection of vodkas and its highly "hyped", all-you-can-eat Sunday brunch buffet; "the decor is pretty basic" but "the courtyard is nice" with its coveted location on a quiet cobblestone square in the Marais.

Pizzeria d'Auteuil *Italian*   ▽ 17 | 11 | 11 | €38

16ᵉ | 81, rue la Fontaine (Michel-Ange-Auteuil) | 01 42 88 00 86

"Overflowing with regulars" from the ritzy 16th, "this pizzeria is in fact a real Italian restaurant"; "yes, the food is good, but it's best not to go hungry" since you'll probably have to wait for service that "runs the gamut from passable to scandalous"; in any case, the "cool crowd" doesn't care that "the welcome is not their strong suit" and the decor's "uninteresting", as the ambiance is always "convivial."

Pizzetta (La) ⊠ *Italian*   – | – | – | M

9ᵉ | 22, av Trudaine (Anvers/Pigalle) | 01 48 78 14 08 | fax 01 48 78 14 08 | www.lapizzetta.fr

Sardinian chef Riccardo Podda packs them into this stylish Italian in a well-heeled corner of the 9th; though the pretty 19th-century stucco moldings and mirrored walls from a previous tenant remain, the furnishings are strictly Milanese minimalist; good pizzas and pastas for modest prices have made it a hit.

	FOOD	DECOR	SERVICE	COST

Planet Hollywood ● *American*   7 | 12 | 9 | €30

8ᵉ | 78, av des Champs-Elysées (Franklin D. Roosevelt/George V) | 01 53 83 78 27 | fax 01 45 62 02 84 | www.planethollywood.com

Yanks who are "homesick for American atmosphere" can count on the fact that this Champs-Elysées chainster is "just like any other Planet Hollywood" with a "lot of stuff to look at" and a "muscular burger" starring on a menu of born-in-the-USA eats; but patriotism has its limits for foes who "avoid this joint" – with "mediocre" cooking and "deplorable service", it's "the reason why the French think we're pagans."

Ploum ✷ *Japanese/New French*   – | – | – | M

10ᵉ | 20, rue Alibert (Goncourt) | 01 42 00 11 90 | www.ploum.fr

Decorated "with huge windows and raw interiors" – like "a UFO that seems to have landed in the middle of nowhere" – this "odd but cute eatery" "near the Canal Saint-Martin" comes bearing "creative, delicious Japanese–New French fusion cuisine" and some of the "freshest sushi in town."

Point Bar ✷Ⓜ *New French*   ∇ 21 | 15 | 20 | €32

1ᵉʳ | 40, pl du Marché St-Honoré (Pyramides) | 01 42 61 76 28 | fax 01 42 96 46 90

This "unpretentious bistro" in the Marché Saint-Honoré gains points galore with New French dishes "carefully prepared" from "quality products" (some grown in the owner's own garden) and "pretty", contemporary decor; the "cute young staff" is led by proprietor Alice Bardet, a renowned chef's daughter who "really makes you feel like an old friend."

Polichinelle Cafe *Bistro*   – | – | – | M

11ᵉ | 64-66, rue de Charonne (Charonne) | 01 58 30 63 52

Yet another in the growing number of eateries that is rapidly turning the 11th into neo-bistro central, this amiable neighborhood place pleases its regulars with a relaxed atmosphere and modest prices for dishes cooked with a lot of loving care; there's live entertainment every Sunday in the ever-bustling bar.

Polidor ● *Bistro*   15 | 15 | 14 | €27

6ᵉ | 41, rue Monsieur-le-Prince (Luxembourg/Odéon) | 01 43 26 95 34 | fax 01 43 26 22 79

"Steeped in history", this "old bistro" (est. 1845) near the Luxembourg Gardens is where students, starving artists and tourists "looking for the 'authentic' Paris" "sit elbow-to-elbow" at "communal tables" to eat "very average", albeit very "cheap", "comfort meals" of French "staples" ("regular diners keep napkins in cubbyholes in the back"); old-timers opine it "hasn't changed in 40 years" – "even the waitresses seem the same" with their "genuine rude service."

Pomponette (A la) ●✷ *Bistro*   – | – | – | M

18ᵉ | 42, rue Lepic (Abbesses/Blanche) | 01 46 06 08 36 | fax 01 42 52 95 44 | www.alapomponette.fr

"A real Montmartre institution, managed by the fourth generation" of the clan that opened it in 1909, this vet serves "good, familial" traditional bistro cuisine in "very Montmartre decor" – "the walls are adorned by works of local painters who were short of cash (and sometimes of talent)"; the "honest neighborhood ambiance" is accented by a concert of Parisian *chansons* once a month.

Pomze ⓩ New French

▽ 19 | 17 | 20 | €38

8e | 109, bd Haussmann (Miromesnil/St-Augustin) | 01 42 65 65 83 | fax 01 42 65 30 03 | www.pomze.com

"Admirers of William Tell" and apple addicts are thrilled to the core by this "wonderfully inventive" "concept" eatery in the 8th, where the New French menu "is built around *la pomme* in all its forms", adding "subtle flavors" to dishes from starters to dessert; augmenting them is an impressive selection of – what else? – "the best ciders" from around France; N.B. there's also a ground-floor gourmet shop.

Port Alma ⓩ Ⓜ Seafood

20 | 15 | 20 | €77

16e | 10, av de New York (Alma Marceau) | 01 47 23 75 11 | fax 01 47 20 42 92

Aficionados drop anchor at this 16th-arrondissement port facing the Seine, saying the "fresh" fish dishes are "as good as seafood gets when not in the Mediterranean" (the "magnificent view of the Eiffel Tower" leaves no doubt that you're in Paris); while it's "pricey", the "attentive service", "relaxed" ambiance and recently refreshed "blue-for-the-sea" contemporary decor make it "worth the trip."

Potager du Roy (Le) ⓩ Ⓜ Classic French

22 | 18 | 18 | €52

Versailles | 1, rue du Maréchal-Joffre (RER Versailles-Rive Gauche) | 01 39 50 35 34 | fax 01 30 21 69 30

Visitors to Versailles hail this "lovely retreat" near the palace, where the chef makes "exceptional" Traditional French "cuisine with a touch of originality", giving "a place of honor to vegetables" (the name refers to the royal garden); the decor is equally "classic" – though perhaps the tables are "a little too close together" – and while it's "a little dear", you won't need a king's ransom to pay the bill.

Pouilly Reuilly ⓩ Bistro

▽ 19 | 17 | 19 | €55

Le Pré-St-Gervais | 68, rue André Joineau (Hoche) | 01 48 45 14 59 | fax 01 48 45 93 93

It's just east of the city in Le Pré-Saint-Gervais, but suburban surveyors say this old bistro can be "out of this world" for "heavy", "typical French food" (think organ meats, blood sausage and giant éclairs); as they walk through to the post-war dining room, customers get a close-up look at the kitchen – but be advised that it stops taking orders after 9:45 PM.

Poulbot Gourmet ⓩ Bistro

– | – | – | M

18e | 39, rue Lamarck (Lamarck-Caulaincourt) | 01 46 06 86 00 | fax 01 46 06 63 14

In a neighborhood known for tourist traps, this "time capsule" in Montmartre surprises with reasonably priced, "carefully" prepared Classic French dishes, "kind" service and cozy bistro decor with prints by renowned illustrator Francisque Poulbot, who once lived on this street.

	FOOD	DECOR	SERVICE	COST

Poule au Pot (La) ◑Ⓜ *Bistro*
21 | 19 | 21 | €43

1er | 9, rue Vauvilliers (Châtelet-Les Halles/Louvre-Rivoli) |
01 42 36 32 96 | fax 01 40 91 90 64 | www.lapouleaupot.fr

There's "a chicken in every pot" – or nearly – at this "classic spot" in
Les Halles, a "local place" where peckish diners can count on "large
portions" of the "signature dish", as well as onion soup, bone marrow,
profiteroles and other bistro faves; the service is "very amiable", right
up until closing time at 5 AM

☑ Pré Catelan (Le) ⑤Ⓜ *Haute Cuisine*
26 | 28 | 25 | €137

16e | Bois de Boulogne, Route de Suresnes (Porte Maillot) |
01 44 14 41 14 | fax 01 45 24 43 25 | www.lenotre.fr

Given its setting "in a fairy-tale park" with a "sumptuous" "fireplace
in the winter" and a "terrace in the summer", some might suspect
this vet of turning into "a tourist trap" – but instead, almost all are
"thrilled" by the "truly wonderful experience", thanks to chef Frédéric
Anton's "amazing" Haute Cuisine with a light, contemporary touch
and the "classy" service; while the "outrageously expensive" bill
makes it preferable "if someone else is paying", this is "the perfect
splurge"; N.B. it was slated to unveil a new look in spring 2007,
which may outdate the Decor score.

NEW Pré Salé (Le) ⑤ *Northern France*
- | - | - | M

1er | 9, rue d'Argenteuil (Pyramides/Louvre-Palais Royale) |
01 42 60 56 22

This 1st-arrondissement newcomer provides a nod to Normandy,
both in the photos adorning its sunny beige and bordeaux decor and
in its creative dishes that have a Haute Cuisine flourish; its name refers to the region's famed salt marshland-raised lamb, so baby
sheep is, not surprisingly, the specialty here; bankers and business
types are already pre-sold at lunch, but at quieter nights it becomes
the happy secret of knowing locals.

Press Café ⑤ *Bistro*
- | - | - | I

2e | 89, rue Montmartre (Sentier) | 01 40 26 07 30 |
www.presscafe.net

A stone's throw from the offices of Agence France-Presse (hence, its
name), this "nice neighborhood bistro" in the 2nd delights journalists and other pressed locals with "exceptional service and food"
consisting of simple fare – foie gras, hand-cut beef tartare, chocolate mousse – at prices so low they're newsworthy.

Pré Verre (Le) ⑤Ⓜ *New French*
23 | 14 | 18 | €37

5e | 8, rue Thénard (Maubert-Mutualité) | 01 43 54 59 47 |
www.lepreverre.com

Diners "who like to be surprised" "wait in line" for a table at this
"young, animated" Latin Quarter New French, which "has achieved
cult culinary status by reinventing classics" with a "fusion of spices"
that "get you traveling without moving" – and all for an "unbeatable
price" too; but no matter how "crowded" and "noisy" the "narrow"
main room gets, claustrophobic clients should "avoid at all costs"
the "smoke-filled, low-ceilinged basement."

Procope (Le) ● *Classic French*

	FOOD	DECOR	SERVICE	COST
	16	22	17	€52

6ᵉ | 13, rue de l'Ancienne Comédie (Odéon) | 01 40 46 79 00 |
fax 01 40 46 79 09 | www.procope.com

"You have to eat in this 17th-century establishment once, just to check it off your list" – for this Classic French in Saint-Germain is practically "a museum" with its "portrait-laden walls, apartment-sized rooms" and antiques (you "like the idea of dining next to Voltaire's desk"?); once patronized by "luminaries of literature, the arts" and politics, it's "now frequented largely by tourists" – "the servers are clearly fed up with them" – and critics call the cuisine "great for history buffs, but not for gourmets."

P'tit Troquet (Le) ⊠ *Bistro*

	FOOD	DECOR	SERVICE	COST
	23	18	23	€41

7ᵉ | 28, rue de l'Exposition (Ecole Militaire) | 01 47 05 80 39 |
fax 01 47 05 80 39

"Expect to feel right at home" at this "beau ideal for the small, family-run bistro" near the Champs de Mars, complete with zinc bar and "menu written daily on a chalkboard"; the "art deco decor" "is somewhat tattered, but that doesn't detract" from the "simple, well-executed" "authentic French flavors"; "a terrific value", it's "a touchstone for cozy, casual dining."

Publicis Drugstore ● *Brasserie*

	FOOD	DECOR	SERVICE	COST
	12	14	12	€38

8ᵉ | 133, av des Champs-Elysées (Charles de Gaulle-Etoile/George V) |
01 44 43 77 64 | fax 01 44 43 79 02 | www.publicisdrugstore.com

A "sweeping glass front affords excellent people-watching" (and allows diners "to be seen") at this brasserie in the "beautifully renovated" Drugstore complex; long hours make it "popular with the late-night club crowd" and consumers cruising the Champs, but despite consulting chef Alain Ducasse's input, many find the "basic" "comfort dishes" "below expectations"; overall prescription: "don't go for the food", but for the "marvelous" location.

Pure Café ● *Eclectic*

	FOOD	DECOR	SERVICE	COST
	-	-	-	M

11ᵉ | 14, rue Jean Macé (Faidherbe-Chaligny) | 01 43 71 47 22 |
fax 01 43 71 47 22

There are no guarantees you'll spot French actress Julie Delpy, but still this intimate bistro, featured in the film *Before Sunset*, makes a "lovely, casual date" (or reunion) place, thanks to its "inventive, refined" Eclectic fare, "inexpensive drinks" from a horseshoe-shaped bar and "relaxed setting", courtesy of its "great, off-the-beaten-track location" in the 11th.

Pur'Grill *New French*

	FOOD	DECOR	SERVICE	COST
	∇ 25	25	26	€88

2ᵉ | Park Hyatt Paris-Vendôme | 5, rue de la Paix (Opéra) |
01 58 71 12 34 | fax 01 58 71 10 32 |
www.paris.vendome.hyatt.com

With the arrival of chef Jean-François Rouquette (ex Les Muses) this dinner-only grill in the Park Hyatt Paris-Vendôme, with a "sublime" circular decor by Ed Tuttle, has become "one of the best [institutional] restaurants in Paris"; the edgy New French menu offers "amazing" food, "superbly executed" "with appropriately attentive service"; "as befits a hotel" eatery, the "prices are steep" but it's "particularly good for dining alone."

Quai (Le) *New French* − | − | − | M
7ᵉ | Quai Anatole France - Port de Solférino (Solférino) |
01 44 18 04 39 | fax 01 44 18 09 52 | www.restaurantlequai.com
"Nothing better than being on a barge on a beautiful day" say sea-faring surveyors of this houseboat moored at the foot of the Musée d'Orsay; "charming servers" offer "enjoyable" New French lunches seven days a week, in a glass-enclosed room or outside on the Seine-side terrace where the splendid view lets "you wave to the *bateaux-mouches* passing by."

Quai Ouest ● *Eclectic* 17 | 21 | 14 | €46
Saint-Cloud | 1200, quai Marcel Dassault (Pont-de-St-Cloud) |
01 46 02 35 54 | fax 01 46 02 33 02
"When your goal is to eat on the water", "you can often find a table" in this spacious Seine-side barge in Saint-Cloud, a "buzzy" spot where TV types and hipsters enjoy "a good view over the river"; although "the decor beats the food", the Eclectic fare is "reliable" enough, and the Sunday brunch complete "with a clown" is "a must for children"; but since "the boat sounds like a playground" then, those *sans enfants* might stick to the other six days of the week.

404 (Le) ● *Moroccan* 21 | 25 | 18 | €40
3ᵉ | 69, rue des Gravilliers (Arts et Métiers) | 01 42 74 57 81 |
fax 01 42 74 03 41
With "dramatic lighting and a harem feel", "the decor's sumptuous, the atmosphere's always happening and the cooking's really good" at this "dark" Moroccan just north of Les Halles; true, it's "increasingly touristy", "noisy" and "cramped (barely room for your elbows)", and the "smiling-joker" servers can be "rushed"; but even if you "just go there for the ambiance", this "den of seduction" is one to "enjoy."

R. ●⊘⚡ *New French* 17 | 21 | 16 | €54
15ᵉ | 6-8, rue de la Cavalerie (La Motte-Picquet-Grenelle) |
01 45 67 06 85 | fax 01 45 67 55 72 | www.le-r.fr
A "strange elevator" takes a "fashionable young crowd" up to this table with a Tibetan Zen decor in the 15th; it's best known for the "incredible" sight it offers of Paris' trademark landmark, and though pessimists pout the panorama "is the only attraction", optimists opine the "New French menu doesn't disappoint"; in any case, it's a "nice choice for a romantic night out" – though "if you're alone and reserve a table on the terrace, the Eiffel Tower will keep you company."

Radis Roses Restaurant ⚡M *New French* − | − | − | M
9ᵉ | 68, rue Rodier (Anvers) | 01 48 78 03 20
This tiny, modern addition to the ever-trendier 9th is a friendly, "very casual" spot, whose New French menu features specialties from the Drôme region of southern France, such as small raviolis stuffed with anything from foie gras to chocolate; there's a New York feeling to the hip little room, enhanced by the fact that it's entirely nonsmoking.

Ragueneau (Le) *Classic French/Tearoom* — — — I

1ᵉʳ | 202, rue St-Honoré (Palais Royal-Musée du Louvre) | 01 42 60 29 20 | fax 01 42 60 29 70 | www.ragueneau.fr

Immortalized as a poetry-loving pastry chef in *Cyrano de Bergerac*, the real Ragueneau operated a shop here steps from Palais Royal in the 17th century; obviously, it's changed hands since then, but it still serves "delicious *pâtisseries* to go" or to consume in the ground-floor tea salon; meanwhile, "very passable" Classic French meals are available upstairs in a restaurant with theatrical decor of chandeliers and red velvet curtains.

Ravi ●⊠ *Indian* ∇ 24 21 23 €51

7ᵉ | 50, rue de Verneuil (Rue du Bac) | 01 42 61 17 28 | fax 01 42 61 12 18

Supporters of the subcontinent make a pilgrimage to this "intimate Indian" in the swank 7th, whose "startlingly good" "traditional" cuisine many say might be the "best in Paris"; the "small room with no windows" is "dark", "but that can be very romantic"; so the hefty "price is the only fly in the curry" ("my mouth never wanted to leave but my wallet cried otherwise").

Rech (Le) ⊠ *Classic French/Seafood* ∇ 14 11 15 €52

17ᵉ | 62, av des Ternes (Charles de Gaulle-Etoile/Ternes) | 01 45 72 29 47 | fax 01 45 72 41 60 | www.rech.fr

A 17th-arrondissement fixture since 1925, this brasserie offers oysters and "fish, superbly prepared and served"; skeptics say the rest of the Classic French "cuisine is a little rocky" these days; however, that should soon change, as chef-restaurateur Alain Ducasse is slated to assume command in March 2007 (not reflected in the scores).

Réconfort (Le) *New French* ∇ 17 23 16 €43

3ᵉ | 37, rue de Poitou (St-Sébastien Froissart) | 01 49 96 09 60 | fax 01 49 96 09 62

In the northern Marais, a "good mix of clientele" frequents this "festive" spot with "whimsical decor" reminiscent of a "maharajah's palace"; "unfortunately, atmosphere can only make up for so much" fume foes who find a "lack of coherence" in the "innovative French" menu and too much "attitude at the door"; on the plus side, "menus are slipped into paperback books, so if your friends arrive late you can read while you wait."

Refectoire (Le) *Bistro* — — — I

11ᵉ | 80, bd Richard Lenoir (Richard Lenoir/St-Ambroise) | 01 48 06 74 85

Its name means 'school cafeteria', but it's more like recess at this "reasonably priced" venue in a quiet part of the 11th, decorated with old school chairs, paper place mats and molecular light fixtures; while some praise the "simple, tasty" modern bistro fare, most of the class contends "you don't come here for the mediocre cuisine or the calm (bring earplugs), but for the fun ambiance, the pretty girls and the neighborhood" trendoids – and the restroom, a veritable sound and light show.

	FOOD	DECOR	SERVICE	COST

Régalade (La) 🅢 *Bistro*
23 | 14 | 17 | €45

14e | 49, av Jean Moulin (Alésia) | 01 45 45 68 58 | fax 01 45 40 96 74
The man who made it a "must-do", chef "Yves Camdeborde, has moved on" – "but you can't see or taste [much] difference" declare disciples of this bistro deep in the 14th; it's "still a winner" for "massive portions" of "stupendous" "Classic French country food" "at a fraction of the price" of others; it's also still "crowded and chaotic" with service that's "a bit grumpy"; but "just thinking about the terrine" "that comes as an all-you-can-eat amuse-bouche" keeps 'em coming back.

☑ Relais d'Auteuil "Patrick Pignol" 🅢 *Haute Cuisine*
26 | 20 | 23 | €112

16e | 31, bd Murat (Michel-Ange-Molitor/Porte d'Auteuil) | 01 46 51 09 54 | fax 01 40 71 05 03
A "belle clientele from the neighborhood" near the Porte d'Auteuil and French Open fans with a hunger for Haute Cuisine know that, though this warm-colored corner "doesn't have the aura of the big names", it remains "one of the best culinary experiences in Paris", thanks to a "family's passion" for "perfection", from M'sieur Pignol's "exquisite" cooking to Madame's "kind service"; P.S. the game and "truffle dishes in season will bring you to your knees."

☑ Relais de l'Entrecôte (Le) ● *Steak*
23 | 14 | 19 | €34

6e | 20, rue St-Benoit (St-Germain-des-Prés) | 01 45 49 16 00 | fax 01 45 49 29 75
8e | 15, rue Marbeuf (Franklin D. Roosevelt) | 01 49 52 07 17 | fax 01 47 23 34 98
www.relais-entrecote.com
"Vegetarians, do not even bother" coming to these "packed" "Paris landmarks" in the 6th and the 8th, where "your only choice is rare, medium or well-done" "all-you-can-eat entrecôte" with a "divine" "secret sauce" and "perfectly crunchy" fries on a set menu, plus "amazing desserts" as an option; since you can't reserve, "go early because the lines get long fast", and be ready for the "old-fashioned waitresses" "who throw you out as soon as you've swallowed the last mouthful."

Relais de Venise (Le) ● *Steak*
22 | 14 | 17 | €37

17e | 271, bd Péreire (Porte Maillot) | 01 45 74 27 97
"No surprises" await at this steakhouse at Porte Maillot, an "address handed down from generation to generation", where "the wait for a table is interminable" and then the "friendly but abrupt" waitresses are almost too "quick"; the fixed menu stars an "eternal entrecôte" with "mysterious sauce" that has "spies the world over trying to find out the recipe", along with "terrific frites" ("whatever you do, don't ask for ketchup!"); P.S. the "bargain price" includes "second helpings."

Relais du Parc (Le) 🅢 Ⓜ *Haute Cuisine*
- | - | - | VE

16e | Sofitel Le Parc | 55-57, av Raymond Poncaré (Victor Hugo/ Trocadero) | 01 44 05 66 10 | fax 01 44 05 66 39 | www.sofitel.com
Experience the remembrance of things past with this recently reopened Haute Cuisine hotel dining room, whose menu features a few signature dishes from two chefs who successively worked there

in the '90s – Joël Robuchon and Alain Ducasse (whatever happened to those guys?); admittedly, it's a gimmick, but it may well suit the suits of the 16th, as does the seasonally changing decor and the "beautiful" interior courtyard; N.B. 59 Poincaré, the hotel's former eatery, is now reserved for private parties.

☑ Relais Louis XIII 🚫Ⓜ️ *Haute Cuisine* | 25 | 24 | 24 | €97 |

6ᵉ | 8, rue des Grands-Augustins (Odéon/St-Michel) | 01 43 26 75 96 | fax 01 44 07 07 80 | www.relaislouis13.com
Patrons pledge fealty to this "sleeper" in the 6th for classic Haute Cuisine in a "lovely old house" with 17th-century paintings, where Louis XIII was proclaimed king; the current sovereign, chef-owner Manuel Martinez, produces "astounding" fare that's "expensive" but "worth every euro", as is the "wonderful" wine list; the "accommodating staff" and "formal" ambiance make it " fantastic to celebrate any grand occasion", "to luxuriate with a lover" or even "to take grandma."

Relais Plaza (Le) ⚫ *Brasserie/Eclectic* | 22 | 22 | 21 | €84 |

8ᵉ | Hôtel Plaza-Athénée | 25, av Montaigne (Alma Marceau/ Franklin D. Roosevelt) | 01 53 67 64 00 | fax 01 53 67 66 66 | www.plaza-athenee-paris.com
"A chic clientele and celebrities" add a "touch of glamour" to this "sophisticated, intimate" art deco "brasserie deluxe"; "the more casual dining experience of the Plaza-Athénée", it's run by the same chefs behind the main restaurant, and their "seductive" Eclectic fare inspires clients to confide "you feel like you're cheating – Alain Ducasse–inspired dishes at a fraction of the price."

☑ Réminet (Le) *New French* | 25 | 18 | 22 | €47 |

5ᵉ | 3, rue des Grands-Degrés (Maubert-Mutualité/St-Michel) | 01 44 07 04 24
"No longer a secret" but "still a great find", this "sweet little place" "looking out on Ile Saint-Louis" is "one of the best choices in the Latin Quarter"; despite a recent change of ownership, it still offers "exceptional", "inventive" New French food at an "outstanding price/quality" ratio; it's "warm, cozy" and "perfect for a romantic dinner" if you don't mind that it's "packed with Americans."

Rendez-vous des Chauffeurs (Au) 🚫Ⓜ️ *Bistro* | - | - | - | I |

18ᵉ | 11, rue des Portes-Blanches (Marcadet-Poissonniers) | 01 42 64 04 17
Nothing changes (not even the menu) at this century-old "bistro with a real sense of neighborhood" – in this case, an unpretentious and un-touristy part of the 18th; this "rustic", "convivial" place has "no decor" to speak of but copious portions of "simply wonderful food" (including hand-cut fries that some call "the best in the world") at "very gentle prices."

Renoma Café Gallery ⚫ *Italian* | - | - | - | E |

8ᵉ | 32, av George V (George V) | 01 47 20 46 19 | fax 01 40 70 90 71 | www.renoma-cafe.com
This trendy Golden Triangle table/lounge for fashionistas "seems to have found its cruising speed": clients "go for the ambiance rather

than the food" – which recently switched to Italian cuisine, served "by
debutants" (albeit "with a smile") – preferring to groove on the
"modern" decor and photo gallery, the perfect-for-people-watching
"pretty terrace on the Avenue George V," and the event-packed evenings featuring fortune tellers, live music and massages.

Repaire de Cartouche (Le) 🛅 Ⓜ *Bistro* | 19 | 10 | 15 | €45 |

11ᵉ | 8, bd Filles du Calvaine (St-Sébastien Froissart) |
01 47 00 25 86 | fax 01 43 38 85 91

The robust dishes at this "traditional" table "with a French countryside feel" in the 11th are a surefire recipe "for beating off the chill of
a Paris winter" including "game cooked with brio" and other "tasty
bistro food"; "the price is very right too" – though "what's in the
plate is more interesting" than the "down-at-the-heels decor."

Restaurant de la Tour 🛅 Ⓜ *Classic French* | – | – | – | M |

15ᵉ | 6, rue Desaix (Dupleix/La Motte-Picquet-Grenelle) |
01 43 06 04 24 | fax 01 44 49 05 66

A short walk from the Tour Eiffel to which its name refers, this "cute"
family-run Classic French is a "nice" respite for tired tourists after
they battle the lines to the top of the Tower; it's especially "fun for
lunch" with a "sunny ambiance" that comes from the warm
Provençal colors in the dining room.

Restaurant de l'Hôtel (Le) 🛅 Ⓜ *Classic French* | – | – | – | E |

(fka Le Bélier)

6ᵉ | L'Hôtel | 13, rue des Beaux-Arts (St-Germain-des-Prés) |
01 44 41 99 01 | fax 01 43 25 64 81 | www.l-hotel.com

Past guests Oscar Wilde (who expired here) and singer Mistinguett
would have appreciated decorator Jacques Garcia's go-for-baroque
decor for the intimate dining room at this historic hotel in Saint-
Germain; frequented by "gallery owners and well-heeled locals", it's
"*très* Parisian" and "romantic", even if the Classic French food is "ok,
not great"; but the recent arrival of chef Philippe Belissent (ex
Ledoyen) may improve things.

Restaurant du Marché 🛅 *Bistro* | – | – | – | M |

15ᵉ | 59, rue de Dantzig (Porte de Versailles) | 01 48 28 31 55 |
fax 01 48 28 18 31

This longstanding, low-key bistro in the 15th draws locals with oft-
changing, "good, unpretentious country cuisine", vaguely rustic,
classic decor of red banquettes, pewter bar and archetypical
blackboard, and Saturday morning cooking classes led by chef-
owner Francis Lévêque.

Restaurant du Musée d'Orsay Ⓜ *Classic French* | 16 | 23 | 16 | €36 |

7ᵉ | Musée d'Orsay | 1, rue de Légion d'Honneur (Solférino) |
01 45 49 47 03 | fax 01 42 22 34 12 | www.museedorsay.fr

When Manet and Monet start to merge in your mind, the Musée
d'Orsay's eatery offers a "regal" "respite from museum overload"

with a "stunning" river view and belle epoque decor of "painted ceilings, crystal chandeliers and mirrored walls" that, while recently lightened up, is "just as interesting" as the institution itself; the Classic French fare is a bit "institutional" too, but even if "the food's better on an airplane, you couldn't ask for a prettier place to sit after a day of Impressionist art."

Restaurant du
Palais Royal 🅉 *Classic French*

19 | 20 | 18 | €62

1ᵉʳ | 110, Galerie de Valois (Bourse/Palais Royal-Musée du Louvre) | 01 40 20 00 27 | fax 01 40 20 00 82 | www.restaurantdupalaisroyal.com

"What better decor than the leaf-dappled shade of the Jardins du Palais Royal?" sigh surveyors seduced by the "magnificent terrace" of this Classic French overlooking one of the city's prettiest gardens; some find it might be a little "too expensive" for food that's just "above average", but all reviewers agree that it is absolutely "idyllic on a beautiful summer evening."

Restaurant GR5 🅉 *Alpine*

15 | 9 | 15 | €30

16ᵉ | 19, rue Gustave Courbet (Rue de la Pompe) | 01 47 27 09 84
17ᵉ | 14, rue Saussier-Leroy (Ternes) | 01 47 66 15 11

"In case of an irresistible desire for fondue or raclette, make a bee-line" to the nearest of these two Savoyard tables in the 16th and 17th, a "great value" for stick-to-your-ribs, melted-cheese meals; named for an alpine footpath, either is "a good address when the cold weather hits" with a "convivial ambiance that feels like home" (assuming you live in a "noisy, tight" place decorated with red-checkered tablecloths and old-fashioned skis).

Restaurant Manufacture 🅉 *Bistro*

▽ 19 | 17 | 15 | €44

Issy-les-Moulineaux | 30, rue Ernest Renar (Corentin-Celton/Porte de Versailles) | 01 40 93 08 98 | fax 01 40 93 57 22 |
www.restaurantmanufacture.com

A "canteen for the TV-industry types working nearby", this "cool" loft space in Issy-les-Moulineaux has a "superb" setting (and camera-worthy terrace) dating from its former life as a tobacco factory; the "reliably good" bistro food is "a clever mix of traditional products and modern flavors" on a menu that "changes with the seasons."

Resto (Le) 🅉 *Classic French*

- | - | - | M

8ᵉ | 10, rue de Castellane (Madeleine) | 01 40 07 99 99 | fax 01 40 07 99 49
Those seeking a stopover while shopping around the Madeleine might well find it in this intimate enclave, which juxtaposes Classic French cuisine with retro-chic decor of aluminum foil wallpaper and '50s-style tables and chairs; the market-fresh menu changes weekly and the staff is friendly, but definitely reserve at lunchtime, since it's on a key corner in the 8th.

Reuan Thai *Thai*

- | - | - | I

11ᵉ | 36, rue de l'Orillon (Belleville) | 01 43 55 15 82
It's a short trip from Belleville to Bangkok at this Thai table that cooks up "spicy" specialties such as green mango salad with catfish

or seafood in a banana leaf; expats and locals often count on it for a budget-friendly, last-minute dinner to take out or eat in, in the traditional, colorful setting seven days a week.

Riad (Le) *Moroccan*
Neuilly-sur-Seine | 42, av Charles de Gaulle (Les Sablons/Porte Maillot) | 01 46 24 42 61 | fax 01 46 40 19 91

This upscale Moroccan's "exotic atmosphere" stands out in the ultra-bourgeois neighborhood of Neuilly, where locals laud its "genuine North African flavors", along with the "solicitous service" of its "friendly staff" amid "intimate", eye-pleasing decor of silk-covered banquettes and marble columns.

NEW Ribouldingue 🛇 M *Classic French*
5e | 10, rue St-Julien-le-Pauvre (St-Michel) | 01 46 33 98 80 | fax 0146 54 09 34

The name of this Latin Quarter newcomer means 'a binge', so get set to go on a spree of funky, earthy French comfort foods like lamb brains, pig's snout and cow's udder (for the timid, the menu also offers less offal dishes like *côte de boeuf* for two); the fussy wood paneling on the walls of the tiny dining room (left over from the previous tenant) provides an elegant, if incongruous, setting for the rustic fare.

River Café *Classic/New French*

FOOD	DECOR	SERVICE	COST
15	19	15	€50

Issy-les-Moulineaux | 146, quai de Stalingrad (RER Issy-Val de Seine) | 01 40 93 50 20 | fax 01 41 46 19 45 | www.lerivercafe.net

"Superb" Seine-seeing is the daily special on this "beautiful houseboat" "permanently moored" in Issy-les-Moulineaux, "so agreeable for dining on a summer evening" with "mini-terraces on each side"; but seafarers admit that – unlike the view – the combo of Classic and New French cooking is "not inspirational" and "you have to have time to spare" because the deck hands are in no hurry to serve.

Robe et le Palais (La) 🛇 *Wine Bar/Bistro*
1er | 13, rue des Lavandières-Ste-Opportune (Châtelet-Les Halles) | 01 45 08 07 41 | fax 01 45 08 07 41

"The French wine list is as thick as a telephone book" at this "informal", "convivial" little *bistrot à vins* in the 1st, where an "extensive" choice of vintages complements "wonderful" classics "in generous portions for the price"; it's ideal "for dinner among friends", and the "delightful staff" ensures "you'll never feel hurried if you want to stay all night and get sloshed on a regional label."

Robert et Louise 🛇 M 🍴 *Bistro*
3e | 64, rue Vieille-du-Temple (Rambuteau) | 01 42 78 55 89

"You feel like you're in the Middle Ages" at this Marais mainstay where "meat dishes are cooked over an open fire in the back"; this unpretentious bistro's "beauty is the inexpensive and simple food", rather than "rustic" decor of farmhouse tables and checkered curtains, reminiscent of "the great-grandparents' kitchen" – and "beware, the toilets [also] harken back a few centuries" when a hole in the floor sufficed.

	FOOD	DECOR	SERVICE	COST

Roi du Pot-au-Feu (Le) 🛽 *Bistro* ▽ 15 | 11 | 14 | €47

9e | 34, rue Vignon (Havre-Caumartin/Madeleine) | 01 47 42 37 10
"Real pot-au-feu" fans make a pilgrimage to this "small, cozy" bistro for princely portions of the hearty "traditional dish" and other "beefy" "French staples"; while its 1930s setting almost "seems too kitschy", it's a "must-do" "for a meal to put you to sleep or to last you all day" shopping nearby on the Grands Boulevards.

Romantica (La) 🛽 *Italian* 21 | 19 | 20 | €45

Clichy | 73, bd Jean Jaurès (Mairie-de-Clichy) | 01 47 37 29 71 | fax 01 47 37 76 32 | www.claudiopuglia.com
Latin food lovers say this idyllic Italian in the Clichy suburbs "lives up to its name", with a flower-filled courtyard, "very friendly" service and "excellent" pasta; "don't miss the house specialty", tagliolini flambéed tableside in a Parmesan wheel, but "be warned" that this filling dish might leave you "too sleepy to be romantic afterwards."

Rosimar 🛽 *Spanish* – | – | – | M

16e | 26, rue Poussin (Michel-Ange-Auteuil/Porte d'Auteuil) | 01 45 27 74 91 | fax 01 45 20 75 05
"Almost everyone's a regular, yet newcomers are well treated" at this "neighborhood place" *près de* Porte d'Auteuil; "authentic Catalan cuisine", "world-class paella" (order it when you book) and a "heart-warming welcome" make up for the "mirrored" but "gloomy decor."

Rôtisserie d'en Face (La) 🛽 *Bistro* 22 | 16 | 20 | €51

6e | 2, rue Christine (Odéon/St-Michel) | 01 43 26 40 98 | fax 01 43 54 22 71 | www.jacques-cagna.com
Diners whose appetites are richer than their wallets make a habit of Jacques Cagna's "casual", "always buzzing" bistro in Saint-Germain supplying "simple, excellently prepared food for a fraction of the price" of the chef-owner's Haute Cuisine table nearby; but if the menu is full of "solid" Gallic "staples" (notably "rotisserie chicken to beat the band"), the clientele is too close to home – seems like "every person in the restaurant is American!"

Rôtisserie du Beaujolais (La) Ⓜ *Bistro* 22 | 16 | 20 | €46

5e | 19, quai de la Tournelle (Jussieu/Pont-Marie) | 01 43 54 17 47 | fax 01 56 24 43 71 | www.tourdargent.com
Overlooking the Seine, this "bustling" bistro might be "next to La Tour d'Argent", but it's "completely different" from its grandiose parent; it's "one heck of a lot more reasonable", with "down-home" Beaujolais fare, including "perfectly cooked meat" from a rotisserie overlooking the room, and a "cramped but charming" atmosphere made even more "homey" by the "owners' cat, named Beaujolais, often sleeping next to the bar" ("admire the feline and you'll get a better table").

Rotonde (La) ➋ *Brasserie* 14 | 13 | 15 | €44

6e | 105, bd du Montparnasse (Vavin) | 01 43 26 48 26 | fax 01 46 34 52 40 | www.rotondemontparnasse.com
In Montparnasse, a "neighborhood populated by famous cafes from a bygone era", this "elegant old-time brasserie" is a "favorite" for its

"ruby-red decor" and "padded little nooks"; while critics carp the cuisine's "correct" but "expensive" for its "not-exceptional" nature, at least the "genuinely surly but efficient waiters" add to the authentic atmosphere of yore.

Rouge St-Honoré *Eclectic* ▽ 15 | 15 | 17 | €32
(fka Rouge Tomate)
1er | 34, pl du Marché St-Honoré (Pyramides/Tuileries) | 01 42 61 16 09 | fax 01 42 61 17 01

"*Toujours la tomate*" is the theme of this Eclectic with a grocery decor and tomato-centric menu; fruit-throwers jeer it's a "cute idea" that's "more trendy than tasty", but others opine "*pourquoi pas?*", provided "you find yourself in the neighborhood" of the Place du Marché Saint-Honoré.

Rouge Vif (Le) 🅩 *Southwest* ▽ 17 | 14 | 23 | €43
7e | 48, rue de Verneuil (Musée d'Orsay/Solférino) | 01 42 86 81 87 | www.lerougevif.com

There's almost "nothing not to like" about this "small, sweet" place near the Musée d'Orsay, where you get "a grand welcome" and the "simple" Southwestern bistro "menu changes frequently"; it's true, the choices are "limited" –and, some say, "only adequate" – but "the owners (who also serve you) are as gracious as can be", ensuring a "vibrant" atmosphere.

Rubis (Le) 🅩 *Wine Bar/Bistro* ▽ 17 | 10 | 16 | €22
1er | 10, rue du Marché St-Honoré (Tuileries) | 01 42 61 03 34

Here's one ruby (*rubis*) that's a real "gem" declare devotees who haunt this "essential" wine bar steps from the Place du Marché Saint-Honoré; it "hasn't changed in 25 years", but still overflows with "atmosphere, true French personality", a "sublime value-for-money lunch" of classic Gallic fare (or just charcuterie and cheese plates at night) and an inexpensive selection of Beaujolais that's drunk liberally around "barrels on the sidewalk when it's nice out."

Rucola (La) 🅩 *Italian* - | - | - | M
17e | 198, bd Malesherbes (Wagram) | 01 44 40 04 50 | fax 01 47 63 13 20

Ever since two employees from Sormani opened this "good Italian in the 17th", the cozy, candlelit dining room with a chalkboard menu and bottles of red stashed in the walls has been "packed" with regulars who praise the "very Italian atmosphere", the "price/quality ratio" and the *delizioso* dishes that represent a new region every two weeks.

Rue Balzac ◑🅩 *New French* 18 | 16 | 17 | €63
8e | 3-5, rue Balzac (George V) | 01 53 89 90 91 | fax 01 53 89 90 94

In the 8th, "Johnny's restaurant" remains a "place to be seen", thanks to the co-ownership of France's eternal rocker, Johnny Hallyday ("you come across him here sometimes"); a "hip crowd" circulates amid the "funky" red-and-blue decor and "original" New French food, and if critics carp the portions, available in both full and half sizes, are "meager for the cost", at least that's "good for your diet."

Rughetta (La) ● *Italian*   ▽ 17 | 9 | 11 | €38
18ᵉ | 41, rue Lepic (Abbesses/Blanche) | 01 42 23 41 70

"Always packed with the young crowd and celebrities" from the neighborhood, this "lively" Montmartre trattoria serves "very good" pizza and pasta that are redolent of Rome; so what if "the personnel is not always nice" and the decor is minimal – "the terrace is really cool in the summer."

Sale e Pepe ●❍⑤Ⓜ *Italian*   - | - | - | I
18ᵉ | 30, rue Ramey (Château Rouge/Jules Joffrin) | 01 46 06 08 01 | fax 01 42 62 45 49

"You'll feel at home as heaping portions of pasta are served onto your plate from a steaming sauté pan" at this "very affordable" Sicilian in the 18th, where "a bubby Italian duo greets you" then treats you to "fantastic pizza and pastas" made with "fresh ingredients", "but don't expect a menu, as the chef typically brings out whatever he's compelled to prepare"; clean air is part of the "good atmosphere" here, since the only smoking allowed is from the pizza oven.

☑ Salon d'Hélène ⑤Ⓜ *Southwest*   25 | 20 | 19 | €74
6ᵉ | 4, rue d'Assas (Sèvres-Babylone) | 01 42 22 00 11 | fax 01 42 22 25 40

The "more relaxed (and lower-priced) eatery of top chef Hélène Darroze" draws an "ever-so-chic young set" from the stylish 6th who call her "tapas system" "sensational", featuring "a wide selection" of Southwestern small plates" "creatively paired and plated" (ok, so "a few combinations border on the bizarre, but most are deliciously successful"); some salon-goers slam the "frosty" service and "uncomfortable seating" ("ask for a banquette when you reserve") but don't be put off – "the place is really worth it."

Samiin *Korean*   - | - | - | M
7ᵉ | 74, av de Breteuil (Sèvres-Lecourbe) | 01 47 34 58 96 | www.samiin.com

Adventurous eaters delight in this young "jewelry box of a place", not far from Ecole Militaire, whose inventive and "flavorful" Korean dishes go beyond the stereotypical barbecue ("their take on tiramisu is a work of art"); the ambiance is "sweet and intimate", with minimalist-chic decor and servers in updated traditional garb.

NEW San ⑤Ⓜ *Italian*   - | - | - | M
3ᵉ | 27, bd du Temple (République) | 01 44 61 73 45 | fax 01 44 61 73 45 | www.sanristorante.com

Ditching all of the decor clichés of the pizzeria genre (instead of murals of Vesuvius and a visible wood-burning oven, there's a loftlike scene of designer tableware, red chairs and movies projected on the white walls), this hip pie palace near the Place de la République pulls in young trendsters; pizzas with imaginative toppings and sassy service give the place a lot of buzz, and everyone appreciates that you don't knead too much dough to eat well here.

	FOOD	DECOR	SERVICE	COST

Sardegna a Tavola Ⓩ *Italian*

	22	11	14	€48

12ᵉ | 1, rue de Cotte (Ledru-Rollin) | 01 44 75 03 28 | fax 01 44 75 03 02

It's not rare to be surrounded by Italian families enjoying this crowded, "superb" Sardinian out in the 12th; regulars ignore the "brusque" service and concentrate on the "finesse" of the "creative preparations" and regional wines, saying "enormous portions" ("sharing's encouraged") make the "inflated prices" a little easier to swallow.

Sarladais (Le) Ⓩ *Southwest*

	-	-	-	M

8ᵉ | 2, rue de Vienne (St-Augustin) | 01 45 22 23 62 | fax 01 45 22 23 62 | www.lesarladais.com

Patrons who venture into this "unassuming" venue "off the beaten path" near the Gare Saint-Lazare are "amazed" to dig into a "tremendous cassoulet" and other seafood-oriented, "consistent" classics from the Southwest; the staff "serves with easy assurance", and the "cozy" digs make it "dependable" for a business lunch or hearty dinner.

Saudade Ⓩ *Portugese*

	-	-	-	M

1ᵉʳ | 34, rue des Bourdonnais (Châtelet-Les Halles) | 01 42 36 03 65 | fax 01 42 36 30 71 | www.restaurantsaudade.com

With a name that means nostalgia, this "piece of Portugal in the heart of Paris" near Châtelet pacifies those pining for pork stir-fried with clams, cod and other classics; the formal dining room with traditional azulejo tiles resounds with live fado music the first Tuesday of each month.

Sauvignon (Au) *Sandwiches/Wine Bar*

	15	11	15	€29

7ᵉ | 80, rue des Sts-Pères (Sèvres-Babylone) | 01 45 48 49 02 | fax 01 45 49 41 00

"A chic crowd" that spends more on shopping than eating "grabs a quick lunch" or après-store munchie at this "delightful" *bar à vins* with "lovely tartines" (open-face sandwiches) "and a wonderful selection of wines by the glass"; "such a deal you will not find elsewhere" rave bargain-hunters, "especially considering the neighborhood" (the tony 7th).

Saveurs de Claude (Aux) Ⓩ *Classic/New French*

	-	-	-	M

6ᵉ | 12, rue Stanislas (Notre-Dame-des-Champs/Vavin) | 01 45 44 41 74 | fax 01 45 44 41 95

Chef-owner Claude Lamain honed his skills working with Guy Savoy before opening this "small neighborhood bistro" in Montparnasse with a concise Classic and New French menu (including a "very good" chocolate dessert sampler); the relaxed ambiance owes much to "pleasant, unrushed service" and "well-spaced tables" in an intimate room with low lighting and a stripped-down art deco design.

Saveurs du Marché (Aux) Ⓩ *Bistro*

	-	-	-	M

Neuilly-sur-Seine | 4, rue de l'Eglise (Pont-de-Neuilly) | 01 47 45 72 11 | fax 01 46 37 72 13

This "good little" place in posh suburban Neuilly boasts fresh, often organic products from the nearby local *marché* (market) and "pleasing" Classic French dishes by chef-owner David Cheleman, who cut his teeth working with Jean-Pierre Vigato (Apicius); naturally, the menu at this black-and-beige modern bistro changes monthly, but often includes a caramel French toast for dessert.

Sawadee 🅜 *Thai* ▽ 18 | 14 | 18 | €33

15ᵉ | 53, av Emile Zola (Charles Michels) | 01 45 77 68 90 | www.sawadee-paris.com

"If you're into Thai cuisine, this is one of the best places to go" say Siamese specialists of this "neighborhood favorite" in the 15th; though the offerings include "nothing original", at least it's the "real [thing], not an imitation", and the decor looks authentic too, with golden Buddhas and other exotic memorabilia; the "room does get loud and smoky, however."

Scheffer (Le) 🅜 *Bistro* 15 | 10 | 15 | €36

16ᵉ | 22, rue Scheffer (Trocadéro) | 01 47 27 81 11

This "classic", "family-run" "bustling little bistro" near Trocadéro is a "rare" survivor of the "old Paris", "always packed" with rememberers of things past who lap up the traditional atmosphere (tiled floor, posters, etc.) and "simple" meals, "like food you'd get in a French home where someone can cook"; prices are "most reasonable" as well, even if the "service is very fast" – maybe to keep up with the crowds.

Scoop *Eclectic* - | - | - | I

1ᵉʳ | 154, rue St-Honoré (Louvre-Rivoli/Palais Royal) | 01 42 60 31 84 | fax 01 42 36 01 81 | www.scoopcafe.com

The latest scoop from the Rue Saint-Honoré lunch crowd is this "*très chic*" sandwich counter/espresso bar/ice cream parlor, serving "ample portions" of Eclectic eats (from frittata to chicken mole) made with "fresh ingredients", plus the "best frozen custard on the planet"; the cool, contempo-coffeehouse setting, with red couches and white ergonomic chairs, now also features an international grocery.

Sébillon ◑ *Brasserie* 19 | 18 | 17 | €50

Neuilly-sur-Seine | 20, av Charles de Gaulle (Les Sablons/Porte Maillot) | 01 46 24 71 31 | fax 01 46 24 43 50 | www.rest-gj.com

A "polished crowd" from the Neuilly suburbs flocks to this "traditional, constant" brasserie for "satisfying" Classic French fare, especially the "signature" "all-you-care-to-eat" lamb and white beans, sliced at table "like at a Sunday home-cooked dinner in the country"; some bleat that the "old-style" waiters are "all attitude", but this place is still hard to beat for "a hearty meal at reasonable prices"; P.S. its 8th-arrondissement sibling, still under the same management, "is now a steakhouse called L'Ascot."

16 Haussmann (Le) 🅜 *New French* 21 | 18 | 21 | €38

9ᵉ | Hôtel Ambassador | 16, bd Haussmann (Chaussée d'Antin/Richelieu-Drouot) | 01 44 83 40 58 | fax 01 44 83 40 57 | www.hotelambassador-paris.com

Boasting an audacious "yellow, red and blue" color scheme, the "attractive contemporary decor" is only one of the reasons that this hotel eatery is "a wonderful surprise"; the "modern French cuisine's excellent" too, and the "friendly, helpful service" is welcome "after power-shopping in the nearby department stores" of the 9th.

Senderens *Brasserie/New French* — | — | — | VE

8ᵉ | 9, pl de la Madeleine (Madeleine) | 01 42 65 22 90 | fax 01 42 65 06 23 | www.senderens.fr

Chef-owner Alain Senderens created a stir when he decided to "reinvent" Lucas Carton in the 8th as a brasserie (which he did as our Survey closed); the "chic" decor now features metallic leather chairs, an undulating fabric ceiling and Corian-topped tables, the New French menu runs to "modern" dishes like curried lamb shoulder and service is "more casual"; lovers of the old landmark "will be shocked" by this "legend downscaled to reality", but fans urge "take a chance and go."

Sens ⏺🅢 *Mediterranean* — | — | — | E

8ᵉ | 23, rue de Ponthieu (Franklin D. Roosevelt) | 01 42 25 95 00 | fax 01 42 25 95 02 | www.lacompagniedescomptoirs.com

The Pourcel twins, chef-owners behind Montpellier's famed Jardin des Sens, take on the affluent Golden Triangle with this slick see-and-be-seen venue; the futuristic gray decor, topped by a glass-roofed bar, creates a chic background to the designer thread-garbed clientele consuming the seafood-oriented Med specialties, brought by befittingly blasé staffers.

NEW Sensing (Le) 🅢 *Haute Cuisine* — | — | — | E

6ᵉ | 19, rue Brea (Vavin) | 01 43 27 08 80 | fax 01 43 26 99 27 | www.restaurant-sensing.com

Chef-restaurateur Guy Martin is aiming to wow the senses with his slickly designed new Haute Cuisine venture in Montparnasse – all minimalist and modern, with tobacco-colored walls, limestone floors and a curving wrought-iron staircase; in the kitchen, Rémi Van Peteghem, Martin's former second at Grand Véfour, produces a contemporary yet sensual tasting-plates mix-and-match menu for a mélange of media types, fashionistas and gastronauts; service from young waiters in well-cut dark suits displays a definite dash.

Senso 🅢 *New French/Southwest* 17 | 16 | 17 | €65

8ᵉ | Hôtel de la Trémoille | 16, rue de la Trémoille (Alma Marceau/ Franklin D. Roosevelt) | 01 56 52 14 14 | fax 01 56 52 14 13 | www.hotel-tremoille.com

"The place to meet for an under-the-radar power lunch" confide customers of this "contemporary" venue in the 8th, run and decorated by Terence Conran in cool shades of ivory and gray; white-collar types with a "new-wave" sensibility appreciate the "well-spaced" tables as much as the "quality" New French–Southwestern dishes – though non–expense-accounters find the food "kind of pricey for what it is."

7ème Sud ⏺ *Mediterranean/Moroccan* 17 | 17 | 16 | €33

7ᵉ | 159, rue de Grenelle (La Tour-Maubourg) | 01 44 18 30 30 | fax 01 44 18 07 42

16ᵉ | 56, rue de Boulainvillers (La Muette) | 01 45 20 18 32

"Very BCBG" (French for 'preppy'), this pair, each an "understated" "cross between a cafe and a restaurant" in the 7th and 16th arrondissements, is "always a good time" if you're "loud, hip and young"; big at brunch, the "sunny" Med-Moroccan menu is "on the high side of average" and the "service is nice – even toward Americans who don't speak French well"; no wonder many "wish they could be a regular" here.

Sept Quinze (Le) 🗷 *Mediterranean/Provence*   18 | 13 | 18 | €40
15ᵉ | 29, av Lowendal (Cambronne/Ségur) | 01 43 06 23 06
A "fashionably dressed crowd" populates this "crowded" but still "charming" site straddling the 7th and the 15th arrondissements; the "affordable" cuisine, though officially Med-Provençal, has a "California-creative" air to it – perhaps reflecting that the "ever-vivacious" chef/co-owner has run restaurants in San Francisco; however, the way it gets "busy, noisy" and "smoky" would make most Bay Area residents blanch.

Severo (Le) *Steak*   ▽ 22 | 10 | 16 | €43
14ᵉ | 8, rue des Plantes (Mouton-Duvernet) | 01 45 40 40 91
"Meat eaters and wine drinkers unite" at this small site in the 14th, where the owner, "formerly a butcher", emphasizes beef (in fact that's all he serves) and ages it too, offering it up with a selection of some of "the best varietals in France"; the atmosphere is "typical Parisian" bistro, from the blackboards on the walls to the "service that lacks friendliness."

Sinago (Le) 🗷 *Cambodian*   - | - | - | I
9ᵉ | 17, rue de Maubeuge (Cadet/Notre-Dame-de-Lorette) | 01 48 78 11 14
Converts to Cambodian cuisine caution you "must reserve" ahead for this "friendly neighborhood favorite" in the 9th; it's a Phnom-enal address for "excellent", authentic Khmer dishes, even if the narrow room with a slightly incongruous decor of wood paneling and rigging from an old Breton boat is "mediocre."

6 New York 🗷 *New French*   20 | 19 | 19 | €57
16ᵉ | 6, av de New York (Alma Marceau) | 01 40 70 03 30 | fax 01 40 70 04 77
In the 16th, just across the river from the Eiffel Tower, this "chic", "Zen-like address" is "kind of trendy – but the New French cuisine is really" "sophisticated" and "well-made"; some say the staff "could be less handsome and more professional", and regret the "lack of risk"-taking by the kitchen (especially since it's co-owned by Apicius' Jean-Pierre Vigato); but most feel that for "business or pleasure" this Seine-side scenester is "enjoyable on all levels."

Sizin ●🗷 *Turkish*   - | - | - | M
9ᵉ | 47, rue St-Georges (St-Georges) | 01 44 63 02 28 | www.sizin-restaurant.com
"Not your corner kebab joint" bellow Byzantine experts of this "family restaurant" in the 9th, decorated with old postcards of Istanbul, where a "warm, welcoming staff serves fine Turkish cuisine" and wines as "authentic" as they are unusual.

		FOOD	DECOR	SERVICE	COST

Soleil (Le) **M** *Bistro*

17 | 14 | 15 | €42

Saint-Ouen | 109, av Michelet (Porte de Clignancourt) |
01 40 10 08 08 | fax 01 40 10 16 85

Famished flea-market hunters frequent this "perfect luncheon spot
after a morning of shopping" in Saint-Ouen, a "plain and simple
place" with "old-fashioned" decor from Les Puces and a blackboard
menu of "traditional" bistro food (in particular, "the large wheel of
country butter is a hit"); but some hagglers huff "prices are not so
high, but not so cheap" anymore, and the service is "middling."

NEW Soleil (Le) **S M** *Mediterranean*

– | – | – | M

7e | 153, rue de Grenelle (La Tour-Maubourg) | 01 45 51 54 12

With a cheerful Provençal decor, including cracked tile floor and
wrought-iron furniture, this traditional bistro near Les Invalides
feels so authentically Southern French that you half expect to catch
a glimpse of the Mediterranean when you look out the picture windows up front; run by the same team as Le Soleil in Saint-Ouen, the
kitchen serves up seasonal produce cooked with inspiration from
the Midi, Spain and Italy, served by a couple of charming waitresses.

Sologne (La) **S** *Classic French*

– | – | – | E

12e | 164, av Daumesnil (Daumesnil) | 01 43 07 68 97 |
fax 01 43 44 66 23

Redolent of the forested region it's named for, this "provincial bastion
in Paris" seems miles away from its location in the 12th – both for its
rustic, "flavorful" Classic French cuisine and its "timeworn" decor of
exposed-stone walls and round tables; "unhurried service" adds to
an atmosphere that's "calm (maybe too much so)" for scenesters.

Sora Lena **S** *Italian/Mediterranean*

– | – | – | E

17e | 18, rue Bayen (Ternes) | 01 45 74 73 73 | fax 01 45 74 73 52

Christened for the grandma of the two brothers who own it, this table near the Place des Ternes is "fashionable", with a celebrity
crowd; nevertheless, "superb risotto" and other "excellent" Med-
Southern Italian dishes emerge from the kitchen of an ex-Sormani
chef; the "warm welcome" extends to the cozy, loungelike decor.

Sormani **S** *Italian*

24 | 18 | 21 | €97

17e | 4, rue du Général Lanrezac (Charles de Gaulle-Etoile) |
01 43 80 13 91 | fax 01 40 55 07 37

"Everyone raves" that this "institution" near the Etoile is one of "the
best Italians in Paris"; with "divine" dishes often "bathed in truffles",
it's "as close to Italy as you are going to get without going there" (but
don't expect an economic advantage, since the "prices are astounding"); the Venetian-style, "lively red decor partially offsets" the "op-
pressive" air generated by the number of "business and older patrons."

Sot l'y Laisse (Le) **S M** *Bistro*

– | – | – | M

11e | 70, rue Alexandre Dumas (Alexandre Dumas) | 01 40 09 79 20
| fax 01 40 09 79 20

Named for a particularly choice morsel of poultry, this yellow-toned,
"lovely discovery in a lost corner of Paris" south of Père Lachaise is

	FOOD	DECOR	SERVICE	COST

a "charming bistro", with fare that combines "finesse and simplicity" and a "superb wine list"; all's served with "remarkable gentility" in "truly warm" digs.

☑ Soufflé (Le) ☒ *Classic French*

	22	17	21	€43

1ᵉʳ | 36, rue du Mont-Thabor (Concorde) | 01 42 60 27 19 | fax 01 42 60 54 98

"Soufflé lovers" feel like they're "dining on and in the clouds" when they visit this "old-school" "staple" in the 1st; "you can go crazy and have one for all three courses" ("never knew they came in so many different types") "or mix-and-match with perfectly good" Classic French food; "ok, so it's touristy", and the "rather dull decor could deflate your evening", but this piece of "puffed heaven" pleases most; P.S. "the Grand Marnier dessert version comes with the entire bottle, so don't deny yourself."

Soupière (La) ☒ *Classic French*

	-	-	-	E

17ᵉ | 154, av de Wagram (Wagram) | 01 46 22 80 10 | fax 01 46 22 27 09

This "little storefront restaurant at the top of Wagram" is an underground favorite for fungiophiles who find "the creative chef has an incomparable talent for preparing wild mushrooms" (especially in autumn) on a menu of "exceptional" Classic French cuisine; a "warm" "familial ambiance" prevails, despite the "no-frills" decor.

Spicy ● *New French*

	15	15	16	€41

8ᵉ | 8, av Franklin D. Roosevelt (Franklin D. Roosevelt/St-Philippe-du-Roule) | 01 56 59 62 59 | fax 01 56 59 62 50 | www.spicyrestaurant.com

"Financial analysts, gallery owners and a few famous actors" grab an "informal business lunch" at this 8th-arrondissement address for "copious" portions of New French cuisine, since "value this good is difficult to find in the neighborhood"; clients give kudos to the "original" international wine list, "friendly staff and pleasant decor", but protest the place "needs to change its name", since the Asian-inflected fare is "anything but spicy."

Spoon, Food & Wine ☒ *Eclectic/New French*

	23	20	21	€69

8ᵉ | Hôtel Marignan | 14, rue de Marignan (Franklin D. Roosevelt) | 01 40 76 34 44 | fax 01 40 76 34 37 | www.spoon.tm.fr

"The most original menu in Paris" "zigzags across the continents" with "creative mix-and-match selections" at this "über-hip Alain Ducasse gem" in the 8th; a "chic" crowd happily "drops a small fortune" for "bite-size" portions of Eclectic eats "with a New French twist" and "an extensive list of new world wines"; while the "service is pretty decent", some complain that "getting the waiter's attention can be more challenging than deciphering the menu" (the easily confused "just get the tasting" option).

NEW Spring ☒ *Bistro*

	-	-	-	M

9ᵉ | 28, rue de la Tour d'Auvergne (Anvers) | 01 45 96 05 72

Before going out on his own with this 16-seater, Chicago native Daniel Rose cooked with the likes of Paul Bocuse and Yannick Alléno at Le Meurice; now, with the help of a single waitress, he nightly produces a contemporary bistro menu in a cozy room decorated with Asian puppets that's putting a spring into the step of the bobos who frequent this trendy part of the 9th.

Square (Le) ◨ *Classic French* | 16 | 14 | 15 | €44 |

7e | 31, rue St-Dominique (Invalides/Solférino) | 01 45 51 09 03 | fax 01 45 50 48 70

This "chic", "lively" "hot spot" covers all the right angles with a "noisy", "friendly vibe" provided by a "young crowd" and "charming servers"; while the Classic French food is "perfectly fine", folks come "more for fun than cuisine"; still, the "great prix fixes" offer a "bang for your buck" that's "nice in a neighborhood" (the 7th) where "reasonable" is rare.

Square (Le) ◨ *Classic/New French* | - | - | - | M |

18e | 227 bis, rue Marcardet (Guy Moquet) | 01 53 11 08 41

A hipster crowd is making a straight line for this casual, "excellent" address off the beaten track in the 18th, where huge blackboards present the day's offerings, an inventive mix of Classic and New French fare; "a fine time" can be had wherever one perches: a bar area with banquettes, a dining room with wooden bistro tables overlooking a patio garden or the garden itself, with vine-covered walls.

Square Trousseau (Le) ●◨Ⓜ *Bistro* | 18 | 16 | 13 | €39 |

12e | 1, rue Antoine Vollon (Bastille/Ledru-Rollin) | 01 43 43 06 00 | fax 01 43 43 00 66

"People eating well in a bustling atmosphere" "sets the scene" in this near-"perfect little bistro on the corner of a lovely square" "a few blocks from Bastille"; it's a "treasure" for "hearty" "*cuisine grand-mère*" and an authentic turn-of-the-century "retro setting" with banquettes, molded ceilings and a zinc bar; but "service is harried", and "ask for the nonsmoking room or you'll eat in a cloud of smoke."

Stella (Le) ● *Brasserie* | 16 | 14 | 16 | €46 |

16e | 133, av Victor Hugo (Rue de la Pompe/Victor Hugo) | 01 56 90 56 00 | fax 01 56 90 56 01

The 16th welcomes the "renaissance of a classic" brasserie that's "found its rhythm" again after a "difficult reopening" in 2003; it's "nice and casual" in a "bourgeois" sort of way, with "kind, professional waiters", platters that will "fulfill your shellfish need" and a "reliable, authentic neighborhood feel" that on the Avenue Victor Hugo translates as "the height of Parisian snobbery."

☑ Stella Maris ◨ *Classic French* | 25 | 20 | 22 | €76 |

8e | 4, rue Arsène Houssaye (Charles de Gaulle-Etoile) | 01 42 89 16 22 | fax 01 42 89 16 01 | www.stellamarisparis.com

Tateru Yoshino – "a remarkable chef" who trained with the likes of Robuchon and Gagnaire – brings "creativity" and a Japanese "mastery of technique" to Classic French cuisine in his small place in the 8th; gourmets grin his interpretation of such national treasures as tête de veau and lièvre à la royale is "irreproachable", the "service

	FOOD	DECOR	SERVICE	COST

exceptional" and a "successful" "recent face-lift" has warmed the "formerly cold" decor; given all this, "prices aren't so bad."

Stéphane Gaborieau-Le Pergolèse ☒ Haute Cuisine
| | - | - | - | VE |

16e | 40, rue Pergolèse (Argentine) | 01 45 00 21 40 | fax 01 45 00 81 31 | www.lepergolese.com

A veteran of luxury hotels in Lyon and southern France, chef-owner Stéphane Gaborieau now runs this plush old-timer in the 16th, instilling new life into the classic Haute Cuisine menu with dishes like lobster ravioli and gingered-apple nems; the redone dining room features wood-paneled walls hung with paintings and tables adorned with linens as starchy as the formal servers.

Stéphane Martin ☒ Ⓜ Classic French
| | ▽ 24 | 14 | 14 | €46 |

15e | 67, rue des Entrepreneurs (Charles Michels/Commerce) | 01 45 79 03 31 | fax 01 45 79 44 69

Chef-owner Stéphane Martin's table has become a "local favorite" in the 15th arrondissement, "perfect for dinner with friends, clients or parents" who return often because the "inventive" Classic French menu – an "unbeatable value" – "changes regularly" yet always features "quality recipes" and a "good choice of wines at all prices"; adorned with velvet curtains and armchairs, the room has a cozy feel and is entirely nonsmoking.

Strapontins (Les) Ⓜ Classic French
| | - | - | - | M |

10e | 16, av Richerand (Bonsergent/République) | 01 42 41 94 79 | fax 01 42 41 74 49

A young and funky crowd battles it out for a "table in the sun" on the "calm, pretty little terrace" of this casual Classic French "just off the Canal" Saint-Martin and "overlooking the 16th-century walls of the Hôpital Saint-Louis"; a few disgruntled diners feel that it "doesn't try hard to entice customers, but they tend to come anyway."

Stresa (Le) ☒ Italian
| | 22 | 17 | 21 | €95 |

8e | 7, rue Chambiges (Alma Marceau) | 01 47 23 51 62

The "stars" come out to this "wonderful" Italian in the 8th, where it's "tough to get a table" unless "you know someone" (or, better yet, are someone); the refined cuisine is "highly recommended for cognoscenti", though prices are so high the figures "while in euros, seem to be in lira", and some say simply "do not go" unless you get off on "clients who spend their time looking at each other in an aquarium of mirrors."

Studio (The) ❶ Tex-Mex
| | - | - | - | M |

4e | 41, rue du Temple (Hôtel-de-Ville/Rambuteau) | 01 42 74 10 38 | fax 01 42 41 50 34 | www.the-studio.fr

"Food is not the star" at this Tex-Mex in the Marais, but the setting, "nestled in a 17th-century courtyard" next to a dancing school, is a feast for the eyes; voyeuristic visitors recommend you "go here only in summer – you'll eat outside, and watching the dance classes around you is great."

Suave Ⓩ *Vietnamese* | – | – | – | I |

13ᵉ | 20, rue de la Providence (Corvisart/Tolbiac) | 01 45 89 99 27 | fax 01 45 81 34 60

Reservations are imperative at this "very small" but "cute" site near Butte-aux-Cailles, often "crowded" with fans of "great Vietnamese food" prepared with finesse; a suave use of fresh herbs and spices in the specialties makes it stand out in a neighborhood filled with Asian eateries.

Sud (Le) Ⓩ *Mediterranean/Provence* | 15 | 19 | 13 | €51 |

17ᵉ | 91, bd Gouvion-St-Cyr (Porte Maillot) | 01 45 74 02 77 | fax 01 45 74 35 36 | www.lesud.fr

"Ah, the sound of crickets in the middle of a Paris winter" sigh surveyors who "feel like they're on vacation" at this Provençal oasis "next to the traffic jams of Porte Maillot"; "exotic Med cuisine and a mix of colors in the plate" reflect the "southern ambiance" of the "under-the-olive-trees" decor; given the "correct, but nothing more" service, the bill is "a little pricey, but worth it" – and many must agree, since the place can get as "crowded" as Aix in August.

Suffren (Le) ☻ *Brasserie* | 14 | 12 | 17 | €38 |

15ᵉ | 84, av de Suffren (La Motte-Piquet Grenelle) | 01 45 66 97 86 | fax 01 47 34 68 82

This family-owned, "bustling brasserie" in the 15th has long been a "popular", "reliable neighborhood standard"; regulars report that this place "delivers what it promises: well-executed versions of basic French fare" along with "great people-watching" from a large sun-filled terrace.

Suite (La) *Classic French* | 12 | 22 | 13 | €64 |

8ᵉ | 40, av George V (George V) | 01 53 57 49 49 | fax 01 53 57 49 48 | www.lasuite.fr

"A nightclub first and foremost" concur clients of this site in the 8th, where a "frosty welcome" ("you can enter, you can't") ensures that only "fabulous people" get in; the privileged few admire the "hottest waitresses in Paris" ("when they finally reach your table") and the "funky interior" (slated to be revamped in early 2007), but say the "expensive" French food, which recently took a more traditional turn, is "a mere afterthought"; then again, if you're looking to eat, "maybe you want to go to a real restaurant."

Table d'Anvers (La) Ⓩ *Classic French* | 21 | 16 | 18 | M |

9ᵉ | 2, pl d'Anvers (Anvers) | 01 48 78 35 21 | fax 01 45 26 66 67 | www.latabledanvers.com

Patrons praise "this pleasant, relaxed" place for its "interesting", "delicious" Classic French menu "attentively served" in "quiet surroundings"; the location is great for a postprandial stroll – "you can waddle at will through Montmartre, climbing off those calories" – and fresh owners have installed a more reasonably priced menu and new retro bistro look, which should silence voters who found prices somewhat "elevated" and "the decor not up to the level of the cuisine."

	FOOD	DECOR	SERVICE	COST

NEW Table de Babette (La) 🗷 *Creole* — | — | — | E
16ᵉ | 32, rue de Longchamp (Boissière/Trocadéro) | 01 45 53 00 07 | fax 01 45 53 00 15

Though *antillaise* (West Indian) cooking in Paris is usually found in casual settings that echo the easygoing islands, TV chef Babette de Rozières is aiming to unveil its upper-crust side; to that end, her colonial Louisiana dining room – home to the late Jamin in the 16th – is formal, elegant and hushed, and the kitchen does a rather urbane take on such French Caribbean–Creole classics as *féroce martiniquaise* (a mash of avocado, crab and cayenne pepper) and stewed pork in five-spice powder; service is leisurely and prices lofty.

🗷 Table de Joël Robuchon (La) *Haute Cuisine* 26 | 20 | 24 | €105
16ᵉ | Hôtel Pont Royal | 16, av Bugeaud (Victor Hugo) | 01 56 28 16 16 | fax 01 56 28 16 78

Because "Joël Robuchon is brilliant", a "*très chic* crowd" willingly pays "*très chic* prices" for his "breathtaking" Haute Cuisine venture in the 16th; offered in both regular and "small tasting portions", "the food seems similar to that at his Atelier", but "you can reserve a table" here; malcontents murmur the "modern decor is a little bland", but others like the lack of "glitz"; and when you add in the "professional" servers and a sommelier who's "a master in his own right", the total is a "remarkable experience."

Table d'Hédiard (La) 🗷 *New French* 22 | 19 | 20 | €42
8ᵉ | 21, pl de la Madeleine (Madeleine) | 01 43 12 88 99 | fax 01 43 12 88 98 | www.hediard.fr

"Pick up groceries and get a quick bite to eat" at this New French "perched above a wonderful gourmet shop" in the 8th; all through the day, there's "light, fresh food and divine desserts" (though "it can be difficult to swallow the prices"); the "staff's attitude" ranges from "affected" to "attentive", but overall, it's a "wonderful place for resting those weary, overworked tourist feet."

Table du Baltimore (La) 🗷 *Haute Cuisine* — | — | — | E
16ᵉ | Sofitel Demeure Hôtel Baltimore | 88, bis av Kléber (Boissière) | 01 44 34 54 34 | fax 01 44 34 54 44 | www.sofitel.com

"Always reliable" for a "business lunch or dinner", this "nicely appointed restaurant" near Trocadéro provides a "comfortable" setting (including "great air-conditioning, a rare thing in Paris"), "attentive service" and a "nice wine list"; but there are tempered tributes for the Haute Cuisine: "good, even very good, but not extraordinary."

🗷 Table du Lancaster (La) *Haute Cuisine* 25 | 25 | 23 | €110
8ᵉ | Hôtel Lancaster | 7, rue de Berri (George V/Franklin Roosevelt) | 01 40 76 40 18 | fax 01 40 76 40 00 | www.hotel-lancaster.fr

Gastronomes are "delighted to have [Rhône Valley chef] Michel Troisgros in Paris" overseeing this "great addition to the restaurant scene" in an "elegant" boutique hotel near the Champs; the "intimate, luxurious" "Asian-inspired setting" provides backdrop for the "interesting tastes" from around the globe; both the Haute Cuisine and the "friendly service" can be "strained", but "the few disappointments" are offset by "superb gustatory moments."

Table Lauriston (La) *Classic French* ▽ 17 | 12 | 18 | €58
16ᵉ | 129, rue Lauriston (Trocadéro) | 01 47 27 00 07

This table near Trocadéro is "a truly wonderful addition to the arrondissement" thanks to the "memorable" Classic French creations by chef-owner Serge Barbey (who trained with Bernard Loiseau and Guy Savoy), along with Mme. Barbey's "kind reception" and the "surroundings with a range of warm colors accented in silver"; it's "a place to return to" (and fans can do so seven days a week).

☑ Taillevent ☒ *Haute Cuisine* 28 | 28 | 28 | €159
8ᵉ | 15, rue Lamennais (Charles de Gaulle-Etoile/George V) | 01 44 95 15 01 | fax 01 42 25 95 18 | www.taillevent.com

Again Paris' No. 1 for Food and Popularity, this "mythic" site in the 8th is "as much a landmark as the Eiffel Tower"; chef Alain Solivérès' classic Haute Cuisine is "exquisite", "no detail is missed" by "consummate host"-owner Jean-Claude Vrinat's staff ("I was squinting because I'd forgotten my glasses, and a waiter presented various pairs on a silver tray") and the "sumptuous" setting now boasts "a refreshing contemporary style"; "reservations are not only required but difficult", but the "memories will last the rest of your life."

Taïra ☒ *Japanese/New French* ▽ 23 | 8 | 15 | €51
17ᵉ | 10, rue des Acacias (Argentine) | 01 47 66 74 14 | fax 01 47 66 74 14

Fin fans find "first-rate fish" – and forgive the "sad-looking room" – at this "discreet, exceptional address" near the Etoile; Nippon native Taïra Kurihara's "unique" menu, a "Japanese adaptation of French cuisine", is so "superb" and "well priced" "it's a scandal this phenomenally talented chef is ignored by the media" (except by us, of course).

Tan Dinh ☒⇥ *Vietnamese* 22 | 14 | 20 | €64
7ᵉ | 60, rue de Verneuil (Rue du Bac/Solférino) | 01 45 44 04 84 | fax 01 45 44 36 93

A "fashionable", "dedicated clientele" adds to the cachet of this "sedate Vietnamese charmer" in the 7th, where the cuisine is "delicate", the "service refined" and an "amazing wine list (particularly the Burgundies) keeps customers coming back"; malcontents mumble that it's "overrated" and the "portions are small" for the price – which, by the way, requires a pocketful of cash, because "they don't accept credit cards."

Tang ☒Ⓜ *Chinese* 17 | 13 | 16 | €65
16ᵉ | 125, rue de la Tour (Rue de la Pompe) | 01 45 04 35 35 | fax 01 45 04 58 19

This chichi Chinese in the 16th enjoys a "reputation as the best" in Paris, and while many feel it's merited, thanks to the "solicitous" owner and "memorable" food from a menu that offers "a lot of choice", scores side with the sizable number of dissidents who declare it "too expensive" for dishes that are merely "good."

Tante Louise ☒ *Burgundy*

22 | 18 | 20 | €69

8ᵉ | 41, rue Boissy-d'Anglas (Concorde/Madeleine) | 01 42 65 06 85 | fax 01 42 65 28 19 | www.bernard-loiseau.com

"Near the Madeleine", this "luxury bistro" specializing in "traditional Burgundian"–Classic French cuisine "cooked to perfection" remains a "good bet for a business lunch or a date" and a "favorite standby" with "the American Embassy crowd nearby"; its "cozy" setting with wood paneling and big armchairs is ideal on "a coolish winter evening", even if the staff seems "attentive and perfunctory at the same time."

Tante Marguerite ☒ *Bistro*

21 | 16 | 22 | €59

7ᵉ | 5, rue de Bourgogne (Assemblée Nationale/Invalides) | 01 45 51 79 42 | fax 01 47 53 79 56 | www.bernard-loiseau.com

Tante Louise's cousin, Marguerite, is another "cozy" upscale bistro serving "excellent" Classic French food and a Burgundy-heavy wine list that comprise "great value in an expensive neighborhood" near the Assemblée Nationale; followers say "forget" the "elegant but boring" decor, for the cuisine and waiters who "anticipate your every need" make this auntie "a winner" for "a quiet dinner with friends."

NEW Tarmac (Le) ◗ *Brasserie/Eclectic*

– | – | – | I

12ᵉ | 33, rue de Lyon (Gare de Lyon) | 01 43 41 97 70 | www.tarmac-paris.com

Coming in for a landing in the 12th, this large new brasserie sports minimalistic mod decor that features photos and projections of planes and airport signs; the Eclectic menu cruises between classics and trendy dishes, and for bargain-fliers, there's an 18-euro lunch (three courses, each with three choices) that changes daily.

Tastevin Ⓜ *Classic French*

23 | 20 | 23 | €64

Maisons-Laffitte | 9, av Eglé (RER Maisons-Laffitte) | 01 39 62 11 67 | fax 01 39 62 73 09

It may be "hard to get to without a car" but that doesn't stop clients who "come back religiously over the decades" to this family-run "historic restaurant" serving "well-prepared" Classic French cuisine in a century-old house and "beautiful" gardens in Maisons-Laffitte; admirers appreciate the "quiet" setting ("don't go if you're younger than 35") and "special personal service" in this "old-world" "treasure."

Taverna de Gli Amici ◗☒ *Italian*

– | – | – | I

7ᵉ | 16, rue du Bac (Rue du Bac) | 01 42 60 37 74 | fax 01 42 60 37 74

Like the name says, this Italian near the Musée d'Orsay is "a great place to meet with friends", with simple trattoria decor and a menu featuring a "big antipasto and cheese selection", an extensive list of wines "served in beautiful huge glasses" and a staff that "gives you really good advice"; the late hours please *amici* living la dolce vita.

Taverne de Maître Kanter ◗ *Brasserie*

10 | 10 | 12 | €33

1ᵉʳ | 16, rue Coquillière (Châtelet-Les Halles/Louvre-Rivoli) | 01 42 36 74 24 | fax 01 42 21 42 31 | www.tmk-leshalles.com

Alsace comes to Les Halles in this "loud and noisy" two-story tavern with a facade like a mountain ski resort and "basic" brasserie fare, including "hearty" regional dishes like choucroute and flammen-küche; the "waiters look stressed" (no wonder, when the kitchen is open round the clock), and some joke it "should be named 'Taverne d'Ordinaire'"; still, a half-liter of Kanterbräu beer is "ideal on the terrace when the weather's nice."

Taverne du Sergent Recruteur (La) ● *Classic French*

FOOD	DECOR	SERVICE	COST
14	15	16	€41

4ᵉ | 41, rue St-Louis-en-l'Ile (Port Marie) | 01 43 54 75 42 | fax 01 44 07 02 58 | www.lesergentrecruteur.com

There are "more tourists jammed in [here] than in Notre Dame" at this Ile Saint-Louis veteran that "attempts to re-create Middle Ages communal dining" with "ye olde" decor of beamed stone walls, farm tools and long wood tables; "excellent baskets of charcuterie, [crudités] and cheese are provided when you sit down", but otherwise the Classic French fare's fairly "marginal" and some feel it's "from a former era and should be left there"; still, with "the right group and sufficient wine, it can be fun."

Taverne Henri IV (La) 🗷 *Wine Bar/Bistro*

FOOD	DECOR	SERVICE	COST
17	16	18	€29

1ᵉʳ | 13, pl du Pont-Neuf (Pont-Neuf) | 01 43 54 27 90 | fax 01 43 54 27 90

"Curators and carpenters sit side by side for a glass" at this "working man's wine bar" on the tip of Ile de la Cité, a "historical institution" and "an old favorite" of many (including writer Georges Simenon); to accompany the "nice selection of wines at good prices", present-day patrons tuck into "homey platters of country pâtés, cheeses" and charcuterie, noting the "owners have spruced up the tired old decor" (it's still "nothing spectacular", though).

Télégraphe (Le) *Classic French*

FOOD	DECOR	SERVICE	COST
20	23	18	€72

7ᵉ | 41, rue de Lille (Rue du Bac/Solférino) | 01 42 92 03 04 | fax 01 42 92 02 77 | www.letelegraphe.fr

A former "telegraph ladies' home", this Classic French in the 7th is "perhaps Paris' best kosher restaurant" say fans who fawn over the "fabulous" art nouveau decor and "great garden eating"; but while it's "truly an interesting place to dine", critical correspondents contend the "crazy prices" are "not merited by the food and service."

Temps au Temps (Le) 🗷 🅼 *Bistro*

FOOD	DECOR	SERVICE	COST
▽ 26	14	21	€33

11ᵉ | 13, rue Paul Bert (Faidherbe-Chaligny) | 01 43 79 63 40 | fax 01 43 79 63 40 | www.tempsautemps.com

Time passes quickly at this "corner of paradise" run by a "wonderful couple" in the 11th, a "convivial" "address with a grand chef" who's earning accolades for his "astonishing" bistro cuisine; "reserve well in advance" because the "tiny" clock-filled room ("only 26 places") is "always full."

Temps des Cerises (Le) ●🌒🗷 *Bistro*

FOOD	DECOR	SERVICE	COST
▽ 18	17	18	€26

13ᵉ | 18, rue de la Butte-aux-Cailles (Place d'Italie) | 01 45 89 69 48 | fax 01 45 88 18 53

Socialists eat up this "lively legacy of the Paris Commune days" in Butte-aux-Cailles, a bistro "run as a cooperative" where "all the staff, from chef to dishwasher, are owners" and patrons sit together at "large tables"; it's "gruff, earthy and genuine" – right down to the "Turkish toilets" – but the "generous portions" of "hearty Traditional French fare" are cheap enough for the masses.

Terminus Nord ● Brasserie

FOOD	DECOR	SERVICE	COST
15	18	16	€41

10ᵉ | 23, rue de Dunkerque (Gare du Nord) | 01 42 85 05 15 | fax 01 40 16 13 98 | www.terminusnord.com

"Exuding the bustle and expectation of its namesake across the road", the Gare du Nord, this "classic" brasserie with its "fin de siècle decor" is "the perfect spot for Eurostar travelers" to "go back in time"; while the food quality can be "random", passengers profess that the "platters of briny seafood are always a safe bet" and the "rushed", white-aproned waiters are "fun to watch."

Terrasse Mirabeau (La) ⊠ Bistro

FOOD	DECOR	SERVICE	COST
–	–	–	M

16ᵉ | 5, pl de Barcelone (Javel/Mirabeau) | 01 42 24 41 51 | fax 01 42 24 43 48 | www.terrasse-mirabeau.com

What "a revelation" rave epicureans who "dream of going all the time" to this contemporary bistro in the 16th near the Seine; the kitchen's "superb creativity" – including "excellent terrines" and "imaginative fish dishes" – matches the sleek maroon-and-chocolate-colored decor with "real paintings on the tabletops" and big bay windows overlooking a "very pleasant terrace."

Terres de Truffes Classic French

FOOD	DECOR	SERVICE	COST
–	–	–	VE

8ᵉ | 21, rue Vignon (Madeleine) | 01 53 43 80 44 | fax 01 42 66 18 20 | www.terresdetruffes.com

"If you love les truffes, rush" to this black diamond mine near the Madeleine, a "small but elegant" eatery/shop run by restaurateur Clément Bruno; truffle buffs treat themselves to an "outstanding" Classic French menu featuring the desirable delicacy in all its varieties and in dishes from starter to dessert (even ice cream); prices are more than justified by the "generous quantities" and "exceptional quality."

Terroir (Le) ⊠ Bistro

FOOD	DECOR	SERVICE	COST
–	–	–	E

13ᵉ | 11, bd Arago (Les Gobelins) | 01 47 07 36 99

"A perennial favorite" of "local people" and tourists on the trail of a "real French restaurant", this bistro in the 13th serves "no trendy nonsense, just top-rate traditional cooking" in "high-priced" but "incredible portions" ("try the terrine de maison and see if you can even eat anything else"); "hearty regional wines", plus a "warm welcome", round out the "marvelous" experience.

Tête Ailleurs (La) ⊠ Mediterranean

FOOD	DECOR	SERVICE	COST
–	–	–	M

4ᵉ | 20, rue Beautreillis (St-Paul/Sully Morland) | 01 42 72 47 80 | fax 01 42 74 66 85 | www.lateteailleurs-restaurant-paris.com

Southern warmth is served at this "casual", "charming" Marais table with "very good Med cooking" and an "eager-to-please staff" that inspires surveyors to call this "one of the friendliest places in town"; the "bright, arty decor" combines rich orange shades with exposed-stone walls and natural light from a glass rooftop.

Thanksgiving 🅜 *Cajun/Creole* — 15 | 12 | 17 | €37

4e | 20, rue St-Paul (St-Paul) | 01 42 77 68 28 | fax 01 42 77 70 83 |
www.thanksgivingparis.com

This "cute little haven" in the Marais may be "nice for homesick
Americans at Thanksgiving", but connoisseurs of Cajun-Creole
cooking are generally "not impressed" by the "overpriced" fare; "the
owners are very sweet" and the boutique is "the place to shop for
U.S. foods you can't get in Europe", but "if you must go, brunch" is
the best bet at this bayou bistro.

Thierry Burlot 🅢 *New French* — ▽ 24 | 20 | 20 | €50
(aka Le Quinze)

15e | 8, rue Nicolas Charlet (Pasteur) | 01 42 19 08 59

Namesake owner Burlot has an enthusiastic following, both at the
Cristal Room where he is head chef, and here in the 15th at his own
New French table, a "great find" for "gourmet, creative food" "at unexpectedly reasonable prices"; regulars "love the contemporary decor" and the "precise flavors" of his "inventive" menu, confiding that
"the caramel ice cream is a life-altering experience."

Thiou *Thai* — 18 | 17 | 16 | €59

7e | 49, quai d'Orsay (Invalides) | 01 40 62 96 50 |
fax 01 40 62 97 30 🅢
8e | 12, av George V (Alma Marceau) | 01 47 20 89 56 |
fax 01 47 20 76 16

Petit Thiou 🅢 *Thai*

7e | 3, rue Surcouf (Invalides) | 01 40 62 96 70

Eponymous chef Thiou has created an empire of "upscale, sexy" Thai
tables, but her "delicate food with a touch of originality" is proof this
"still-trendy" chain is "not content to be just a show-biz canteen" –
in fact, the marinated grilled beef "will make you cry, it's so good";
"if you want to see famous" names, head to the Quai d'Orsay branch
or the Comptoir with its Asian decor in the 8th; the "cheaper" Rue
Surcouf site is "the same, but without the beautiful people."

Thoumieux 🅢 *Bistro/Southwest* — 15 | 16 | 16 | €41

7e | Hôtel Thoumieux | 79, rue St-Dominique (Invalides/La Tour-
Maubourg) | 01 47 05 49 75 | fax 01 47 05 36 96 | www.thoumieux.com

"Time stands still at this landmark of bistro cuisine" run by the same
family for four generations near Les Invalides, with "decor as old-
fashioned and run-down as the waiters" and "absolutely reliable"
"heavy Gallic delicacies" from the Southwest; detractors declare this
"big" vet is "living on its reputation", but to supporters it's still "worth
a visit for the cassoulet" that "ranks first for both greasy and yummy."

Timbre (Le) 🅢🅜 *Bistro* — 22 | 14 | 23 | €37

6e | 3, rue St-Beuve (Vavin) | 01 45 49 10 40 | fax 01 45 78 20 35 |
www.restaurantletimbre.com

Timbre means postage stamp, "a perfect name" for this "minuscule"
"marvel" near the Luxembourg Gardens, where "you definitely get
to know your neighbors" and also get to "watch the chef in full creative mode" doing "scrumptious" bistro dishes in an open kitchen;

	FOOD	DECOR	SERVICE	COST

chef-owner Chris Wright "may be British but the food and experience couldn't be more French", and while "the decor is not a priority", the atmosphere's "cozy" and the service "much better than at the post office."

Timgad (Le) *Moroccan*

| | 22 | 20 | 19 | €63 |

17ᵉ | 21, rue Brunel (Argentine) | 01 45 74 23 70 | fax 01 40 68 76 46 | www.timgad-paris.com

Couscous critics call this "refined, exotic" table in the 17th "one of the best Moroccans in town", serving "melt-in-the-mouth" couscous and other dishes "of exemplary finesse"; "step into the restaurant and you are right in the heart of Marrakech", thanks to "amazing" decor of hand-carved plaster and service that reflects "authentic warmth"; but the "exceptional meal" does come with an "exceptional price."

Tire-Bouchon (Le) ⑤ *Bistro*

| | 18 | 13 | 16 | €37 |

15ᵉ | 62, rue des Entrepreneurs (Charles Michels) | 01 40 59 09 27 | fax 01 40 59 09 27

"What a little jewel of a place" hail habitués of this New French bistro that's "well worth the trip to the 15th" for "refined, inventive" dishes offering an "unsurpassed value" at the price; "the smile of Madame" creates "a nice ambiance" that warms up the "simple", red-and-yellow decor; P.S. "with only seven tables", better reserve.

Titi Parisien (Le) Ⓜ *Bistro*

| | ▽ 16 | 15 | 15 | €48 |

7ᵉ | 96, bd de la Tour Maubourg (Ecole Militaire/La Tour-Maubourg) | 01 44 18 36 37

Carnivores sink their teeth into this "laid-back but chic" bistro with a "lovely view on Les Invalides" and a menu featuring "high-quality" beef and a choice of sauces; the 1930s-style decor is "cozy" and the "young vibe" is a welcome "addition to the bourgeois neighborhood."

Toi ❶ *New French*

| | - | - | - | M |

8ᵉ | 27, rue du Colisée (Franklin D. Roosevelt/St-Philippe-du-Roule) | 01 42 56 56 58 | fax 01 42 56 09 60 | www.restaurant-toi.com

Everything old is new again, like the "flashy, love-it-or-hate-it" 1970s orange-and-purple decor at this club near the Champs; it offers "trendy" lounge dining in armchairs or couches and a house DJ spinning cool tunes; but style sentries say the overall experience is "more amusing than appetizing", given that the New French menu "isn't very long, in contrast to the service that takes a little *too* long."

Tokyo Eat ❶Ⓜ *New French*

| | 12 | 20 | 12 | €38 |

16ᵉ | Palais de Tokyo | 13, av du President Wilson (Iéna) | 01 47 20 00 29 | fax 01 47 20 05 62 | www.palaisdetokyo.com

Modern-art buffs satisfy their appetites late into the night at "one of Paris' hippest spots", the "chic canteen" of the Palais de Tokyo museum; the New French menu touches on "varied flavors" from around the globe, but the star of the show is the "exceptional setting", with spaceshiplike lamps hanging from the high ceilings, and the "sublime terrace", whose "view of the Seine and Eiffel Tower" is outright "magic"; P.S. "if it seems too dear, you can grab a sandwich" at Idem, the downstairs cafeteria.

Tong Yen ● *Chinese*

FOOD	DECOR	SERVICE	COST
20	11	17	€64

8e | 1 bis, rue Jean Mermoz (Franklin D. Roosevelt) | 01 42 25 04 23 |
fax 01 45 63 51 57

"The smartest woman in the restaurant business", chef-owner
Thérèse Luong, has built this "classic" Chinese near the Champs
into "the chicest Asian eatery in Paris", because she "makes you feel
like a celebrity when you walk in" (indeed, politicians and power
brokers are among her regulars); her clientele confesses that the
"very kitsch", authentic '60s decor "could use a lift", but her "delicious,
light" dishes are unfailingly "first-rate."

Tonnelle Saintongeaise (La) Ⓢ *Classic French*

FOOD	DECOR	SERVICE	COST
-	-	-	E

Neuilly-sur-Seine | 32, bd Vital-Bouhot (Pont-de-Levallois) |
01 46 24 43 15 | fax 01 46 24 36 33

With its "charming location", complete with "a terrace right in the
middle of Ile de la Jatte", this Classic French is a comfortable hangout (its covered courtyard is agreeable "even in stormy summer
weather"); the menu offers "dishes that are simple but always adequate", including specialties from the chef's native Charente and a
hand-cut steak tartare that's a "must for raw-meat lovers."

Toque (La) Ⓢ *Classic French*

FOOD	DECOR	SERVICE	COST
▽ 23	18	20	€91

17e | 16, rue de Tocqueville (Villiers) | 01 42 27 97 75 |
fax 01 47 63 97 69

"Loyal followers" of chef-owner Jacky Joubert have been coming to
his small establishment in the 17th for over a quarter-century to
partake of "outstanding" Classic French cuisine in intimate alcoves
underneath the clouds of a trompe l'oeil ceiling; despite the high
tabs, they say it's "great value" in a "warm", if "conservative, atmosphere" "for a business meal" or simply an "enjoyable evening."

Ⓩ Tour d'Argent (La) Ⓜ *Haute Cuisine*

FOOD	DECOR	SERVICE	COST
25	28	26	€141

5e | 15-17, quai de la Tournelle (Cardinal Lemoine/Pont Marie) |
01 43 54 23 31 | fax 01 44 07 12 04 | www.latourdargent.com

Dining at this Haute Cuisine "legend" is "pure theater", thanks to its
"enchanting setting" with "an unparalleled view of Notre Dame" in
the 5th; the numbered "duck is a must", accompanied by a bottle
from the "fabled" *cave* (try to "tour it after dinner"); some sniff this
tower is "for the birds" and arguably "Paris' most expensive, elegant
tourist trap", but the savvy "go at lunch – that's when the natives go,
and the tab is much kinder."

Tournesol (Le) *Bistro*

FOOD	DECOR	SERVICE	COST
13	15	13	€42

16e | 2, av de Lamballe (Passy) | 01 45 25 95 94 |
fax 01 45 25 43 09

"Always full with a trendy clientele from the neighborhood" and the
nearby Maison de la Radio, this "lively" spot in prosperous Passy
serves up lots of ambiance and "loud music" – along with a generally
"banal" bistro menu that's best basically for a "quick meal"; however, the "nice sidewalk terrace" facing the Seine is a major "perk"
on sunny days.

	FOOD	DECOR	SERVICE	COST

Z Train Bleu (Le) *Classic French* — **19** **27** **19** **€64**

12ᵉ | Gare de Lyon (Gare de Lyon) | 01 43 43 09 06 | fax 01 43 43 97 96 |
www.le-train-bleu.com

"Take a trip back in time to the days of luxury locomotive travel" say
travelers to this "art nouveau masterpiece" with its "theatrical atmosphere" and "entrancing frescos" in the Gare de Lyon; although
the Classic French "food doesn't live up to the decor", it has gotten
"a little more creative" of late, and the "service is polite"; and with
"champagne and good spirits in profusion" the experience is "un-
missable, even without a train ticket."

NEW 35° Ouest 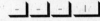 *Seafood* — **-** **-** **-** **E**

7ᵉ | 35, rue de Verneuil (Rue du Bac) | 01 42 86 98 88 | fax 01 42 86 00 65
Deep pockets are de rigueur at this new, elegant establishment just
off the Rue du Bac – the brainchild of the former owner of Gaya Rive
Gauche; within its contemporary, celadon walls, it offers up traditional seafood graced with creative touches to a well-heeled crowd of
older locals; the proprietor himself guarantees the gracious service.

Tricotin ● *Asian* — **-** **-** **-** **I**

13ᵉ | 15, av de Choisy (Porte de Choisy) | 01 45 84 74 44
Dumpling devotees line up for a table at this "superior" "canteen-style
Asian" in Chinatown, where two dining rooms with different menus
but the same "minimal decor" are always "crowded" with "lots of admirers" who dig their chopsticks into "amazingly good" (and "inexpensive") Chinese, Vietnamese or Thai dishes, plus "quality dim sum."

Triporteur (Le) Ⓢ *Bistro* — **-** **-** **-** **M**

15ᵉ | 4, rue de Dantzig (Convention) | 01 45 32 82 40
"The owner clearly loves food, and loves sharing his passion for it"
at this "neighborhood bistro" located on an "excellent spot on a
quiet street" in the 15th; the seasonally changing, Classic French-
Southwestern specialties are listed on the prototypical blackboard
menu, amid a setting decorated with casual bric-a-brac, including a
hard-to-miss delivery tricycle (*triporteur*) over the door.

Z Trois Marches (Les) Ⓢ Ⓜ *Haute Cuisine* — **26** **26** **24** **€88**

Versailles | Hôtel Trianon Palace | 1, bd de la Reine (RER Versailles-Rive
Droite) | 01 39 50 13 21 | fax 01 30 21 01 25 | www.trianonpalace.fr
"Society's upper echelons" "eat as though they were at the Versailles
court" at this Haute Cuisine hideaway near the Sun King's old stomping grounds; a "remarkable chef" creates "inventive and succulent"
dishes in a "sumptuous palace" "with a view on the park" and "Marie
Antoinette's sheep-grazing meadow"; adding to the "royal" treatment
are "flawless service", "a stunning wine list" and "three enormous
cheese carts" that make the "phenomenal prices" "worth every euro."

Troquet (Le) Ⓢ Ⓜ *Basque/New French* — **23** **13** **18** **€42**

15ᵉ | 21, rue François Bonvin (Sèvres-Lecourbe/Volontaire) |
01 45 66 89 00 | fax 01 45 66 89 83
"Reserve well in advance if you hope to score a table" at this "neighborhood gathering spot", a "boisterous" "family-run" "slice of authentic

Paris", where "the tables are packed tight" with admirers of the "imaginative" New French fare with "superb Basque" accents; the 15th-arrondissement "location is out of the way", but the menu offers "a moderate four-course prix fixe" that's "never the same meal twice."

Trou Gascon (Au) 🛇 *Southwest* — 24 | 17 | 23 | €72

12ᵉ | 40, rue Taine (Daumesnil) | 01 43 44 34 26 | fax 01 43 07 80 55 | www.autrogascon.fr

Foie gras fanatics feel "the heart of Alain Dutournier's genius" lies in this small, modern site "way off the beaten path" in the "far-from-fancy" 12th, where the celebrated chef-owner serves "delicious, refined" Southwestern fare that's "the essence of authentic country cuisine", along with a "wonderful and unusual wine list" and a "huge Armagnac collection"; a few quack it "could use a face-lift", but to the majority, it's "still a standout."

NEW Truc Café (Le) Ⓜ *Wine Bar/Bistro* — – | – | – | M

18ᵉ | 58, rue du Poteau (Jules Joffrin) | 01 42 52 64 09

Generously served Classic French dishes and an Italian-oriented wine list have made this *bistrot à vins* in a gentrifying Montmartre neighborhood a hit with a trendy young crowd; changing contemporary art exhibitions and a pretty, quiet little garden out back please as much as the smiling service and modest prices.

Truffe Noire (La) 🛇 *Classic French* — 20 | 14 | 16 | €79

Neuilly-sur-Seine | 2, pl Parmentier (Les Sablons/Porte Maillot) | 01 46 24 94 14 | fax 01 46 24 94 60 | www.truffe-noire.com

Neuilly's nobility gets its dose of decadent eats at this "very Classic" French that's maintained a "consistently high quality over the years", though now with refurbished decor that features modern banquettes and Murano chandeliers; the "fine" cuisine, including a tasting menu featuring the fabulous fungus, might be "a little pricey" – but "you have to shell out if you want to eat truffles", *n'est-ce pas?*

Truffière (La) 🛇Ⓜ *Classic/New French* — 24 | 23 | 23 | €74

5ᵉ | 4, rue Blainville (Cardinal Lemoine/Place Monge) | 01 46 33 29 82 | fax 01 46 33 64 74 | www.latruffiere.com

"Truffles, great wine, great cheese – this is the life" sigh those seduced by this "elegant", "extremely *romantique*" 17th-century vaulted cellar in the 5th, where the New and Classic French menu offers fungus "in abundance", as well as *fromage* "from a tray so huge the waiters have trouble rolling it around the room"; a few warn to "watch the wine list or it can get very expensive", and be mindful that, while it might feel like "old-world Paris" here, "you may very well run into your neighbors from Ft. Worth."

Trumilou (Le) *Bistro* — 19 | 14 | 19 | €29

4ᵉ | 84, quai de l'Hôtel de Ville (Hôtel-de-Ville/Pont-Marie) | 01 42 77 63 98 | fax 01 48 04 91 89

"Other than its location across from the Seine, there's nothing fancy" here – and that pleases budget eaters who make a beeline for this "boisterous", "friendly", "funky bargain of a place", serving "decent old-style" bistro food in the 4th; sure, the "eclectic decor" is looking "a little tattered", but it's "just the thing to soothe an artist's soul."

Tsé-Yang ◐ *Chinese*

| 21 | 21 | 17 | €60 |

16ᵉ | 25, av Pierre 1er de Serbie (Alma Marceau/Iéna) | 01 47 20 70 22 | fax 01 49 52 03 68

Practically a time zone away from its Chinatown cousins, this swank 16th-arrondissement table draws an upscale clientele who claim it's "the only restaurant where you eat *real* Chinese cuisine"; the "refined", "creative" Beijing and Shanghai specialties are "worth the elegant price"; but some suspect it pays to be a party member, since the servers "are friendly to regulars and overlook those who aren't"; P.S. a recent switch from "magnificient" imperial decor to a more modern black-and-gold setting may outdate the Decor score.

Tsukizi ⊠ Ⓜ *Japanese*

| - | - | - | M |

6ᵉ | 2 bis, rue des Ciseaux (Mabillon/St-Germain-des-Prés) | 01 43 54 65 19

"A lot of Japanese" clients and others "who miss real sushi" get a taste of Tokyo in the heart of Saint-Germain at this "tiny counter" where expats from the old country "manage and cook" the "very fresh products"; zealots even praise the "Zen ambiance" (the critical just call it "cramped").

Uitr *Seafood*

| - | - | - | M |

15ᵉ | 1, pl Falguière (Pasteur/Pernety) | 01 47 34 12 24 | fax 01 47 34 12 34

Oyster eaters can binge on bivalves all year round, singly or by the dozen, at this "good-value" annex of seafooder La Cagouille in the 15th; the "fresh products" are "prepared with talent" and served amid nautical decor; there's a substantial collection of whiskies to wash 'em down with.

NEW Unico ⊠ Ⓜ *Argentinean*

| - | - | - | E |

11ᵉ | 15, rue Paul Bert (Faidherbe-Chaligny) | 01 43 67 68 08 | www.resto-unico.com

Occupying the orange-tiled premises of a '70s-vintage former butcher shop not far from the Bastille, this South American is off with a gallop as one of the town's hottest new tables; what's pulling the trendy young crowd are authentic starters like Argentine sausages, followed by imported pampas beef and wines; service is young and friendly, even if the prices could make a gaucho groucho.

Vagenende ◐ *Brasserie*

| 15 | 22 | 16 | €50 |

6ᵉ | 142, bd St-Germain (Mabillon/Odéon) | 01 43 26 68 18 | fax 01 40 51 73 38 | www.vagenende.fr

Commonly called "the poor man's Maxim's", this century-old brasserie in the 6th is "a feast for the eyes" with a "stunningly authentic", "almost edible" art nouveau interior; less mouthwatering is the menu of "acceptable-but-ordinary food", despite an "outstanding" raw bar; nonetheless, the "bustling" ambiance, the "great-for-people-watching" location and the late-night service make it "a fine place for an off-hour meal, just to soak in the decor."

Vaudeville (Le) ● *Brasserie*

	FOOD	DECOR	SERVICE	COST
	17	20	16	€49

2ᵉ | 29, rue Vivienne (Bourse) | 01 40 20 04 62 | fax 01 40 20 14 35 | www.vaudevilleparis.com

A "stylish clientele" enhances the "glittering" "marble and mosaic" setting of this art deco spot "across from the Bourse" in the 2nd arrondissement, a "lively late-night brasserie" with a "special-occasion feel"; despite "desultory service", seafood lovers say this is "the best of the Groupe Flo" chain, with the "good", "basic" menu enhanced by "giant platters of *fruits de mer*" that have 'em rolling in the aisles.

Verre Bouteille (Le) ● *Wine Bar/Bistro*

	FOOD	DECOR	SERVICE	COST
	–	–	–	M

17ᵉ | 85, av des Ternes (Porte Maillot) | 01 45 74 01 02 | fax 01 47 63 07 02 | www.leverrebouteille.com

Carnivores who "crave beef tartare in the middle of the night" steak their claim to this "unpretentious" wine bar in the 17th, which goes strong until 5 AM; amid the bistro bites, the aforementioned raw meat "is excellent – chopped, not ground", and there's a range of vinos by the glass.

Verre Volé (Le) *Wine Bar/Bistro*

	FOOD	DECOR	SERVICE	COST
	▽ 14	14	18	€27

10ᵉ | 67, rue de Lancry (République) | 01 48 03 17 34

Vino-inclined reviewers "run, don't walk" to this "jovial" wine bar on the banks of the Canal Saint-Martin and "while away the afternoon" or evening sampling from a gently priced list of "intelligently and passionately chosen" young varietals alongside "simple" dishes such as oysters or charcuterie; the room is "*tout petite*" so it can be "hard to find a free table", but at least the cheek-to-jowl ambiance ensures it's always "high-spirited."

NEW Versance (Le) Ⓢ Ⓜ *Classic/New French*

	FOOD	DECOR	SERVICE	COST
	–	–	–	E

2ᵉ | 16, rue Feydeau (Bourse) | 01 45 08 00 08 | fax 01 45 08 47 99 | www.leversance.fr

Young chef Samuel Cavagnis roamed the world for several years before setting up shop at this elegant gray-and-white duplex near the old Bourse, or stock market (and indeed, prices are for those with substantial portfolios); his produce-driven French cuisine blends the traditional and the new, as does the decor, which juxtaposes contemporary furniture with a stained-glass window and 19th-century moldings; it's as appropriate for a business meal as for a romantic tête-à-tête.

Viaduc Café (Le) ● *Classic/New French*

	FOOD	DECOR	SERVICE	COST
	▽ 12	18	13	€35

12ᵉ | 43, av Daumesnil (Bastille/Gare de Lyon) | 01 44 74 70 70 | fax 01 44 74 70 71 | www.viaduc-cafe.fr

The trip is "hip" at this "lovely-to-look at" eatery with stone walls and high ceilings built "under the arches of a former railroad viaduct" in the 12th; it's "understandably popular" for its "original" decor and a "beautiful" large terrace open until the wee hours in summer, despite the "just fair" Classic–New French cuisine (though a new chef arrived post-Survey); still, it's "not about the food" here –

"the whole point of the place is to get a tan and to be seen"; P.S. "great jazz brunch" on Sundays.

Vieille Fontaine Rôtisserie (La) M *Classic/New French*   ▽ 20 | 21 | 22 | €38

Maisons-Laffitte | 8, av Grétry (RER Maisons-Laffitte) | 01 39 62 01 78 | fax 01 39 62 13 43 | www.viellefontaine.com

With an "agreeable setting in the park of Maisons Laffitte", this restaurant in a Second Empire–era mansion attracts locals as well as weekenders to the country with "very fine" Classic and New French cuisine and a staff that's "a delight"; this aristocratic estate is especially "wonderful" "in good weather, when the terrace overlooking the garden is lovely."

Vieux Bistro (Le) *Lyon*   20 | 16 | 19 | €44

4e | 14, rue du Cloître Notre-Dame (Cité) | 01 43 54 18 95 | fax 01 44 07 35 63 | www.lamaree.fr

"Don't let its location fool you", "on touristy Restaurant Row" "in the shadows of Notre Dame", because "this is the real stuff" – "a quintessential bistro" with "homey atmosphere" and "ample portions" of "solid, tasteful, earthy" Lyonnais cuisine; some non-Gallic guests grumble "they push tourists to the rear", but in any case, "the outdoor tables are the best" "for the view" of the cathedral; "if you time it right you can even eat while listening to the choir sing."

Vieux Chêne (Au) Z *Bistro*   – | – | – | M

11e | 7, rue du Dahomey (Faidherbe-Chaligny) | 01 43 71 67 69

Most patrons "say positive things" about this young "neo-bistro" on a quiet street in the 11th – citing in particular the "good" New French cuisine (e.g. the signature soft cod with soy sauce), the "*very* good wines" and cognacs and the reasonable prices; the decor is pleasantly retro, conjuring up a circa-1900 room with cast-iron columns, woody accents and walls that show the patina of time.

Villa Corse (La) Z *Corsica*   16 | 16 | 14 | €48

15e | 164, bd de Grenelle (Cambronne/La Motte-Picquet-Grenelle) | 01 53 86 70 81 | fax 01 53 86 90 73 🕐

NEW 16e | 141, av de Malakoff (Porte Maillot) | 01 40 67 18 44 M

No need to be Corsican to feel "like you're at home" at this "intimate" address in the 15th, specializing in an "interesting variety" of "flavorful, copious" dishes and charcuterie from the Ile de Beauté; the "lovely library" area, adorned with "comfortable club chairs" and "warm and cozy" ambiance, is "quite the spot for a dinner à deux", though some say the service can be just a little "coarse"; N.B. a 16th-arrondissement offshoot opened last autumn.

Village d'Ung et Li Lam ● *Chinese/Thai*   – | – | – | M

8e | 10, rue Jean Mermoz (Franklin D. Roosevelt) | 01 42 25 99 79 | fax 01 42 25 12 06

Village people call this original Oriental outpost in the 8th "a must in Paris", as much for the "ultrakitsch decor" (kind of "Asia meets the Champs-Elysées", with a six-ton aquarium on the ceiling) as for the "quality" Chinese-Thai cuisine and "charming welcome."

Village Kabyle ⚠M *North African* | – | – | – | I |

18ᵉ | 4, rue Aimé Lavy (Jules Joffrin) | 01 42 55 03 34 | fax 01 45 86 68 35
Nomads who wander into the upper reaches of the 18th can pitch their tents for a desert meal at the more "modest" (and less expensive) of the two eateries run by Wally le Saharien; he specializes in Kabyle dishes, notably an "outstanding" dry couscous that "you don't get anywhere else" (or not easily, anyway); "family-style service" and a "charming" Algerian setting also make this a worthwhile oasis.

Villaret (Le) ❶⚠ *Bistro* | 23 | 14 | 19 | €48 |

11ᵉ | 13, rue Ternaux (Oberkampf/Parmentier) | 01 43 57 89 76
"Crowded" with customers who crow "this is what a bistro is all about", this "friendly, informal" table "in the middle of nowhere in the 11th" "packs it in late" with patrons who "leave satiated" by the "satisfying", "varied" Classic French fare with "modern touches" and an "exceptional" wine list, all of a "quality amazing for the price"; "lace curtains dress up" the "simple" digs.

Vinci (Le) ⚠ *Classic French/Italian* | – | – | – | E |

16ᵉ | 23, rue Paul Valéry (Victor Hugo) | 01 45 01 68 18 | fax 01 45 01 60 37
Suits in the 16th know this "small" site adorned with well-spaced tables and reddish tones as "one of the best deals in the neighborhood", "deserving its loyal clientele" with prix fixes that are "champion for value"; its Joël Robuchon–trained chef cooks up "excellent" dishes that combine "Italian inspiration" and Classic French savoir faire.

Vin dans les voiles (Le) ⚠ *Wine Bar/Bistro* | – | – | – | I |

16ᵉ | 8, rue Chapu (Exelmans) | 01 46 47 83 98 | fax 01 46 47 83 98 | www.vindanslesvoiles.com
"Wines are taken seriously by the *patron*" of this "relaxed", "hospitable" spot in the southern 16th with a thirst-inducing list of reds and whites to taste alongside a blackboard menu of simple bistro dishes; the "small" room can get "a bit cramped when crowded", but the "excellent values" ferment an intoxicating ambiance.

Vin des Pyrenees ❶ *Classic French* | 16 | 17 | 16 | €32 |

4ᵉ | 25, rue Beautrellis (St-Paul/Bastille) | 01 42 72 64 94 | fax 01 42 71 19 62
Perfect for a "festive meal among friends", this Marais bistro draws a "trendy", "younger crowd" that likes the "convivial" ambiance and "simple" Classic French menu with "lots of meat"; the room (with a "large" smoke-free area) is arrayed "*à l'ancienne*" with wooden tables, old postcards and "bottles in wire-covered cubbyholes"; the staff's "mostly friendly", and "the owners are always at hand."

Vinea Café (Le) ❶ *Classic French* | – | – | – | M |

12ᵉ | 26-28, Cour St-Emilion (Cour St-Emilion) | 01 44 74 09 09 | fax 01 44 74 06 66 | www.vinea-cafe.com
Day-trippers to the shops and cinemas of the "happening scene" of the Cour Saint-Emilion, a renovated district of 19th-century wine storehouses, can grab a noon meal from the "nicely priced lunch menu" or a late dinner of Classic French cuisine at this "historic

stone building" (an old *cave*) with a "very pleasant terrace"; however, critics caution the "inconsistent" quality makes prices seem "high."

Vin et Marée *Seafood*
17 | 12 | 15 | €45

1er | 165, rue St-Honoré (Palais Royal-Musée du Louvre) | 01 42 86 06 96 | fax 01 42 86 06 97

7e | 71, av de Suffren (La Motte-Picquet-Grenelle) | 01 47 83 27 12 | fax 01 43 06 62 35

11e | 276, bd Voltaire (Nation) | 01 43 72 31 23 | fax 01 40 09 05 24

14e | 108, av du Maine (Gaîté) | 01 43 20 29 50 | fax 01 43 27 84 11

16e | 183, bd Murat (Porte de St-Cloud) | 01 46 47 91 39 | fax 01 46 47 69 07

This "chain of simple" seafooders has cast a wide net throughout the city, and its clients trust the "consistent quality" of the "standard fare" from a "tuna steak big enough for Ahab" to a "gigantesque" baba "with a good bottle of rum generously left at the table"; some carp about the "inattentive" service that leaves them fishing around for a waiter, and the "spacious" settings that seem slightly "sterile" – though entirely smoke-free now.

20 de Bellechasse (Le) ●🗷 *Bistro*
17 | 13 | 16 | €37

7e | 20, rue de Bellechasse (Solférino) | 01 47 05 11 11

Near the Musée d'Orsay, this "adorable neighborhood place" pulls a "smart young crowd" with "jet-set" hopes that likes the "simple but good bistro food", including "well-priced daily specials"; sparked by the "warm service", the "ambiance is always cheerful."

🆕 21 🗷🅼 *Seafood*
– | – | – | E

6e | 21, rue Mazarine (Odéon) | 01 46 33 76 90

After stints at Le Duc and his own eponymous restaurant, Paul Minchelli – a prince among *poisson* preparers – makes his comeback with this charming if pricey seafood bistro in the heart of Saint-Germain-des-Près (on the site of the late La Cafetière); popular with the area's antiques dealers and book editors, the intimate place offers a premium catch-of-the-day menu that's distinguished by the co-chef/owner's signature minimalist approach to fish and shellfish.

Vin sur Vin 🗷 *New French*
21 | 18 | 19 | €66

7e | 20, rue de Monttessuy (Alma Marceau/Ecole Militaire) | 01 47 05 14 20

Like "a private home" with an incredibly well-stocked cellar, this "tiny jewel" near the Champ de Mars has only 20 seats, a "high-quality" New French menu and a choice of 600 labels from an "outstanding, realistically priced wine list"; some say the staff's "a bit stiff", but fans "feel the warmth"; oh, and "don't forget to check the humidor for a [cigar on your] stroll to the *Tour Eiffel*" after dinner.

Violon d'Ingres (Le) 🗷🅼 *Bistro*
24 | 21 | 21 | M

7e | 135, rue St-Dominique (Ecole Militaire) | 01 45 55 15 05 | fax 01 45 55 48 42 | www.leviolondingres.com

Chef-owner Christian Constant transports fans (including "a lot of Americans") to "foodie heaven" at his "chic" table in the 7th; his constant supervision of the kitchen ensures "near perfection" on the plate, while wife Catherine oversees service in the "long, narrow" dining room; dissenters deem it "disappointing" ("we observed it's different if you are 'known'") but most marvel at "this most memorable meal"; N.B. a post-Survey menu switch from Haute Cuisine to upscale bistro fare, plus new brasserie-chic decor, is not reflected in the above scores.

	FOOD	DECOR	SERVICE	COST

Virgin Café ● Classic French

	9	10	8	€29

8e | Virgin Megastore | 52-60, av des Champs-Elysées (Franklin D. Roosevelt) | 01 42 56 15 96 | fax 01 45 53 50 41

Virgin Megastore shoppers flipping through the stacks can grab "a quick bite" between tracks at this "nice but noisy" space where "you can feel like you're 20" watching music videos, or take in the "view of the Champs"; the "simple", "snack"-like Classic French fare is "adequate", but the "rushed" staff strikes some "as inexperienced as a virgin."

Vivres (Les) Ⓢ Ⓜ Classic French

	–	–	–	I

9e | 28, rue Pétrelle (Anvers) | 01 42 80 26 10

The lower-priced annex of chef-owner Jean-Luc André's Le Pétrelle next door in the 9th has the charm of a small country grocery, with bouquets of flowers and vegetables, a handful of tables and shelves of preserves decorating the small room; eat in or take away the simple, Classic French eats like maman used to make.

Voltaire (Le) Ⓢ Ⓜ Bistro

	22	21	21	€68

7e | 27, quai Voltaire (Rue du Bac) | 01 42 61 17 49

"A place to go with your rich Parisian aunt", this "intimate and divine" address "on the banks of the Seine" is a "quintessential bistro" where "well-heeled" Left Bankers order "highly recommended" if "rather pricey" fare from "the most classical French menu you can come across"; a roomful of "regular patrons" creates a "clubby" air, and while the service is "great if you are known", the "uninitiated" reproach the staff for being a little "rude to tourists and newcomers."

Wadja Ⓢ Bistro

	21	13	19	€31

6e | 10, rue de la Grande-Chaumière (Vavin) | 01 46 33 02 02 | fax 01 46 33 02 02

"An authentic neighborhood experience", reminiscent of the days when Montparnasse was starving artist central, this "utilitarian"-looking "postcard bistro" serves up "creative and delicious" Classic French food on a true "bang-for-the-back" menu; the "extensive" wine list is an equally "terrific value."

Waknine Ⓢ New French

	▽ 14	16	15	€37

16e | 9, av Pierre 1er de Serbie (Iéna) | 01 47 23 48 18 | fax 01 47 23 87 33 | www.waknine.fr

The welcoming armchairs "fill up at lunch time" in this "chic" and "charming" 16th-arrondissement address where "always smiling" servers deliver "slightly fusion" New French food; the room can get "noisy" at noon or during impromptu "TGIF wine gatherings", but there's a "softer ambiance at night" and at afternoon tea too.

	FOOD	DECOR	SERVICE	COST

Wally Le Saharien 🗷 🅼 *North African*
▽ | 18 | 15 | 17 | €44

9ᵉ | 36, rue Rodier (Anvers/Notre-Dame-de-Lorette) |
01 42 85 51 90 | fax 01 42 85 51 90

"People come from all over Paris" to this exotic in the 9th arrondissement in search of what many consider "the best couscous
in Paris", an "extreme" version as "dry" as the Sahara it hails from,
along with other "unforgettable" dishes from Wally's native Algeria;
at dinner a tasting menu is the sole option, which guarantees "an exceptional evening" to some, though foes find the lack of choice
"hard to swallow."

Water Bar
Colette (Le) 🗷 *Italian/New French*
13 | 17 | 15 | €31

1ᵉʳ | 213, rue St-Honoré (Tuileries) | 01 55 35 33 93 |
fax 01 55 35 33 99 | www.colette.fr

"Rich women shopping in the neighborhood" maintain their fashion-
friendly figures with "light and fresh" Italian–New French nibbles accompanied by an assortment of "mineral waters with strange
names" at this "spare" cafe in the "super-trendy" store Colette; detractors dismiss it as an "amusing but expensive" "fad" that won't
die – "nice bottles, but a bit too much attitude."

Wepler ● *Brasserie*
15 | 12 | 14 | €47

18ᵉ | 14, pl de Clichy (Place de Clichy) | 01 45 22 53 24 |
fax 01 44 70 07 50 | www.wepler.com

"One of the last [independent] big brasseries in Paris", this "legendary" address "in the heart of the Place de Clichy" remains a "temple of tradition" where the "famous" *fruits de mer* "has a place of
honor all year long"; detractors declare the decor is "nothing extraordinary" and the menu "unoriginal", but if you "stick with the oysters
you won't be disappointed."

Willi's Wine Bar 🗷 *Wine Bar/Bistro*
19 | 16 | 19 | €46

1ᵉʳ | 13, rue des Petits-Champs (Palais Royal-Musée du Louvre/
Pyramides) | 01 42 61 05 09 | fax 01 47 03 36 93 |
www.williswinebar.com

"When the English fall for wine, they do it right" toast tipplers in
tribute to this "crowded" "oenophiles' stalwart" near the Palais
Royal; decorated with "annual posters for sale", the small room
buzzes with the sounds of "Anglo-Saxon chatting", lubricated by
"little-known gems" from British owner Mark Williamson's "wide-
ranging list"; though the "food is only a secondary reason to go", the
market-"fresh" menu offers "fairly solid" Gallic fare.

Wok Cooking ● *Asian*
- | - | - | I

11ᵉ | 25, rue des Taillandiers (Bastille) | 01 55 28 88 77 |
fax 01 48 10 04 65

The "original concept" of this interactive Asian in the Bastille bar
strip is that you "make your own stir-fry" by "picking your ingredients"
and watching as "the chef cooks them in front of you"; energetic eaters say it's "fun" and appealingly "cheap", even if the pine-and-plastic
setting feels a little "clinical."

W Restaurant (Le) ☒ *Haute Cuisine* — | — | — | VE

8ᵉ | Hôtel Warwick | 5, rue de Berri (George V) | 01 45 61 82 08 |
fax 01 45 63 75 81 | www.warwickhotels.com

A few steps off the Champs, this Haute Cuisine table is a choice destination for client lunches when quality cuisine can clinch the deal;
the kitchen "deserves kudos" for the "fresh" fare prepared with a
Mediterranean accent, as does the "efficient service" say surveyors
willing to "overlook" the "corporate-chic and cold decor" and the uninspiring "location at the back of an international hotel."

Yen *Japanese* 19 | 15 | 17 | €45

6ᵉ | 22, rue St-Benoît (St-Germain-des-Prés) | 01 45 44 11 18 |
fax 01 45 44 19 48

Gourmands ready for "something other than sushi" nippon over to
this Saint-Germain Japanese for "elaborate", "unconventional" offerings, including "the best soba in Paris", in a coolly "Zen atmosphere"
where "the regulars go upstairs"; but cost-conscious customers
complain that "small" portions and "expensive" tabs mean "you'll
have a yen after eating here . . . for something to eat."

Yugaraj *Indian* 19 | 14 | 19 | €56

6ᵉ | 14, rue Dauphine (Pont-Neuf/Odéon) | 01 43 26 44 91 |
fax 01 46 33 50 77

At what's "reputed to be the best Indian in Paris" (certainly, one of
the "rare good ones"), "attentive personnel" serve an "original"
menu of "delicate, flavorful" fare prepared with top-notch ingredients like Bresse chicken, accompanied by a "great wine list"; carved
statues and colonial antiques make for "authentic" subcontinental
surroundings, though the "very pricey" bill more closely matches
the spiffy Saint-Germain quarter outside.

Zébra Square ◑ *Classic French* 12 | 18 | 13 | €54

16ᵉ | 3, pl Clément-Ader (Passy/RER Kennedy-Radio France) |
01 44 14 91 91 | fax 01 45 27 18 34 | www.zebrasquare.com

"Your reception will depend on how well you're known" at this
"meeting place for young, dynamic professionals" "on expense ac-
counts", including many regulars from the Maison de la Radio just
steps away; though conservatives quip it's "more cold than cool",
the "contemporary" (and "noisy") setting is "better than the food" –
rather "ordinary" Classic French cuisine (the specialty tartares are
touted, though); but you'll only find out "if the staff stops preening
long enough to take your order."

☑ Ze Kitchen Galerie ☒ *Eclectic* 23 | 20 | 21 | €57

6ᵉ | 4, rue des Grands-Augustins (St-Michel) | 01 44 32 00 32 |
fax 01 44 32 00 33 | www.zekitchengalerie.fr

"William Ledeuil has found his groove" rave habitués of this "hip"
Eclectic in Saint-Germain, where the co-chef/owner creates "light",
"witty" dishes with "Asian influences" that "blend perfectly with local
products" – in short, "what good fusion cooking is all about"; an "open
kitchen" is part of the "minimalist art-gallery decor", and the "good-
natured staff" adds to the "stimulating vibe" of a "zeeelicious" time.

Zéphyr (Le) ● *Bistro*

FOOD	DECOR	SERVICE	COST
-	-	-	M

20ᵉ | 1, rue du Jourdain (Jourdain) | 01 46 36 65 81 | fax 01 40 33 10 89 | www.lezephyr.com

Its name means gentle breeze, but this one in the far reaches of Belleville blows hot and cold; the refined and "inventive" bistro fare is "scrumptious" to some palates, "disappointing" to others; still, this neighborhood hangout remains a popular place "to meet with close friends" and admire the superbly preserved art deco interior.

Zeyer (Le) ● *Brasserie*

FOOD	DECOR	SERVICE	COST
15	15	15	€51

14ᵉ | 62, rue d'Alésia (Alésia) | 01 45 40 43 88 | fax 01 45 40 64 51

Alésia residents have long frequented this "good old" brasserie for "large portions" of "reliable" albeit "middling", traditional eats (exception: the "excellent choucroute"); service is "fast, if unfriendly", and the 1930s-meets-1970s decor feels "a little dated" to some, though the big windows offer a "splendid view onto the church" in the square.

Zinc-Zinc 🄱 *Bistro*

FOOD	DECOR	SERVICE	COST
▽ 14	17	15	€39

Neuilly-sur-Seine | 209 ter, av Charles de Gaulle (Pont de Neuilly) | 01 40 88 36 06 | fax 01 47 38 16 21 | www.zinczinc.com

The "young" guns of Neuilly pack into this "trendy" spot for "smart lunches and cool dinners" or else belly up to the bar "after work for tapas" and a cocktail; they praise the "consistent quality" of the bistro fare but especially the scene, a modish Manhattanesque setting that "can get a bit crowded, noisy and smoky" at prime time.

Zo ●🄱 *Eclectic*

FOOD	DECOR	SERVICE	COST
15	16	15	€43

8ᵉ | 13, rue Montalivet (Champs-Elysées-Clémenceau) | 01 42 65 18 18 | fax 01 42 65 10 91 | www.restaurantzo.com

Fusionistas from the "posh neighborhood" around the Faubourg Saint-Honoré have made this "happening" table their "local hangout" with an "Eclectic menu" that meanders from the Mediterranean to Japan and a bar that specializes in fruity vodkas; for a restaurant *à la mode,* it's "affordable", and the "warm ambiance" makes it "good for a party" or "casual dinner."

Zygomates (Les) 🄱🄼 *Bistro*

FOOD	DECOR	SERVICE	COST
-	-	-	I

12ᵉ | 7, rue de Capri (Daumesnil/Michel Bizot) | 01 40 19 93 04 | fax 01 44 73 46 63 | www.leszygomates.fr

Patrons are beaming in this century-old charcuterie-turned-eatery, with its "charming setting" of trompe l'oeil and etched glass, "excellent value" menu of "delicious" Classic French cooking and "friendly service befitting the name", which means the muscles used to smile; its location in the 12th might be a little "far from the center", yet clients still come, cheering "the old Paris bistro lives on."

INDEXES

French Cuisines

Includes restaurant names, neighborhoods and Food ratings. ☑ indicates places with the highest ratings, popularity and importance.

BISTRO

Abadache	**17ᵉ**	‑
Absinthe	**1ᵉʳ**	19
🆕 Accolade	**17ᵉ**	‑
A et M	**16ᵉ**	15
Affriolé	**7ᵉ**	21
☑ Allard	**6ᵉ**	22
Allobroges	**20ᵉ**	20
☑ Ami Louis	**3ᵉ**	26
Ami Marcel	**15ᵉ**	21
Ampère	**17ᵉ**	15
AOC	**5ᵉ**	19
Ardoise	**1ᵉʳ**	23
Assiette	**14ᵉ**	20
Astier	**11ᵉ**	22
Atelier Maître Albert	**5ᵉ**	21
Aub. Nicolas Flamel	**3ᵉ**	20
Babylone	**7ᵉ**	‑
Bar des Théâtres	**8ᵉ**	13
Bastide Odéon	**6ᵉ**	20
☑ Benoît	**4ᵉ**	24
Beurre Noisette	**15ᵉ**	21
🆕 Bis du Severo	**14ᵉ**	‑
Bistral	**17ᵉ**	23
Bistro 121	**15ᵉ**	20
Bistro de Breteuil	**7ᵉ**	18
Bistro/Deux Théâtres	**9ᵉ**	15
Bistro du 17ème	**17ᵉ**	16
Bistro Melrose	**17ᵉ**	‑
Bistro St. Ferdinand	**17ᵉ**	16
Bistrot Baracane	**4ᵉ**	23
Bistrot d'à Côté	**multi. loc.**	20
Bistrot d'André	**15ᵉ**	‑
Bistrot de l'Etoile Laur.	**16ᵉ**	19
Bistrot de l'Etoile Niel	**17ᵉ**	19
Bistrot de l'Université	**7ᵉ**	15
Bistrot de Paris	**7ᵉ**	19
Bistrot des Dames	**17ᵉ**	15
Bistrot des Vignes	**16ᵉ**	13
Bistrot d'Henri	**6ᵉ**	17
Bistrot du Cap	**15ᵉ**	‑
Bistrot du Dôme	**multi. loc.**	19
Bistrot du Peintre	**11ᵉ**	16
Bistrot du Sommelier	**8ᵉ**	20
Bistrot Papillon	**9ᵉ**	20
Bistrot Paul Bert	**11ᵉ**	20

Bistrot Vivienne	**2ᵉ**	15
Bon Accueil	**7ᵉ**	24
Boucherie Roulière	**6ᵉ**	‑
Boulangerie	**20ᵉ**	20
Buisson Ardent	**5ᵉ**	20
Butte Chaillot	**16ᵉ**	20
Café Burq	**18ᵉ**	‑
Café Constant	**7ᵉ**	22
Café d'Angel	**17ᵉ**	19
Café de l'Industrie	**11ᵉ**	13
Café de Mars	**7ᵉ**	16
Café du Commerce	**15ᵉ**	13
Café la Jatte	**Neuilly**	14
Café Moderne	**2ᵉ**	22
Café Ruc	**1ᵉʳ**	14
Caméléon	**6ᵉ**	‑
Camille	**3ᵉ**	20
🆕 Cantine de Quentin	**10ᵉ**	‑
Carte Blanche	**9ᵉ**	‑
Cave de l'Os à Moëlle	**15ᵉ**	20
Cave Gourmande	**19ᵉ**	24
Cerisaie	**14ᵉ**	24
Chardenoux	**11ᵉ**	15
Charpentiers	**6ᵉ**	18
Chez André	**8ᵉ**	20
Chez Denise	**1ᵉʳ**	23
Chez Fred	**17ᵉ**	‑
☑ Chez Georges	**2ᵉ**	21
Chez Gérard	**Neuilly**	19
Chez L'Ami Jean	**7ᵉ**	22
Chez la Vieille	**1ᵉʳ**	22
Chez Léna et Mimile	**5ᵉ**	‑
Chez Léon	**17ᵉ**	17
Chez Maître Paul	**6ᵉ**	20
Chez Marcel	**6ᵉ**	21
Chez Papinou	**Neuilly**	‑
Chez Paul	**11ᵉ**	20
Chez Paul	**13ᵉ**	17
Chez Pauline	**1ᵉʳ**	21
Chez Ramulaud	**11ᵉ**	22
Chez René	**5ᵉ**	21
Chez Savy	**8ᵉ**	21
Christine	**6ᵉ**	23
Cinq Mars	**7ᵉ**	‑
Clou	**17ᵉ**	‑
Comptoir du Relais	**6ᵉ**	22

Contre-Allée | 14ᵉ	24
Coupe Gorge | 4ᵉ	-
Crus de Bourgogne | 2ᵉ	-
D'Chez Eux | 7ᵉ	22
2 Pieces Cuisine | 18ᵉ	-
Dix Vins | 15ᵉ	16
Dos de la Baleine | 4ᵉ	16
Duc de Richelieu | 12ᵉ	-
Ebauchoir | 12ᵉ	-
Entracte | 18ᵉ	-
Entredgeu | 17ᵉ	21
Epi d'Or | 1ᵉʳ	21
☑ Epi Dupin | 6ᵉ	23
Escargot Montorgueil | 1ᵉʳ	18
Fins Gourmets | 7ᵉ	21
☑ Fontaine de Mars | 7ᵉ	21
Fontaines | 5ᵉ	18
Fous d'en Face | 4ᵉ	18
Frugier | 16ᵉ	-
Gauloise | 15ᵉ	16
Gavroche | 2ᵉ	21
Gorille Blanc | 7ᵉ	-
Gourmets des Ternes | 8ᵉ	19
Grange Batelière | 9ᵉ	-
Grille | 10ᵉ	-
Grille St-Germain | 6ᵉ	17
Joséphine/Dumonet | 6ᵉ	23
Lescure | 1ᵉʳ	16
☑ Lyonnais | 2ᵉ	22
Maison du Jardin | 6ᵉ	22
Mathusalem | 16ᵉ	14
Mesturet | 2ᵉ	-
Moissonnier | 5ᵉ	22
Mon Vieil Ami | 4ᵉ	24
Moulin à Vent | 5ᵉ	22
Muscade | 1ᵉʳ	-
Noces de Jeannette | 2ᵉ	-
O à la Bouche | 14ᵉ	17
Oeillade | 7ᵉ	15
Olivades | 7ᵉ	22
Opportun | 14ᵉ	-
Oudino | 7ᵉ	-
Ourcine | 13ᵉ	21
Paul, Restaurant | 1ᵉʳ	19
Pères et Filles | 6ᵉ	12
Perraudin | 5ᵉ	16
Petites Sorcières | 14ᵉ	-
Petit Marguery | 13ᵉ	22
NEW Petit Pamphlet | 3ᵉ	-
Petit Pascal | 13ᵉ	-
Petit Pergolèse | 16ᵉ	15
Petit Pontoise | 5ᵉ	23
Petit Prince de Paris | 5ᵉ	21
Petit Rétro | 16ᵉ	20
Petit Riche | 9ᵉ	16
Polichinelle Cafe | 11ᵉ	-
Polidor | 6ᵉ	15
Pomponette | 18ᵉ	-
Pouilly Reuilly | St-Gervais	19
Poulbot Gourmet | 18ᵉ	-
Poule au Pot | 1ᵉʳ	21
Press Café | 2ᵉ	-
P'tit Troquet | 7ᵉ	23
Pure Café | 11ᵉ	-
Refectoire | 11ᵉ	-
Régalade | 14ᵉ	23
Rendez-vous/Chauff. | 18ᵉ	-
Repaire de Cartouche | 11ᵉ	19
Rest. du Marché | 15ᵉ	-
Rest. Manufacture | Issy-les-Moul.	19
Robert et Louise | 3ᵉ	-
Roi du Pot-au-Feu | 9ᵉ	15
Rôtiss. d'en Face | 6ᵉ	22
Rôtiss. du Beaujolais | 5ᵉ	22
Rouge Vif | 7ᵉ	17
Saveurs du Marché | Neuilly	-
Scheffer | 16ᵉ	15
Soleil | St-Ouen	17
NEW Soleil | 7ᵉ	-
Sot l'y Laisse | 11ᵉ	-
NEW Spring | 9ᵉ	-
Square Trousseau | 12ᵉ	18
Suite | 8ᵉ	12
Temps au Temps | 11ᵉ	26
Temps des Cerises | 13ᵉ	18
Terrasse Mirabeau | 16ᵉ	-
Terroir | 13ᵉ	-
Thoumieux | 7ᵉ	15
Timbre | 6ᵉ	22
Tire-Bouchon | 15ᵉ	18
Titi Parisien | 7ᵉ	16
Tournesol | 16ᵉ	13
Triporteur | 15ᵉ	-
Trumilou | 4ᵉ	19
Vieux Bistro | 4ᵉ	20
Vieux Chêne | 11ᵉ	-
Villaret | 11ᵉ	23
20 de Bellechasse | 7ᵉ	17
Violon d'Ingres | 7ᵉ	24
Voltaire | 7ᵉ	22
Wadja | 6ᵉ	21

Restaurant	Score
Zéphyr	20e	–
Zinc-Zinc	Neuilly	14
Zygomates	12e	–

BRASSERIE

Restaurant	Score
Arbuci	6e	15
Aub. Dab	16e	16
Ballon des Ternes	17e	15
Boeuf sur le Toit	8e	16
Z Bofinger	4e	20
Bouillon Racine	6e	14
Brass. Balzar	5e	18
Brass. de l'Ile St. Louis	4e	16
Brass. du Louvre	1er	18
Brass. Flo	10e	17
Brass. Julien	10e	17
Brass. La Lorraine	8e	16
Brass. L'Européen	12e	–
Z Brass. Lipp	6e	17
Brass. Lutétia	6e	17
Brass. Mollard	8e	16
Charlot - Roi des Coq.	9e	15
Chez Francis	8e	14
Chez Georges-Maillot	17e	15
Chez Jenny	3e	17
Chez Les Anges	7e	–
Chien qui Fume	1er	17
Closerie des Lilas	6e	16
Congrès Maillot	17e	14
Costes	1er	17
Z Coupole	14e	18
Editeurs	6e	15
Flandrin	16e	13
Gallopin	2e	15
Garnier	8e	22
Grand Café	9e	15
Grand Colbert	2e	18
Marty	5e	17
Mascotte	18e	–
Petit Bofinger	multi. loc.	16
Petit Lutétia	6e	16
Petit Zinc	6e	20
Pied de Cochon	1er	18
Publicis Drugstore	8e	12
Rech	17e	14
Relais Plaza	8e	22
Rotonde	6e	14
Sébillon	Neuilly	19
Senderens	8e	–
Stella	16e	16
Suffren	15e	14

Restaurant	Score
NEW Tarmac	12e	–
Tav. de Maître Kanter	1er	10
Terminus Nord	10e	15
Vagenende	6e	15
Vaudeville	2e	17
Wepler	18e	15
Zeyer	14e	15

CLASSIC

Restaurant	Score
Aiguière	11e	–
Aimant du Sud	13e	–
Z Allard	6e	22
Altitude 95	7e	16
Z Ami Louis	3e	26
Amognes	11e	23
Appart'	8e	15
NEW Arome	8e	–
Aub. Bressane	7e	17
Aub. de la Reine Blanche	4e	20
Aub. du Champ de Mars	7e	23
Aub. du Clou	9e	13
Auguste	7e	19
Autobus Imperial	1er	–
Bacchantes	9e	–
Z Bar Vendôme	1er	21
Basilic	7e	14
Beaujolais d'Auteuil	16e	15
Biche au Bois	12e	21
Bistro de Breteuil	7e	18
Bistro St. Ferdinand	17e	16
Bistrot d'à Côté	multi. loc.	20
Bistrot d'André	15e	–
Bistrot d'Henri	6e	17
Boeuf Couronné	19e	17
Bon Accueil	7e	24
Bon Saint Pourçain	6e	17
NEW Brass. Printemps	9e	–
Buisson Ardent	5e	20
Café Beaubourg	4e	15
Café Charbon	11e	11
Café de Flore	6e	15
Café de la Musique	19e	–
Café de la Paix	9e	19
Café de la Poste	4e	16
Café de l'Esplanade	7e	17
Café Faubourg	8e	17
Café Guitry	9e	–
Café Le Petit Pont	5e	24
Z Café Les Deux Magots	6e	15
Café Marly	1er	15
Café Terminus	8e	–

subscribe to zagat.com

Cap Seguin | **Boulogne**	–	Hangar | 3ᵉ	20
Carte Blanche | 9ᵉ	–	Harold | 17ᵉ	–
Caveau du Palais | 1ᵉʳ	21	Huîtrier | 17ᵉ	–
Caves Pétrissans | 17ᵉ	21	Ile | **Issy-les-Moul.**	16
Céladon | 2ᵉ	24	Ilot Vache | 4ᵉ	21
Chai 33 | 12ᵉ	12	Jardin des Cygnes | 8ᵉ	20
Chalet de Neuilly | **Neuilly**	–	NEW Jardinier | 9ᵉ	–
Chalet des Iles | 16ᵉ	15	Jardins de Bagatelle | 16ᵉ	17
Chapeau Melon | 19ᵉ	–	Je Thé . . . Me | 15ᵉ	22
Chartier | 9ᵉ	13	Joséphine/Dumonet | 6ᵉ	23
Chaumière en l'Ile | 4ᵉ	22	Z Jules Verne | 7ᵉ	23
NEW Chez Cécile | 8ᵉ	–	Kiosque | 16ᵉ	14
Chez Clément | **multi. loc.**	12	Z Ladurée | **multi. loc.**	22
Chez Denise | 1ᵉʳ	23	Lavinia | 1ᵉʳ	17
Chez Françoise | 7ᵉ	15	Ma Bourgogne | 4ᵉ	17
Chez Gégène | **Joinville**	–	Macéo | 1ᵉʳ	21
Chez Grisette | 18ᵉ	–	Maison de l'Amér. Latine | 7ᵉ	17
Chez Léna et Mimile | 5ᵉ	–	Marc Annibal de Coconnas | 4ᵉ	17
Chez Nénesse | 3ᵉ	19	Marlotte | 6ᵉ	20
Christine | 6ᵉ	23	Martel | 10ᵉ	16
Cigale Recamier | 7ᵉ	22	Mathusalem | 16ᵉ	14
Citrus Etoile | 8ᵉ	–	Maupertu | 7ᵉ	20
Closerie des Lilas | 6ᵉ	16	Maxim's | 8ᵉ	20
Comédiens | 9ᵉ	–	Méditerranée | 6ᵉ	19
Cordonnerie | 1ᵉʳ	–	Monsieur Lapin | 14ᵉ	20
Coupe-Chou | 5ᵉ	20	Moulin de la Galette | 18ᵉ	–
Da Rosa | 6ᵉ	19	Murat | 16ᵉ	15
Dauphin | 1ᵉʳ	23	Natacha | 14ᵉ	21
Deux Canards | 10ᵉ	18	Nos Ancêtres/Gaulois | 4ᵉ	10
2 Pieces Cuisine | 18ᵉ	–	Z Obélisque | 8ᵉ	23
Drouant | 2ᵉ	–	Oenothèque | 9ᵉ	–
Ecluse | **multi. loc.**	14	Orangerie | 4ᵉ	–
Z Espadon | 1ᵉʳ	25	Orénoc | 17ᵉ	–
Etoile | 16ᵉ	18	Os à Moëlle | 15ᵉ	23
Ferme St-Simon | 7ᵉ	22	Ourcine | 13ᵉ	21
Fermette Marbeuf | 8ᵉ	18	Papilles | 5ᵉ	22
NEW Ferrandaise | 6ᵉ	–	Parc aux Cerfs | 6ᵉ	17
Flora Danica | 8ᵉ	18	Passage/Carm. | 11ᵉ	–
Flore en l'Ile | 4ᵉ	16	Passiflore | 16ᵉ	23
Florimond | 7ᵉ	24	Paul Chêne | 16ᵉ	22
Fontaine Gaillon | 2ᵉ	19	Paul, Restaurant | 1ᵉʳ	19
Fouquet's | 8ᵉ	17	Pavillon Montsouris | 14ᵉ	18
Gare | 16ᵉ	14	Pearl | 13ᵉ	–
Z Gérard Besson | 1ᵉʳ	25	Père Claude | 15ᵉ	18
Gitane | 15ᵉ	14	Pères et Filles | 6ᵉ	12
Gorille Blanc | 7ᵉ	–	Petit Châtelet | 5ᵉ	19
Grande Armée | 16ᵉ	12	Petit Colombier | 17ᵉ	17
Grand Louvre | 1ᵉʳ	18	Petite Chaise | 7ᵉ	19
Grange Batelière | 9ᵉ	–	Petite Tour | 16ᵉ	16
Guinguette/Neuilly | **Neuilly**	15	Petit Pascal | 13ᵉ	–
Guirlande de Julie | 3ᵉ	–	Petit Rétro | 16ᵉ	20

Chamarré | 7e	24
NEW Chateaubriand | 11e	-
Chez Catherine | 8e	23
Chez Michel | 10e	23
Chiberta | 8e	23
Citrus Etoile | 8e	-
Clos des Gourmets | 7e	24
Clos Morillons | 15e	-
Clovis | 8e	19
Cottage Marcadet | 18e	21
NEW Cou de la Girafe | 8e	-
Z Cristal Room | 16e	19
Cuisine | 7e	21
Delicabar | 7e	15
Z 1728 | 8e	16
Dôme du Marais | 4e	18
Don Juans | 3e	-
Doobie's | 8e	12
Famille | 18e	16
NEW First | 1er	-
NEW Gazzetta | 12e	-
Georgette | 9e	20
Gourmand | 6e	23
Harold | 17e	-
Harumi | 15e	-
Z Hélène Darroze | 6e	23
NEW Hier & Aujourd'hui | 17e	-
Z Hiramatsu | 16e	27
NEW Hôtel Amour | 9e	-
Ile | Issy-les-Moul.	16
Jardin | 8e	22
Jean | 9e	19
Jumeaux | 11e	-
Kodo | 4e	-
Les Saveurs de Flora | 8e	22
Libre Sens | 8e	16
Macéo | 1er	21
Magnolias | Perreux	22
Maison du Jardin | 6e	22
Z Michel Rostang | 17e	27
Montalembert | 7e	17
Murano | 3e	17
Musichall | 8e	15
O à la Bouche | 14e	17
NEW Ombres | 7e	-
Ourcine | 13e	21
Pershing | 8e	15
Petite Cour | 6e	18
Petit Marché | 3e	22
NEW Petit Monsieur | 11e	-
Petit Pergolèse | 16e	15

Petit Poucet | **Levallois**	16
Pétrelle | 9e	-
Pinxo | 1er	20
Ploum | 10e	-
Point Bar | 1er	21
Pomze | 8e	19
Pré Verre | 5e	23
Pur'Grill | 2e	25
Quai | 7e	-
R. | 15e	17
Radis Roses | 9e	-
Réconfort | 3e	17
Z Réminet | 5e	25
River Café | **Issy-les-Moul.**	15
Rue Balzac | 8e	18
Saveurs de Claude | 6e	-
16 Haussmann | 9e	21
Senderens | 8e	-
NEW Sensing | 6e	-
Senso | 8e	17
6 New York | 16e	20
Spicy | 8e	15
Spoon, Food & Wine | 8e	23
Square | 18e	-
Table d'Hédiard | 8e	22
Taïra | 17e	23
Thierry Burlot | 15e	24
Tire-Bouchon | 15e	18
Toi | 8e	-
Tokyo Eat | 16e	12
Troquet | 15e	23
Truffière | 5e	24
NEW Versance | 2e	-
Viaduc Café | 12e	12
Vieille Fontaine Rôtiss. | **Maisons-Laff.**	20
Vieux Chêne | 11e	-
Vin sur Vin | 7e	21
Waknine | 16e	14
Water Bar Colette | 1er	13

HAUTE CUISINE

Z Alain Ducasse | 8e	28
Z Ambroisie | 4e	27
Z Apicius | 8e	26
Z Arpège | 7e	26
Astor | 8e	20
Z Atelier de Joël Robuchon | 7e	27
Z Bristol | 8e	27
Z Carré des Feuillants | 1er	25
Cazaudehore | **St-Germain-Laye**	20

Restaurant	Rating
▣ Cinq	8e	28
Dominique Bouchet	8e	24
▣ Elysées	8e	26
▣ Grand Véfour	1er	27
▣ Guy Savoy	17e	28
▣ Hiramatsu	16e	27
▣ Jacques Cagna	6e	26
▣ Lapérouse	6e	21
▣ Lasserre	8e	27
Laurent	8e	24
Maison Blanche	8e	19
Maxan	8e	-
▣ Meurice	1er	26
Montparnasse 25	14e	24
Muses	9e	-
Ormes	7e	24
Paris	6e	19
▣ Pavillon/Gr. Cascade	16e	22
▣ Pavillon Ledoyen	8e	26
▣ Pierre Gagnaire	8e	28
▣ Pré Catelan	16e	26
▣ Relais d'Auteuil	16e	26
Relais du Parc	16e	-
▣ Relais Louis XIII	6e	25
NEW Sensing	6e	-
Stéphane Gaborieau	16e	-
▣ Table de Joël Robuchon	16e	26
Table du Baltimore	16e	-
▣ Table du Lancaster	8e	25
▣ Taillevent	8e	28
▣ Tour d'Argent	5e	25
▣ Trois Marches	Versailles	26
W Restaurant	8e	-

REGIONAL

ALPINE
Chalet de Neuilly	Neuilly	-
Rest. GR5	multi. loc.	15

ALSACE/JURA
Alsace	8e	15
Alsaco	9e	18
▣ Bofinger	4e	20
Chez Jenny	3e	17
Chez Maître Paul	6e	20
Epicure 108	17e	-

AUVERGNE
Ambassade/Auvergne	3e	19
Aub. Aveyronnaise	12e	-
Bath's	17e	-
Bistrot à Vins Mélac	11e	16
Chantairelle	5e	-
Chez Gérard	Neuilly	19
Lozère	6e	18
Mascotte	18e	-
Nemrod	6e	15

AVEYRON
Ambassade/Auvergne	3e	19
Aub. Aveyronnaise	12e	-
Chez Savy	8e	21

BASQUE
Bascou	3e	22
Basilic	7e	14
Casa Alcalde	15e	15
Chez L'Ami Jean	7e	22
Pamphlet	3e	23
Troquet	15e	23

BRITTANY
Crêperie de Josselin	14e	21

BURGUNDY
Ma Bourgogne	4e	17
Tante Louise	8e	22

CORSICA
Alivi	4e	17
Casa Olympe	9e	23
Cosi (Le)	5e	17
Main d'Or	11e	21
Villa Corse	multi. loc.	16

GASCONY
Braisière	17e	24
Comte de Gascogne	Boulogne	25

LYON
Aub. Pyrénées Cévennes	11e	21
▣ Benoît	4e	24
Chez Fred	17e	-
Chez Marcel	6e	21
Chez René	5e	21
Duc de Richelieu	12e	-
▣ Lyonnais	2e	22
Moissonnier	5e	22
Opportun	14e	-
Vieux Bistro	4e	20

NORTHERN FRANCE
Graindorge	17e	22
NEW Pré Salé	1er	-

PROVENCE
Aimant du Sud	13e	-
Bastide Odéon	6e	20
Bistro de l'Olivier	8e	20

Casa Olympe	9ᵉ	23
182 Rive Droite	16ᵉ	12
Chez Janou	3ᵉ	20
Fish La Boissonnerie	6ᵉ	21
Jardin	8ᵉ	22
Olivades	7ᵉ	22
Petit Niçois	7ᵉ	19
Sept Quinze	15ᵉ	18
Sud	17ᵉ	15

SOUTHWEST

Ami Pierre	11ᵉ	19
Assiette	14ᵉ	20
Aub. Etchégorry	13ᵉ	20
Aub. Pyrénées Cévennes	11ᵉ	21
Bistrot Baracane	4ᵉ	23
Café Faubourg	8ᵉ	17
Cerisaie	14ᵉ	24
Chez L'Ami Jean	7ᵉ	22
Chez Papa	multi. loc.	18
Dauphin	1ᵉʳ	23
D'Chez Eux	7ᵉ	22
Diapason	18ᵉ	16
Domaine de Lintillac	multi. loc.	–
Fins Gourmets	7ᵉ	21
☒ Fontaine de Mars	7ᵉ	21
Gamin de Paris	4ᵉ	18
Gitane	15ᵉ	14
☒ Hélène Darroze	6ᵉ	23
Il Etait une Oie	17ᵉ	17
J'Go	9ᵉ	18
Languedoc	5ᵉ	19
Maison Courtine	14ᵉ	21
Mesturet	2ᵉ	–
Oulette	12ᵉ	21
Pamphlet	3ᵉ	23
Pasco	7ᵉ	–
Rouge Vif	7ᵉ	17
☒ Salon d'Hélène	6ᵉ	25
Sarladais	8ᵉ	–
Senso	8ᵉ	17
Thoumieux	7ᵉ	15
Triporteur	15ᵉ	–
Trou Gascon	12ᵉ	24

SEAFOOD

Autour du Mont	15ᵉ	–
Autour du Saumon	multi. loc.	–
Ballon et Coquillages	17ᵉ	–
Bar à Huîtres	multi. loc.	18
Bistrot Bigorneau	16ᵉ	15

Bistrot de Marius	8ᵉ	17
Bistrot du Cap	15ᵉ	–
Bistrot du Dôme	multi. loc.	19
Brass. L'Européen	12ᵉ	–
Brass. Lutétia	6ᵉ	17
Cabane	17ᵉ	–
Cagouille	14ᵉ	21
Cap Vernet	8ᵉ	18
144 Petrossian	7ᵉ	22
☒ Coupole	14ᵉ	18
Dessirier	17ᵉ	21
Divellec	7ᵉ	23
Dôme	14ᵉ	22
Duc	14ᵉ	24
Ecailler du Bistrot	11ᵉ	–
Espadon Bleu	6ᵉ	19
Fables de La Fontaine	7ᵉ	21
Fish La Boissonnerie	6ᵉ	21
Fontaine Gaillon	2ᵉ	19
Frégate	12ᵉ	–
Garnier	8ᵉ	22
Gaya	7ᵉ	22
Goumard	1ᵉʳ	24
Jarrasse	Neuilly	–
Luna	8ᵉ	24
Maison Prunier	16ᵉ	22
☒ Marée	8ᵉ	25
Marée de Versailles	Versailles	21
Marius	16ᵉ	20
Marius et Janette	8ᵉ	21
Méditerranée	6ᵉ	19
Pétrus	17ᵉ	–
Pichet de Paris	8ᵉ	20
Port Alma	16ᵉ	20
Rech	17ᵉ	14
Sarladais	8ᵉ	–
NEW 35° Ouest	7ᵉ	–
Uitr	15ᵉ	–
Vin et Marée	multi. loc.	17
NEW 21	6ᵉ	–
Wepler	18ᵉ	15

SHELLFISH

Ballon des Ternes	17ᵉ	15
Ballon et Coquillages	17ᵉ	–
Bar à Huîtres	multi. loc.	18
Cabane	17ᵉ	–
Charlot - Roi des Coq.	9ᵉ	15
Dôme	14ᵉ	22
Ecaille de la Fontaine	2ᵉ	–
Ecailler du Bistrot	11ᵉ	–

Garnier | 8ᵉ	22
Huîtrerie Régis | 6ᵉ	–
Huîtrier | 17ᵉ	–
Marée de Versailles | **Versailles**	21
Marius | 16ᵉ	20
Marius et Janette | 8ᵉ	21
Pichet de Paris | 8ᵉ	20
Rech | 17ᵉ	14
Stella | 16ᵉ	16
Terminus Nord | 10ᵉ	15
Uitr | 15ᵉ	–

STEAK

Boeuf Couronné | 19ᵉ	17
Boucherie Roulière | 6ᵉ	–
Devèz | 8ᵉ	14
Gavroche | 2ᵉ	21
Gourmets des Ternes | 8ᵉ	19
Hippopotamus | **multi. loc.**	10
Louchebem | 1ᵉʳ	14
☑ Relais/l'Entrecôte | **multi. loc.**	23
Relais de Venise | 17ᵉ	22
NEW Ribouldingue | 5ᵉ	–
Severo | 14ᵉ	22
Titi Parisien | 7ᵉ	16

WINE BARS/BISTROS

Ami Pierre | 11ᵉ	19
Bacchantes | 9ᵉ	–
Baratin | 20ᵉ	–
Baron Rouge | 12ᵉ	19
Bistrot à Vins Mélac | 11ᵉ	16
Bistrot du Sommelier | 8ᵉ	20

Bons Crus | 1ᵉʳ	–
Bouchons/Fr. Cl./Colbert | **multi. loc.**	19
Bourguignon du Marais | 4ᵉ	22
Café Burq | 18ᵉ	–
Café du Passage | 11ᵉ	–
Cave de l'Os à Moëlle | 15ᵉ	20
Caves Pétrissans | 17ᵉ	21
Chai 33 | 12ᵉ	12
Chapeau Melon | 19ᵉ	–
Chez Grisette | 18ᵉ	–
Cloche des Halles | 1ᵉʳ	16
Clown Bar | 11ᵉ	19
Coude Fou | 4ᵉ	16
Couleurs de Vigne | 15ᵉ	–
Dix Vins | 15ᵉ	16
Ecluse | **multi. loc.**	14
Enoteca | 4ᵉ	22
Juvéniles | 1ᵉʳ	17
Lavinia | 1ᵉʳ	17
Legrand Filles et Fils | 2ᵉ	–
Louis Vin | 5ᵉ	–
Mauzac | 5ᵉ	–
Oenothèque | 9ᵉ	–
NEW Petit Monsieur | 11ᵉ	–
Robe et le Palais | 1ᵉʳ	–
Rubis | 1ᵉʳ	17
Sauvignon | 7ᵉ	15
Tav. Henri IV | 1ᵉʳ	17
NEW Truc Café | 18ᵉ	–
Verre Bouteille | 17ᵉ	–
Verre Volé | 10ᵉ	14
Vin dans les voiles | 16ᵉ	–
Willi's Wine Bar | 1ᵉʳ	19

subscribe to zagat.com

Other Cuisines

Includes restaurant names, neighborhoods and Food ratings. ☑ indicates places with the highest ratings, popularity and importance.

AMERICAN

Breakfast in America	multi. loc.	13
Buffalo Grill	multi. loc.	9
Coffee Parisien	multi. loc.	15
Joe Allen	1er	14
Meating	17^e	19
Planet Hollywood	8^e	7

ARGENTINEAN

Anahï	3^e	22
El Palenque	5^e	20
NEW Unico	11^e	-

ARMENIAN

Diamantaires	9^e	-

ASIAN

Asian	8^e	16
☑ Buddha Bar	8^e	16
Epicure 108	17^e	-
Orénoc	17^e	-
Passy Mandarin	multi. loc.	16
Tricotin	13^e	-
Wok Cooking	11^e	-

ASIAN FUSION

Orénoc	17^e	-
Passiflore	16^e	23

BELGIAN

Graindorge	17^e	22
Léon/Bruxelles	multi. loc.	15

CAJUN

Thanksgiving	4^e	15

CAMBODIAN

Coin des Gourmets	5^e	16
Kambodgia	16^e	18
Mousson	1er	-
Sinago	9^e	-

CAVIAR

☑ Caviar Kaspia	8^e	26
144 Petrossian	7^e	22
Maison du Caviar	8^e	21
Maison Prunier	16^e	22

CHINESE

(* dim sum specialist)

Chen Soleil d'Est	15^e	24
Chez Ly	17^e	-
Chez Vong	1er	20
China Club	12^e	16
Davé	1er	19
Délices de Szechuen	7^e	16
Diep	8^e	20
Elysées Hong Kong	16^e	-
Lao Tseu	7^e	18
Mandarin/Neuilly	Neuilly	-
Mirama	5^e	16
New Nioullaville*	11^e	16
Nouveau Village Tao	13^e	14
Tang	16^e	17
Tong Yen	8^e	20
Tsé-Yang	16^e	21
Village d'Ung/Li Lam	8^e	-

CREOLE

NEW Table de Babette	16^e	-
Thanksgiving	4^e	15

DANISH

Copenhague	8^e	20
Flora Danica	8^e	18
Petite Sirène/Copen.	9^e	20

DESSERT

☑ Angelina	1er	20
A Priori Thé	2^e	16
Café Lenôtre	8^e	19
Dalloyau	multi. loc.	23
Deux Abeilles	7^e	18
Flore en l'Ile	4^e	16
Jean-Paul Hévin	1er	24
☑ Ladurée	multi. loc.	22
Loir dans la Théière	4^e	18
Mariage Frères	multi. loc.	21
☑ Soufflé	1er	22
Table d'Hédiard	8^e	22

EASTERN EUROPEAN

Chez Marianne	4^e	18
Patrick Goldenberg	17^e	15
Pitchi Poï	4^e	-

ECLECTIC

Ampère | 17ᵉ	15
Apollo | 14ᵉ	14
Autour du Saumon | multi. loc.	–
Berkeley | 8ᵉ	12
🆕 Black Calavados | 8ᵉ	–
Café Etienne Marcel | 2ᵉ	13
Café Fusion | 13ᵉ	–
Café la Jatte | Neuilly	14
ⓩ Caviar Kaspia | 8ᵉ	26
Chez Prune | 10ᵉ	12
Cook Book | 7ᵉ	–
Costes | 1ᵉʳ	17
Doobie's | 8ᵉ	12
Durand Dupont | Neuilly	9
Eugène | 8ᵉ	–
Fumoir | 1ᵉʳ	15
ⓩ Georges | 4ᵉ	18
Indigo Square | Bagnolet	–
Juvéniles | 1ᵉʳ	17
Kong | 1ᵉʳ	14
Mandala Ray | 8ᵉ	15
Mandalay | Levallois	–
Market | 8ᵉ	20
No Stress Café | 9ᵉ	–
Paradis du Fruit | multi. loc.	13
Pearl | 13ᵉ	–
Pershing | 8ᵉ	15
Pure Café | 11ᵉ	–
Quai Ouest | St-Cloud	17
Relais Plaza | 8ᵉ	22
Rouge St-Honoré | 1ᵉʳ	15
Scoop | 1ᵉʳ	–
Spoon, Food & Wine | 8ᵉ	23
🆕 Tarmac | 12ᵉ	–
ⓩ Ze Kitchen Galerie | 6ᵉ	23
Zo | 8ᵉ	15

ETHIOPIAN

Entoto | 13ᵉ	–

GREEK

Délices d'Aphrodite | 5ᵉ	18
Diamantaires | 9ᵉ	–
Mavrommatis | 5ᵉ	22

HAMBURGERS

Coffee Parisien | multi. loc.	15
Indiana Café | multi. loc.	8
Joe Allen | 1ᵉʳ	14
Planet Hollywood | 8ᵉ	7

INDIAN

Annapurna | 8ᵉ	19
Indra | 8ᵉ	18
Maharajah | 5ᵉ	16
New Jawad | 7ᵉ	16
Ravi | 7ᵉ	24
Yugaraj | 6ᵉ	19

INDONESIAN

Djakarta | 1ᵉʳ	19

IRISH

Carr's | 1ᵉʳ	12

ISRAELI

As du Fallafel | 4ᵉ	24

ITALIAN

(N=Northern; S=Southern)

Amici Miei | 11ᵉ	19
Barlotti | 1ᵉʳ	15
Bartolo | 6ᵉ	18
Beato | 7ᵉ	18
Bel Canto | multi. loc.	15
Bellini | 16ᵉ	18
Bocconi | 8ᵉ	22
Ca d'Oro | N | 1ᵉʳ	–
Caffé Minotti | 7ᵉ	23
Caffé Toscano | 7ᵉ	–
Cailloux | 13ᵉ	16
🆕 Carmine | 7ᵉ	–
Carpaccio | 8ᵉ	22
Casa Bini | N | 6ᵉ	20
Cherche Midi | 6ᵉ	18
Chez Livio | Neuilly	13
Chez Vincent | 19ᵉ	22
🆕 Cibus | 1ᵉʳ	–
Curieux Spaghetti Bar | 4ᵉ	–
Da Mimmo | 10ᵉ	15
Dell Orto | 9ᵉ	–
Emporio Armani | N | 6ᵉ	18
Enoteca | 4ᵉ	22
Enzo | 14ᵉ	–
Fellini | S | multi. loc.	19
Filo Delle Stagioni | 3ᵉ	–
Findi | 8ᵉ	17
Finzi | 8ᵉ	20
Fontanarosa | 15ᵉ	19
Giulio Rebellato | N | 16ᵉ	20
Gli Angeli | 3ᵉ	19
Grand Venise | 15ᵉ	22
I Golosi | 9ᵉ	20

Il Barone	14e	–
Il Cortile	N	1er	21
Il Viccolo	6e	17
Lei	7e	18
NEW Mori Venice Bar	N	2e	24
Ostéria	4e	–
Osteria Ascolani	18e	–
Paolo Petrini	N	17e	21
Paris Seize	16e	14
Perron	7e	22
Pizzeria d'Auteuil	16e	17
Pizzetta	9e	–
Renoma Café	8e	–
Romantica	Clichy	21
Rucola	17e	–
Rughetta	18e	17
Sale e Pepe	S	18e	–
NEW San	3e	–
Sardegna a Tavola	12e	22
Sora Lena	S	17e	–
Sormani	17e	24
Stresa	8e	22
Tav. de Gli Amici	7e	–
Vinci	16e	–
Water Bar Colette	1er	13

JAPANESE

(* sushi specialist)

Aida	7e	–
Azabu	6e	20
Benkay*	15e	23
Bound	8e	–
Foujita*	1er	14
Higuma	1er	18
Inagiku	5e	–
Isami*	4e	27
Issé*	1er	18
Kai	1er	–
Kaïten*	8e	19
Kifune*	17e	–
Kinugawa*	multi. loc.	25
Kodo	4e	–
Lô Sushi*	8e	14
Matsuri	multi. loc.	12
Orient-Extrême*	6e	20
NEW Ozu	16e	–
Ploum	10e	–
Taïra	17e	23
Tsukizi	6e	–
Yen	6e	19

JEWISH

Patrick Goldenberg	17e	15
Pitchi Poï	4e	–

KOREAN

Samiin	7e	–

KOSHER

Patrick Goldenberg	17e	15
Télégraphe	7e	20

LEBANESE

Al Dar	multi. loc.	22
Al Diwan	8e	19
Escale du Liban	4e	–
Fakhr el Dine	multi. loc.	17
Fleurs de Thym	4e	–
Liza	2e	–
Mont Liban	17e	–
Noura	multi. loc.	18

MEDITERRANEAN

Don Juans	3e	–
NEW Gazzetta	12e	–
Pasco	7e	–
Sens	8e	–
7ème Sud	multi. loc.	17
Sept Quinze	15e	18
NEW Soleil	7e	–
Sora Lena	17e	–
Sud	17e	15
Tête Ailleurs	4e	–

MEXICAN

Anahuacalli	5e	21

MIDDLE EASTERN

Chez Marianne	4e	18

MOROCCAN

Al Mounia	16e	16
Andy Wahloo	3e	12
Atlas	5e	18
Chez Omar	3e	21
Comptoir	1er	16
El Mansour	8e	20
Etoile Marocaine	8e	18
Mansouria	11e	19
Martel	10e	16
Oum el Banine	16e	–
Pied de Chameau/Al Nour	3e	–
404	3e	21
Riad	Neuilly	–

OTHER CUISINES

7ème Sud	multi. loc.	17
Timgad	17e	22

NORTH AFRICAN

Boule Rouge	9e	-
Village Kabyle	18e	-
Wally Le Saharien	9e	18

PAKISTANI

New Jawad	7e	16

PAN-LATIN

Barrio Latino	12e	11
Barroco	6e	-

PIZZA

Amici Miei	11e	19
Bartolo	6e	18
Da Mimmo	10e	15
Enzo	14e	-
Pizzeria d'Auteuil	16e	17
Pizzetta	9e	-
Rughetta	18e	17
Sale e Pepe	18e	-

PORTUGUESE

Saudade	1er	-

RUSSIAN

☑ Caviar Kaspia	8e	26
Daru	8e	-
Maison du Caviar	8e	21

SANDWICHES

BE Boulangépicier	multi. loc.	22
Café Very/Dame	multi. loc.	13
Cosi	6e	19
Ferme	1er	-
Lina's	multi. loc.	15
Sauvignon	7e	15

SEAFOOD

Autour du Saumon	multi. loc.	-
Copenhague	8e	20
Sens	8e	-

SEYCHELLES

Coco de Mer	5e	22

SOUTH AFRICAN

Chamarré	7e	24
Moulin de la Galette	18e	-

SOUTHEAST ASIAN

Baan-Boran	1er	21
Baie d'Ha Long	16e	-
Banyan	15e	25
Blue Elephant	11e	19
Chez Ly	17e	-
Chieng Mai	5e	17
Davé	1er	19
Diep	8e	20
Erawan	15e	20
Khun Akorn	11e	19
Kim Anh	15e	21
Lac-Hong	16e	19
Lao Siam	19e	23
Nouveau Village Tao	13e	14
Palanquin	6e	18
Paradis Thai	13e	18
Reuan Thai	11e	-
Sawadee	15e	18
Suave	13e	-
Tan Dinh	7e	22
Thiou/Petit Thiou	multi. loc.	18
Village d'Ung/Li Lam	8e	-

SPANISH

Bellota-Bellota	7e	19
Casa Alcalde	15e	15
Casa Tina	16e	12
Chez Ramona	20e	-
Fogón	6e	20
Rosimar	16e	-

STEAKHOUSES

Buffalo Grill	multi. loc.	9
Meating	17e	19
NEW Unico	11e	-

TEX-MEX

Indiana Café	multi. loc.	8
Studio	4e	-

THAI

Baan-Boran	1er	21
Banyan	15e	25
Blue Elephant	11e	19
Chez Ly	17e	-
Chieng Mai	5e	17
Erawan	15e	20
Khun Akorn	11e	19
Lao Siam	19e	23
Nouveau Village Tao	13e	14
Paradis Thai	13e	18

subscribe to zagat.com

Reuan Thai | 11e	‑
Sawadee | 15e	18
Thiou/Petit Thiou | **multi. loc.**	18
Village d'Ung/Li Lam | 8e	‑

TURKISH

Sizin | 9e	‑

VIETNAMESE

Baie d'Ha Long | 16e	‑
Coin des Gourmets | 5e	16

Davé | 1er	19
Indochine | 1er	16
Kambodgia | 16e	18
Kim Anh | 15e	21
Lac-Hong | 16e	19
Palanquin | 6e	18
Suave | 13e	‑
Tan Dinh | 7e	22

OTHER CUISINES

Locations

Includes restaurant names, cuisines and Food ratings. ☑ indicates places with the highest ratings, popularity and importance.

Paris

1ST ARRONDISSEMENT

Absinthe	*Bistro*	19
☑ Angelina	*Tea*	20
Ardoise	*Bistro*	23
Atelier Berger	*New Fr.*	21
Autobus Imperial	*Classic Fr.*	–
Baan-Boran	*Thai*	21
Barlotti	*Italian*	15
☑ Bar Vendôme	*Classic Fr.*	21
Bons Crus	*Wine Bar/Bistro*	–
Brass. du Louvre	*Brass.*	18
Ca d'Oro	*Italian*	–
Café Marly	*Classic/New Fr.*	15
Café Ruc	*Bistro*	14
Café Very/Dame	*Sandwiches*	13
☑ Carré des Feuillants	*Haute Cuisine*	25
Carr's	*Irish*	12
Cartes Postales	*New Fr.*	19
Caveau du Palais	*Classic Fr.*	21
Chez Denise	*Bistro*	23
Chez la Vieille	*Bistro*	22
Chez Pauline	*Bistro*	21
Chez Vong	*Chinese*	20
Chien qui Fume	*Brass.*	17
NEW Cibus	*Italian*	–
Cloche des Halles	*Wine Bar/Bistro*	16
Comptoir	*Moroccan*	16
Cordonnerie	*Classic Fr.*	–
Costes	*Eclectic*	17
Dauphin	*Southwest*	23
Davé	*Chinese/Viet.*	19
Djakarta	*Indonesian*	19
Ecluse	*Wine Bar/Bistro*	14
Epi d'Or	*Bistro*	21
Escargot Montorgueil	*Bistro*	18
☑ Espadon	*Classic Fr.*	25
Fellini	*Italian*	19
Ferme	*Sandwiches*	–
NEW First	*New Fr.*	–
Foujita	*Jap.*	14
Fumoir	*Eclectic*	15
☑ Gérard Besson	*Classic Fr.*	25
Goumard	*Seafood*	24

Grand Louvre	*Classic Fr.*	18
☑ Grand Véfour	*Haute Cuisine*	27
Higuma	*Jap.*	18
Hippopotamus	*Steak*	10
Il Cortile	*Italian*	21
Indochine	*Viet.*	16
Issé	*Jap.*	18
Jean-Paul Hévin	*Dessert/Tea.*	24
Joe Allen	*American*	14
Juvéniles	*Wine Bar/Bistro*	17
Kai	*Jap.*	–
☑ Kinugawa	*Jap.*	25
Kong	*Eclectic*	14
Lavinia	*Classic Fr.*	17
Léon/Bruxelles	*Belgian*	15
Lescure	*Bistro*	16
Louchebem	*Steak*	14
Macéo	*Classic/New Fr.*	21
Matsuri	*Jap.*	12
☑ Meurice	*Haute Cuisine*	26
Mousson	*Cambodian*	–
Muscade	*Bistro/Tea.*	–
Paradis du Fruit	*Eclectic*	13
Paul, Restaurant	*Bistro*	19
Pharamond	*Classic Fr.*	18
Pied de Cochon	*Brass.*	18
Pierre au Palais Royal	*Classic Fr.*	16
Pinxo	*New Fr.*	20
Point Bar	*New Fr.*	21
Poule au Pot	*Bistro*	21
NEW Pré Salé	*N. France*	–
Ragueneau	*Classic Fr./Tea.*	–
Rest. du Palais Royal	*Classic Fr.*	19
Robe et le Palais	*Wine Bar/Bistro*	–
Rouge St-Honoré	*Eclectic*	15
Rubis	*Wine Bar/Bistro*	17
Saudade	*Portugese*	–
Scoop	*Eclectic*	–
☑ Soufflé	*Classic Fr.*	22
Tav. de Maître Kanter	*Brass.*	10
Tav. Henri IV	*Wine Bar/Bistro*	17
Vin et Marée	*Seafood*	17
Water Bar Colette	*Italian/New Fr.*	13
Willi's Wine Bar	*Wine Bar/Bistro*	19

2ND ARRONDISSEMENT

Angl'Opera	*New Fr.*	21
A Priori Thé	*Tea*	16
Bistrot Vivienne	*Bistro*	15
Café Etienne Marcel	*Eclectic*	13
Café Moderne	*Bistro*	22
Céladon	*Classic Fr.*	24
Chez Clément	*Classic Fr.*	12
Ⓩ Chez Georges	*Bistro*	21
Crus de Bourgogne	*Bistro*	–
Domaine de Lintillac	*Southwest*	–
Drouant	*Classic Fr.*	–
Ecaille de la Fontaine (L')	*Shellfish*	–
Fontaine Gaillon	*Classic Fr.*	19
Gallopin	*Brass.*	15
Gavroche	*Bistro*	21
Grand Colbert	*Brass.*	18
Hippopotamus	*Steak*	10
Legrand Filles et Fils	*Wine Bar/Bistro*	–
Lina's	*Sandwiches*	15
Liza	*Lebanese*	–
Ⓩ Lyonnais	*Lyon*	22
Mesturet	*Southwest*	–
NEW Mori Venice Bar	*Italian*	–
Noces de Jeannette	*Bistro*	–
Noura	*Lebanese*	18
Paradis du Fruit	*Eclectic*	13
Passy Mandarin	*Asian*	16
Press Café	*Bistro*	–
Pur'Grill	*New Fr.*	25
Vaudeville	*Brass.*	17
NEW Versance	*Classic/New Fr.*	–

3RD ARRONDISSEMENT

Ambassade/Auvergne	*Auvergne*	19
Ⓩ Ami Louis	*Bistro*	26
Anahï	*Argent.*	22
Andy Wahloo	*Moroccan*	12
Aub. Nicolas Flamel	*Bistro*	20
Bar à Huîtres	*Seafood*	18
Bascou	*Basque*	22
Buffalo Grill	*Steakhouse*	9
Camille	*Bistro*	20
Chez Janou	*Provence*	20
Chez Jenny	*Alsace*	17
Chez Nénesse	*Classic Fr.*	19
Chez Omar	*Moroccan*	21
Don Juans	*New Fr.*	–

Filo Delle Stagioni	*Italian*	–
Gli Angeli	*Italian*	19
Guirlande de Julie	*Classic Fr.*	–
Hangar	*Classic Fr.*	20
Indiana Café	*Tex-Mex*	8
Murano	*New Fr.*	17
Pamphlet	*Basque/Southwest*	23
Petit Marché	*New Fr.*	22
NEW Petit Pamphlet	*Bistro*	–
Pied de Chameau	*Moroccan*	–
404	*Moroccan*	21
Réconfort	*New Fr.*	17
Robert et Louise	*Bistro*	–
NEW San	*Italian*	–

4TH ARRONDISSEMENT

Alivi	*Corsica*	17
Ⓩ Ambroisie	*Haute Cuisine*	27
As du Fallafel	*Mideast.*	24
Aub. de la Reine Blanche	*Classic/New Fr.*	20
Autour du Saumon	*Seafood*	–
Bel Canto	*Italian*	15
Ⓩ Benoît	*Lyon*	24
Bistrot Baracane	*Southwest*	23
Bistrot du Dôme	*Seafood*	19
Ⓩ Bofinger	*Brass.*	20
Bourguignon du Marais	*Wine Bar/Bistro*	22
Brass. de l'Ile St. Louis	*Brass.*	16
Breakfast in America	*Amer.*	13
Café Beaubourg	*Classic Fr.*	15
Café de la Poste	*Classic Fr.*	16
Café Very/Dame	*Sandwiches*	13
Chaumière en l'Ile	*Classic Fr.*	22
Chez Clément	*Classic Fr.*	12
Chez Marianne	*Mideast.*	18
Coude Fou	*Wine Bar/Bistro*	16
Coupe Gorge	*Bistro*	–
Curieux Spaghetti Bar	*Italian*	–
Dalloyau	*Dessert/Tea.*	23
Dôme du Marais	*New Fr.*	18
Dos de la Baleine	*Bistro*	16
Enoteca	*Italian*	22
Escale du Liban	*Lebanese*	–
Fleurs de Thym	*Lebanese*	–
Flore en l'Ile	*Classic Fr.*	16
Fous d'en Face	*Bistro*	18
Gamin de Paris	*Southwest*	18
Ⓩ Georges	*Eclectic*	18
Hippopotamus	*Steak*	10

LOCATIONS

Ilot Vache	*Classic Fr.*	21
🅩 Isami	*Jap.*	27
Kodo	*Jap./New Fr.*	-
Léon/Bruxelles	*Belgian*	15
Loir dans la Théière	*Dessert/Tea.*	18
Ma Bourgogne	*Burgundy*	17
Marc Annibal de Coconnas	*Classic Fr.*	17
Mariage Frères	*Dessert/Tea.*	21
Mon Vieil Ami	*Bistro*	24
Nos Ancêtres/Gaulois	*Classic Fr.*	10
Orangerie	*Classic Fr.*	-
Ostéria	*Italian*	24
Petit Bofinger	*Brass.*	16
Pitchi Poï	*East. European*	-
Studio	*Tex-Mex*	-
Tav. du Sgt. Recruteur	*Classic Fr.*	14
Tête Ailleurs	*Med.*	-
Thanksgiving	*Cajun/Creole*	15
Trumilou	*Bistro*	19
Vieux Bistro	*Lyon*	20
Vin des Pyrenees	*Classic Fr.*	16

5TH ARRONDISSEMENT

Al Dar	*Lebanese*	22
Anahuacalli	*Mex.*	21
AOC	*Bistro*	19
Atelier Maître Albert	*Bistro*	21
Atlas	*Moroccan*	18
Bar à Huîtres	*Seafood*	18
Bouchons/Fr. Cl./Colbert	*Wine Bar/Bistro*	19
Brass. Balzar	*Brass.*	18
Breakfast in America	*Amer.*	13
Buffalo Grill	*Steakhouse*	9
Buisson Ardent	*Classic Fr.*	20
Café Le Petit Pont	*Classic Fr.*	24
Chantairelle	*Auvergne*	-
Chez Léna et Mimile	*Bistro*	-
Chez René	*Lyon*	21
Chieng Mai	*Thai*	17
Coco de Mer	*Seychelles*	22
Coin des Gourmets	*Cambodian/Viet.*	16
Cosi (Le)	*Corsica*	17
Coupe-Chou	*Classic Fr.*	20
Délices d'Aphrodite	*Greek*	18
El Palenque	*Argent.*	20
Fontaines	*Bistro*	18

Hippopotamus	*Steak*	10
Inagiku	*Jap.*	-
Languedoc	*Southwest*	19
Louis Vin	*Wine Bar/Bistro*	-
Maharajah	*Indian*	16
Marty	*Brass.*	17
Mauzac	*Wine Bar/Bistro*	-
Mavrommatis	*Greek*	22
Mirama	*Chinese*	16
Moissonnier	*Lyon*	22
Moulin à Vent	*Bistro*	22
Papilles	*Classic Fr.*	22
Paradis du Fruit	*Eclectic*	13
Perraudin	*Bistro*	16
Petit Châtelet	*Classic Fr.*	19
Petit Pontoise	*Bistro*	23
Petit Prince de Paris	*Bistro*	21
Pré Verre	*New Fr.*	23
🅩 Réminet	*New Fr.*	25
NEW Ribouldingue	*Classic Fr.*	-
Rôtiss. du Beaujolais	*Bistro*	22
🅩 Tour d'Argent	*Haute Cuisine*	25
Truffière	*Classic/New Fr.*	24

6TH ARRONDISSEMENT

Alcazar	*New Fr.*	17
🅩 Allard	*Bistro*	22
Arbuci	*Brass.*	15
Azabu	*Jap.*	20
Barroco	*Pan-Latin*	-
Bartolo	*Italian*	18
Bastide Odéon	*Provence*	20
Bistrot d'Henri	*Bistro*	17
Bon Saint Pourçain	*Classic Fr.*	17
Boucherie Roulière	*Bistro*	-
Bouillon Racine	*Brass.*	14
🅩 Bouquinistes	*New Fr.*	21
🅩 Brass. Lipp	*Brass.*	17
Brass. Lutétia	*Brass.*	17
Café de Flore	*Classic Fr.*	15
🅩 Café Les Deux Magots	*Classic Fr.*	15
Caméléon	*Bistro*	-
Casa Bini	*Italian*	20
Charpentiers	*Bistro*	18
Cherche Midi	*Italian*	18
Chez Clément	*Classic Fr.*	12
Chez Maître Paul	*Alsace*	20
Chez Marcel	*Lyon*	21
Christine	*Bistro*	23
Closerie des Lilas	*Classic Fr.*	16

Coffee Parisien | *Amer.*	15
Comptoir du Relais | *Bistro*	22
Cosi | *Sandwiches*	19
Dalloyau | *Dessert/Tea.*	23
Da Rosa | *Classic Fr.*	19
Ecluse | *Wine Bar/Bistro*	14
Editeurs | *Brass.*	15
Emporio Armani | *Italian*	18
☒ Epi Dupin | *Bistro*	23
Espadon Bleu | *Seafood*	19
NEW Ferrandaise | *Classic Fr.*	–
Fish La Boissonnerie | *Provence*	21
Fogón | *Spanish*	20
Gourmand | *New Fr.*	23
Grille St-Germain | *Bistro*	17
☒ Hélène Darroze | *New French/Southwest*	23
Hippopotamus | *Steak*	10
Huîtrerie Régis | *Shellfish*	–
Il Viccolo | *Italian*	17
Indiana Café | *Tex-Mex*	8
☒ Jacques Cagna | *Haute Cuisine*	26
Joséphine/Dumonet | *Bistro*	23
☒ Ladurée | *Classic Fr./Tea.*	22
☒ Lapérouse | *Haute Cuisine*	21
Léon/Bruxelles | *Belgian*	15
Lozère | *Auvergne*	18
Maison du Jardin | *Bistro*	22
Mariage Frères | *Dessert/Tea.*	21
Marlotte | *Classic Fr.*	20
Méditerranée | *Classic Fr.*	19
Nemrod | *Auvergne*	15
Noura | *Lebanese*	18
Orient-Extrême | *Jap.*	20
Palanquin | *Viet.*	18
Paradis du Fruit | *Eclectic*	13
Parc aux Cerfs | *Classic Fr.*	17
Paris | *Haute Cuisine*	19
Pères et Filles | *Bistro*	12
Petite Cour | *New Fr.*	18
Petit Lutétia | *Brass.*	16
Petit St. Benoît | *Classic Fr.*	15
Petit Zinc | *Brass.*	20
Polidor | *Bistro*	15
Procope | *Classic Fr.*	16
☒ Relais/l'Entrecôte | *Steak*	23
☒ Relais Louis XIII | *Haute Cuisine*	25
Rest. de l'Hôtel | *Classic Fr.*	–
Rôtiss. d'en Face | *Bistro*	22

Rotonde | *Brass.*	14
☒ Salon d'Hélène | *Southwest*	25
Saveurs de Claude | *Classic/ New Fr.*	–
NEW Sensing | *Haute Cuisine*	–
Timbre | *Bistro*	22
Tsukizi | *Jap.*	–
Vagenende | *Brass.*	15
NEW 21 | *Seafood*	–
Wadja | *Bistro*	21
Yen | *Jap.*	19
Yugaraj | *Indian*	19
☒ Ze Kitchen Galerie | *Eclectic*	23

7TH ARRONDISSEMENT

Affriolé | *Bistro*	21
Aida | *Jap.*	–
Altitude 95 | *Classic Fr.*	16
☒ Arpège | *Haute Cuisine*	26
☒ Atelier de Joël Robuchon | *Haute Cuisine*	27
Aub. Bressane | *Classic Fr.*	17
Aub. du Champ de Mars | *Classic Fr.*	23
Auguste | *Classic Fr.*	19
Babylone | *Bistro*	–
Bamboche | *New Fr.*	18
Basilic | *Basque*	14
Beato | *Italian*	18
Bellota-Bellota | *Spanish*	19
Bistro de Breteuil | *Bistro*	18
Bistrot de l'Université | *Bistro*	15
Bistrot de Paris | *Bistro*	19
Bon Accueil | *Bistro*	24
Café Constant | *Bistro*	22
Café de l'Esplanade | *Classic/ New Fr.*	17
Café de Mars | *Bistro*	16
Caffé Minotti | *Italian*	23
Caffé Toscano | *Italian*	–
NEW Carmine | *Italian*	–
144 Petrossian | *Seafood*	22
Chamarré | *New Fr.*	24
Chez Françoise | *Classic Fr.*	15
Chez L'Ami Jean | *Basque/Bistro*	22
Chez Les Anges | *Brass.*	–
Cigale Recamier | *Classic Fr.*	22
Cinq Mars | *Bistro*	–
Clos des Gourmets | *New Fr.*	24
Cook Book | *Eclectic*	–
Cuisine | *New Fr.*	21
D'Chez Eux | *Southwest*	22

LOCATIONS

Delicabar | *New Fr.* — 15

Délices de Szechuen | *Chinese* — 16

Deux Abeilles | *Dessert/Tea.* — 18

Divellec | *Seafood* — 23

Domaine de Lintillac | *Southwest* — -

Fables de La Fontaine | *Seafood* — 21

Ferme St-Simon | *Classic Fr.* — 22

Fins Gourmets | *Southwest* — 21

Florimond | *Classic Fr.* — 24

Z Fontaine de Mars | *Southwest* — 21

Gaya | *Seafood* — 22

Gorille Blanc | *Bistro* — -

Z Jules Verne | *Classic Fr.* — 23

Lao Tseu | *Chinese* — 18

Lei | *Italian* — 18

Lina's | *Sandwiches* — 15

Maison de l'Amér. Latine | *Classic Fr.* — 17

Maupertu | *Classic Fr.* — 20

Montalembert | *New Fr.* — 17

New Jawad | *Indian/Pakistani* — 16

Oeillade | *Bistro* — 15

Olivades | *Provence* — 22

NEW Ombres | *New Fr.* — -

Ormes | *Haute Cuisine* — 24

Oudino | *Bistro* — -

Pasco | *Med./Southwest* — -

Perron | *Italian* — 22

Petite Chaise | *Classic Fr.* — 19

Petit Niçois | *Provence* — 19

P'tit Troquet | *Bistro* — 23

Quai | *New Fr.* — -

Ravi | *Indian* — 24

Rest. du Musée d'Orsay | *Classic Fr.* — 16

Rouge Vif | *Southwest* — 17

Samiin | *Korean* — -

Sauvignon | *Sandwiches/Wine Bar* — 15

7ème Sud | *Med./Moroccan* — 17

NEW Soleil | *Bistro/Med.* — -

Square | *Classic Fr.* — 16

Tan Dinh | *Viet.* — 22

Tante Marguerite | *Bistro* — 21

Tav. de Gli Amici | *Italian* — -

Télégraphe | *Classic Fr.* — 20

Thiou/Petit Thiou | *Thai* — 18

Thoumieux | *Bistro/Southwest* — 15

Titi Parisien | *Bistro* — 16

NEW 35° Ouest | *Seafood* — -

Vin et Marée | *Seafood* — 17

20 de Bellechasse | *Bistro* — 17

Vin sur Vin | *New Fr.* — 21

Violon d'Ingres | *Bistro* — 24

Voltaire | *Bistro* — 22

8TH ARRONDISSEMENT

Z Alain Ducasse | *Haute Cuisine* — 28

Al Diwan | *Lebanese* — 19

Alsace | *Alsace* — 15

Z Ambassadeurs | *New Fr.* — 27

Z Angle du Faubourg | *New Fr.* — 23

Annapurna | *Indian* — 19

Z Apicius | *Haute Cuisine* — 26

Appart' | *Classic Fr.* — 15

NEW Arome | *Classic/New Fr.* — -

Asian | *Asian* — 16

Astor | *Haute Cuisine* — 20

Avenue | *New Fr.* — 18

Bar des Théâtres | *Bistro* — 13

BE Boulangépicier | *Sandwiches* — 22

Berkeley | *Eclectic* — 12

Bistro de l'Olivier | *Provence* — 20

Bistrot de Marius | *Seafood* — 17

Bistrot du Sommelier | *Wine Bar/Bistro* — 20

NEW Black Calavados | *Eclectic* — -

Bocconi | *Italian* — 22

Boeuf sur le Toit | *Brass.* — 16

Bouchons/Fr. Cl./Colbert | *Wine Bar/Bistro* — 19

Bound | *Jap./New Fr.* — -

Brass. La Lorraine | *Brass.* — 16

Brass. Mollard | *Brass.* — 16

Z Bristol | *Haute Cuisine* — 27

Z Buddha Bar | *Asian* — 16

Café Faubourg | *Classic Fr.* — 17

Café Lenôtre | *New Fr.* — 19

Café M | *New Fr.* — 16

Café Terminus | *Classic Fr.* — -

Cap Vernet | *New Fr.* — 18

Carpaccio | *Italian* — 22

Z Caviar Kaspia | *Russian* — 26

Chez André | *Bistro* — 20

Chez Catherine | *New Fr.* — 23

NEW Chez Cécile | *Classic Fr.* — -

Chez Clément | *Classic Fr.* — 12

Chez Francis | *Brass.* — 14

Chez Papa | *Southwest* — 18

Chez Savy | *Aveyron* — 21

Chiberta | *New Fr.* — 23

Z Cinq | *Haute Cuisine* — 28

Citrus Etoile | *Classic/New Fr.* –

Clovis | *New Fr.* 19

Copenhague | *Danish* 20

☒ **NEW** Cou de la Girafe | *New Fr.* –

Dalloyau | *Dessert/Tea.* 23

Daru | *Russian* –

Devèz | *Steak* 14

Diep | *Asian* 20

☒ 1728 | *New Fr.* 16

Dominique Bouchet | *Haute Cuisine* 24

Doobie's | *Eclectic/New Fr.* 12

Ecluse | *Wine Bar/Bistro* 14

El Mansour | *Moroccan* 20

☒ Elysées | *Haute Cuisine* 26

Etoile Marocaine | *Moroccan* 18

Eugène | *Eclectic* –

Fakhr el Dine | *Lebanese* 17

Fermette Marbeuf | *Classic Fr.* 18

Findi | *Italian* 17

Finzi | *Italian* 20

Flora Danica | *Danish* 18

Fouquet's | *Classic Fr.* 17

Garnier | *Brass.* 22

Gourmets des Ternes | *Bistro* 19

Hippopotamus | *Steak* 10

Indiana Café | *Tex-Mex* 8

Indra | *Indian* 18

Jardin | *New Fr./Provence* 22

Jardin des Cygnes | *Classic Fr.* 20

Kaïten | *Jap.* 19

☒ Kinugawa | *Jap.* 25

☒ Ladurée | *Classic Fr./Tea.* 22

☒ Lasserre | *Haute Cuisine* 27

Laurent | *Haute Cuisine* 24

Léon/Bruxelles | *Belgian* 15

Les Saveurs de Flora | *New Fr.* 22

Libre Sens | *New Fr.* 16

Lina's | *Sandwiches* 15

Lô Sushi | *Jap.* 14

Luna | *Seafood* 24

Maison Blanche | *Haute Cuisine* 19

Maison du Caviar | *Russian* 21

Mandala Ray | *Eclectic* 15

☒ Marée | *Seafood* 25

Mariage Frères | *Dessert/Tea.* 21

Marius et Janette | *Seafood* 21

Market | *Eclectic* 20

Maxan | *Haute Cuisine* –

Maxim's | *Classic Fr.* 20

Musichall | *New Fr.* 15

☒ Obélisque | *Classic Fr.* 23

Paradis du Fruit | *Eclectic* 13

☒ Pavillon Ledoyen | *Haute Cuisine* 26

Pershing | *Eclectic/New Fr.* 15

Pichet de Paris | *Seafood* 20

☒ Pierre Gagnaire | *Haute Cuisine* 28

Planet Hollywood | *American* 7

Pomze | *New Fr.* 19

Publicis Drugstore | *Brass.* 12

☒ Relais/l'Entrecôte | *Steak* 23

Relais Plaza | *Brass./Eclectic* 22

Renoma Café | *Italian* –

Resto | *Classic Fr.* –

Rue Balzac | *New Fr.* 18

Sarladais | *Southwest* –

Senderens | *Brass./New Fr.* –

Sens | *Med.* –

Senso | *New Fr./Southwest* 17

Spicy | *New Fr.* 15

Spoon, Food & Wine | *Eclectic/New Fr.* 23

☒ Stella Maris | *Classic Fr.* 25

Stresa | *Italian* 22

Suite | *Classic Fr.* 12

Table d'Hédiard | *New Fr.* 22

☒ Table du Lancaster | *Haute Cuisine* 25

☒ Taillevent | *Haute Cuisine* 28

Tante Louise | *Burgundy* 22

Terres de Truffes | *Classic Fr.* –

Thiou/Petit Thiou | *Thai* 18

Toi | *New Fr.* –

Tong Yen | *Chinese* 20

Village d'Ung/Li Lam | *Chinese/Thai* –

Virgin Café | *Classic Fr.* 9

W Restaurant | *Haute Cuisine* –

Zo | *Eclectic* 15

9TH ARRONDISSEMENT

Alsaco | *Alsace* 18

Aub. du Clou | *Classic Fr.* 13

Bacchantes | *Wine Bar/Bistro* –

BE Boulangépicier | *Sandwiches* 22

Bistro/Deux Théâtres | *Bistro* 15

Bistrot Papillon | *Bistro* 20

Boule Rouge | *African* –

NEW Brass. Printemps | *Classic Fr.* –

Buffalo Grill | *Steakhouse* 9

Café de la Paix | *Classic Fr.*	19
Café Guitry | *Classic Fr.*	–
Carte Blanche | *Bistro*	–
Casa Olympe | *Corsica/ Provence*	23
Charlot - Roi des Coq. | *Brass.*	15
Chartier | *Classic Fr.*	13
Comédiens | *Classic Fr.*	–
Dell Orto | *Italian*	–
Diamantaires | *Armenian/Greek*	–
Domaine de Lintillac | *Southwest*	–
Georgette | *Bistro*	20
Grand Café | *Brass.*	15
Grange Batelière | *Classic Fr.*	–
NEW Hôtel Amour | *New Fr.*	–
I Golosi | *Italian*	20
Indiana Café | *Tex-Mex*	8
NEW Jardinier | *Classic Fr.*	–
Jean | *New Fr.*	19
J'Go | *Southwest*	18
Z Ladurée | *Classic Fr./Tea.*	22
Léon/Bruxelles | *Belgian*	15
Lina's | *Sandwiches*	15
Muses | *Haute Cuisine*	–
No Stress Café | *Eclectic*	–
Oenothèque | *Wine Bar/Bistro*	–
Petite Sirène/Copen. | *Danish*	20
Petit Riche | *Bistro*	16
Pétrelle | *New Fr.*	–
Pizzetta | *Italian*	–
Radis Roses | *New Fr.*	–
Roi du Pot-au-Feu | *Bistro*	15
16 Haussmann | *New Fr.*	21
Sinago | *Cambodian*	–
Sizin | *Turkish*	–
NEW Spring | *Bistro*	–
Table d'Anvers | *Classic Fr.*	21
Vivres | *Classic Fr.*	–
Wally Le Saharien | *North African*	18

10TH ARRONDISSEMENT

Brass. Flo | *Brass.*	17
Brass. Julien | *Brass.*	17
Buffalo Grill | *Steakhouse*	9
NEW Cantine de Quentin | *Wine Bar/Bistro*	–
Chez Michel | *New Fr.*	23
Chez Papa | *Southwest*	18
Chez Prune | *Eclectic*	12
Da Mimmo | *Italian*	15
Deux Canards | *Classic Fr.*	18
Grille | *Bistro*	–
Hippopotamus | *Steak*	10
Martel | *Classic Fr./Moroccan*	16
Ploum | *Jap./New Fr.*	–
Strapontins | *Classic Fr.*	–
Terminus Nord | *Brass.*	15
Verre Volé | *Wine Bar/Bistro*	14

11TH ARRONDISSEMENT

Aiguière | *Classic Fr.*	–
Amici Miei | *Italian*	19
Ami Pierre | *Southwest*	19
Amognes | *Classic Fr.*	23
Astier | *Bistro*	22
Aub. Pyrénées Cévennes | *Southwest*	21
Bistrot à Vins Mélac | *Wine Bar/Bistro*	16
Bistrot du Peintre | *Bistro*	16
Bistrot Paul Bert | *Bistro*	20
Blue Elephant | *Thai*	19
Café Charbon | *Classic Fr.*	11
Café de l'Industrie | *Bistro*	13
Café du Passage | *Wine Bar/Bistro*	–
Chardenoux | *Bistro*	15
NEW Chateaubriand | *New Fr.*	–
Chez Paul | *Bistro*	20
Chez Ramulaud | *Bistro*	22
Clown Bar | *Wine Bar/Bistro*	19
Ecailler du Bistrot (L') | *Seafood*	–
Ecluse | *Wine Bar/Bistro*	14
Indiana Café | *Tex-Mex*	8
Jumeaux | *New Fr.*	–
Khun Akorn | *Thai*	19
Léon/Bruxelles | *Belgian*	15
Main d'Or | *Corsica*	21
Mansouria | *Moroccan*	19
New Nioullaville | *Chinese*	16
Paradis du Fruit | *Eclectic*	13
Passage/Carm. | *Wine Bar/Bistro*	–
NEW Petit Monsieur | *New Fr.*	–
Polichinelle Cafe | *Bistro*	–
Pure Café | *Eclectic*	–
Refectoire | *Bistro*	–
Repaire de Cartouche | *Bistro*	19
Reuan Thai | *Thai*	–
Sot l'y Laisse | *Bistro*	–
Temps au Temps | *Bistro*	26
NEW Unico | *Argent.*	–

Vieux Chêne	*Bistro*	–
Villaret	*Bistro*	23
Vin et Marée	*Seafood*	17
Wok Cooking	*Asian*	–

12TH ARRONDISSEMENT

Aub. Aveyronnaise	*Auvergne*	–
Baron Rouge	*Wine Bar/Bistro*	19
Barrio Latino	*Pan-Latin*	11
Biche au Bois	*Bistro*	21
Brass. L'Européen	*Brass.*	–
Chai 33	*Wine Bar/Bistro*	12
China Club	*Chinese*	16
Duc de Richelieu	*Lyon*	–
Ebauchoir	*Bistro*	–
Frégate	*Seafood*	–
NEW Gazzetta	*Med./New Fr.*	–
Lina's	*Sandwiches*	15
Oulette	*Southwest*	21
Sardegna a Tavola	*Italian*	22
Sologne	*Classic Fr.*	–
Square Trousseau	*Bistro*	18
NEW Tarmac	*Brass./Eclectic*	–
Z Train Bleu	*Classic Fr.*	19
Trou Gascon	*Southwest*	24
Viaduc Café	*Classic/New Fr.*	12
Vinea Café	*Classic Fr.*	–
Zygomates	*Bistro*	–

13TH ARRONDISSEMENT

Aimant du Sud	*Classic Fr.*	–
Aub. Etchégorry	*Southwest*	20
Z Avant Goût	*New Fr.*	25
BIOArt	*New Fr.*	–
Buffalo Grill	*Steakhouse*	9
Café Fusion	*Eclectic*	–
Cailloux	*Italian*	16
Chez Paul	*Bistro*	17
Entoto	*Ethiopian*	–
Léon/Bruxelles	*Belgian*	15
Nouveau Village Tao	*Chinese/Thai*	14
Ourcine	*Classic/New Fr.*	21
Paradis Thai	*Thai*	18
Pearl	*Classic Fr./Eclectic*	–
Petit Marguery	*Bistro*	22
Petit Pascal	*Bistro*	–
Suave	*Viet.*	–
Temps des Cerises	*Bistro*	18
Terroir	*Bistro*	–
Tricotin	*Asian*	–

14TH ARRONDISSEMENT

Amuse Bouche	*New Fr.*	17
Apollo	*Eclectic*	14
Assiette	*Bistro*	20
Bar à Huîtres	*Seafood*	18
Bel Canto	*Italian*	15
NEW Bis du Severo	*Bistro*	–
Bistrot du Dôme	*Seafood*	19
Buffalo Grill	*Steakhouse*	9
Cagouille	*Seafood*	21
Cerisaie	*Southwest*	24
Chez Clément	*Classic Fr.*	12
Chez Papa	*Southwest*	18
Contre-Allée	*Bistro*	24
Z Coupole	*Brass.*	18
Crêperie de Josselin	*Brittany*	21
Dôme	*Seafood*	22
Duc	*Seafood*	24
Enzo	*Italian*	–
Hippopotamus	*Steak*	10
Il Barone	*Italian*	–
Indiana Café	*Tex-Mex*	8
Léon/Bruxelles	*Belgian*	15
Maison Courtine	*Southwest*	21
Monsieur Lapin	*Classic Fr.*	20
Montparnasse 25	*Haute Cuisine*	24
Natacha	*Classic Fr.*	21
O à la Bouche	*Bistro*	17
Opportun	*Lyon*	–
Paradis du Fruit	*Eclectic*	13
Pavillon Montsouris	*Classic Fr.*	18
Petites Sorcières	*Bistro*	–
Régalade	*Bistro*	23
Severo	*Steak*	22
Vin et Marée	*Seafood*	17
Zeyer	*Brass.*	15

15TH ARRONDISSEMENT

Ami Marcel	*Bistro*	21
Autour du Mont	*Seafood*	–
Autour du Saumon	*Seafood*	–
Banyan	*Thai*	25
Benkay	*Jap.*	23
Beurre Noisette	*Bistro*	21
Bistro 121	*Bistro*	20
Bistro d'Hubert	*Bistro*	20
Bistrot d'André	*Bistro*	–
Bistrot du Cap	*Seafood*	–
Buffalo Grill	*Steakhouse*	9
Café du Commerce	*Bistro*	13

Restaurant		Rating
Casa Alcalde	*Basque/Spanish*	15
Cave de l'Os à Moëlle	*Bistro*	20
Chen Soleil d'Est	*Chinese*	24
Chez Clément	*Classic Fr.*	12
Chez Papa	*Southwest*	18
Clos Morillons	*New Fr.*	–
Couleurs de Vigne	*Wine Bar/Bistro*	–
Dalloyau	*Dessert/Tea.*	23
Dix Vins	*Bistro/Wine Bar*	16
Erawan	*Thai*	20
Fellini	*Italian*	19
Fontanarosa	*Italian*	19
Gauloise	*Bistro*	16
Gitane	*Southwest*	14
Grand Venise	*Italian*	22
Harumi	*New Fr.*	–
Hippopotamus	*Steak*	10
Je Thé . . . Me	*Classic Fr.*	22
Kim Anh	*Viet.*	21
Os à Moëlle	*Classic Fr.*	23
Père Claude	*Classic Fr.*	18
R.	*New Fr.*	17
Rest. de la Tour	*Classic Fr.*	–
Rest. du Marché	*Bistro*	–
Sawadee	*Thai*	18
Sept Quinze	*Med./Provence*	18
Stéphane Martin	*Classic Fr.*	24
Suffren	*Brass.*	14
Thierry Burlot	*New Fr.*	24
Tire-Bouchon	*Bistro*	18
Triporteur	*Bistro*	–
Troquet	*Basque/New Fr.*	23
Uitr	*Seafood*	–
Villa Corse	*Corsica*	16

16TH ARRONDISSEMENT

Restaurant		Rating
A et M	*Bistro*	15
NEW Alain Bourgade	*New Fr.*	–
Al Dar	*Lebanese*	22
Al Mounia	*Moroccan*	16
☑ Astrance	*New Fr.*	27
Aub. Dab	*Brass.*	16
Baie d'Ha Long	*Viet.*	–
Beaujolais d'Auteuil	*Classic Fr.*	15
Bellini	*Italian*	18
Bistrot Bigorneau	*Seafood*	15
Bistrot de l'Etoile Laur.	*Bistro*	19
Bistrot des Vignes	*Bistro*	13
Bon	*New Fr.*	15
Butte Chaillot	*Bistro*	20

Restaurant		Rating
Casa Tina	*Spanish*	12
182 Rive Droite	*New Fr.*	12
Chalet des Iles	*Classic Fr.*	15
Coffee Parisien	*Amer.*	15
☑ Cristal Room	*New Fr.*	19
Elysées Hong Kong	*Chinese*	–
Etoile	*Classic Fr.*	18
Fakhr el Dine	*Lebanese*	17
Flandrin	*Brass.*	13
Frugier	*Bistro*	–
Gare	*Classic Fr.*	14
Giulio Rebellato	*Italian*	20
Grande Armée	*Classic Fr.*	12
☑ Hiramatsu	*Haute Cuisine*	27
Jardins de Bagatelle	*Classic Fr.*	17
Kambodgia	*SE Asian*	18
Kiosque	*Classic Fr.*	14
Lac-Hong	*Viet.*	19
Maison Prunier	*Seafood*	22
Marius	*Seafood*	20
Mathusalem	*Bistro*	14
Matsuri	*Jap.*	12
Murat	*Classic Fr.*	15
Noura	*Lebanese*	18
Oum el Banine	*Moroccan*	–
NEW Ozu	*Jap.*	–
Paris Seize	*Italian*	14
Passiflore	*Asian/Classic Fr.*	23
Passy Mandarin	*Asian*	16
Paul Chêne	*Classic Fr.*	22
☑ Pavillon/Gr. Cascade	*Haute Cuisine*	22
Petite Tour	*Classic Fr.*	16
Petit Pergolèse	*Bistro*	15
Petit Rétro	*Bistro*	20
Petit Victor Hugo	*Classic Fr.*	14
Pizzeria d'Auteuil	*Italian*	17
Port Alma	*Seafood*	20
☑ Pré Catelan	*Haute Cuisine*	26
☑ Relais d'Auteuil	*Haute Cuisine*	26
Relais du Parc	*Haute Cuisine*	–
Rest. GR5	*Alpine*	15
Rosimar	*Spanish*	–
Scheffer	*Bistro*	15
7ème Sud	*Med./Moroccan*	17
6 New York	*New Fr.*	20
Stella	*Brass.*	16
Stéphane Gaborieau	*Haute Cuisine*	–
NEW Table de Babette	*Creole*	–

Table de Joël Robuchon | *Haute Cuisine* Ⓩ 26

Table du Baltimore | *Haute Cuisine* –

Table Lauriston | *Classic Fr.* 17

Tang | *Chinese* 17

Terrasse Mirabeau | *Bistro* –

Tokyo Eat | *New Fr.* 12

Tournesol | *Bistro* 13

Tsé-Yang | *Chinese* 21

Villa Corse | *Corsica* 16

Vinci | *Classic Fr./Italian* –

Vin dans les voiles | *Wine Bar/Bistro* –

Vin et Marée | *Seafood* 17

Waknine | *New Fr.* 14

Zébra Square | *Classic Fr.* 12

17TH ARRONDISSEMENT

Abadache | *Bistro* –

NEW Accolade | *Bistro* –

Ampère | *Bistro* 15

Autour du Saumon | *Seafood* –

Ballon des Ternes | *Brass.* 15

Ballon et Coquillages | *Seafood* –

Baptiste | *New Fr.* 19

Bath's | *Auvergne/New French* –

Bistral | *Bistro* 23

Bistro du 17ème | *Bistro* 16

Bistro Melrose | *Bistro* –

Bistro St. Ferdinand | *Bistro* 16

Bistrot d'à Côté | *Bistro* 20

Bistrot de l'Etoile Niel | *Bistro* 19

Bistrot des Dames | *Bistro* 15

Braisière | *Gascony* 24

Buffalo Grill | *Steakhouse* 9

Cabane | *Seafood* –

Café d'Angel | *Bistro* 19

Caïus | *New Fr.* 18

Caves Pétrissans | *Wine Bar/Bistro* 21

Chez Clément | *Classic Fr.* 12

Chez Fred | *Lyon* –

Chez Georges-Maillot | *Brass.* 15

Chez Léon | *Bistro* 17

Chez Ly | *Chinese/Thai* –

Clou | *Bistro* –

Congrès Maillot | *Brass.* 14

Dessirier | *Seafood* 21

Ecluse | *Wine Bar/Bistro* 14

Entredgeu | *Bistro* 21

Epicure 108 | *Alsace/Asian* –

Graindorge | *Belgian/N. France* 22

Ⓩ Guy Savoy | *Haute Cuisine* 28

Harold | *Classic/New Fr.* –

NEW Hier & Aujourd'hui | *New Fr.* –

Huîtrier | *Classic Fr.* –

Il Etait une Oie | *Southwest* 17

Kifune | *Jap.* –

Léon/Bruxelles | *Belgian* 15

Lina's | *Sandwiches* 15

Meating | *Steakhouse* 19

Ⓩ Michel Rostang | *New Fr.* 27

Mont Liban | *Lebanese* –

Orénoc | *Asian/Classic Fr.* –

Paolo Petrini | *Italian* 21

Paradis du Fruit | *Eclectic* 13

Patrick Goldenberg | *Eastern European* 15

Petit Bofinger | *Brass.* 16

Petit Colombier | *Classic Fr.* 17

Pétrus | *Classic Fr.* –

Rech | *Classic Fr./Seafood* 14

Relais de Venise | *Steak* 22

Rest. GR5 | *Alpine* 15

Rucola | *Italian* –

Sora Lena | *Italian/Med.* –

Sormani | *Italian* 24

Soupière | *Classic Fr.* –

Sud | *Med./Provence* 15

Taïra | *Jap./New Fr.* 23

Timgad | *Moroccan* 22

Toque | *Classic Fr.* 23

Verre Bouteille | *Wine Bar/Bistro* –

18TH ARRONDISSEMENT

Café Burq | *Wine Bar/Bistro* –

Chez Grisette | *Wine Bar/Bistro* –

Cottage Marcadet | *New Fr.* 21

2 Pièces Cuisine | *Bistro* –

Diapason | *Southwest* 16

Entracte | *Bistro* –

Famille | *New Fr.* 16

Mascotte | *Auvergne* –

Moulin de la Galette | *Classic Fr.* –

Osteria Ascolani | *Italian* –

Pomponette | *Bistro* –

Poulbot Gourmet | *Bistro* –

Rendez-vous/Chauff. | *Bistro* –

Rughetta | *Italian* 17

Sale e Pepe | *Italian* –

Square | *Classic/New Fr.* –

LOCATIONS

NEW Truc Café | *Wine Bar/Bistro* | –

Village Kabyle | *North African* | –

Wepler | *Brass.* | 15

19TH ARRONDISSEMENT

Boeuf Couronné | *Classic Fr.* | 17

Buffalo Grill | *Steakhouse* | 9

Café de la Musique | *Classic Fr.* | –

Cave Gourmande | *Bistro* | 24

Chapeau Melon | *Classic Fr./Eclectic* | –

Chez Vincent | *Italian* | 22

Lao Siam | *Thai* | 23

20TH ARRONDISSEMENT

Allobroges | *Bistro* | 20

Baratin | *Wine Bar/Bistro* | –

Boulangerie | *Bistro* | 20

Chez Ramona | *Spanish* | –

Zéphyr | *Bistro* | –

Outlying Areas

BAGNOLET

Indigo Square | *Eclectic* | –

BOUGIVAL

Camélia | *New Fr.* | –

BOULOGNE-BILLANCOURT

Cap Seguin | *Classic Fr.* | –

Chez Clément | *Classic Fr.* | 12

Comte de Gascogne | *Gascony* | 25

Dalloyau | *Dessert/Tea.* | 23

CLICHY

Romantica | *Italian* | 21

ISSY-LES-MOULINEAUX

Ile | *Classic/New Fr.* | 16

Rest. Manufacture | *Bistro* | 19

River Café | *Classic/New Fr.* | 15

JOINVILLE-LE-PONT

Chez Gégène | *Classic Fr.* | –

LA DÉFENSE

Petit Bofinger | *Brass.* | 16

LE PRÉ-ST-GERVAIS

Pouilly Reuilly | *Bistro* | 19

LEVALLOIS-PERRET

Mandalay | *Eclectic* | –

Petit Poucet | *New Fr.* | 16

MAISONS-LAFFITTE

Tastevin | *Classic Fr.* | 23

Vieille Fontaine Rôtiss. | *Classic/New Fr.* | 20

NEUILLY-SUR-SEINE

Bel Canto | *Italian* | 15

Bistrot d'à Côté | *Bistro* | 20

Café la Jatte | *Eclectic* | 14

Chalet de Neuilly | *Alpine/Classic Fr.* | –

Chez Gérard | *Auvergne* | 19

Chez Livio | *Italian* | 13

Chez Papinou | *Bistro* | –

Coffee Parisien | *Amer.* | 15

Durand Dupont | *Eclectic* | 9

Guinguette/Neuilly | *Classic Fr.* | 15

Jarrasse | *Seafood* | –

Lina's | *Sandwiches* | 15

Mandarin/Neuilly | *Chinese* | –

Matsuri | *Jap.* | 12

Paradis du Fruit | *Eclectic* | 13

Riad | *Moroccan* | –

Saveurs du Marché | *Bistro* | –

Sébillon | *Brass.* | 19

Tonnelle Saintongeaise | *Classic Fr.* | –

Truffe Noire | *Classic Fr.* | 20

Zinc-Zinc | *Bistro* | 14

PERREUX-SUR-MARNE

Magnolias | *New Fr.* | 22

PUTEAUX

Hippopotamus | *Steak* | 10

SAINT-CLOUD

Quai Ouest | *Eclectic* | 17

SAINT-GERMAIN-EN-LAYE

Cazaudehore | *Haute Cuisine* | 20

SAINT-OUEN

Soleil | *Bistro* | 17

VERSAILLES

Marée de Versailles | *Seafood* | 21

Potager du Roy | *Classic Fr.* | 22

Z Trois Marches | *Haute Cuisine* | 26

VINCENNES

Petit Bofinger | *Brass.* | 16

Special Features

Listings cover the best in each category and include restaurant names, locations and Food ratings. Multi-location restaurants' features may vary by branch. ☒ indicates places with the highest ratings, popularity and importance.

ADDITIONS

(Properties added since the last edition of the book)

Accolade | 17ᵉ   ⌐
Alain Bourgade | 16ᵉ   ⌐
Arome | 8ᵉ   ⌐
Autour du Mont | 15ᵉ   ⌐
Baratin | 20ᵉ   ⌐
Bath's | 17ᵉ   ⌐
Bis du Severo | 14ᵉ   ⌐
Black Calavados | 8ᵉ   ⌐
Boucherie Roulière | 6ᵉ   ⌐
Brass. Printemps | 9ᵉ   ⌐
Cantine de Quentin | 10ᵉ   ⌐
Carmine | 7ᵉ   ⌐
Chapeau Melon | 19ᵉ   ⌐
Chez Cécile | 8ᵉ   ⌐
Chez Ramona | 20ᵉ   ⌐
Cibus | 1ᵉʳ   ⌐
Cou de la Girafe | 8ᵉ   ⌐
2 Pieces Cuisine | 18ᵉ   ⌐
Ferrandaise | 6ᵉ   ⌐
First | 1ᵉʳ   ⌐
Gazzetta | 12ᵉ   ⌐
Grange Batelière | 9ᵉ   ⌐
Hier & Aujourd'hui | 17ᵉ   ⌐
Hôtel Amour | 9ᵉ   ⌐
Huîtrerie Régis | 6ᵉ   ⌐
Jardinier | 9ᵉ   ⌐
Mori Venice Bar | 2ᵉ   ⌐
Ombres | 7ᵉ   ⌐
Oudino | 7ᵉ   ⌐
Ozu | 16ᵉ   ⌐
Petit Monsieur | 11ᵉ   ⌐
Petit Pamphlet | 3ᵉ   ⌐
Petit Pascal | 13ᵉ   ⌐
Pétrelle | 9ᵉ   ⌐
Pétrus | 17ᵉ   ⌐
Pizzetta | 9ᵉ   ⌐
Pré Salé | 1ᵉʳ   ⌐
Ribouldingue | 5ᵉ   ⌐
San | 3ᵉ   ⌐
Sensing | 6ᵉ   ⌐
Soleil | 7ᵉ   ⌐
Spring | 9ᵉ   ⌐

Table de Babette | 16ᵉ   ⌐
Tarmac | 12ᵉ   ⌐
35° Ouest | 7ᵉ   ⌐
Truc Café | 18ᵉ   ⌐
Unico | 11ᵉ   ⌐
Versance | 2ᵉ   ⌐
21 | 6ᵉ   ⌐
Vivres | 9ᵉ   ⌐

BREAKFAST

(See also Hotel Dining)

Alsace | 8ᵉ   15
☒ Angelina | 1ᵉʳ   20
A Priori Thé | 2ᵉ   16
Autour du Saumon | multi. loc.   ⌐
Avenue | 8ᵉ   18
Bar des Théâtres | 8ᵉ   13
Berkeley | 8ᵉ   12
Brass. Balzar | 5ᵉ   18
Brass. La Lorraine | 8ᵉ   16
NEW Brass. Printemps | 9ᵉ   ⌐
Breakfast in America | multi. loc.   13
Café Beaubourg | 4ᵉ   15
Café de Flore | 6ᵉ   15
Café de la Musique | 19ᵉ   ⌐
Café de l'Esplanade | 7ᵉ   17
Café Lenôtre | 8ᵉ   19
Café Le Petit Pont | 5ᵉ   24
☒ Café Les Deux Magots | 6ᵉ   15
Café Marly | 1ᵉʳ   15
Café Ruc | 1ᵉʳ   14
Camille | 3ᵉ   20
Cazaudehore | St-Germain-Laye   20
Chez Clément | multi. loc.   12
Chez Prune | 10ᵉ   12
Cloche des Halles | 1ᵉʳ   16
Congrès Maillot | 17ᵉ   14
Couleurs de Vigne | 15ᵉ   -
☒ Coupole | 14ᵉ   18
☒ Cristal Room | 16ᵉ   19
Dalloyau | multi. loc.   23
Deux Abeilles | 7ᵉ   18
Dôme | 14ᵉ   22
Duc de Richelieu | 12ᵉ   -
Editeurs | 6ᵉ   15

SPECIAL FEATURES

Ferme | 1er [–]
Flandrin | 16e [13]
Flore en l'Ile | 4e [16]
Fontaines | 5e [18]
Fouquet's | 8e [17]
Gavroche | 2e [21]
Grand Café | 9e [15]
Grande Armée | 16e [12]
Grille St-Germain | 6e [17]
Ⓩ Ladurée | **multi. loc.** [22]
Lina's | **multi. loc.** [15]
Loir dans la Théière | 4e [18]
Ma Bourgogne | 4e [17]
Main d'Or | 11e [21]
Mascotte | 18e [19]
Murat | 16e [16]
Nemrod | 6e [12]
Noura | 16e [14]
Point Bar | 1er [18]
Pomze | 8e [15]
Procope | 6e [16]
Publicis Drugstore | 8e [14]
Rotonde | 6e [22]
Rue Balzac | 8e [10]
Sauvignon | 7e [15]
Stella | 16e [–]
Suffren | 15e [17]
Table d'Hédiard | 8e [12]
Tav. de Maître Kanter | 1er [9]
Terminus Nord | 10e [15]
Tricotin | 13e [12]
Vaudeville | 2e [15]
Viaduc Café | 12e [14]
Virgin Café | 8e
Wepler | 18e
Zébra Square | 16e
Zeyer | 14e
Zinc-Zinc | **Neuilly**

BRUNCH

Alcazar | 6e [17]
Ⓩ Angelina | 1er [20]
Appart' | 8e [15]
A Priori Thé | 2e [16]
Asian | 8e [16]
Barlotti | 1er [15]
Barrio Latino | 12e [11]
Berkeley | 8e [12]
Blue Elephant | 11e [19]
Bon | 16e [15]
Brass. Lutétia | 6e [17]

Breakfast in America | 5e [13]
Café Beaubourg | 4e [15]
Café Charbon | 11e [11]
Café de la Musique | 19e [–]
Café de l'Industrie | 11e [13]
Café Etienne Marcel | 2e [13]
Café la Jatte | **Neuilly** [14]
Café Le Petit Pont | 5e [24]
Carr's | 1er [12]
Chai 33 | 12e [12]
Chez Prune | 10e [12]
Comptoir | 1er [16]
Curieux Spaghetti Bar | 4e [–]
Delicabar | 7e [15]
Doobie's | 8e [12]
Durand Dupont | **Neuilly** [9]
Editeurs | 6e [15]
Ferme | 1er [–]
Findi | 8e [17]
Flora Danica | 8e [18]
Flore en l'Ile | 4e [16]
Fouquet's | 8e [17]
Fumoir | 1er [15]
Gare | 16e [14]
Harold | 17e [–]
Jardin des Cygnes | 8e [20]
Joe Allen | 1er [14]
Kiosque | 16e [14]
Kodo | 4e [–]
Lina's | **multi. loc.** [15]
Liza | 2e [–]
Loir dans la Théière | 4e [18]
Mariage Frères | 6e [21]
Market | 8e [20]
Murano | 3e [17]
No Stress Café | 9e [–]
Paradis du Fruit | **multi. loc.** [13]
Pershing | 8e [15]
Pied de Chameau/Al Nour | 3e [–]
Pitchi Poï | 4e [12]
Publicis Drugstore | 8e [–]
Quai | 7e [–]
404 | 3e [21]
Refectoire | 11e [–]
Renoma Café | 8e [–]
Rouge St-Honoré | 1er [15]
Scoop | 1er [–]
7ème Sud | **multi. loc.** [17]
Spicy | 8e [15]
Studio | 4e [–]
Télégraphe | 7e [20]

Thanksgiving | 4^e	15
Viaduc Café | 12^e	12
Vinea Café | 12^e	-
Virgin Café | 8^e	9
Wepler | 18^e	15
W Restaurant | 8^e	-
Zébra Square | 16^e	12

BUSINESS DINING

☑ Ami Louis | 3^e	26
☑ Angle du Faubourg | 8^e	23
Angl'Opera | 2^e	21
☑ Astrance | 16^e	27
Auguste | 7^e	19
Bistro St. Ferdinand | 17^e	16
Bistrot de l'Etoile Laur. | 16^e	19
Bistrot de l'Etoile Niel | 17^e	19
Boeuf Couronné | 19^e	17
Boeuf sur le Toit | 8^e	16
Buisson Ardent | 5^e	20
Café de l'Esplanade | 7^e	17
Café Faubourg | 8^e	17
Caffé Minotti | 7^e	23
Cap Vernet | 8^e	18
Caves Pétrissans | 17^e	21
Céladon | 2^e	24
144 Petrossian | 7^e	22
Chez André | 8^e	20
Chez Les Anges | 7^e	-
Chez Pauline | 1er	21
Chez Savy | 8^e	21
Chiberta | 8^e	23
Clos des Gourmets | 7^e	24
Copenhague | 8^e	20
Costes | 1er	17
Cuisine | 7^e	21
Dessirier | 17^e	21
Divellec | 7^e	23
Dôme | 14^e	22
Dôme du Marais | 4^e	18
Dominique Bouchet | 8^e	24
Drouant | 2^e	-
Duc | 14^e	24
Flora Danica | 8^e	18
Fouquet's | 8^e	17
Frugier | 16^e	-
Gaya | 7^e	22
Georgette | 9^e	20
☑ Gérard Besson | 1er	25
Goumard | 1er	24
Graindorge | 17^e	22

☑ Guy Savoy | 17^e	28
☑ Hélène Darroze | 6^e	23
Il Cortile | 1er	21
Issé | 1er	18
☑ Jules Verne | 7^e	23
☑ Lapérouse | 6^e	21
Les Saveurs de Flora | 8^e	22
Macéo | 1er	21
Maison Blanche | 8^e	19
Mansouria | 11^e	19
☑ Marée | 8^e	25
Marius | 16^e	20
Marty | 5^e	17
Maxan | 8^e	-
Meating | 17^e	19
☑ Meurice | 1er	26
Montalembert | 7^e	17
NEW Mori Venice Bar | 2^e	-
Paris | 6^e	19
Paris Seize | 16^e	14
Pasco | 7^e	-
Petit Bofinger | 4^e	16
Petit Marguery | 13^e	22
Petit Pergolèse | 16^e	15
Pétrus | 17^e	-
Pichet de Paris | 8^e	20
Pierre au Palais Royal | 1er	16
☑ Pierre Gagnaire | 8^e	28
Pomze | 8^e	19
NEW Pré Salé | 1er	-
Pur'Grill | 2^e	25
☑ Relais Louis XIII | 6^e	25
☑ Salon d'Hélène | 6^e	25
Sébillon | **Neuilly**	19
16 Haussmann | 9^e	21
Senso | 8^e	17
Sormani | 17^e	24
☑ Stella Maris | 8^e	25
Stresa | 8^e	22
☑ Table de Joël Robuchon | 16^e	26
☑ Table du Lancaster | 8^e	25
Table Lauriston | 16^e	17
Tan Dinh | 7^e	22
Tante Louise | 8^e	22
Terrasse Mirabeau | 16^e	-
Thierry Burlot | 15^e	24
☑ Train Bleu | 12^e	19
NEW 35º Ouest | 7^e	-
Trou Gascon | 12^e	24
Vagenende | 6^e	15
Vaudeville | 2^e	17

SPECIAL FEATURES

NEW Versance	2e	–
Vin et Marée	multi. loc.	17
Voltaire	7e	22
W Restaurant	8e	–

CATERING

Al Dar	16e	22
Al Diwan	8e	19
Anahuacalli	5e	21
A Priori Thé	2e	16
Ardoise	1er	23
As du Fallafel	4e	24
Asian	8e	16
Atlas	5e	18
Autobus Imperial	1er	–
Autour du Saumon	multi. loc.	–
☒ Avant Goût	13e	25
Baan-Boran	1er	21
Baie d'Ha Long	16e	–
Banyan	15e	25
BE Boulangépicier	8e	22
Bellota-Bellota	7e	19
Bistral	17e	23
Bistro 121	15e	20
Bistrot de l'Etoile Niel	17e	19
Blue Elephant	11e	19
Boule Rouge	9e	–
Butte Chaillot	16e	20
Caffé Toscano	7e	–
Caïus	17e	18
Casa Tina	16e	12
Cave Gourmande	19e	24
144 Petrossian	7e	22
Chez Marianne	4e	18
Chez Michel	10e	23
Chez Vong	1er	20
Coco de Mer	5e	22
Coffee Parisien	multi. loc.	15
Coin des Gourmets	5e	16
Cook Book	7e	–
Cosi	6e	19
Dalloyau	multi. loc.	23
Da Mimmo	10e	15
Daru	8e	–
Délices d'Aphrodite	5e	18
Deux Abeilles	7e	18
☒ 1728	8e	16
Enoteca	4e	22
Escale du Liban	4e	–
Etoile Marocaine	8e	18
Fakhr el Dine	multi. loc.	17
Filo Delle Stagioni	3e	–
Findi	8e	17
Flora Danica	8e	18
Fogón	6e	20
Foujita	1er	14
Higuma	1er	18
Il Etait une Oie	17e	17
Inagiku	5e	–
☒ Jacques Cagna	6e	26
Jarrasse	Neuilly	–
Joséphine/Dumonet	6e	23
Khun Akorn	11e	19
Kim Anh	15e	21
☒ Kinugawa	1er	25
Lao Siam	19e	23
Lao Tseu	7e	18
Les Saveurs de Flora	8e	22
Lina's	multi. loc.	15
Maharajah	5e	16
Maison du Caviar	8e	21
☒ Marée	8e	25
Marlotte	6e	20
Martel	10e	16
Matsuri	multi. loc.	12
Mavrommatis	5e	22
☒ Meurice	1er	26
Mirama	5e	16
Musichall	8e	15
New Jawad	7e	16
New Nioullaville	11e	16
Noura	multi. loc.	18
Oenothèque	9e	–
Oum el Banine	16e	–
Pamphlet	3e	23
Passy Mandarin	16e	16
Patrick Goldenberg	17e	15
Petite Cour	6e	18
Petite Tour	16e	16
Pitchi Poï	4e	–
Pomze	8e	19
Quai	7e	–
404	3e	21
Ragueneau	1er	–
Rech	17e	14
☒ Relais d'Auteuil	16e	26
☒ Relais Louis XIII	6e	25
Repaire de Cartouche	11e	19
Rest. de la Tour	15e	–
Rest. du Marché	15e	–
Rest. du Palais Royal	1er	19
Reuan Thai	11e	–

subscribe to zagat.com

Riad | **Neuilly**	–
Rosimar | 16ᵉ	–
Rucola | 17ᵉ	–
Samiin | 7ᵉ	–
Sardegna a Tavola | 12ᵉ	22
Sauvignon | 7ᵉ	15
Saveurs de Claude | 6ᵉ	–
Sawadee | 15ᵉ	18
Scoop | 1ᵉʳ	–
Sologne | 12ᵉ	–
Stéphane Martin | 15ᵉ	24
Table d'Hédiard | 8ᵉ	22
Timgad | 17ᵉ	22
Tong Yen | 8ᵉ	20
Village d'Ung/Li Lam | 8ᵉ	–
Village Kabyle | 18ᵉ	–
Wally Le Saharien | 9ᵉ	18
Zéphyr | 20ᵉ	–
Zo | 8ᵉ	15

CELEBRITY CHEFS

Z Alain Ducasse | *Alain Ducasse* | 8ᵉ	28
Z Ambroisie | *Bernard Pacaud* | 4ᵉ	27
Z Apicius | *Jean-Pierre Vigato* | 8ᵉ	26
Z Arpège | *Alain Passard* | 7ᵉ	26
Z Astrance | *Pascal Barbot* | 16ᵉ	27
Z Atelier de Joël Robuchon | *Joël Robuchon* | 7ᵉ	27
Z Benoît | *Alain Ducasse* | 4ᵉ	24
Bistrot d'à Côté | *Michel Rostang* | **multi. loc.**	20
Z Bouquinistes | *Guy Savoy* | 6ᵉ	21
Z Bristol | *Eric Frechon* | 8ᵉ	27
Z Butte Chaillot | *Guy Savoy* | 16ᵉ	20
Z Carré des Feuillants | *Alain Dutournier* | 1ᵉʳ	25
Chiberta | *Guy Savoy* | 8ᵉ	23
Z Cinq | *Philippe Legendre* | 8ᵉ	28
Comptoir du Relais | *Yves Camdeborde* | 6ᵉ	22
Drouant | *Antoine Westermann* | 2ᵉ	–
Z Elysées | *Eric Briffard* | 8ᵉ	26
Z Espadon | *Michel Roth* | 1ᵉʳ	25
Fables de La Fontaine | *Christian Constant* | 7ᵉ	21
Gaya | *Pierre Gagnaire* | 7ᵉ	22
Z Grand Véfour | *Guy Martin* | 1ᵉʳ	27
Z Guy Savoy | *Guy Savoy* | 17ᵉ	28
Z Hélène Darroze | *Hélène Darroze* | 6ᵉ	23
Z Hiramatsu | *Hiroyuki Hiramatsu* | 16ᵉ	27
Z Jacques Cagna | *Jacques Cagna* | 6ᵉ	26
Z Lasserre | *Jean-Louis Nomicos* | 8ᵉ	27
Z Lyonnais | *Alain Ducasse* | 2ᵉ	22
Market | *Jean-Georges Vongerichten* | 8ᵉ	20
Z Michel Rostang | *Michel Rostang* | 17ᵉ	27
Mon Vieil Ami | *Antoine Westermann* | 4ᵉ	24
Z Pavillon Ledoyen | *Christian Le Squer* | 8ᵉ	26
Z Pierre Gagnaire | *Pierre Gagnaire* | 8ᵉ	28
Pinxo | *Alain Dutournier* | 1ᵉʳ	20
Publicis Drugstore | *Alain Ducasse* | 8ᵉ	12
Z Salon d'Hélène | *Hélène Darroze* | 6ᵉ	25
Senderens | *Alain Senderens* | 8ᵉ	–
NEW Sensing | *Guy Martin* | 6ᵉ	–
Spoon, Food & Wine | *Alain Ducasse* | 8ᵉ	23
Z Table de Joël Robuchon | *Joël Robuchon* | 16ᵉ	26
Z Table du Lancaster | *Michel Troisgros* | 8ᵉ	25
Z Taillevent | *Alain Solivérès* | 8ᵉ	28
Trou Gascon | *Alain Dutournier* | 12ᵉ	24
NEW 21 | *Paul Minchelli* | 6ᵉ	–
Violon d'Ingres | *Christian Constant* | 7ᵉ	24
Z Ze Kitchen Galerie | *William Ledeuil* | 6ᵉ	23

CHEESE TRAYS

Aiguière | 11ᵉ	–
Aimant du Sud | 13ᵉ	–
NEW Alain Bourgade | 16ᵉ	–
Z Alain Ducasse | 8ᵉ	28
Alivi | 4ᵉ	17
Altitude 95 | 7ᵉ	16
Z Ambroisie | 4ᵉ	27
Ami Marcel | 15ᵉ	21
Amognes | 11ᵉ	23
Ampère | 17ᵉ	15
Z Apicius | 8ᵉ	26
NEW Arome | 8ᵉ	–

SPECIAL FEATURES

Restaurant	Rating	Restaurant	Rating
☑ Arpège | 7ᵉ	26	Chez Maître Paul | 6ᵉ	20
Astier | 11ᵉ	22	Chez Nénesse | 3ᵉ	19
Astor | 8ᵉ	20	Chez Papinou | **Neuilly**	-
Atelier Berger | 1er	21	Chez Ramulaud | 11ᵉ	22
☑ Atelier de Joël Robuchon | 7ᵉ	27	Chez René | 5ᵉ	21
Aub. Dab | 16ᵉ	16	Chiberta | 8ᵉ	23
Bacchantes | 9ᵉ	-	☑ Cinq | 8ᵉ	28
Ballon des Ternes | 17ᵉ	15	Citrus Etoile | 8ᵉ	-
Ballon et Coquillages | 17ᵉ	-	Cloche des Halles | 1er	16
☑ Bar Vendôme | 1er	21	Closerie des Lilas | 6ᵉ	16
Bath's | 17ᵉ	-	Clou | 17ᵉ	-
Beaujolais d'Auteuil | 16ᵉ	15	Clovis | 8ᵉ	19
Bel Canto | **multi. loc.**	15	Comédiens | 9ᵉ	-
Bistral | 17ᵉ	23	Congrès Maillot | 17ᵉ	14
Bistro 121 | 15ᵉ	20	Cook Book | 7ᵉ	-
Bistrot à Vins Mélac | 11ᵉ	16	Copenhague | 8ᵉ	20
Bistrot du Sommelier | 8ᵉ	20	Cordonnerie | 1er	-
Boeuf Couronné | 19ᵉ	17	Cosi (Le) | 5ᵉ	17
Bon Accueil | 7ᵉ	24	Cottage Marcadet | 18ᵉ	21
Bons Crus | 1er	-	Dalloyau | 8ᵉ	23
Bouchons/Fr. Cl./Colbert | 8ᵉ	19	Diapason | 18ᵉ	16
Bouillon Racine | 6ᵉ	14	Divellec | 7ᵉ	23
Bound | 8ᵉ	-	Dôme | 14ᵉ	22
Bourguignon du Marais | 4ᵉ	22	Dôme du Marais | 4ᵉ	18
Braisière | 17ᵉ	24	Drouant | 2ᵉ	-
Brass. du Louvre | 1er	18	Duc de Richelieu | 12ᵉ	-
Brass. Flo | 10ᵉ	17	☑ Elysées | 8ᵉ	26
Brass. Lutétia | 6ᵉ	17	Epicure 108 | 17ᵉ	-
Café de l'Industrie | 11ᵉ	13	Epi d'Or | 1er	21
Café du Passage | 11ᵉ	-	☑ Espadon | 1er	25
Café Faubourg | 8ᵉ	17	Ferme St-Simon | 7ᵉ	22
Café Fusion | 13ᵉ	-	Fermette Marbeuf | 8ᵉ	18
Café Terminus | 8ᵉ	-	Fins Gourmets | 7ᵉ	21
Camélia | **Bougival**	-	Fontaine Gaillon | 2ᵉ	19
NEW Carmine | 7ᵉ	-	Fontaines | 5ᵉ	18
☑ Carré des Feuillants | 1er	25	Fouquet's | 8ᵉ	17
Caveau du Palais | 1er	21	Frugier | 16ᵉ	-
Caves Pétrissans | 17ᵉ	21	Garnier | 8ᵉ	22
☑ Caviar Kaspia | 8ᵉ	26	Giulio Rebellato | 16ᵉ	20
Cazaudehore | St-Germain-Laye	20	Goumard | 1er	24
Céladon | 2ᵉ	24	Graindorge | 17ᵉ	22
Chantairelle | 5ᵉ	-	Grand Café | 9ᵉ	15
Chaumière en l'Ile | 4ᵉ	22	☑ Grand Véfour | 1er	27
Chez André | 8ᵉ	20	Grille | 10ᵉ	-
Chez Catherine | 8ᵉ	23	☑ Guy Savoy | 17ᵉ	28
Chez Françoise | 7ᵉ	15	☑ Hélène Darroze | 6ᵉ	23
Chez Fred | 17ᵉ	-	Huîtrerie Régis | 6ᵉ	-
☑ Chez Georges | 2ᵉ	21	I Golosi | 9ᵉ	20
Chez Léon | 17ᵉ	17	Il Cortile | 1er	21
Chez Les Anges | 7ᵉ	-	☑ Jacques Cagna | 6ᵉ	26
		Jardin | 8ᵉ	22

Jardin des Cygnes | 8e	20
Jarrasse | **Neuilly**	-
Jean | 9e	19
Joséphine/Dumonet | 6e	23
⚡ Jules Verne | 7e	23
Kodo | 4e	-
⚡ Lasserre | 8e	27
Laurent | 8e	24
Lavinia | 1er	17
Les Saveurs de Flora | 8e	22
Louchebem | 1er	14
Macéo | 1er	21
Magnolias | **Perreux**	22
Main d'Or | 11e	21
Maison Blanche | 8e	19
Maison du Jardin | 6e	22
Marc Annibal de Coconnas | 4e	17
⚡ Marée | 8e	25
Marlotte | 6e	20
Mascotte | 18e	-
Maupertu | 7e	20
Meating | 17e	19
Mesturet | 2e	-
⚡ Meurice | 1er	26
⚡ Michel Rostang | 17e	27
Moissonnier | 5e	22
Montparnasse 25 | 14e	24
Murano | 3e	17
Muses | 9e	-
Nos Ancêtres/Gaulois | 4e	10
No Stress Café | 9e	-
Oenothèque | 9e	-
Oudino | 7e	-
Paolo Petrini | 17e	21
Papilles | 5e	22
Paris | 6e	19
Passage/Carm. | 11e	-
Passiflore | 16e	23
Paul Chêne | 16e	22
⚡ Pavillon/Gr. Cascade | 16e	22
⚡ Pavillon Ledoyen | 8e	26
Pavillon Montsouris | 14e	18
Petit Colombier | 17e	17
Petite Sirène/Copen. | 9e	20
NEW Petit Monsieur | 11e	-
Petit Pascal | 13e	-
Pétrelle | 9e	-
Pichet de Paris | 8e	20
⚡ Pierre Gagnaire | 8e	28
Point Bar | 1er	21
Polichinelle Cafe | 11e	-

Pomze | 8e	19
Port Alma | 16e	20
Poule au Pot | 1er	21
Press Café | 2e	-
Procope | 6e	16
Pure Café | 11e	-
Ragueneau | 1er	-
⚡ Relais d'Auteuil | 16e	26
Relais de Venise | 17e	22
Relais du Parc | 16e	-
⚡ Relais Louis XIII | 6e	25
⚡ Réminet | 5e	25
Rendez-vous/Chauff. | 18e	-
Romantica | **Clichy**	21
Rôtiss. du Beaujolais | 5e	22
⚡ Salon d'Hélène | 6e	25
Sardegna a Tavola | 12e	22
Sauvignon | 7e	15
Sébillon | **Neuilly**	19
16 Haussmann | 9e	21
Sot l'y Laisse | 11e	-
⚡ Soufflé | 1er	22
Soupière | 17e	-
Stella | 16e	16
Stéphane Gaborieau | 16e	-
⚡ Table de Joël Robuchon | 16e	26
Table du Baltimore | 16e	-
⚡ Table du Lancaster | 8e	25
Table Lauriston | 16e	17
Tante Louise | 8e	22
NEW Tarmac | 12e	-
Tastevin | **Maisons-Laff.**	23
Tav. de Gli Amici | 7e	-
Tav. Henri IV | 1er	17
Tête Ailleurs | 4e	-
Thoumieux | 7e	15
Timbre | 6e	22
Tokyo Eat | 16e	12
⚡ Tour d'Argent | 5e	25
⚡ Train Bleu | 12e	19
⚡ Trois Marches | **Versailles**	26
Trou Gascon | 12e	24
Truffe Noire | **Neuilly**	20
Truffière | 5e	24
Vaudeville | 2e	17
NEW Versance | 2e	-
Vieux Chêne | 11e	-
Villaret | 11e	23
Vin dans les voiles | 16e	-
Vin des Pyrenees | 4e	16
Violon d'Ingres | 7e	24

SPECIAL FEATURES

Vivres	9e	–
Waknine	16e	14
Wepler	18e	15
Willi's Wine Bar	1er	19
W Restaurant	8e	–
Zéphyr	20e	–
Zo	8e	15

CHILD-FRIENDLY

(Alternatives to the usual fast-food places; * children's menu available)

Aiguière*	11e	–
Alcazar*	6e	17
Altitude 95*	7e	16
Ampère	17e	15
Amuse Bouche	14e	17
Anahuacalli*	5e	21
A Priori Thé*	2e	16
Asian*	8e	16
☑ Atelier de Joël Robuchon	7e	27
Atlas*	5e	18
Aub. Dab*	16e	16
Autour du Saumon*	multi. loc.	–
Bar à Huîtres*	multi. loc.	18
☑ Bar Vendôme*	1er	21
BE Boulangépicier*	8e	22
BIOArt*	13e	–
Bistro 121	15e	20
Bistro de Breteuil*	7e	18
Bistrot d'André*	15e	–
Bistrot du Dôme*	14e	19
Boeuf sur le Toit*	8e	16
☑ Bofinger*	4e	20
Brass. du Louvre*	1er	18
Brass. Julien*	10e	17
Brass. Lutétia*	6e	17
Brass. Mollard*	8e	16
Breakfast in America	5e	13
Buffalo Grill*	multi. loc.	9
Café de la Musique	19e	–
Café de la Paix*	9e	19
Café Very/Dame*	multi. loc.	13
Chai 33*	12e	12
Chalet de Neuilly*	Neuilly	–
Chalet des Iles*	16e	15
Chez Clément*	multi. loc.	12
Chez Jenny*	3e	17
Chez Livio*	Neuilly	13
Congrès Maillot*	17e	14
Cook Book*	7e	–
☑ Coupole*	14e	18
Fouquet's*	8e	17
Gare*	16e	14
Gauloise*	15e	16
Gitane	15e	14
Hippopotamus*	multi. loc.	10
Indiana Café*	multi. loc.	8
J'Go*	9e	18
Kiosque*	16e	14
☑ Ladurée	8e	22
Languedoc	5e	19
Léon/Bruxelles*	multi. loc.	15
Monsieur Lapin	14e	20
Orénoc*	17e	–
Paradis Thai	13e	18
Pavillon Montsouris*	14e	18
Pearl*	13e	–
Petit Bofinger*	multi. loc.	16
Petite Cour	6e	18
Petite Sirène/Copen.	9e	20
Petite Tour*	16e	16
Petit Poucet*	Levallois	16
Pied de Cochon	1er	18
Planet Hollywood*	8e	7
Point Bar*	1er	21
Port Alma	16e	20
Procope	6e	16
Quai Ouest	St-Cloud	17
☑ Relais/l'Entrecôte	multi. loc.	23
Rest. du Musée d'Orsay*	7e	16
Rest. du Palais Royal	1er	19
River Café	Issy-les-Moul.	15
Rôtiss. d'en Face	6e	22
Rôtiss. du Beaujolais	5e	22
Rotonde*	6e	14
Sardegna a Tavola	12e	22
Sébillon*	Neuilly	19
Spicy*	8e	15
Studio*	4e	–
Tang	16e	17
Tav. de Maître Kanter*	1er	10
Terminus Nord*	10e	15
☑ Train Bleu*	12e	19
Trumilou	4e	19
Vagenende*	6e	15
Vaudeville*	2e	17
Viaduc Café*	12e	12
Vieux Bistro	4e	20
Village d'Ung/Li Lam*	8e	–
Virgin Café*	8e	9
Wepler*	18e	15

SPECIAL FEATURES

Planet Hollywood	**8**ᵉ	7
Suite	**8**ᵉ	12
Vinea Café	**12**ᵉ	–

DINING ALONE

(Other than hotels and places with counter service)

Aimant du Sud	**13**ᵉ	–
Alcazar	**6**ᵉ	17
Alsace	**8**ᵉ	15
Ami Marcel	**15**ᵉ	21
Ampère	**17**ᵉ	15
Amuse Bouche	**14**ᵉ	17
☑ Arpège	**7**ᵉ	26
As du Fallafel	**4**ᵉ	24
Assiette	**14**ᵉ	20
Aub. Bressane	**7**ᵉ	17
Azabu	**6**ᵉ	20
Ballon des Ternes	**17**ᵉ	15
Bar à Huîtres	**multi. loc.**	18
Bar des Théâtres	**8**ᵉ	13
Bistrot à Vins Mélac	**11**ᵉ	16
Bistrot de Marius	**8**ᵉ	17
Bistrot du Peintre	**11**ᵉ	16
Boeuf sur le Toit	**8**ᵉ	16
Bouchons/Fr. Cl./Colbert	**multi. loc.**	19
Bouillon Racine	**6**ᵉ	14
Bourguignon du Marais	**4**ᵉ	22
Brass. de l'Ile St. Louis	**4**ᵉ	16
Breakfast in America	**5**ᵉ	13
Buisson Ardent	**5**ᵉ	20
Cabane	**17**ᵉ	–
Ca d'Oro	**1**ᵉʳ	–
Café Beaubourg	**4**ᵉ	15
Café de Flore	**6**ᵉ	15
Café de la Poste	**4**ᵉ	16
Café de l'Industrie	**11**ᵉ	13
Café du Commerce	**15**ᵉ	13
Café du Passage	**11**ᵉ	–
Café Lenôtre	**8**ᵉ	19
☑ Café Les Deux Magots	**6**ᵉ	15
Café Marly	**1**ᵉʳ	15
Caméléon	**6**ᵉ	–
Camille	**3**ᵉ	20
Cap Vernet	**8**ᵉ	18
Carr's	**1**ᵉʳ	12
Charlot - Roi des Coq.	**9**ᵉ	15
Charpentiers	**6**ᵉ	18
Chartier	**9**ᵉ	13
Chez Catherine	**8**ᵉ	23
☑ Chez Georges	**2**ᵉ	21

Chez Jenny	**3**ᵉ	17
Chez la Vieille	**1**ᵉʳ	22
Chez Maître Paul	**6**ᵉ	20
Chez Marcel	**6**ᵉ	21
Chez Marianne	**4**ᵉ	18
Closerie des Lilas	**6**ᵉ	16
Coffee Parisien	**multi. loc.**	15
Congrès Maillot	**17**ᵉ	14
Cosi	**6**ᵉ	19
☑ Coupole	**14**ᵉ	18
Curieux Spaghetti Bar	**4**ᵉ	–
Delicabar	**7**ᵉ	15
Deux Canards	**10**ᵉ	18
Duc de Richelieu	**12**ᵉ	–
Durand Dupont	**Neuilly**	9
Ecluse	**multi. loc.**	14
Emporio Armani	**6**ᵉ	18
Entracte	**18**ᵉ	–
Epi d'Or	**1**ᵉʳ	21
Escargot Montorgueil	**1**ᵉʳ	18
Fakhr el Dine	**multi. loc.**	17
Ferme	**1**ᵉʳ	–
Fins Gourmets	**7**ᵉ	21
Fish La Boissonnerie	**6**ᵉ	21
Fous d'en Face	**4**ᵉ	18
Fumoir	**1**ᵉʳ	15
Gauloise	**15**ᵉ	16
Georgette	**9**ᵉ	20
☑ Isami	**4**ᵉ	27
Jarrasse	**Neuilly**	–
Jean	**9**ᵉ	19
Je Thé . . . Me	**15**ᵉ	22
Joe Allen	**1**ᵉʳ	14
Joséphine/Dumonet	**6**ᵉ	23
☑ Ladurée	**multi. loc.**	22
Languedoc	**5**ᵉ	19
Lao Tseu	**7**ᵉ	18
Legrand Filles et Fils	**2**ᵉ	–
Lina's	**multi. loc.**	15
Lô Sushi	**8**ᵉ	14
Ma Bourgogne	**4**ᵉ	17
Marty	**5**ᵉ	17
Maupertu	**7**ᵉ	20
Mauzac	**5**ᵉ	–
Maxan	**8**ᵉ	–
Moulin à Vent	**5**ᵉ	22
Mousson	**1**ᵉʳ	–
Nemrod	**6**ᵉ	15
No Stress Café	**9**ᵉ	–
Oenothèque	**9**ᵉ	–
Pamphlet	**3**ᵉ	23

Papilles | 5ᵉ	22
Paradis Thai | 13ᵉ	18
Pasco | 7ᵉ	-
Pères et Filles | 6ᵉ	12
Perraudin | 5ᵉ	16
Petit Bofinger | 4ᵉ	16
Petit Colombier | 17ᵉ	17
Petite Chaise | 7ᵉ	19
Petite Sirène/Copen. | 9ᵉ	20
Petit Lutétia | 6ᵉ	16
Petit Marguery | 13ᵉ	22
Petit Pergolèse | 16ᵉ	15
Petit Rétro | 16ᵉ	20
Petit Riche | 9ᵉ	16
Polidor | 6ᵉ	15
Poule au Pot | 1ᵉʳ	21
P'tit Troquet | 7ᵉ	23
Repaire de Cartouche | 11ᵉ	19
Rest. du Marché | 15ᵉ	-
Roi du Pot-au-Feu | 9ᵉ	15
Rubis | 1ᵉʳ	17
Sologne | 12ᵉ	
Suffren | 15ᵉ	14
Table d'Hédiard | 8ᵉ	22
Tan Dinh | 7ᵉ	22
Tav. Henri IV | 1ᵉʳ	17
Terminus Nord | 10ᵉ	15
Vagenende | 6ᵉ	15
Viaduc Café | 12ᵉ	12
Vieux Bistro | 4ᵉ	20
Vieux Chêne | 11ᵉ	-
Vin et Marée | **multi. loc.**	17
Vin sur Vin | 7ᵉ	21
Wepler | 18ᵉ	15
Wok Cooking | 11ᵉ	-
Zéphyr | 20ᵉ	-

ENTERTAINMENT

(Call for days and times of performances)

Alivi | Corsican | 4ᵉ	17
Annapurna | sitar | 8ᵉ	19
Arbuci | DJ/jazz | 6ᵉ	15
Asian | DJ | 8ᵉ	16
Avenue | DJ | 8ᵉ	18
Barlotti | DJ | 1ᵉʳ	15
Barrio Latino | salsa | 12ᵉ	11
Barroco | live music | 6ᵉ	-
☑ Bar Vendôme | piano | 1ᵉʳ	21
Bel Canto | opera | **multi. loc.**	15
Berkeley | DJ | 8ᵉ	12
Café Charbon | concerts | 11ᵉ	11

Café Faubourg | piano | 8ᵉ	17
Café Le Petit Pont | jazz | 5ᵉ	24
Carr's | Irish | 1ᵉʳ	12
NEW Chez Cécile | jazz | 8ᵉ	-
Chez Françoise | live music | 7ᵉ	15
Chez Gégène | dancing | **Joinville**	-
China Club | concerts | 12ᵉ	16
Diamantaires | orchestra | 9ᵉ	-
Djakarta | Balinese | 1ᵉʳ	19
Indigo Square | live music | **Bagnolet**	-
Jardin | harp | 8ᵉ	22
Jardin des Cygnes | piano | 8ᵉ	20
☑ Jules Verne | piano | 7ᵉ	23
☑ Lasserre | piano | 8ᵉ	27
Mandala Ray | DJ | 8ᵉ	15
Maxim's | piano | 8ᵉ	20
Musichall | varies | 8ᵉ	15
Nos Ancêtres/Gaulois | guitar | 4ᵉ	10
Passage/Carm. | debates | 11ᵉ	-
Pied de Chameau/Al Nour | snake charmer/dancers | 3ᵉ	-
Polichinelle Cafe | concerts | 11ᵉ	-
Quai Ouest | clown | **St-Cloud**	17
Relais Plaza | jazz | 8ᵉ	22
Saudade | Fado | 1ᵉʳ	-
Viaduc Café | jazz | 12ᵉ	12
Zébra Square | DJ | 16ᵉ	12
Zo | DJ | 8ᵉ	15

FAMILY-STYLE

Aimant du Sud | 13ᵉ	-
☑ Allard | 6ᵉ	22
Allobroges | 20ᵉ	20
Ampère | 17ᵉ	15
Ardoise | 1ᵉʳ	23
Babylone | 7ᵉ	-
Bartolo | 6ᵉ	18
Café du Passage | 11ᵉ	-
Chez Papa | **multi. loc.**	18
Closerie des Lilas | 6ᵉ	16
Flore en l'Ile | 4ᵉ	16
☑ Fontaine de Mars | 7ᵉ	21
Fous d'en Face | 4ᵉ	18
Joséphine/Dumonet | 6ᵉ	23
Marty | 5ᵉ	17
Mon Vieil Ami | 4ᵉ	24
Repaire de Cartouche | 11ᵉ	19
Wok Cooking | 11ᵉ	-

SPECIAL FEATURES

1904 | Vagenende | **6**^e	15
1905 | Bons Crus | **1**^{er}	-
1906 | Rendez-vous/ Chauff. | **18**^e	-
1908 | Chardenoux | **11**^e	15
1909 | Bistrot d'André | **15**^e	-
1909 | Pomponette | **18**^e	-
1910 | Brass. Lutétia | **6**^e	17
1910 | Fontaine de Mars | **7**^e	21
1912 | Benoît | **4**^e	24
1913 | Marty | **5**^e	17
1913 | Zeyer | **14**^e	15
1914 | Sébillon | **Neuilly**	19
1918 | Daru | **8**^e	-
1919 | Chez Marcel | **6**^e	21
1919 | Lescure | **1**^{er}	16
1920 | Closerie des Lilas | **6**^e	16
1920 | Hôtel Amour* | **9**^e	-
1920 | Maison Prunier | **16**^e	22
1920 | Petit Niçois | **7**^e	19
1920 | Tournesol | **16**^e	13
1922 | Café du Commerce | **15**^e	13
1923 | Chez Savy | **8**^e	21
1923 | Thoumieux | **7**^e	15
1924 | Ami Louis | **3**^e	26
1924 | Bristol | **8**^e	27
1925 | Biche au Bois | **12**^e	21
1925 | Grand Venise | **15**^e	22
1925 | Guinguette/Neuilly | **Neuilly**	15
1925 | Petit Lutétia | **6**^e	16
1925 | Rech | **17**^e	14
1925 | Terminus Nord | **10**^e	15
1926 | Chez Georges-Maillot | **17**^e	15
1927 | Caviar Kaspia | **8**^e	26
1927 | Coupole | **14**^e	18
1928 | Cazaudehore | **St-Germain-Laye**	20
1929 | Diamantaires | **9**^e	-
1929 | Jardin des Cygnes | **8**^e	20
1929 | Petit Colombier | **17**^e	17
1929 | Tante Louise | **8**^e	22
1929 | Zéphyr | **20**^e	-
1930 | Allard | **6**^e	22
1930 | Garnier | **8**^e	22
1930 | Trumilou | **4**^e	19
1931 | Chez L'Ami Jean | **7**^e	22
1932 | Chiberta | **8**^e	23
1932 | Crus de Bourgogne | **2**^e	-
1935 | Epi d'Or | **1**^{er}	21
1935 | Poule au Pot | **1**^{er}	21

1935 | Truffe Noire | **Neuilly**	20
1936 | Relais Plaza | **8**^e	22
1937 | Chez André | **8**^e	20
1937 | Chez Léna et Mimile | **5**^e	-
1939 | Voltaire | **7**^e	22
1940 | Flandrin | **16**^e	13
1942 | Lasserre | **8**^e	27
1942 | Méditerranée | **6**^e	19
1945 | Aub. Bressane | **7**^e	17
1945 | Chez Fred | **17**^e	-
1945 | Chez Paul | **11**^e	20
1945 | Pied de Cochon | **1**^{er}	18
1946 | Chez Maître Paul | **6**^e	20
1946 | Taillevent | **8**^e	28
1947 | Moulin à Vent | **5**^e	22
1948 | Rubis | **1**^{er}	17
1949 | Chez Françoise | **7**^e	15
1950 | Diapason | **18**^e	16
1950 | Terrasse Mirabeau* | **16**^e	-
1951 | Bartolo | **6**^e	18
1951 | Deux Canards | **10**^e	18
1951 | Petit Châtelet | **5**^e	19
1952 | Bistro 121 | **15**^e	20
1954 | Marc Annibal de Coconnas | **4**^e	17
1954 | Sauvignon | **7**^e	15
1955 | Copenhague | **8**^e	20
1956 | Maison du Caviar | **8**^e	21
1956 | Robert et Louise | **3**^e	-

HOLIDAY MEALS

(Special prix fixe meals offered at major holidays)

ⓩ Ambassadeurs | **8**^e	27
ⓩ Ambroisie | **4**^e	27
Amognes | **11**^e	23
ⓩ Apicius | **8**^e	26
ⓩ Arpège | **7**^e	26
Astor | **8**^e	20
ⓩ Atelier de Joël Robuchon | **7**^e	27
ⓩ Benoît | **4**^e	24
ⓩ Bristol | **8**^e	27
ⓩ Café Les Deux Magots | **6**^e	15
144 Petrossian | **7**^e	22
Chen Soleil d'Est | **15**^e	24
Chiberta | **8**^e	23
ⓩ Cinq | **8**^e	28
ⓩ Coupole | **14**^e	18
Daru | **8**^e	-
Diapason | **18**^e	16
Divellec | **7**^e	23
ⓩ Espadon | **1**^{er}	25

SPECIAL FEATURES

Goumard | 1er   24

🅩 Guy Savoy | 17e   28

Huîtrier | 17e   -

Jardins de Bagatelle | 16e   17

🅩 Jules Verne | 7e   23

🅩 Lapérouse | 6e   21

🅩 Lasserre | 8e   27

🅩 Marée | 8e   25

Maxim's | 8e   20

Montparnasse 25 | 14e   24

Paris | 6e   19

🅩 Pavillon/Gr. Cascade | 16e   22

🅩 Pavillon Ledoyen | 8e   26

🅩 Pierre Gagnaire | 8e   28

Potager du Roy | **Versailles**   22

🅩 Pré Catelan | 16e   26

🅩 Relais Louis XIII | 6e   25

Romantica | **Clichy**   21

Rue Balzac | 8e   18

🅩 Salon d'Hélène | 6e   25

Senderens | 8e   -

Sormani | 17e   24

Table d'Anvers | 9e   21

🅩 Taillevent | 8e   28

Tan Dinh | 7e   22

🅩 Tour d'Argent | 5e   25

Trou Gascon | 12e   24

Wally Le Saharien | 9e   18

HOTEL DINING

Four Seasons George V

　🅩 Cinq | 8e   28

Hôtel Ambassador

　16 Haussmann | 9e   21

Hôtel Amour

　NEW Hôtel Amour | 9e   -

Hôtel Astor

　Astor | 8e   20

Hôtel Balzac

　🅩 Pierre Gagnaire | 8e   28

Hôtel Castille Paris

　Il Cortile | 1er   21

Hôtel Concorde St-Lazare

　Café Terminus | 8e   -

Hôtel Costes

　Costes | 1er   17

Hôtel de Crillon

　🅩 Ambassadeurs | 8e   27

　🅩 Obélisque | 8e   23

Hôtel de la Trémoille

　Senso | 8e   17

Hôtel de Ville

　🅩 Benoît | 4e   24

Hôtel du Louvre

　Brass. du Louvre | 1er   18

Hôtel Edouard VII

　Angl'Opera | 2e   21

Hôtel El Dorado

　Bistrot des Dames | 17e   15

Hôtel Hyatt

　Café M | 8e   16

Hôtel Lancaster

　🅩 Table du Lancaster | 8e   25

Hôtel Le Bristol

　🅩 Bristol | 8e   27

Hôtel Lutétia

　Brass. Lutétia | 6e   17

　Paris | 6e   19

Hôtel Marignan

　Spoon, Food & Wine | 8e   23

Hôtel Meurice

　🅩 Meurice | 1er   26

Hôtel Montalembert

　Montalembert | 7e   17

Hôtel Novotel Tour Eiffel

　Benkay | 15e   23

Hôtel Pershing Hall

　Pershing | 8e   15

Hôtel Plaza-Athénée

　🅩 Alain Ducasse | 8e   28

　Relais Plaza | 8e   22

Hôtel Pont Royal

　🅩 Atelier de Joël Robuchon | 27
　7^e

　🅩 Table de Joël Robuchon | 26
　16^e

Hôtel Prince de Galles

　Jardin des Cygnes | 8e   20

Hôtel Ritz

　🅩 Bar Vendôme | 1er   21

　🅩 Espadon | 1er   25

Hôtel Royal Monceau

　Carpaccio | 8e   22

　Jardin | 8e   22

Hôtel Scribe

　Muses | 9e   -

Hôtel Thoumieux

　Thoumieux | 7e   15

Hôtel Trianon Palace

　🅩 Trois Marches | **Versailles**   26

Hôtel Vernet

　🅩 Elysées | 8e   26

Hôtel Warwick		
W Restaurant | 8ᵉ	–	
Hôtel Westminster		
Céladon | 2ᵉ	24	
InterContinental Le Grand Hôtel		
Café de la Paix | 9ᵉ	19	
Le Méridien Etoile		
Orénoc | 17ᵉ	–	
Le Méridien Montparnasse		
Montparnasse 25 | 14ᵉ	24	
L'Hôtel		
Rest. de l'Hôtel | 6ᵉ	–	
Murano Urban Resort		
Murano | 3ᵉ	17	
Park Hyatt Paris-Vendôme		
Pur'Grill | 2ᵉ	25	
Relais St. Germain Hôtel		
Comptoir du Relais | 6ᵉ	22	
Renaissance Paris Vendôme		
Pinxo | 1ᵉʳ	20	
Sofitel Arc de Triomphe		
Clovis | 8ᵉ	19	
Sofitel Demeure Hôtel Baltimore		
Table du Baltimore | 16ᵉ	–	
Sofitel Le Faubourg		
Café Faubourg | 8ᵉ	17	
Sofitel Le Parc		
Relais du Parc | 16ᵉ	–	
Terrass Hotel		
Diapason | 18ᵉ	16	
Westin Hotel		
NEW First | 1ᵉʳ	–	

JACKET REQUIRED

(* Tie also required)

☑ Alain Ducasse* | 8ᵉ	28	
☑ Ambroisie* | 4ᵉ	27	
☑ Arpège | 7ᵉ	26	
☑ Astrance | 16ᵉ	27	
☑ Carré des Feuillants* | 1ᵉʳ	25	
☑ Cinq | 8ᵉ	28	
☑ Espadon* | 1ᵉʳ	25	
☑ Grand Véfour | 1ᵉʳ	27	
☑ Jules Verne* | 7ᵉ	23	
☑ Lasserre | 8ᵉ	27	
Maxim's* | 8ᵉ	20	
☑ Meurice | 1ᵉʳ	26	
☑ Michel Rostang* | 17ᵉ	27	
☑ Pavillon/Gr. Cascade | 16ᵉ	22	
☑ Pavillon Ledoyen | 8ᵉ	26	

☑ Pré Catelan* | 16ᵉ	26	
Relais Plaza | 8ᵉ	22	
☑ Salon d'Hélène | 6ᵉ	25	
☑ Taillevent* | 8ᵉ	28	
☑ Tour d'Argent* | 5ᵉ	25	

LATE DINING

(Weekday closing hour)

Alcazar | 1 AM | 6ᵉ	17	
Al Dar | 12 AM | multi. loc.	22	
Al Diwan | 1 AM | 8ᵉ	19	
Alsace | 24 hrs. | 8ᵉ	15	
Ami Pierre | 12 AM | 11ᵉ	19	
Anahï | 12 AM | 3ᵉ	22	
Andy Wahloo | 12 AM | 3ᵉ	12	
Arbuci | 12 AM | 6ᵉ	15	
As du Fallafel | 12 AM | 4ᵉ	24	
Asian | 12 AM | 8ᵉ	16	
☑ Atelier de Joël Robuchon | 12 AM | 7ᵉ	27	
Aub. Dab | 2 AM | 16ᵉ	16	
Avenue | 1 AM | 8ᵉ	18	
Bacchantes | 12:30 AM | 9ᵉ	–	
Ballon des Ternes | 12 AM | 17ᵉ	15	
Bar à Huîtres | 2 AM | multi. loc.	18	
Bar des Théâtres | 1 AM | 8ᵉ	13	
Barlotti | 12:30 AM | 1ᵉʳ	15	
Barrio Latino | 12:45 AM | 12ᵉ	11	
Barroco | 12 AM | 6ᵉ	–	
Berkeley | 1 AM | 8ᵉ	12	
Bistro/Deux Théâtres | 12:30 AM | 9ᵉ	15	
Bistro Melrose | 1 AM | 17ᵉ	–	
Bistro St. Ferdinand | 12:30 AM | 17ᵉ	16	
Bistrot Baracane | 12 AM | 4ᵉ	23	
Bistrot de l'Etoile Laur. | 12 AM | 16ᵉ	19	
Bistrot de Paris | 12 AM | 7ᵉ	19	
Bistrot du Peintre | 12 AM | 11ᵉ	16	
NEW Black Calavados | 12 AM | 8ᵉ	–	
Blue Elephant | 12 AM | 11ᵉ	19	
Boeuf Couronné | 12 AM | 19ᵉ	17	
Boeuf sur le Toit | 1 AM | 8ᵉ	16	
☑ Bofinger | 1 AM | 4ᵉ	20	
Bon | 12:30 AM | 16ᵉ	15	
Brass. Balzar | 12 AM | 5ᵉ	18	
Brass. Flo | 12:30 AM | 10ᵉ	17	
Brass. Julien | 1 AM | 10ᵉ	17	
Brass. La Lorraine | 1 AM | 8ᵉ	16	
Brass. L'Européen | 1 AM | 12ᵉ	–	

Murano	12 AM	3e	17
Murat	12 AM	16e	15
Musichall	5 AM	8e	15
New Jawad	12 AM	7e	16
New Nioullaville	12:30 AM	11e	16
Noura	12 AM	multi. loc.	18
Opportun	12 AM	14e	-
Orangerie	12 AM	4e	-
Osteria Ascolani	2 AM	18e	-
Paradis du Fruit	1 AM	multi. loc.	13
Pershing	12 AM	8e	15
Petit Bofinger	varies	4e	16
Petit Marché	12 AM	3e	22
Petit Prince de Paris	12 AM	5e	21
Petit Riche	12:15 AM	9e	16
Petit Zinc	12 AM	6e	20
Pied de Chameau/Al Nour	1 AM	3e	-
Pied de Cochon	24 hrs.	1er	18
Planet Hollywood	1 AM	8e	7
Polidor	12:30 AM	6e	15
Pomponette	12 AM	18e	-
Poule au Pot	5 AM	1er	21
Procope	1 AM	6e	16
Publicis Drugstore	2 AM	8e	12
404	12 AM	3e	21
Renoma Café	varies	8e	-
Rotonde	1 AM	6e	14
Sébillon	12 AM	Neuilly	19
Spicy	12 AM	8e	15
Studio	12:30 AM	4e	-
Suffren	12 AM	15e	14
NEW Tarmac	2 AM	12e	-
Tav. de Maître Kanter	24 hrs.	1er	10
Terminus Nord	1 AM	10e	15
Tong Yen	12:15 AM	8e	20
Tricotin	12 AM	13e	-
Vagenende	1 AM	6e	15
Vaudeville	1 AM	2e	17
Verre Bouteille	varies	17e	-
Viaduc Café	3 AM	12e	12
Village d'Ung/Li Lam	12 AM	8e	-
Vinea Café	12 AM	12e	-
Virgin Café	12 AM	8e	9
Wepler	1 AM	18e	15
Zéphyr	12 AM	20e	-
Zeyer	12:30 AM	14e	15
Zo	12 AM	8e	15

MEET FOR A DRINK

Alcazar	6e	17
Z Angelina	1er	20
Arbuci	6e	15
Autobus Imperial	1er	-
Bar des Théâtres	8e	13
Baron Rouge	12e	19
Bistrot à Vins Mélac	11e	16
Bistrot du Peintre	11e	16
Bistrot Paul Bert	11e	20
NEW Black Calavados	8e	-
Bons Crus	1er	-
Bourguignon du Marais	4e	22
Brass. Balzar	5e	18
Breakfast in America	5e	13
Z Buddha Bar	8e	16
Café Beaubourg	4e	15
Café Burq	18e	-
Café Charbon	11e	11
Café de Flore	6e	15
Café de la Musique	19e	-
Café de l'Esplanade	7e	17
Café de l'Industrie	11e	13
Café du Passage	11e	-
Café la Jatte	Neuilly	14
Café Lenôtre	8e	19
Z Café Les Deux Magots	6e	15
Café Marly	1er	15
Café Ruc	1er	14
Café Very/Dame	multi. loc.	13
Carr's	1er	12
Cave de l'Os à Moëlle	15e	20
Chapeau Melon	19e	-
China Club	12e	16
Cloche des Halles	1er	16
Closerie des Lilas	6e	16
Clown Bar	11e	19
Comptoir	1er	16
Cosi	6e	19
Coude Fou	4e	16
Z Coupole	14e	18
Curieux Spaghetti Bar	4e	-
Dalloyau	multi. loc.	23
Deux Abeilles	7e	18
Dix Vins	15e	16
Dôme	14e	22
Ecluse	multi. loc.	14
Enoteca	4e	22
Etoile	16e	18
Ferme	1er	-
NEW First	1er	-

SPECIAL FEATURES

Fish La Boissonnerie	6ᵉ	21
Fontaines	5ᵉ	18
Fouquet's	8ᵉ	17
Fous d'en Face	4ᵉ	18
Fumoir	1ᵉʳ	15
Gavroche	2ᵉ	21
Grande Armée	16ᵉ	12
Harold	17ᵉ	–
Indiana Café	**multi. loc.**	8
Juvéniles	1ᵉʳ	17
Z Ladurée	**multi. loc.**	22
Legrand Filles et Fils	2ᵉ	–
Lina's	**multi. loc.**	15
Loir dans la Théière	4ᵉ	18
Ma Bourgogne	4ᵉ	17
Mandala Ray	8ᵉ	15
Mauzac	5ᵉ	–
Murano	3ᵉ	17
Musichall	8ᵉ	15
Nemrod	6ᵉ	15
No Stress Café	9ᵉ	–
Oenothèque	9ᵉ	19
Publicis Drugstore	8ᵉ	12
Rest. du Palais Royal	1ᵉʳ	19
River Café	**Issy-les-Moul.**	15
Rubis	1ᵉʳ	17
Sauvignon	7ᵉ	15
Suffren	15ᵉ	14
Viaduc Café	12ᵉ	12
Vinea Café	12ᵉ	–
Vin sur Vin	7ᵉ	21
Virgin Café	8ᵉ	9
Wepler	18ᵉ	15
Willi's Wine Bar	1ᵉʳ	19
Zébra Square	16ᵉ	12
Zo	8ᵉ	15

NO AIR-CONDITIONING

Abadache	17ᵉ	–
NEW Accolade	17ᵉ	–
A et M	16ᵉ	15
Aimant du Sud	13ᵉ	–
Alivi	4ᵉ	17
Alsaco	9ᵉ	18
Z Ami Louis	3ᵉ	26
Ami Pierre	11ᵉ	19
Amognes	11ᵉ	23
Amuse Bouche	14ᵉ	17
Anahuacalli	5ᵉ	21
Z Angelina	1ᵉʳ	20
AOC	5ᵉ	19

Apollo	14ᵉ	14
A Priori Thé	2ᵉ	16
Assiette	14ᵉ	20
Atelier Berger	1ᵉʳ	21
Aub. du Champ de Mars	7ᵉ	23
Aub. Nicolas Flamel	3ᵉ	20
Autour du Mont	15ᵉ	–
Autour du Saumon	**multi. loc.**	–
Babylone	7ᵉ	21
Baratin	20ᵉ	–
Bascou	3ᵉ	22
Biche au Bois	12ᵉ	21
BIOArt	13ᵉ	–
Bistro d'Hubert	15ᵉ	20
Bistrot Baracane	4ᵉ	23
Bistrot d'à Côté	**multi. loc.**	20
Bistrot d'André	15ᵉ	–
Bistrot de l'Université	7ᵉ	15
Bistrot de Marius	8ᵉ	17
Bistrot de Paris	7ᵉ	19
Bistrot des Dames	17ᵉ	15
Bistrot d'Henri	6ᵉ	17
Bistrot Vivienne	2ᵉ	15
Bon Saint Pourçain	6ᵉ	17
Brass. de l'Ile St. Louis	4ᵉ	16
Breakfast in America	5ᵉ	13
Cabane	17ᵉ	–
Ca d'Oro	1ᵉʳ	–
Café Beaubourg	4ᵉ	15
Café Burq	18ᵉ	–
Café Charbon	11ᵉ	11
Café de Mars	7ᵉ	16
Café Le Petit Pont	5ᵉ	24
Café Very/Dame	4ᵉ	13
Cagouille	14ᵉ	21
Cailloux	13ᵉ	16
Caméléon	6ᵉ	–
Cap Seguin	**Boulogne**	–
Carr's	1ᵉʳ	12
Caves Pétrissans	17ᵉ	21
182 Rive Droite	16ᵉ	12
Cerisaie	14ᵉ	24
Chalet de Neuilly	**Neuilly**	–
Chalet des Iles	16ᵉ	15
Chantairelle	5ᵉ	–
Chapeau Melon	19ᵉ	–
Chardenoux	11ᵉ	15
Chaumière en l'Ile	4ᵉ	22
Cherche Midi	6ᵉ	18
NEW Chez Cécile	8ᵉ	–
Chez Françoise	7ᵉ	15

subscribe to zagat.com

Chez Fred	17e	–	
Chez Georges-Maillot	17e	15	
Chez Grisette	18e	–	
Chez la Vieille	1er	22	
Chez Léon	17e	17	
Chez Marcel	6e	21	
Chez Marianne	4e	18	
Chez Michel	10e	23	
Chez Nénesse	3e	19	
Chez Omar	3e	21	
Chez Papinou	Neuilly	–	
Chez Paul	11e	20	
Chez Paul	13e	17	
Chez Pauline	1er	21	
Chez Prune	10e	12	
Chez Ramona	20e	–	
Chez René	5e	21	
NEW Cibus	1er	–	
Cinq Mars	7e	–	
Cloche des Halles	1er	16	
Closerie des Lilas	6e	16	
Clou	17e	–	
Clown Bar	11e	19	
Coco de Mer	5e	22	
Coin des Gourmets	5e	16	
Contre-Allée	14e	24	
Cordonnerie	1er	–	
Cosi	6e	19	
Coupe Gorge	4e	–	
Crus de Bourgogne	2e	–	
Dauphin	1er	23	
Dell Orto	9e	–	
Deux Abeilles	7e	18	
2 Pieces Cuisine	18e	–	
Devèz	8e	14	
Dix Vins	15e	16	
Djakarta	1er	19	
Dôme du Marais	4e	18	
Duc de Richelieu	12e	–	
Durand Dupont	Neuilly	9	
Ecluse	multi. loc.	14	
Entoto	13e	–	
Entracte	18e	–	
Entredgeu	17e	21	
Epi d'Or	1er	21	
Z Epi Dupin	6e	23	
Escargot Montorgueil	1er	18	
Fins Gourmets	7e	21	
Flandrin	16e	13	
Flore en l'Ile	4e	16	
Florimond	7e	24	

Foujita	1er	14	
Fouquet's	8e	17	
Gauloise	15e	16	
Gavroche	2e	21	
Georgette	9e	20	
Gli Angeli	3e	19	
Gorille Blanc	7e	–	
Gourmets des Ternes	8e	19	
Graindorge	17e	22	
Grange Batelière	9e	–	
Guinguette/Neuilly	Neuilly	15	
NEW Hier & Aujourd'hui	17e	–	
Huîtrerie Régis	6e	–	
Il Barone	14e	–	
Il Etait une Oie	17e	17	
Indigo Square	Bagnolet	–	
Jardins de Bagatelle	16e	17	
Jean	9e	19	
Jumeaux	11e	–	
Khun Akorn	11e	19	
Louchebem	1er	14	
Z Lyonnais	2e	22	
Ma Bourgogne	4e	17	
Marius	16e	20	
Martel	10e	16	
Mascotte	18e	–	
Maupertu	7e	20	
Moissonnier	5e	22	
Mon Vieil Ami	4e	24	
Moulin à Vent	5e	22	
Mousson	1er	–	
No Stress Café	9e	–	
Os à Moëlle	15e	23	
Osteria Ascolani	18e	–	
Ourcine	13e	21	
Pasco	7e	–	
Patrick Goldenberg	17e	15	
Paul, Restaurant	1er	19	
Z Pavillon/Gr. Cascade	16e	22	
Pavillon Montsouris	14e	18	
Pères et Filles	6e	12	
Perraudin	5e	16	
Petit Bofinger	17e	16	
Petit Châtelet	5e	19	
Petite Sirène/Copen.	9e	20	
Petit Lutétia	6e	16	
Petit Marché	3e	22	
Petit Marguery	13e	22	
NEW Petit Monsieur	11e	–	
Petit Niçois	7e	19	
Petit Pascal	13e	–	

SPECIAL FEATURES

Petit Poucet | Levallois — 16
Pétrelle | 9e — -
Pharamond | 1er — 18
Pitchi Poï | 4e — -
Pomponette | 18e — -
Ⓩ Pré Catelan | 16e — 26
NEW Pré Salé | 1er — -
Procope | 6e — 16
P'tit Troquet | 7e — 23
Pure Café | 11e — -
Réconfort | 3e — 17
Relais de Venise | 17e — 22
Ⓩ Réminet | 5e — 25
Rendez-vous/Chauff. | 18e — -
Repaire de Cartouche | 11e — 19
Rest. du Marché | 15e — -
Rest. du Palais Royal | 1er — 19
Rest. GR5 | 16e — 15
River Café | Issy-les-Moul. — 15
Robert et Louise | 3e — -
Roi du Pot-au-Feu | 9e — 15
Romantica | Clichy — 21
Rughetta | 18e — 17
Sale e Pepe | 18e — -
Sardegna a Tavola | 12e — 22
Sauvignon | 7e — 15
Saveurs de Claude | 6e — -
Scheffer | 16e — 15
Sept Quinze | 15e — 18
Sinago | 9e — -
Soleil | St-Ouen — 17
Sot l'y Laisse | 11e — -
Square | 18e — -
Square Trousseau | 12e — 18
Strapontins | 10e — -
Tastevin | Maisons-Laff. — 23
Tav. Henri IV | 1er — 17
Temps au Temps | 11e — 26
Temps des Cerises | 13e — 18
Terrasse Mirabeau | 16e — -
Terroir | 13e — -
Thanksgiving | 4e — 15
Timbre | 6e — 22
Tokyo Eat | 16e — 12
Tonnelle Saintongeaise | Neuilly — -
Tournesol | 16e — 13
Ⓩ Train Bleu | 12e — 19
Triporteur | 15e — -
Troquet | 15e — 23
NEW Truc Café | 18e — -
Truffe Noire | Neuilly — 20

Tsukizi | 6e — -
Uitr | 15e — -
Vaudeville | 2e — 17
Verre Volé | 10e — 14
Vieille Fontaine Rôtiss. | Maisons-Laff. — 20
Vieux Chêne | 11e — -
Vin et Marée | 16e — 17
Wadja | 6e — 21
Waknine | 16e — 14
Willi's Wine Bar | 1er — 19
Zéphyr | 20e — -
Zinc-Zinc | Neuilly — 14
Zygomates | 12e — -

NONSMOKING

(As of January 2008 smoking will be banned in all Paris restaurants)

Absinthe | 1er — 19
Aida | 7e — -
NEW Alain Bourgade | 16e — -
Ⓩ Allard | 6e — 22
Altitude 95 | 7e — 16
Amici Miei | 11e — 19
Amognes | 11e — 23
Amuse Bouche | 14e — 17
Anahï | 3e — 22
Anahuacalli | 5e — 21
Ⓩ Angelina | 1er — 20
Ⓩ Angle du Faubourg | 8e — 23
Apollo | 14e — 14
A Priori Thé | 2e — 16
Ardoise | 1er — 23
As du Fallafel | 4e — 24
Assiette | 14e — 20
Ⓩ Astrance | 16e — 27
Ⓩ Atelier de Joël Robuchon | 7e — 27
Aub. Bressane | 7e — 17
Aub. de la Reine Blanche | 4e — 20
Aub. du Champ de Mars | 7e — 23
Auguste | 7e — 19
Autour du Saumon | 15e — -
Ⓩ Avant Goût | 13e — 25
Ballon et Coquillages | 17e — -
Baptiste | 17e — 19
Bar à Huîtres | multi. loc. — 18
Bartolo | 6e — 18
Ⓩ Bar Vendôme | 1er — 21
Beato | 7e — 18
BE Boulangépicier | multi. loc. — 22
Bistral | 17e — 23
Bistro/Deux Théâtres | 9e — 15

Bistrot d'à Côté | **multi. loc.**	20
NEW Black Calavados | **8e**	-
Boeuf Couronné | **19e**	17
Bouchons/Fr. Cl./Colbert | **8e**	19
Z Bouquinistes | **6e**	21
Brass. Julien | **10e**	17
Breakfast in America | **multi. loc.**	13
Z Bristol | **8e**	27
Cabane | **17e**	-
Café Charbon | **11e**	11
Café d'Angel | **17e**	19
Café Ruc | **1er**	14
Café Terminus | **8e**	-
Cailloux | **13e**	16
NEW Cantine de Quentin | **10e**	-
Cap Vernet | **8e**	18
Casa Alcalde | **15e**	15
Casa Tina | **16e**	12
Cave Gourmande | **19e**	24
Cerisaie | **14e**	24
Chalet de Neuilly | **Neuilly**	-
Chaumière en l'Île | **4e**	22
Chez Gégène | **Joinville**	-
Chez Grisette | **18e**	-
Chez Paul | **13e**	17
Chez Prune | **10e**	12
Chez Ramulaud | **11e**	22
Cinq Mars | **7e**	-
Clou | **17e**	-
Clown Bar | **11e**	19
Coffee Parisien | **multi. loc.**	15
Comptoir du Relais | **6e**	22
Cottage Marcadet | **18e**	21
Coude Fou | **4e**	16
Couleurs de Vigne | **15e**	-
Z Coupole | **14e**	18
Cuisine | **7e**	21
Dalloyau | **8e**	23
Da Rosa | **6e**	19
Delicabar | **7e**	15
Deux Canards | **10e**	18
Domaine de Lintillac | **multi. loc.**	-
Ecaille de la Fontaine | **2e**	-
Editeurs | **6e**	15
Entredgeu | **17e**	21
Enzo | **14e**	-
Z Epi Dupin | **6e**	23
Fables de La Fontaine | **7e**	21
Famille | **18e**	16
NEW Ferrandaise | **6e**	-
NEW First | **1er**	-
Fish La Boissonnerie | **6e**	21
Flandrin | **16e**	13
Florimond | **7e**	24
Fogón | **6e**	20
Foujita | **1er**	14
Gamin de Paris | **4e**	18
Gaya | **7e**	22
Gli Angeli | **3e**	19
Gorille Blanc | **7e**	-
Gourmand | **6e**	23
Grille St-Germain | **6e**	17
Hippopotamus | **15e**	10
Z Hiramatsu | **16e**	27
NEW Hôtel Amour | **9e**	-
Huîtrerie Régis | **6e**	-
Indiana Café | **multi. loc.**	8
Indochine | **1er**	16
Z Isami | **4e**	27
Z Jacques Cagna | **6e**	26
Jardin des Cygnes | **8e**	20
Joséphine/Dumonet | **6e**	23
Juvéniles | **1er**	17
Kai | **1er**	-
Kaïten | **8e**	19
Khun Akorn | **11e**	19
Kifune | **17e**	-
Kim Anh | **15e**	21
Lac-Hong | **16e**	19
Z Ladurée | **multi. loc.**	22
Laurent | **8e**	24
Lavinia | **1er**	17
Legrand Filles et Fils | **2e**	-
Lei | **7e**	18
Léon/Bruxelles | **9e**	15
Louis Vin | **5e**	-
Lozère | **6e**	18
Luna | **8e**	24
Ma Bourgogne | **4e**	17
Maison du Caviar | **8e**	21
Mandala Ray | **8e**	15
Marc Annibal de Coconnas | **4e**	17
Mariage Frères | **multi. loc.**	21
Marius et Janette | **8e**	21
Matsuri | **multi. loc.**	12
Maxim's | **8e**	20
Z Meurice | **1er**	26
Mirama | **5e**	16
Mont Liban | **17e**	-
Moulin de la Galette | **18e**	-

SPECIAL FEATURES

Mousson | 1er	–	
Muscade | 1er	–	
Noura | 16e	18	
NEW Ombres | 7e	–	
Oulette | 12e	21	
Paradis du Fruit | **multi. loc.**	13	
Paris Seize | 16e	14	
Passiflore | 16e	23	
Petite Sirène/Copen. | 9e	20	
Petites Sorcières | 14e	–	
Petite Tour | 16e	16	
Petit Niçois | 7e	19	
Petit Pontoise | 5e	23	
Petit Rétro | 16e	20	
Z Pierre Gagnaire | 8e	28	
Ploum | 10e	–	
NEW Pré Salé | 1er	–	
Pré Verre | 5e	23	
P'tit Troquet | 7e	23	
Pure Café | 11e	–	
Quai Ouest | **St-Cloud**	17	
Radis Roses | 9e	–	
Ravi | 7e	24	
Réconfort | 3e	17	
Z Relais/l'Entrecôte | 8e	23	
Relais Plaza | 8e	22	
Z Réminet | 5e	25	
Renoma Café | 8e	–	
Rest. GR5 | 17e	15	
Rest. Manufacture | **Issy-les-Moul.**	19	
Robe et le Palais | 1er	–	
Roi du Pot-au-Feu | 9e	15	
Rubis | 1er	17	
Sale e Pepe | 18e	–	
Saudade | 1er	–	
Scheffer | 16e	15	
NEW Sensing | 6e	–	
7ème Sud | 16e	17	
Severo | 14e	22	
Sinago | 9e	–	
Sora Lena | 17e	–	
Sot l'y Laisse | 11e	–	
Spicy | 8e	15	
NEW Spring | 9e	–	
Stéphane Martin | 15e	24	
Suave | 13e	–	
Z Table de Joël Robuchon | 16e	26	
Z Table du Lancaster | 8e	25	
Taïra | 17e	23	
Tav. du Sgt. Recruteur | 4e	14	

Tav. Henri IV | 1er	17
Temps au Temps | 11e	26
Terminus Nord | 10e	15
Thanksgiving | 4e	15
Thiou/Petit Thiou | 8e	18
Timbre | 6e	22
Toi | 8e	–
NEW 35° Ouest | 7e	–
Tsukizi | 6e	–
NEW Unico | 11e	–
Vieux Bistro | 4e	20
Villa Corse | 16e	16
Vin dans les voiles | 16e	–
Vin des Pyrenees | 4e	16
Vin et Marée | **multi. loc.**	17
NEW 21 | 6e	–
Vivres | 9e	–
Wepler | 18e	15
Willi's Wine Bar | 1er	19
Yugaraj | 6e	19
Z Ze Kitchen Galerie | 6e	23
Zéphyr | 20e	–
Zinc-Zinc | **Neuilly**	14

OPEN SUNDAY

Aida | 7e	–
Alcazar | 6e	17
Al Dar | **multi. loc.**	22
Al Diwan | 8e	19
Alivi | 4e	17
Z Allard | 6e	22
Al Mounia | 16e	16
Alsace | 8e	15
Altitude 95 | 7e	16
Ambassade/Auvergne | 3e	19
Z Ami Louis | 3e	26
Amuse Bouche | 14e	17
Anahï | 3e	22
Anahuacalli | 5e	21
Z Angelina | 1er	20
Angl'Opera | 2e	21
Apollo | 14e	14
Appart' | 8e	15
A Priori Thé | 2e	16
Arbuci | 6e	15
Ardoise | 1er	23
As du Fallafel | 4e	24
Asian | 8e	16
Assiette | 14e	20
Astier | 11e	22
Z Atelier de Joël Robuchon | 7e	27

subscribe to zagat.com

Atelier Maître Albert	5ᵉ	21
Atlas	5ᵉ	18
Aub. Aveyronnaise	12ᵉ	–
Aub. Bressane	7ᵉ	17
Aub. Dab	16ᵉ	16
Aub. de la Reine Blanche	4ᵉ	20
Aub. du Clou	9ᵉ	13
Autour du Saumon	multi. loc.	–
Avenue	8ᵉ	18
Azabu	6ᵉ	20
Baie d'Ha Long	16ᵉ	–
Ballon des Ternes	17ᵉ	15
Ballon et Coquillages	17ᵉ	–
Bamboche	7ᵉ	18
Bar à Huîtres	multi. loc.	18
Bar des Théâtres	8ᵉ	13
Barlotti	1ᵉʳ	15
Baron Rouge	12ᵉ	19
Barrio Latino	12ᵉ	11
Barroco	6ᵉ	–
Bartolo	6ᵉ	18
☑ Bar Vendôme	1ᵉʳ	21
Basilic	7ᵉ	14
Beaujolais d'Auteuil	16ᵉ	15
BE Boulangépicier	8ᵉ	22
Bel Canto	4ᵉ	15
Benkay	15ᵉ	23
☑ Benoît	4ᵉ	24
Berkeley	8ᵉ	12
Bistro 121	15ᵉ	20
Bistro de Breteuil	7ᵉ	18
Bistro de l'Olivier	8ᵉ	20
Bistro/Deux Théâtres	9ᵉ	15
Bistro d'Hubert	15ᵉ	20
Bistro Melrose	17ᵉ	–
Bistro St. Ferdinand	17ᵉ	16
Bistrot d'à Côté	17ᵉ	20
Bistrot d'André	15ᵉ	–
Bistrot de l'Etoile Niel	17ᵉ	19
Bistrot de Marius	8ᵉ	17
Bistrot des Dames	17ᵉ	15
Bistrot des Vignes	16ᵉ	13
Bistrot d'Henri	6ᵉ	17
Bistrot du Cap	15ᵉ	–
Bistrot du Dôme	multi. loc.	19
Bistrot du Peintre	11ᵉ	16
Blue Elephant	11ᵉ	19
Boeuf Couronné	19ᵉ	17
Boeuf sur le Toit	8ᵉ	16
☑ Bofinger	4ᵉ	20
Bon	16ᵉ	15
Boucherie Roulière	6ᵉ	–
Bouchons/Fr. Cl./Colbert	5ᵉ	19
Bouillon Racine	6ᵉ	14
Bound	8ᵉ	–
Brass. Balzar	5ᵉ	18
Brass. de l'Ile St. Louis	4ᵉ	16
Brass. du Louvre	1ᵉʳ	18
Brass. Flo	10ᵉ	17
Brass. Julien	10ᵉ	17
Brass. La Lorraine	8ᵉ	16
Brass. L'Européen	12ᵉ	–
☑ Brass. Lipp	6ᵉ	17
Brass. Lutétia	6ᵉ	17
Brass. Mollard	8ᵉ	16
Breakfast in America	5ᵉ	13
☑ Bristol	8ᵉ	27
☑ Buddha Bar	8ᵉ	16
Buffalo Grill	multi. loc.	9
Butte Chaillot	16ᵉ	20
Ca d'Oro	1ᵉʳ	–
Café Beaubourg	4ᵉ	15
Café Charbon	11ᵉ	11
Café Constant	7ᵉ	22
Café de Flore	6ᵉ	15
Café de la Musique	19ᵉ	–
Café de la Paix	9ᵉ	19
Café de l'Esplanade	7ᵉ	17
Café de l'Industrie	11ᵉ	13
Café du Commerce	15ᵉ	13
Café du Passage	11ᵉ	–
Café Etienne Marcel	2ᵉ	13
Café Faubourg	8ᵉ	17
Café Fusion	13ᵉ	–
Café la Jatte	Neuilly	14
Café Lenôtre	8ᵉ	19
Café Le Petit Pont	5ᵉ	24
☑ Café Les Deux Magots	6ᵉ	15
Café M	8ᵉ	16
Café Marly	1ᵉʳ	15
Café Ruc	1ᵉʳ	14
Café Terminus	8ᵉ	–
Café Very/Dame	multi. loc.	13
Cagouille	14ᵉ	21
Camille	3ᵉ	20
NEW Cantine de Quentin	10ᵉ	–
NEW Carmine	7ᵉ	–
Carpaccio	8ᵉ	22
Carr's	1ᵉʳ	12
Casa Alcalde	15ᵉ	15
Casa Bini	6ᵉ	20
Casa Tina	16ᵉ	12

SPECIAL FEATURES

Restaurant	Rating
Caveau du Palais	1er	21
Cave de l'Os à Moëlle	15e	20
Cazaudehore	St-Germain-Laye	20
182 Rive Droite	16e	12
Chai 33	12e	12
Chalet de Neuilly	Neuilly	-
Chalet des Iles	16e	15
Chardenoux	11e	15
Charlot - Roi des Coq.	9e	15
Charpentiers	6e	18
Chartier	9e	13
Chaumière en l'Ille	4e	22
Cherche Midi	6e	18
Chez André	8e	20
Chez Clément	multi. loc.	12
Chez Francis	8e	14
Chez Françoise	7e	15
Chez Gégène	Joinville	-
Chez Georges-Maillot	17e	15
Chez Janou	3e	20
Chez Jenny	3e	17
Chez Livio	Neuilly	13
Chez Ly	17e	-
Chez Maître Paul	6e	20
Chez Marianne	4e	18
Chez Omar	3e	21
Chez Papa	multi. loc.	18
Chez Papinou	Neuilly	-
Chez Paul	11e	20
Chez Paul	13e	17
Chez Prune	10e	12
Chez Ramona	20e	-
Chieng Mai	5e	17
Chien qui Fume	1er	17
China Club	12e	16
Christine	6e	23
Ⓩ Cinq	8e	28
Closerie des Lilas	6e	16
Clown Bar	11e	19
Coffee Parisien	multi. loc.	15
Coin des Gourmets	5e	16
Comptoir	1er	16
Comptoir du Relais	6e	22
Congrès Maillot	17e	14
Cosi	6e	19
Costes	1er	17
Coude Fou	4e	16
Coupe-Chou	5e	20
Coupe Gorge	4e	-
Ⓩ Coupole	14e	18
Crêperie de Josselin	14e	21
Cuisine	7e	21
Curieux Spaghetti Bar	4e	-
Dalloyau	multi. loc.	23
Da Rosa	6e	19
Dauphin	1er	23
Davé	1er	19
Délices d'Aphrodite	5e	18
Délices de Szechuen	7e	16
Dessirier	17e	21
Devèz	8e	14
Diamantaires	9e	-
Diep	8e	20
Djakarta	1er	19
Dôme	14e	22
Doobie's	8e	12
Drouant	2e	-
Durand Dupont	Neuilly	9
Ecluse	multi. loc.	14
Editeurs	6e	15
Elysées Hong Kong	16e	-
Enoteca	4e	22
Entracte	18e	-
Escale du Liban	4e	-
Escargot Montorgueil	1er	18
Ⓩ Espadon	1er	25
Etoile Marocaine	8e	18
Fables de La Fontaine	7e	21
Fakhr el Dine	8e	17
Fellini	1er	19
Ferme	1er	-
Fermette Marbeuf	8e	18
Filo Delle Stagioni	3e	-
Findi	8e	17
Finzi	8e	20
NEW First	1er	-
Fish La Boissonnerie	6e	21
Flandrin	16e	13
Flora Danica	8e	18
Flore en l'Ile	4e	16
Fogón	6e	20
Ⓩ Fontaine de Mars	7e	21
Fontanarosa	15e	19
Foujita	1er	14
Fouquet's	8e	17
Fumoir	1er	15
Gallopin	2e	15
Gamin de Paris	4e	18
Gare	16e	14
Garnier	8e	22
Gauloise	15e	16

☒ Georges | 4e	18
Giulio Rebellato | 16e	20
Gli Angeli | 3e	19
Goumard | 1er	24
Grand Café | 9e	15
Grand Colbert | 2e	18
Grande Armée | 16e	12
Grand Louvre | 1er	18
Grange Batelière | 9e	-
Grille St-Germain | 6e	17
Guinguette/Neuilly | Neuilly	15
Harold | 17e	-
Harumi | 15e	-
Higuma | 1er	18
Hippopotamus | multi. loc.	10
NEW Hôtel Amour | 9e	-
Huîtrerie Régis | 6e	-
Huîtrier | 17e	-
Ile | Issy-les-Moul.	16
Ilot Vache | 4e	21
Indiana Café | multi. loc.	8
Jardin des Cygnes | 8e	20
Jardins de Bagatelle | 16e	17
Jarrasse | Neuilly	-
Joe Allen | 1er	14
☒ Jules Verne | 7e	23
Kai | 1er	-
Khun Akorn | 11e	19
Kim Anh | 15e	21
Kiosque | 16e	14
Kodo | 4e	-
Kong | 1er	14
☒ Ladurée | multi. loc.	22
Languedoc | 5e	19
Lao Siam | 19e	23
Lao Tseu | 7e	18
Lei | 7e	18
Léon/Bruxelles | multi. loc.	15
Libre Sens | 8e	16
Liza | 2e	-
Loir dans la Théière | 4e	18
Lô Sushi | 8e	14
Louis Vin | 5e	-
Lozère | 6e	18
Ma Bourgogne | 4e	17
Maharajah | 5e	16
Main d'Or | 11e	21
Maison Blanche | 8e	19
Maison du Caviar | 8e	21
Marc Annibal de Coconnas | 4e	17
Mariage Frères | multi. loc.	21
Marius et Janette | 8e	21
Market | 8e	20
Marty | 5e	17
Mascotte | 18e	-
Matsuri | multi. loc.	12
Meating | 17e	19
Méditerranée | 6e	19
Mirama | 5e	16
Monsieur Lapin | 14e	20
Montalembert | 7e	17
Mont Liban | 17e	-
Mon Vieil Ami | 4e	24
NEW Mori Venice Bar | 2e	-
Moulin de la Galette | 18e	-
Murano | 3e	17
Murat | 16e	15
Muscade | 1er	-
Musichall | 8e	15
New Jawad | 7e	16
New Nioullaville | 11e	16
Noces de Jeannette | 2e	-
Nos Ancêtres/Gaulois | 4e	10
No Stress Café | 9e	-
Noura | multi. loc.	18
Nouveau Village Tao | 13e	14
☒ Obélisque | 8e	23
Oeillade | 7e	15
Oenothèque | 9e	-
NEW Ombres | 7e	-
Orangerie | 4e	-
Osteria Ascolani | 18e	-
NEW Ozu | 16e	-
Pamphlet | 3e	23
Paradis du Fruit | multi. loc.	13
Paradis Thai | 13e	18
Parc aux Cerfs | 6e	17
Pasco | 7e	-
Passy Mandarin | multi. loc.	16
Patrick Goldenberg | 17e	15
Paul, Restaurant | 1er	19
☒ Pavillon/Gr. Cascade | 16e	22
Pavillon Montsouris | 14e	18
Pearl | 13e	-
Père Claude | 15e	18
Pères et Filles | 6e	12
Pershing | 8e	15
Petit Bofinger | multi. loc.	16
Petite Chaise | 7e	19
Petite Cour | 6e	18
Petit Lutétia | 6e	16
Petit Marché | 3e	22

SPECIAL FEATURES

Petit Niçois | 7e	19
Petit Pontoise | 5e	23
Petit Poucet | **Levallois**	16
Petit Prince de Paris | 5e	21
Petit Zinc | 6e	20
Pharamond | 1er	18
Pied de Chameau/Al Nour | 3e	-
Pied de Cochon | 1er	18
⊠ Pierre Gagnaire | 8e	28
Pinxo | 1er	20
Pitchi Poï | 4e	-
Pizzeria d'Auteuil | 16e	17
Planet Hollywood | 8e	7
Polichinelle Cafe | 11e	-
Polidor | 6e	15
Poule au Pot | 1er	21
Procope | 6e	16
Publicis Drugstore | 8e	12
Pure Café | 11e	-
Pur'Grill | 2e	25
Quai | 7e	-
Quai Ouest | **St-Cloud**	17
404 | 3e	21
Ragueneau | 1er	-
Réconfort | 3e	17
Refectoire | 11e	-
⊠ Relais/l'Entrecôte | **multi. loc.**	23
Relais de Venise | 17e	22
Relais Plaza | 8e	22
⊠ Réminet | 5e	25
Renoma Café | 8e	-
Rest. du Musée d'Orsay | 7e	16
Reuan Thai | 11e	-
Riad | **Neuilly**	-
River Café | **Issy-les-Moul.**	15
Rôtiss. du Beaujolais | 5e	22
Rotonde | 6e	14
Rouge St-Honoré | 1er	15
Rughetta | 18e	17
Samiin | 7e	-
Sauvignon | 7e	15
Scoop | 1er	-
Sébillon | **Neuilly**	19
Senderens | 8e	-
7ème Sud | **multi. loc.**	17
Severo | 14e	22
Soleil | **St-Ouen**	17
Spicy | 8e	15
Stella | 16e	16

Strapontins | 10e	-
Studio | 4e	-
Suffren | 15e	14
Suite | 8e	12
⊠ Table de Joël Robuchon | 16e	26
⊠ Table du Lancaster | 8e	25
Table Lauriston | 16e	17
NEW Tarmac | 12e	-
Tastevin | **Maisons-Laff.**	23
Tav. de Maître Kanter | 1er	10
Tav. du Sgt. Recruteur | 4e	14
Télégraphe | 7e	20
Terminus Nord | 10e	15
Terres de Truffes | 8e	-
Thanksgiving | 4e	15
Thiou/Petit Thiou | 8e	18
Timgad | 17e	22
Titi Parisien | 7e	16
Toi | 8e	-
Tokyo Eat | 16e	12
Tong Yen | 8e	20
⊠ Tour d'Argent | 5e	25
Tournesol | 16e	13
⊠ Train Bleu | 12e	19
Tricotin | 13e	-
NEW Truc Café | 18e	-
Trumilou | 4e	19
Tsé-Yang | 16e	21
Uitr | 15e	-
Vagenende | 6e	15
Vaudeville | 2e	17
Verre Bouteille | 17e	-
Verre Volé | 10e	14
Viaduc Café | 12e	12
Vieille Fontaine Rôtiss. | **Maisons-Laff.**	20
Vieux Bistro | 4e	20
Village d'Ung/Li Lam | 8e	-
Vin des Pyrenees | 4e	16
Vinea Café | 12e	-
Vin et Marée | **multi. loc.**	17
Virgin Café | 8e	9
Wepler | 18e	15
Wok Cooking | 11e	-
Yen | 6e	19
Yugaraj | 6e	19
Zébra Square | 16e	12
Zéphyr | 20e	-
Zeyer | 14e	15

(G=garden; P=patio; S=sidewalk; T=terrace)

Absinthe | S, T | 1er	19
A et M | S | 16^e	15
Aimant du Sud | S, T | 13^e	–
NEW Alain Bourgade | G | 16^e	–
☑ Alain Ducasse | P | 8^e	28
Al Dar | S, T | multi. loc.	22
Alivi | T | 4^e	17
Alsace | S | 8^e	15
Amici Miei | S | 11^e	19
Amognes | S | 11^e	23
Ampère | S | 17^e	15
AOC | T | 5^e	19
A Priori Thé | P | 2^e	16
Arbuci | S | 6^e	15
Asian | S | 8^e	16
Astier | S | 11^e	22
Atlas | S | 5^e	18
Aub. Aveyronnaise | P, S, T | 12^e	–
Aub. Dab | S | 16^e	16
Aub. du Clou | S, T | 9^e	13
Aub. Etchégorry | S | 13^e	20
Avenue | T | 8^e	18
Baie d'Ha Long | T | 16^e	–
Ballon des Ternes | S, T | 17^e	15
Barlotti | P, S | 1er	15
Bartolo | S, T | 6^e	18
☑ Bar Vendôme | P | 1er	21
Basilic | G, T | 7^e	14
Beaujolais d'Auteuil | S | 16^e	15
BE Boulangépicier | S | 8^e	22
Bel Canto | T | 14^e	15
Berkeley | T | 8^e	12
BIOArt | T | 13^e	–
Bistro de Breteuil | T | 7^e	18
Bistro d'Hubert | T | 15^e	20
Bistro du 17ème | S | 17^e	16
Bistro Melrose | S | 17^e	–
Bistrot à Vins Mélac | S | 11^e	16
Bistrot d'à Côté | S, T | multi. loc.	20
Bistrot de l'Etoile Niel | S, T | 17^e	19
Bistrot de Marius | S | 8^e	17
Bistrot des Dames | G | 17^e	15
Bistrot du Cap | T | 15^e	–
Bistrot du Peintre | T | 11^e	16
Bistrot Vivienne | T | 2^e	15
Bocconi | S | 8^e	22
Bon Accueil | S | 7^e	24
Bon Saint Pourçain | S | 6^e	17
Bouchons/Fr. Cl./Colbert | S | 8^e	19
Bourguignon du Marais | T | 4^e	22
Brass. de l'Ile St. Louis | T | 4^e	16
Brass. du Louvre | T | 1er	18
☑ Bristol | G | 8^e	27
Buisson Ardent | S | 5^e	20
Café Beaubourg | T | 4^e	15
Café Charbon | S | 11^e	11
Café de Flore | S, T | 6^e	15
Café de la Musique | T | 19^e	–
Café de la Paix | S | 9^e	19
Café de l'Esplanade | S | 7^e	17
Café de l'Industrie | S | 11^e	13
Café de Mars | S | 7^e	16
Café du Passage | S | 11^e	–
Café Etienne Marcel | S | 2^e	13
Café Fusion | S | 13^e	–
Café Guitry | T | 9^e	–
Café la Jatte | G, T | Neuilly	14
Café Lenôtre | G, P | 8^e	19
Café Le Petit Pont | T | 5^e	24
☑ Café Les Deux Magots | G, T | 6^e	15
Café Marly | T | 1er	15
Café Ruc | S | 1er	14
Café Very/Dame | T | multi. loc.	13
Cagouille | T | 14^e	21
Cailloux | S | 13^e	16
Camille | S | 3^e	20
Cap Seguin | T | Boulogne	–
Cap Vernet | T | 8^e	18
Carpaccio | T | 8^e	22
Casa Alcalde | S | 15^e	15
Casa Tina | S | 16^e	12
Caves Pétrissans | T | 17^e	21
Cazaudehore | G, T | St-Germain-Laye	20
182 Rive Droite | T | 16^e	12
Chai 33 | T | 12^e	12
Chalet des Iles | G, T | 16^e	15
Chantairelle | G | 5^e	–
Charpentiers | S | 6^e	18
Chaumière en l'Ile | S | 4^e	22
Cherche Midi | S | 6^e	18
Chez André | S | 8^e	20
Chez Francis | S | 8^e	14
Chez Gégène | S, T | Joinville	–
Chez Gérard | S | Neuilly	19
Chez Janou | T | 3^e	20

Restaurant	Rating
Chez Léna et Mimile | T | 5e	–
Chez Les Anges | S | 7e	–
Chez Livio | T | Neuilly	13
Chez Ly | S | 17e	–
Chez Marcel | S | 6e	21
Chez Marianne | S, T | 4e	18
Chez Michel | S | 10e	23
Chez Omar | T | 3e	21
Chez Papa | S | multi. loc.	18
Chez Paul | S | 11e	20
Chez Paul | S | 13e	17
Chez Prune | S | 10e	12
Chez Ramulaud | S | 11e	22
Chez René | T | 5e	21
Chez Savy | S | 8e	21
Chez Vong | T | 1er	20
Chien qui Fume | S, T | 1er	17
Cigale Recamier | T | 7e	22
Z Cinq | T | 8e	28
Cloche des Halles | S, T | 1er	16
Clos des Gourmets | T | 7e	24
Closerie des Lilas | T | 6e	16
Clown Bar | S | 11e	19
Comptoir | S | 1er	16
Contre-Allée | S | 14e	24
Copenhague | T | 8e	20
Cordonnerie | S | 1er	–
Costes | G, P | 1er	17
Coupe-Chou | T | 5e	20
Crus de Bourgogne | S | 2e	–
Dalloyau | S, T | multi. loc.	23
Da Mimmo | S | 10e	15
Da Rosa | T | 6e	19
Daru | S | 8e	–
Dauphin | S | 1er	23
Délices d'Aphrodite | S | 5e	18
Délices de Szechuen | S, T | 7e	16
Deux Abeilles | S | 7e	18
Devèz | S | 8e	14
Diapason | T | 18e	16
Duc de Richelieu | T | 12e	–
Durand Dupont | G | Neuilly	9
Ebauchoir | S | 12e	–
Editeurs | S | 6e	15
El Mansour | S | 8e	20
Entracte | T | 18e	–
Z Epi Dupin | S | 6e	23
Z Espadon | G, T | 1er	25
Eugène | S | 8e	–
Fables de La Fontaine | T | 7e	21
Fakhr el Dine | S | 8e	17
Findi | S | 8e	17
Fins Gourmets | S | 7e	21
Flandrin | S, T | 16e	13
Fleurs de Thym | S | 4e	–
Flora Danica | G, T | 8e	18
Flore en l'Ile | S, T | 4e	16
Florimond | S | 7e	24
Z Fontaine de Mars | S, T | 7e	21
Fontaine Gaillon | T | 2e	19
Fontaines | S, T | 5e	18
Fontanarosa | T | 15e	19
Fouquet's | S, T | 8e	17
Fous d'en Face | S | 4e	18
Fumoir | S | 1er	15
Gallopin | S | 2e	15
Gare | G, T | 16e	14
Gauloise | S, T | 15e	16
Z Georges | T | 4e	18
Gitane | S | 15e	14
Gorille Blanc | S | 7e	–
Gourmets des Ternes | S | 8e	19
Grand Café | S | 9e	15
Grande Armée | S | 16e	12
Grille St-Germain | S | 6e	17
Guinguette/Neuilly | T | Neuilly	15
Guirlande de Julie | S, T | 3e	–
Hangar | S | 3e	20
Harold | S | 17e	–
Hippopotamus | T | 6e	10
Il Cortile | P | 1er	21
Ile | G, T | Issy-les-Moul.	16
Indigo Square | G | Bagnolet	–
Issé | S | 1er	18
Jardin | S, T | 8e	22
Jardin des Cygnes | T | 8e	20
Jardins de Bagatelle | G, T | 16e	17
Jarrasse | S, T | Neuilly	–
Je Thé . . . Me | S, T | 15e	22
Joe Allen | S, T | 1er	14
Joséphine/Dumonet | S | 6e	23
Kaïten | S, T | 8e	19
Khun Akorn | T | 11e	19
Kim Anh | T | 15e	21
Kiosque | S, T | 16e	14
Laurent | G, T | 8e	24
Legrand Filles et Fils | P | 2e	–
Lei | S | 7e	18
Lescure | S, T | 1er	16
Les Saveurs de Flora | S | 8e	22
Ma Bourgogne | S, T | 4e	17
Main d'Or | S | 11e	21

SPECIAL FEATURES

Table d'Anvers | S, T | 9ᵉ — 21
Tastevin | G | **Maisons-Laff.** — 23
Télégraphe | T | 7ᵉ — 20
Temps au Temps | S, T | 11ᵉ — 26
Terrasse Mirabeau | T | 16ᵉ — –
Terroir | S | 13ᵉ — –
Thiou/Petit Thiou | S | 7ᵉ — 18
Titi Parisien | S | 7ᵉ — 16
Tokyo Eat | T | 16ᵉ — 12
Tonnelle Saintongeaise | G | **Neuilly** — –
Tournesol | S | 16ᵉ — 13
Triporteur | S | 15ᵉ — –
☑ Trois Marches | G | **Versailles** — 26
Troquet | S | 15ᵉ — 23
Trumilou | S | 4ᵉ — 19
Vagenende | S, T | 6ᵉ — 15
Vaudeville | S | 2ᵉ — 17
Viaduc Café | S, T | 12ᵉ — 12
Vieille Fontaine Rôtiss. | G | **Maisons-Laff.** — 20
Vieux Bistro | S | 4ᵉ — 20
Vieux Chêne | S | 11ᵉ — –
Vinea Café | T | 12ᵉ — –
20 de Bellechasse | S | 7ᵉ — 17
Wepler | S | 18ᵉ — 15
Zébra Square | S, T | 16ᵉ — 12
Zéphyr | T | 20ᵉ — –
Zo | S | 8ᵉ — 15

PARKING

(V=valet, *=validated)

A et M | V | 16ᵉ — 15
☑ Alain Ducasse | V | 8ᵉ — 28
Al Dar | V | 5ᵉ — 22
Al Diwan | V | 8ᵉ — 19
☑ Ambassadeurs | V | 8ᵉ — 27
☑ Ambroisie | V | 4ᵉ — 27
☑ Apicius | V | 8ᵉ — 26
NEW Arome | V | 8ᵉ — –
Asian | V | 8ᵉ — 16
Astor | V | 8ᵉ — 20
Aub. Bressane | V | 7ᵉ — 17
Avenue | V | 8ᵉ — 18
Barlotti | V | 1ᵉʳ — 15
Barrio Latino | V | 12ᵉ — 11
☑ Bar Vendôme | V | 1ᵉʳ — 21
Bastide Odéon | V | 6ᵉ — 20
Bath's | V | 17ᵉ — –
Bel Canto | V | 14ᵉ — 15
Benkay | V | 15ᵉ — 23

Berkeley | V | 8ᵉ — 12
BIOArt | V | 13ᵉ — –
Bistro 121 | V | 15ᵉ — 20
Bistrot d'à Côté | V | **multi. loc.** — 20
Bistrot de l'Etoile Niel | V | 17ᵉ — 19
Bistrot de Marius | V | 8ᵉ — 17
Bistrot de Paris | V | 7ᵉ — 19
Blue Elephant* | 11ᵉ — 19
Bocconi | V | 8ᵉ — 22
Boeuf Couronné | V | 19ᵉ — 17
Boeuf sur le Toit | V | 8ᵉ — 16
Bon | V | 16ᵉ — 15
Bouchons/Fr. Cl./Colbert | V | 8ᵉ — 19
☑ Bouquinistes | V | 6ᵉ — 21
Brass. Flo | V | 10ᵉ — 17
Brass. Julien | V | 10ᵉ — 17
Brass. La Lorraine | V | 8ᵉ — 16
☑ Bristol | V | 8ᵉ — 27
☑ Buddha Bar | V | 8ᵉ — 16
Café de l'Esplanade | V | 7ᵉ — 17
Café du Commerce | V | 15ᵉ — 13
Café Faubourg | V | 8ᵉ — 17
Café la Jatte | V | **Neuilly** — 14
Café Lenôtre | V | 8ᵉ — 19
Café M | V | 8ᵉ — 16
Café Terminus | V | 8ᵉ — –
Caffé Minotti | V | 7ᵉ — 23
Cap Seguin | V | **Boulogne** — –
Carpaccio | V | 8ᵉ — 22
☑ Carré des Feuillants | V | 1ᵉʳ — 25
Caves Pétrissans | V | 17ᵉ — 21
☑ Caviar Kaspia | V | 8ᵉ — 26
Céladon | V | 2ᵉ — 24
144 Petrossian | V | 7ᵉ — 22
Chalet des Iles | V | 16ᵉ — 15
Chen Soleil d'Est | V | 15ᵉ — 24
Chez Françoise | V | 7ᵉ — 15
Chez Fred | V | 17ᵉ — –
Chez Georges-Maillot | V | 17ᵉ — 15
Chez Jenny | V | 3ᵉ — 17
Chez Les Anges | V | 7ᵉ — –
Chez Livio | V | **Neuilly** — 13
Chez Vong | V | 1ᵉʳ — 20
Chiberta | V | 8ᵉ — 23
Closerie des Lilas | V | 6ᵉ — 16
Clou | V | 17ᵉ — –
Clovis | V | 8ᵉ — 19
Comte de Gascogne | V | **Boulogne** — 25
Congrès Maillot | V | 17ᵉ — 14
Copenhague | V | 8ᵉ — 20

Costes | V | 1er	17
NEW Cou de la Girafe | V | 8^e	-
Z Cristal Room | V | 16^e	19
Dalloyau | V | 8^e	23
Delicabar | V | 7^e	15
Dessirier | V | 17^e	21
Diep | V | 8^e	20
Divellec | V | 7^e	23
Z 1728 | V | 8^e	16
Doobie's | V | 8^e	12
Drouant | V | 2^e	-
Duc | V | 14^e	24
El Mansour | V | 8^e	20
Z Elysées | V | 8^e	26
Escargot Montorgueil | V | 1er	18
Z Espadon | V | 1er	25
Etoile | V | 16^e	18
Findi | V | 8^e	17
NEW First | V | 1er	-
Flandrin | V | 16^e	13
Flora Danica | V | 8^e	18
Fontaine Gaillon | V | 2^e	19
Fouquet's | V | 8^e	17
Gare | V | 16^e	14
Garnier | V | 8^e	22
Z Georges | V | 4^e	18
Z Gérard Besson | V | 1er	25
Goumard | V | 1er	24
Grand Colbert | V | 2^e	18
Grande Armée | V | 16^e	12
Z Grand Véfour | V | 1er	27
Grand Venise | V | 15^e	22
Z Guy Savoy | V | 17^e	28
Z Hélène Darroze | V | 6^e	23
Huîtrier | V | 17^e	-
Il Cortile | V | 1er	21
Ile | V | **Issy-les-Moul.**	16
Z Jacques Cagna | V | 6^e	26
Jardin | V | 8^e	22
Jardin des Cygnes | V | 8^e	20
Jarrasse | V | **Neuilly**	-
Z Jules Verne | V | 7^e	23
Kiosque | V | 16^e	14
Kong | V | 1er	14
Z Lapérouse | V | 6^e	21
Z Lasserre | V | 8^e	27
Laurent | V | 8^e	24
Lei | V | 7^e	18
Liza | V | 2^e	-
Z Lyonnais | V | 2^e	22
Maison Blanche | V | 8^e	19

Maison du Caviar | V | 8^e	21
Maison Prunier | V | 16^e	22
Mandala Ray | V | 8^e	15
Z Marée | V | 8^e	25
Marius | V | 16^e	20
Marius et Janette | V | 8^e	21
Market | V | 8^e	20
Marty | V | 5^e	17
Mathusalem | V | 16^e	14
Maxan | V | 8^e	-
Maxim's | V | 8^e	20
Meating | V | 17^e	19
Méditerranée | V | 6^e	19
Z Meurice | V | 1er	26
Z Michel Rostang | V | 17^e	27
Montalembert | V | 7^e	17
Montparnasse 25 | V | 14^e	24
NEW Mori Venice Bar | V | 2^e	-
Moulin à Vent | V | 5^e	22
Murano | V | 3^e	17
Murat | V | 16^e	15
Muses | V | 9^e	-
Musichall | V | 8^e	15
Z Obélisque | V | 8^e	23
Orangerie | V | 4^e	-
NEW Ozu | V | 16^e	-
Paris | V | 6^e	19
Pasco* | 7^e	-
Passiflore | V | 16^e	23
Paul Chêne | V | 16^e	22
Z Pavillon/Gr. Cascade | V | 16^e	22
Z Pavillon Ledoyen | V | 8^e	26
Pavillon Montsouris | V | 14^e	18
Pershing | V | 8^e	15
Petit Pergolèse | V | 16^e	15
Petit Poucet | V | **Levallois**	16
Pétrus | V | 17^e	-
Z Pierre Gagnaire | V | 8^e	28
Pinxo | V | 1er	20
Z Pré Catelan | V | 16^e	26
Pur'Grill | V | 2^e	25
Quai Ouest | V | **St-Cloud**	17
R. | V | 15^e	17
Rech | V | 17^e	14
Z Relais d'Auteuil | V | 16^e	26
Relais Plaza | V | 8^e	22
River Café | V | **Issy-les-Moul.**	15
Romantica | V | **Clichy**	21
Rôtiss. d'en Face | V | 6^e	22
Rue Balzac | V | 8^e	18

SPECIAL FEATURES

Salon d'Hélène	V	6e	25
NEW San	V	3e	–
Sébillon	V	Neuilly	19
16 Haussmann	V	9e	21
Senderens	V	8e	–
NEW Sensing	V	6e	–
Senso	V	8e	17
6 New York	V	16e	20
NEW Soleil	V	7e	–
Sora Lena	V	17e	–
Sormani	V	17e	24
Spoon, Food & Wine	V	8e	23
Stella	V	16e	16
Sud	V	17e	15
Suite	V	8e	12
NEW Table de Babette	V	16e	–
Z Table de Joël Robuchon	V	16e	26
Table d'Hédiard	V	8e	22
Table du Baltimore	V	16e	–
Z Table du Lancaster	V	8e	25
Z Taillevent	V	8e	28
Tang	V	16e	17
Télégraphe	V	7e	20
Terrasse Mirabeau	V	16e	–
Thiou/Petit Thiou	V	7e	18
Timgad	V	17e	22
Toi	V	8e	–
Tong Yen	V	8e	20
Z Tour d'Argent	V	5e	25
Z Trois Marches	V	Versailles	26
NEW Truc Café	V	18e	–
Truffe Noire	V	Neuilly	20
Villa Corse	V	15e	16
Village d'Ung/Li Lam	V	8e	–
Vin et Marée	V	multi. loc.	17
W Restaurant	V	8e	–
Zébra Square	V	16e	12

PEOPLE-WATCHING

Absinthe	1er	19
Z Alain Ducasse	8e	28
Z Ami Louis	3e	26
Anahï	3e	22
Z Angle du Faubourg	8e	23
Z Arpège	7e	26
Astor	8e	20
Z Astrance	16e	27
Z Atelier de Joël Robuchon	7e	27
Avenue	8e	18
Barlotti	1er	15

Z Benoît	4e	24
Berkeley	8e	12
NEW Black Calavados	8e	–
Brass. Balzar	5e	18
Z Brass. Lipp	6e	17
Z Bristol	8e	27
Café Beaubourg	4e	15
Café de Flore	6e	15
Café de l'Esplanade	7e	17
Café Etienne Marcel	2e	13
Café Guitry	9e	–
Z Café Les Deux Magots	6e	15
Caffè Minotti	7e	23
144 Petrossian	7e	22
NEW Chateaubriand	11e	–
Chez Les Anges	7e	–
Chez Omar	3e	21
Z Cinq	8e	28
Cinq Mars	7e	–
Copenhague	8e	20
Costes	1er	17
Divellec	7e	23
Dôme	14e	22
Drouant	2e	–
Duc	14e	24
Z Elysées	8e	26
Z Epi Dupin	6e	23
Z Espadon	1er	25
Ferme St-Simon	7e	22
Flandrin	16e	13
Fouquet's	8e	17
Gare	16e	14
Gauloise	15e	16
Z Georges	4e	18
Grande Armée	16e	12
Z Grand Véfour	1er	27
Z Guy Savoy	17e	28
Z Hélène Darroze	6e	23
Il Cortile	1er	21
Jarrasse	Neuilly	–
Joséphine/Dumonet	6e	23
Kong	1er	14
Z Lasserre	8e	27
Maison Blanche	8e	19
Maison de l'Amér. Latine	7e	17
Maison Prunier	16e	22
Market	8e	20
Méditerranée	6e	19
Murano	3e	17
Musichall	8e	15
Natacha	14e	21

NEW Ombres | 7e	7
Orangerie | 4e	–
⊠ Pavillon Ledoyen | 8e	26
Pétrelle | 9e	–
⊠ Pierre Gagnaire | 8e	28
⊠ Pré Catelan | 16e	26
Publicis Drugstore | 8e	12
Relais Plaza | 8e	22
Renoma Café | 8e	–
Rest. de l'Hôtel | 6e	–
⊠ Salon d'Hélène | 6e	25
Senderens | 8e	–
Senso | 8e	17
6 New York | 16e	20
Sormani | 17e	24
Spoon, Food & Wine | 8e	23
Square Trousseau | 12e	18
Stresa | 8e	22
⊠ Table de Joël Robuchon | 16e	26
⊠ Table du Lancaster | 8e	25
⊠ Taillevent | 8e	28
Tan Dinh | 7e	22
Terrasse Mirabeau | 16e	–
Thiou/Petit Thiou | 7e	18
Tong Yen | 8e	20
⊠ Tour d'Argent | 5e	25
Voltaire | 7e	22

POWER SCENES

⊠ Alain Ducasse | 8e	28
⊠ Ambassadeurs | 8e	27
⊠ Ambroisie | 4e	27
⊠ Apicius | 8e	26
⊠ Arpège | 7e	26
Assiette | 14e	20
⊠ Atelier de Joël Robuchon | 7e	27
Aub. Bressane | 7e	17
Bar des Théâtres | 8e	13
Bastide Odéon | 6e	20
Beato | 7e	18
⊠ Benoît | 4e	24
Bistrot de l'Etoile Laur. | 16e	19
Bistrot de l'Etoile Niel | 17e	19
Bistrot de l'Université | 7e	15
Bistrot de Marius | 8e	17
Bistrot de Paris | 7e	19
Bistrot d'Henri | 6e	17
Bon Saint Pourçain | 6e	17
Brass. Balzar | 5e	18
⊠ Brass. Lipp | 6e	17
⊠ Bristol | 8e	27

Café de Flore | 6e	15
Café Faubourg | 8e	17
Caffè Minotti | 7e	23
Cagouille | 14e	21
Cap Vernet | 8e	18
Carpaccio | 8e	22
⊠ Carré des Feuillants | 1er	25
Caves Pétrissans | 17e	21
⊠ Caviar Kaspia | 8e	26
Cazaudehore | St-Germain-Laye	20
Céladon | 2e	24
Chen Soleil d'Est | 15e	24
Cherche Midi | 6e	18
Chez Les Anges | 7e	–
Chiberta | 8e	23
Cigale Recamier | 7e	22
Clos des Gourmets | 7e	24
Closerie des Lilas | 6e	16
Comte de Gascogne | Boulogne	25
Copenhague | 8e	20
Costes | 1er	17
⊠ Cristal Room | 16e	19
Dessirier | 17e	21
Divellec | 7e	23
Dôme | 14e	22
Duc | 14e	24
⊠ Elysées | 8e	26
⊠ Espadon | 1er	25
Etoile | 16e	18
Ferme St-Simon | 7e	22
Flandrin | 16e	13
Fouquet's | 8e	17
Gare | 16e	14
Gaya | 7e	22
⊠ Georges | 4e	18
Goumard | 1er	24
Grande Armée | 16e	12
⊠ Grand Véfour | 1er	27
⊠ Guy Savoy | 17e	28
⊠ Hiramatsu | 16e	27
Issé | 1er	18
Jardin | 8e	22
Jarrasse | Neuilly	–
Joséphine/Dumonet | 6e	23
⊠ Jules Verne | 7e	23
⊠ Ladurée | 8e	22
⊠ Lasserre | 8e	27
Laurent | 8e	24
Luna | 8e	24
Maison Blanche | 8e	19

SPECIAL FEATURES

Maison Prunier | 16e	22
☑ Marée | 8e	25
Marius | 16e	20
Marius et Janette | 8e	21
Market | 8e	20
Marlotte | 6e	20
Marty | 5e	17
Mathusalem | 16e	14
Meating | 17e	19
☑ Meurice | 1er	26
☑ Michel Rostang | 17e	27
Montalembert | 7e	17
Montparnasse 25 | 14e	24
NEW Mori Venice Bar | 2e	-
Natacha | 14e	21
☑ Obélisque | 8e	23
Oenothèque | 9e	-
Oulette | 12e	21
Paris | 6e	19
Paul Chêne | 16e	22
☑ Pavillon/Gr. Cascade | 16e	22
☑ Pavillon Ledoyen | 8e	26
Pavillon Montsouris | 14e	18
Perron | 7e	22
Petit Colombier | 17e	17
Petite Tour | 16e	16
Petit Marguery | 13e	22
Petit Poucet | Levallois	16
Petit Rétro | 16e	20
Pétrus | 17e	-
Pichet de Paris | 8e	20
Pierre au Palais Royal | 1er	16
☑ Pierre Gagnaire | 8e	28
Port Alma | 16e	20
☑ Pré Catelan | 16e	26
☑ Relais d'Auteuil | 16e	26
Relais Plaza | 8e	22
Sébillon | Neuilly	19
Senderens | 8e	-
Sormani | 17e	24
☑ Stella Maris | 8e	25
Stresa | 8e	22
Table d'Anvers | 9e	21
☑ Table de Joël Robuchon | 16e	26
☑ Table du Lancaster | 8e	25
☑ Taillevent | 8e	28
Tan Dinh | 7e	22
Tante Marguerite | 7e	21
Terrasse Mirabeau | 16e	-
Tong Yen | 8e	20
Tonnelle Saintongeaise | Neuilly	-

☑ Tour d'Argent | 5e	25
Tsé-Yang | 16e	21
Vieux Bistro | 4e	20
Violon d'Ingres | 7e	24
Voltaire | 7e	22

QUICK BITES

Altitude 95 | 7e	16
☑ Angelina | 1er	20
A Priori Thé | 2e	16
As du Fallafel | 4e	24
Bar des Théâtres | 8e	13
Baron Rouge | 12e	19
Barrio Latino | 12e	11
BE Boulangépicier | 8e	22
BIOArt | 13e	-
Bistrot à Vins Mélac | 11e	16
Bons Crus | 1er	-
NEW Brass. Printemps | 9e	-
Breakfast in America | 5e	13
☑ Buddha Bar | 8e	16
Buffalo Grill | multi. loc.	9
Café Beaubourg | 4e	15
Café de Flore | 6e	15
Café du Commerce | 15e	13
☑ Café Les Deux Magots | 6e	15
Café Marly | 1er	15
Café Very/Dame | multi. loc.	13
Cave de l'Os à Moëlle | 15e	20
Chez Marianne | 4e	18
Chez Papa | multi. loc.	18
Cloche des Halles | 1er	16
Clown Bar | 11e	19
Coffee Parisien | multi. loc.	15
Congrès Maillot | 17e	14
Cosi | 6e	19
Crêperie de Josselin | 14e	21
Dalloyau | multi. loc.	23
Da Rosa | 6e	19
Duc de Richelieu | 12e	-
Ecluse | multi. loc.	14
Emporio Armani | 6e	18
Escale du Liban | 4e	-
Ferme | 1er	-
Fous d'en Face | 4e	18
Fumoir | 1er	15
Garnier | 8e	22
Harold | 17e	-
Indiana Café | multi. loc.	8
Je Thé . . . Me | 15e	22
Joe Allen | 1er	14

Juvéniles | **1ᵉʳ**	17
Léon/Bruxelles | **multi. loc.**	15
Lina's | **multi. loc.**	15
Loir dans la Théière | **4ᵉ**	18
Lô Sushi | **8ᵉ**	14
Ma Bourgogne | **4ᵉ**	17
Maison du Caviar | **8ᵉ**	21
Mariage Frères | **multi. loc.**	21
Mauzac | **5ᵉ**	–
Mesturet | **2ᵉ**	–
Mirama | **5ᵉ**	16
Murat | **16ᵉ**	15
Nemrod | **6ᵉ**	15
Noura | **multi. loc.**	18
Papilles | **5ᵉ**	22
Paradis du Fruit | **5ᵉ**	13
Petite Sirène/Copen. | **9ᵉ**	20
Pinxo | **1ᵉʳ**	20
Press Café | **2ᵉ**	–
Publicis Drugstore | **8ᵉ**	12
Ragueneau | **1ᵉʳ**	–
Rest. du Musée d'Orsay | **7ᵉ**	16
Rubis | **1ᵉʳ**	17
Sauvignon | **7ᵉ**	15
Scoop | **1ᵉʳ**	–
Table d'Hédiard | **8ᵉ**	22
Tav. Henri IV | **1ᵉʳ**	17
Tsukizi | **6ᵉ**	–
Viaduc Café | **12ᵉ**	12
Vinea Café | **12ᵉ**	–
Vin sur Vin | **7ᵉ**	21
Virgin Café | **8ᵉ**	9
Wok Cooking | **11ᵉ**	–

QUIET CONVERSATION

Aiguière | **11ᵉ**	–
Aimant du Sud | **13ᵉ**	–
Alivi | **4ᵉ**	17
⌧ Allard | **6ᵉ**	22
Allobroges | **20ᵉ**	20
Ambassade/Auvergne | **3ᵉ**	19
Ami Marcel | **15ᵉ**	21
Amognes | **11ᵉ**	23
Ampère | **17ᵉ**	15
Amuse Bouche | **14ᵉ**	17
Angl'Opera | **2ᵉ**	21
A Priori Thé | **2ᵉ**	16
Assiette | **14ᵉ**	20
⌧ Astrance | **16ᵉ**	27
Atelier Berger | **1ᵉʳ**	21
⌧ Atelier de Joël Robuchon | **7ᵉ**	27

Aub. du Clou | **9ᵉ**	13
Aub. Pyrénées Cévennes | **11ᵉ**	21
Bamboche | **7ᵉ**	18
Basilic | **7ᵉ**	14
Beato | **7ᵉ**	18
Bellini | **16ᵉ**	18
⌧ Benoît | **4ᵉ**	24
Bistro d'Hubert | **15ᵉ**	20
Bistrot d'à Côté | **multi. loc.**	20
Bistrot d'Henri | **6ᵉ**	17
Bistrot du Peintre | **11ᵉ**	16
Boeuf sur le Toit | **8ᵉ**	16
Bon Saint Pourçain | **6ᵉ**	17
Bouillon Racine | **6ᵉ**	14
⌧ Bouquinistes | **6ᵉ**	21
Brass. Flo | **10ᵉ**	17
Brass. Julien | **10ᵉ**	17
⌧ Brass. Lipp | **6ᵉ**	17
Brass. Mollard | **8ᵉ**	16
Buisson Ardent | **5ᵉ**	20
Butte Chaillot | **16ᵉ**	20
Cabane | **17ᵉ**	–
Ca d'Oro | **1ᵉʳ**	–
Café Charbon | **11ᵉ**	11
Café de l'Industrie | **11ᵉ**	13
Café du Passage | **11ᵉ**	–
Café Faubourg | **8ᵉ**	17
Café Lenôtre | **8ᵉ**	19
⌧ Café Les Deux Magots | **6ᵉ**	15
Café M | **8ᵉ**	16
Café Marly | **1ᵉʳ**	15
Caffè Minotti | **7ᵉ**	23
Caméléon | **6ᵉ**	–
Camélia | **Bougival**	–
Cap Vernet | **8ᵉ**	18
Carpaccio | **8ᵉ**	22
Cartes Postales | **1ᵉʳ**	19
Casa Olympe | **9ᵉ**	23
Cave Gourmande | **19ᵉ**	24
⌧ Caviar Kaspia | **8ᵉ**	26
144 Petrossian | **7ᵉ**	22
Chardenoux | **11ᵉ**	15
Charpentiers | **6ᵉ**	18
Chez Les Anges | **7ᵉ**	–
Chez Maître Paul | **6ᵉ**	20
Chez Pauline | **1ᵉʳ**	21
Chez Ramulaud | **11ᵉ**	22
Chez René | **5ᵉ**	21
Chiberta | **8ᵉ**	23
Cigale Recamier | **7ᵉ**	22
Clos des Gourmets | **7ᵉ**	24

Closerie des Lilas	6e	16	Marc Annibal de Coconnas	4e	17
Copenhague	8e	20	☑ Marée	8e	25
Costes	1er	17	Mariage Frères	**multi. loc.**	21
Coupe-Chou	5e	20	Marlotte	6e	20
☑ Coupole	14e	18	Marty	5e	17
Crus de Bourgogne	2e	–	Maupertu	7e	20
Cuisine	7e	21	Maxan	8e	–
Da Rosa	6e	19	Meating	17e	19
Daru	8e	–	Méditerranée	6e	19
Dauphin	1er	23	Montalembert	7e	17
Délices d'Aphrodite	5e	18	Moulin à Vent	5e	22
Dessirier	17e	21	Moulin de la Galette	18e	–
Diapason	18e	16	Murano	3e	17
Dix Vins	15e	16	Muscade	1er	–
Djakarta	1er	19	No Stress Café	9e	–
Ecaille de la Fontaine	2e	–	☑ Obélisque	8e	23
El Mansour	8e	20	Orangerie	4e	–
Entoto	13e	–	Orénoc	17e	–
Entracte	18e	–	Ormes	7e	24
Epi d'Or	1er	21	Oulette	12e	21
Erawan	15e	20	Pamphlet	3e	23
Escargot Montorgueil	1er	18	Pasco	7e	–
Fins Gourmets	7e	21	Pères et Filles	6e	12
Flora Danica	8e	18	Petit Colombier	17e	17
Flore en l'Ile	4e	16	Petite Chaise	7e	19
☑ Fontaine de Mars	7e	21	Petite Sirène/Copen.	9e	20
Fontanarosa	15e	19	Petit Lutétia	6e	16
Gallopin	2e	15	Petit Marguery	13e	22
Garnier	8e	22	Petit Prince de Paris	5e	21
Gaya	7e	22	Petit Rétro	16e	20
Georgette	9e	20	Pierre au Palais Royal	1er	16
☑ Gérard Besson	1er	25	☑ Pierre Gagnaire	8e	28
Gli Angeli	3e	19	Point Bar	1er	21
Goumard	1er	24	Polidor	6e	15
Graindorge	17e	22	Potager du Roy	**Versailles**	22
Guirlande de Julie	3e	–	Poulbot Gourmet	18e	–
Huîtrier	17e	–	P'tit Troquet	7e	23
Il Cortile	1er	21	Repaire de Cartouche	11e	19
☑ Isami	4e	27	Rest. de l'Hôtel	6e	–
Jean	9e	19	Rest. du Marché	15e	–
Joséphine/Dumonet	6e	23	Rest. du Palais Royal	1er	19
☑ Jules Verne	7e	23	Roi du Pot-au-Feu	9e	15
Jumeaux	11e	–	Rue Balzac	8e	18
Kiosque	16e	14	Sarladais	8e	–
☑ Ladurée	**multi. loc.**	22	Saudade	1er	–
☑ Lapérouse	6e	21	Sébillon	**Neuilly**	19
Legrand Filles et Fils	2e	–	16 Haussmann	9e	21
Macéo	1er	21	Sologne	12e	–
Magnolias	**Perreux**	22	Sot l'y Laisse	11e	–
Maison Blanche	8e	19	☑ Soufflé	1er	22
Mansouria	11e	19	☑ Stella Maris	8e	25

Stresa | 8ᵉ	22
☑ Table du Lancaster | 8ᵉ	25
Taïra | 17ᵉ	23
Tan Dinh | 7ᵉ	22
Tante Louise | 8ᵉ	22
Tête Ailleurs | 4ᵉ	–
Thiou/Petit Thiou | 7ᵉ	18
Titi Parisien | 7ᵉ	16
Trou Gascon | 12ᵉ	24
Tsé-Yang | 16ᵉ	21
Viaduc Café | 12ᵉ	12
Vieux Bistro | 4ᵉ	20
Vin dans les voiles | 16ᵉ	–
Vin sur Vin | 7ᵉ	21

ROMANTIC PLACES

☑ Alain Ducasse | 8ᵉ	28
☑ Allard | 6ᵉ	22
☑ Ambassadeurs | 8ᵉ	27
☑ Ambroisie | 4ᵉ	27
Amognes | 11ᵉ	23
☑ Arpège | 7ᵉ	26
Astor | 8ᵉ	20
☑ Astrance | 16ᵉ	27
Bamboche | 7ᵉ	18
Blue Elephant | 11ᵉ	19
Bouillon Racine | 6ᵉ	14
☑ Bouquinistes | 6ᵉ	21
Brass. Flo | 10ᵉ	17
Brass. Julien | 10ᵉ	17
☑ Bristol | 8ᵉ	27
Buisson Ardent | 5ᵉ	20
Café de Flore | 6ᵉ	15
Café Lenôtre | 8ᵉ	19
☑ Café Les Deux Magots | 6ᵉ	15
Café Marly | 1ᵉʳ	15
Casa Olympe | 9ᵉ	23
☑ Caviar Kaspia | 8ᵉ	26
144 Petrossian | 7ᵉ	22
Chalet des Iles | 16ᵉ	15
Chardenoux | 11ᵉ	15
Chez Pauline | 1ᵉʳ	21
China Club | 12ᵉ	16
Closerie des Lilas | 6ᵉ	16
Copenhague | 8ᵉ	20
Costes | 1ᵉʳ	17
Coupe-Chou | 5ᵉ	20
☑ Coupole | 14ᵉ	18
☑ Cristal Room | 16ᵉ	19
Crus de Bourgogne | 2ᵉ	–
Délices d'Aphrodite | 5ᵉ	18

Dôme | 14ᵉ	22
El Mansour | 8ᵉ	20
☑ Elysées | 8ᵉ	26
Epi d'Or | 1ᵉʳ	21
☑ Espadon | 1ᵉʳ	25
Fakhr el Dine | multi. loc.	17
NEW First | 1ᵉʳ	–
Flora Danica | 8ᵉ	18
☑ Fontaine de Mars | 7ᵉ	21
Gavroche | 2ᵉ	21
☑ Georges | 4ᵉ	18
☑ Grand Véfour | 1ᵉʳ	27
Guirlande de Julie | 3ᵉ	–
☑ Guy Savoy | 17ᵉ	28
Il Cortile | 1ᵉʳ	21
☑ Jacques Cagna | 6ᵉ	26
Jardin | 8ᵉ	22
Jardins de Bagatelle | 16ᵉ	17
Joséphine/Dumonet | 6ᵉ	23
☑ Jules Verne | 7ᵉ	23
☑ Ladurée | multi. loc.	22
☑ Lapérouse | 6ᵉ	21
☑ Lasserre | 8ᵉ	27
Laurent | 8ᵉ	24
Ma Bourgogne | 4ᵉ	17
Macéo | 1ᵉʳ	21
Maison Blanche | 8ᵉ	19
Maison de l'Amér. Latine | 7ᵉ	17
Mandala Ray | 8ᵉ	15
Mansouria | 11ᵉ	19
Marc Annibal de Coconnas | 4ᵉ	17
Marty | 5ᵉ	17
Maxim's | 8ᵉ	20
Méditerranée | 6ᵉ	19
☑ Meurice | 1ᵉʳ	26
Moulin de la Galette | 18ᵉ	–
Muscade | 1ᵉʳ	–
Orangerie | 4ᵉ	–
Paul, Restaurant | 1ᵉʳ	19
☑ Pavillon/Gr. Cascade | 16ᵉ	22
☑ Pavillon Ledoyen | 8ᵉ	26
Pavillon Montsouris | 14ᵉ	18
Petit Prince de Paris | 5ᵉ	21
Potager du Roy | Versailles	22
Poulbot Gourmet | 18ᵉ	–
☑ Pré Catelan | 16ᵉ	26
☑ Relais Louis XIII | 6ᵉ	25
Rest. de l'Hôtel | 6ᵉ	–
Romantica | Clichy	21
Rughetta | 18ᵉ	17
Sormani | 17ᵉ	24

SPECIAL FEATURES

Square Trousseau | **12ᵉ**	18
🔲 Stella Maris | **8ᵉ**	25
Tan Dinh | **7ᵉ**	22
Tête Ailleurs | **4ᵉ**	–
Timgad | **17ᵉ**	22
🔲 Tour d'Argent | **5ᵉ**	25
🔲 Train Bleu | **12ᵉ**	19
🔲 Trois Marches | **Versailles**	26
Trou Gascon | **12ᵉ**	24
NEW Versance | **2ᵉ**	–

SINGLES SCENES

Absinthe | **1ᵉʳ**	19
A et M | **16ᵉ**	15
Alsace | **8ᵉ**	15
Alsaco | **9ᵉ**	18
Amici Miei | **11ᵉ**	19
🔲 Angle du Faubourg | **8ᵉ**	23
Apollo | **14ᵉ**	14
Astor | **8ᵉ**	20
Aub. du Clou | **9ᵉ**	13
Autobus Imperial | **1ᵉʳ**	–
Bar des Théâtres | **8ᵉ**	13
Barlotti | **1ᵉʳ**	15
Baron Rouge | **12ᵉ**	19
Barrio Latino | **12ᵉ**	11
Berkeley | **8ᵉ**	12
Bistro/Deux Théâtres | **9ᵉ**	15
Bistrot à Vins Mélac | **11ᵉ**	16
Bistrot d'à Côté | **17ᵉ**	20
NEW Black Calavados | **8ᵉ**	–
Bon | **16ᵉ**	15
Brass. Balzar | **5ᵉ**	18
🔲 Buddha Bar | **8ᵉ**	16
Café Beaubourg | **4ᵉ**	15
Café Burq | **18ᵉ**	–
Café de Flore | **6ᵉ**	15
Café de la Paix | **9ᵉ**	19
Café de l'Esplanade | **7ᵉ**	17
Café du Passage | **11ᵉ**	–
Café Etienne Marcel | **2ᵉ**	13
Café la Jatte | **Neuilly**	14
Café Lenôtre | **8ᵉ**	19
🔲 Café Les Deux Magots | **6ᵉ**	15
Café M | **8ᵉ**	16
Café Marly | **1ᵉʳ**	15
Café Ruc | **1ᵉʳ**	14
Carr's | **1ᵉʳ**	12
Cave de l'Os à Moëlle | **15ᵉ**	20
182 Rive Droite | **16ᵉ**	12
NEW Chateaubriand | **11ᵉ**	–

Cherche Midi | **6ᵉ**	18
Chez Gégène | **Joinville**	–
China Club | **12ᵉ**	16
Cinq Mars | **7ᵉ**	–
Closerie des Lilas | **6ᵉ**	16
Clown Bar | **11ᵉ**	19
Comédiens | **9ᵉ**	–
Costes | **1ᵉʳ**	17
Curieux Spaghetti Bar | **4ᵉ**	–
Delicabar | **7ᵉ**	15
Emporio Armani | **6ᵉ**	18
Enoteca | **4ᵉ**	22
Etoile | **16ᵉ**	18
Fumoir | **1ᵉʳ**	15
Grille St-Germain | **6ᵉ**	17
Joe Allen | **1ᵉʳ**	14
Kiosque | **16ᵉ**	14
Kong | **1ᵉʳ**	14
Loir dans la Théière | **4ᵉ**	18
Lô Sushi | **8ᵉ**	14
Mandala Ray | **8ᵉ**	15
Murano | **3ᵉ**	17
Murat | **16ᵉ**	15
Musichall | **8ᵉ**	15
Natacha | **14ᵉ**	21
Pinxo | **1ᵉʳ**	20
Press Café | **2ᵉ**	–
Rest. de l'Hôtel | **6ᵉ**	–
Rubis | **1ᵉʳ**	17
Sauvignon | **7ᵉ**	15
Vinea Café | **12ᵉ**	–
Zo | **8ᵉ**	15

SLEEPERS

(Good to excellent food, but little known)

Affriolé | **7ᵉ**	21
Al Dar | **multi. loc.**	22
Allobroges | **20ᵉ**	20
Ami Marcel | **15ᵉ**	21
Amognes | **11ᵉ**	23
Anahï | **3ᵉ**	22
Anahuacalli | **5ᵉ**	21
Angl'Opera | **2ᵉ**	21
Assiette | **14ᵉ**	20
Astier | **11ᵉ**	22
Astor | **8ᵉ**	20
Atelier Berger | **1ᵉʳ**	21
Aub. de la Reine Blanche | **4ᵉ**	20
Aub. du Champ de Mars | **7ᵉ**	23
Aub. Etchégorry | **13ᵉ**	20

Aub. Nicolas Flamel	3ᵉ	20	Chez Savy	8ᵉ	21
Aub. Pyrénées Cévennes	11ᵉ	21	Chez Vincent	19ᵉ	22
☑ Avant Goût	13ᵉ	25	Chez Vong	1ᵉʳ	20
Azabu	6ᵉ	20	Chiberta	8ᵉ	23
Baan-Boran	1ᵉʳ	21	Coco de Mer	5ᵉ	22
Banyan	15ᵉ	25	Comptoir du Relais	6ᵉ	22
Bascou	3ᵉ	22	Comte de Gascogne	Boulogne	25
BE Boulangépicier	multi. loc.	22	Contre-Allée	14ᵉ	24
Benkay	15ᵉ	23	Copenhague	8ᵉ	20
Beurre Noisette	15ᵉ	21	Cottage Marcadet	18ᵉ	21
Biche au Bois	12ᵉ	21	Crêperie de Josselin	14ᵉ	21
Bistral	17ᵉ	23	Cuisine	7ᵉ	21
Bistro 121	15ᵉ	20	Dauphin	1ᵉʳ	23
Bistro de l'Olivier	8ᵉ	20	Dessirier	17ᵉ	21
Bistro d'Hubert	15ᵉ	20	Dominique Bouchet	8ᵉ	24
Bistrot Baracane	4ᵉ	23	Duc	14ᵉ	24
Bistrot d'à Côté	multi. loc.	20	El Mansour	8ᵉ	20
Bistrot du Sommelier	8ᵉ	20	El Palenque	5ᵉ	20
Bistrot Papillon	9ᵉ	20	☑ Elysées	8ᵉ	26
Bistrot Paul Bert	11ᵉ	20	Entredgeu	17ᵉ	21
Bocconi	8ᵉ	22	Epi d'Or	1ᵉʳ	21
Boulangerie	20ᵉ	20	Erawan	15ᵉ	20
Bourguignon du Marais	4ᵉ	22	Fables de La Fontaine	7ᵉ	21
Braisière	17ᵉ	24	Fins Gourmets	7ᵉ	21
Buisson Ardent	5ᵉ	20	Finzi	8ᵉ	20
Café Le Petit Pont	5ᵉ	24	Florimond	7ᵉ	24
Café Moderne	2ᵉ	22	Fogón	6ᵉ	20
Caffè Minotti	7ᵉ	23	Garnier	8ᵉ	22
Camille	3ᵉ	20	Gavroche	2ᵉ	21
Carpaccio	8ᵉ	22	Gaya	7ᵉ	22
Casa Bini	6ᵉ	20	Georgette	9ᵉ	20
Casa Olympe	9ᵉ	23	☑ Gérard Besson	1ᵉʳ	25
Caveau du Palais	1ᵉʳ	21	Giulio Rebellato	16ᵉ	20
Cave de l'Os à Moëlle	15ᵉ	20	Gourmand	6ᵉ	23
Cave Gourmande	19ᵉ	24	Graindorge	17ᵉ	22
Caves Pétrissans	17ᵉ	21	Grand Venise	15ᵉ	22
☑ Caviar Kaspia	8ᵉ	26	Hangar	3ᵉ	20
Cazaudehore		20	I Golosi	9ᵉ	20
St-Germain-Laye			Il Cortile	1ᵉʳ	21
Céladon	2ᵉ	24	Ilot Vache	4ᵉ	21
144 Petrossian	7ᵉ	22	☑ Isami	4ᵉ	27
Cerisaie	14ᵉ	24	Jardin	8ᵉ	22
Chamarré	7ᵉ	24	Jardin des Cygnes	8ᵉ	20
Chaumière en l'Ile	4ᵉ	22	Jean-Paul Hévin	1ᵉʳ	24
Chen Soleil d'Est	15ᵉ	24	Je Thé . . . Me	15ᵉ	22
Chez Catherine	8ᵉ	23	Joséphine/Dumonet	6ᵉ	23
Chez L'Ami Jean	7ᵉ	22	Kim Anh	15ᵉ	21
Chez la Vieille	1ᵉʳ	22	Lao Siam	19ᵉ	23
Chez Marcel	6ᵉ	21	☑ Lapérouse	6ᵉ	21
Chez Pauline	1ᵉʳ	21	Les Saveurs de Flora	8ᵉ	22
Chez Ramulaud	11ᵉ	22	Luna	8ᵉ	24

SPECIAL FEATURES

Bistrot de l'Etoile Laur.	16e	19	Jules Verne	7e	23
Bistrot du Sommelier	8e	20	Kinugawa	multi. loc.	25
Blue Elephant	11e	19	Lapérouse	6e	21
Bristol	8e	27	Lasserre	8e	27
Buddha Bar	8e	16	Laurent	8e	24
Camélia	Bougival	–	Les Saveurs de Flora	8e	22
Carré des Feuillants	1er	25	Magnolias	Perreux	22
Cartes Postales	1er	19	Maharajah	5e	16
Casa Tina	16e	12	Mansouria	11e	19
Céladon	2e	24	Marée	8e	25
144 Petrossian	7e	22	Mavrommatis	5e	22
Chamarré	7e	24	Maxan	8e	–
Chen Soleil d'Est	15e	24	Meurice	1er	26
NEW Chez Cécile	8e	–	Michel Rostang	17e	27
Chez L'Ami Jean	7e	22	Mont Liban	17e	–
Chez Marianne	4e	18	Montparnasse 25	14e	24
Chez Michel	10e	23	Muses	9e	–
Chez Vincent	19e	22	Noura	16e	18
Chiberta	8e	23	O à la Bouche	14e	17
Chieng Mai	5e	17	Olivades	7e	22
Cinq	8e	28	Orient-Extrême	6e	20
Clovis	8e	19	Ormes	7e	24
Coco de Mer	5e	22	Os à Moëlle	15e	23
Coin des Gourmets	5e	16	NEW Ozu	16e	–
Comte de Gascogne	Boulogne	25	Paris	6e	19
Copenhague	8e	20	Passy Mandarin	16e	16
Cristal Room	16e	19	Pavillon/Gr. Cascade	16e	22
Cuisine	7e	21	Pavillon Ledoyen	8e	26
D'Chez Eux	7e	22	Petit Colombier	17e	17
Dominique Bouchet	8e	24	Petit Marguery	13e	22
Elysées	8e	26	Pierre Gagnaire	8e	28
Epicure 108	17e	–	Planet Hollywood	8e	7
Espadon	1er	25	Potager du Roy	Versailles	22
NEW Ferrandaise	6e	–	Pré Catelan	16e	26
Filo Delle Stagioni	3e	–	Pur'Grill	2e	25
Fogón	6e	20	Relais d'Auteuil	16e	26
Fouquet's	8e	17	Relais Louis XIII	6e	25
NEW Gazzetta	12e	–	Réminet	5e	25
Gérard Besson	1er	25	Romantica	Clichy	21
Gourmand	6e	23	Salon d'Hélène	6e	25
Graindorge	17e	22	NEW San	3e	–
Grand Colbert	2e	18	Sawadee	15e	18
Grand Véfour	1er	27	16 Haussmann	9e	21
Guy Savoy	17e	28	Senderens	8e	–
Hélène Darroze	6e	23	NEW Sensing	6e	–
Hiramatsu	16e	27	Sologne	12e	–
Inagiku	5e	–	NEW Spring	9e	–
Jacques Cagna	6e	26	Stella Maris	8e	25
Jardin	8e	22	Stéphane Gaborieau	16e	–
Jean	9e	19	Table d'Anvers	9e	21
Je Thé . . . Me	15e	22	NEW Table de Babette	16e	–

SPECIAL FEATURES

☑ Table de Joël Robuchon | 16^e	26
Table du Baltimore | 16^e	–
☑ Table du Lancaster | 8^e	25
☑ Taillevent | 8^e	28
Taïra | 17^e	23
Tang | 16^e	17
Tante Louise | 8^e	22
Tante Marguerite | 7^e	21
Terrasse Mirabeau | 16^e	–
Thierry Burlot | 15^e	24
Tire-Bouchon | 15^e	18
☑ Trois Marches | **Versailles**	26
Troquet | 15^e	23
Truffe Noire | **Neuilly**	20
Truffière | 5^e	24
Villaret | 11^e	23
Violon d'Ingres | 7^e	24
Wally Le Saharien | 9^e	18
W Restaurant | 8^e	–
Zéphyr | 20^e	–

TEEN APPEAL

Absinthe | 1er	19
Alcazar | 6^e	17
Al Dar | **multi. loc.**	22
Altitude 95 | 7^e	16
Anahï | 3^e	22
Anahuacalli | 5^e	21
☑ Angelina | 1er	20
Annapurna | 8^e	19
Apollo | 14^e	14
Appart' | 8^e	15
Arbuci | 6^e	15
As du Fallafel | 4^e	24
Asian | 8^e	16
Aub. du Clou | 9^e	13
Autobus Imperial | 1er	–
☑ Avant Goût | 13^e	25
Avenue | 8^e	18
Bar des Théâtres | 8^e	13
Baron Rouge | 12^e	19
Barrio Latino | 12^e	11
Bartolo | 6^e	18
Bascou | 3^e	22
Berkeley | 8^e	12
BIOArt | 13^e	–
Bistrot à Vins Mélac | 11^e	16
Bistrot Baracane | 4^e	23
Bistrot d'André | 15^e	–
Bistrot des Dames | 17^e	15
Bistrot du Peintre | 11^e	16

Blue Elephant | 11^e	19
Bon | 16^e	15
Boulangerie | 20^e	20
Breakfast in America | 5^e	13
☑ Buddha Bar | 8^e	16
Buffalo Grill | **multi. loc.**	9
Café Beaubourg | 4^e	15
Café Burq | 18^e	–
Café Charbon | 11^e	11
Café de la Musique | 19^e	–
Café de la Poste | 4^e	16
Café de l'Esplanade | 7^e	17
Café de l'Industrie | 11^e	13
Café de Mars | 7^e	16
Café du Commerce | 15^e	13
Café du Passage | 11^e	–
Café la Jatte | **Neuilly**	14
Café Lenôtre | 8^e	19
Café Marly | 1er	15
Café Ruc | 1er	14
Café Very/Dame | **multi. loc.**	13
Cailloux | 13^e	16
Carr's | 1er	12
182 Rive Droite | 16^e	12
Chalet des Iles | 16^e	15
Chartier | 9^e	13
Chez Clément | **multi. loc.**	12
Chez L'Ami Jean | 7^e	22
Chez Marianne | 4^e	18
Chez Omar | 3^e	21
Chez Papa | **multi. loc.**	18
Chez Paul | 11^e	20
Chez Prune | 10^e	12
Chez Vong | 1er	20
China Club | 12^e	16
Clown Bar | 11^e	19
Coco de Mer | 5^e	22
Coffee Parisien | **multi. loc.**	15
Coin des Gourmets | 5^e	16
Comptoir | 1er	16
Contre-Allée | 14^e	24
Cosi | 6^e	19
Costes | 1er	17
Coude Fou | 4^e	16
☑ Coupole | 14^e	18
Crêperie de Josselin | 14^e	21
Curieux Spaghetti Bar | 4^e	–
Delicabar | 7^e	15
Délices d'Aphrodite | 5^e	18
Dix Vins | 15^e	16
Durand Dupont | **Neuilly**	9

Emporio Armani | 6^e	18
Enoteca | 4^e	22
Entoto | 13^e	-
Entracte | 18^e	-
Erawan | 15^e	20
Etoile | 16^e	18
Ferme | 1er	-
Fish La Boissonnerie | 6^e	21
Fogón | 6^e	20
☑ Fontaine de Mars | 7^e	21
Fontaines | 5^e	18
Fous d'en Face | 4^e	18
Fumoir | 1er	15
Gamin de Paris | 4^e	18
☑ Georges | 4^e	18
Gli Angeli | 3^e	19
Grande Armée | 16^e	12
Grille St-Germain | 6^e	17
Hangar | 3^e	20
Hippopotamus | **multi. loc.**	10
Ile | **Issy-les-Moul.**	16
Indiana Café | **multi. loc.**	8
☑ Isami | 4^e	27
Joe Allen | 1er	14
Jumeaux | 11^e	-
Kiosque | 16^e	14
Kong | 1er	14
Lao Siam | 19^e	23
Léon/Bruxelles | **multi. loc.**	15
Lina's | **multi. loc.**	15
Loir dans la Théière | 4^e	18
Lô Sushi | 8^e	14
Ma Bourgogne | 4^e	17
Mandala Ray | 8^e	15
Mauzac | 5^e	-
Mavrommatis | 5^e	22
Mirama | 5^e	16
Murat | 16^e	15
Natacha | 14^e	21
No Stress Café | 9^e	-
Ostéria | 4^e	24
Paradis du Fruit | 5^e	13
Paradis Thai | 13^e	18
Petite Sirène/Copen. | 9^e	20
Pied de Cochon | 1er	18
Planet Hollywood | 8^e	7
Polidor | 6^e	15
Press Café | 2^e	-
Quai Ouest | **St-Cloud**	17
404 | 3^e	21
Refectoire | 11^e	-

Rendez-vous/Chauff. | 18^e	-
Renoma Café | 8^e	-
River Café | **Issy-les-Moul.**	15
Rubis | 1er	17
NEW San | 3^e	-
Sardegna a Tavola | 12^e	22
Sauvignon | 7^e	15
16 Haussmann | 9^e	21
Sept Quinze | 15^e	18
Spicy | 8^e	15
Spoon, Food & Wine | 8^e	23
Square Trousseau | 12^e	18
Tav. de Maître Kanter | 1er	10
Télégraphe | 7^e	20
Thiou/Petit Thiou | 7^e	18
Tricotin | 13^e	-
Trumilou | 4^e	19
Vagenende | 6^e	15
Vaudeville | 2^e	17
Viaduc Café | 12^e	12
Vinea Café | 12^e	-
Virgin Café | 8^e	9
Water Bar Colette | 1er	13
Wok Cooking | 11^e	-
Yen | 6^e	19
Zébra Square | 16^e	12
Zéphyr | 20^e	-
Zo | 8^e	15

THEME RESTAURANTS

Aub. Nicolas Flamel | 3^e	20
Bar à Huîtres | **multi. loc.**	18
Barrio Latino | 12^e	11
Bel Canto | **multi. loc.**	15
Bellota-Bellota | 7^e	19
Bistrot d'André | 15^e	-
Breakfast in America | 5^e	13
☑ Buddha Bar | 8^e	16
Café de la Musique | 19^e	-
Chez Clément | **multi. loc.**	12
Coco de Mer | 5^e	22
Léon/Bruxelles | **multi. loc.**	15
Lina's | **multi. loc.**	15
Monsieur Lapin | 14^e	20
Nos Ancêtres/Gaulois | 4^e	10
Paradis du Fruit | 5^e	13
Planet Hollywood | 8^e	7
Pomze | 8^e	19
Rouge St-Honoré | 1er	15
Virgin Café | 8^e	9
Wok Cooking | 11^e	-

SPECIAL FEATURES

SPECIAL FEATURES

Chantairelle	5e	–
Charlot - Roi des Coq.	9e	15
Chaumière en l'Ille	4e	22
Chez Clément	8e	12
Chez Francis	8e	14
Chez Fred	17e	–
Chez Gégène	**Joinville**	–
Chez Léna et Mimile	5e	–
Chez Paul	13e	17
Chez Prune	10e	12
Chien qui Fume	1er	17
Christine	6e	23
Ⓩ Cinq	8e	28
Cloche des Halles	1er	16
Clos des Gourmets	7e	24
Comptoir	1er	16
Copenhague	8e	20
Cosi (Le)	5e	17
Dalloyau	6e	23
Dauphin	1er	23
D'Chez Eux	7e	22
Delicabar	7e	15
Délices de Szechuen	7e	16
Diapason	18e	16
Divellec	7e	23
Duc de Richelieu	12e	–
Durand Dupont	**Neuilly**	9
Emporio Armani	6e	18
Ⓩ Espadon	1er	25
Etoile	16e	18
Fables de La Fontaine	7e	21
NEW First	1er	–
Flora Danica	8e	18
Flore en l'Ile	4e	16
Ⓩ Fontaine de Mars	7e	21
Fontaine Gaillon	2e	19
Fontaines	5e	18
Fouquet's	8e	17
Fous d'en Face	4e	18
Fumoir	1er	15
Ⓩ Georges	4e	18
Gli Angeli	3e	19
Gourmand	6e	23
Grand Café	9e	15
Grande Armée	16e	12
Ⓩ Grand Véfour	1er	27
Guirlande de Julie	3e	–
Il Cortile	1er	21
Ile	**Issy-les-Moul.**	16
Ⓩ Isami	4e	27
Jardins de Bagatelle	16e	17
Ⓩ Jules Verne	7e	23
Khun Akorn	11e	19
Kiosque	16e	14
Kong	1er	14
Ⓩ Ladurée	8e	22
Ⓩ Lapérouse	6e	21
Ⓩ Lasserre	8e	27
Lavinia	1er	17
Legrand Filles et Fils	2e	–
Léon/Bruxelles	**multi. loc.**	15
Maison Blanche	8e	19
Maison de l'Amér. Latine	7e	17
Marc Annibal de Coconnas	4e	17
Marius	16e	20
Market	8e	20
Marty	5e	17
Maupertu	7e	20
Mauzac	5e	–
Mavrommatis	5e	22
Méditerranée	6e	19
Moissonnier	5e	22
Montalembert	7e	17
Moulin de la Galette	18e	–
Muscade	1er	–
NEW Ombres	7e	–
NEW Ozu	16e	–
Papilles	5e	22
Parc aux Cerfs	6e	17
Pasco	7e	–
Paul, Restaurant	1er	19
Ⓩ Pavillon/Gr. Cascade	16e	22
Ⓩ Pavillon Ledoyen	8e	26
Pères et Filles	6e	12
Pershing	8e	15
Petit Bofinger	17e	16
Petit Châtelet	5e	19
Petite Cour	6e	18
Petit Marché	3e	22
Petit Pergolèse	16e	15
Petit Poucet	**Levallois**	16
Petit Zinc	6e	20
Pied de Cochon	1er	18
Pitchi Poï	4e	–
Point Bar	1er	21
Port Alma	16e	20
Pouilly Reuilly	**St-Gervais**	19
Poule au Pot	1er	21
Procope	6e	16
Pure Café	11e	–
Quai	7e	–
Quai Ouest	**St-Cloud**	17

VISITORS ON EXPENSE ACCOUNT

SPECIAL FEATURES

Orangerie | **4e**	–
Orénoc | **17e**	–
Oulette | **12e**	21
⊠ Pavillon Ledoyen | **8e**	26
Petit Colombier | **17e**	17
Pétrus | **17e**	–
Pierre au Palais Royal | **1er**	16
⊠ Pierre Gagnaire | **8e**	28
Pomze | **8e**	19
⊠ Pré Catelan | **16e**	26
⊠ Relais Louis XIII | **6e**	25
Relais Plaza | **8e**	22
Senderens | **8e**	–
⊠ Stella Maris | **8e**	25
Table d'Anvers | **9e**	21
⊠ Table de Joël Robuchon | **16e**	26
⊠ Table du Lancaster | **8e**	25
⊠ Taillevent | **8e**	28
⊠ Taïra | **17e**	23
Tante Marguerite | **7e**	21
Terrasse Mirabeau | **16e**	–
⊠ Tour d'Argent | **5e**	25
⊠ Trois Marches | **Versailles**	26
Trou Gascon | **12e**	24
W Restaurant | **8e**	–

WATERSIDE

BIOArt | **13e**	–
Bons Crus | **1er**	–
Brass. de l'Ile St. Louis | **4e**	16
Buffalo Grill | **13e**	9
Cap Seguin | **Boulogne**	–
Chalet des Iles | **16e**	15
Chez Gégène | **Joinville**	–
Chez Prune | **10e**	12
Guinguette/Neuilly | **Neuilly**	15
Petit Poucet | **Levallois**	16
Quai | **7e**	–
Quai Ouest | **St-Cloud**	17
River Café | **Issy-les-Moul.**	15

WINNING WINE LISTS

⊠ Alain Ducasse | **8e**	28
⊠ Ambassadeurs | **8e**	27
⊠ Ambroisie | **4e**	27
⊠ Atelier de Joël Robuchon | **7e**	27
Bistrot du Sommelier | **8e**	20
Bistrot Paul Bert | **11e**	20
Bouchons/Fr. Cl./Colbert | **multi. loc.**	19
Bourguignon du Marais | **4e**	22

⊠ Bristol | **8e**	27
Café Burq | **18e**	–
Café Lenôtre | **8e**	19
Cagouille | **14e**	21
⊠ Carré des Feuillants | **1er**	25
Cave de l'Os à Moëlle | **15e**	20
Caves Pétrissans | **17e**	21
144 Petrossian | **7e**	22
Chai 33 | **12e**	12
Chapeau Melon | **19e**	–
⊠ Cinq | **8e**	28
Coupe Gorge | **4e**	–
Dessirier | **17e**	21
Divellec | **7e**	23
Drouant | **2e**	–
Ecluse | **multi. loc.**	14
⊠ Elysées | **8e**	26
Enoteca | **4e**	22
Ferme St-Simon | **7e**	22
Fish La Boissonnerie | **6e**	21
Fogón | **6e**	20
⊠ Gérard Besson | **1er**	25
⊠ Grand Véfour | **1er**	27
⊠ Guy Savoy | **17e**	28
⊠ Hélène Darroze | **6e**	23
Il Cortile | **1er**	21
⊠ Jacques Cagna | **6e**	26
Jardin | **8e**	22
Joséphine/Dumonet | **6e**	23
⊠ Jules Verne | **7e**	23
⊠ Lasserre | **8e**	27
Laurent | **8e**	24
Lavinia | **1er**	17
Legrand Filles et Fils | **2e**	–
Macéo | **1er**	21
⊠ Marée | **8e**	25
Maxim's | **8e**	20
⊠ Meurice | **1er**	26
⊠ Michel Rostang | **17e**	27
Montparnasse 25 | **14e**	24
Muses | **9e**	–
Oenothèque | **9e**	–
Oulette | **12e**	21
Paris | **6e**	19
⊠ Pavillon/Gr. Cascade | **16e**	22
⊠ Pavillon Ledoyen | **8e**	26
Petit Marguery | **13e**	22
Pierre au Palais Royal | **1er**	16
⊠ Pierre Gagnaire | **8e**	28
⊠ Relais Louis XIII | **6e**	25
Saudade | **1er**	–

SPECIAL FEATURES

Wine Vintage Chart

This chart, based on our 0 to 30 scale, is designed to help you select wine. The ratings (by **Howard Stravitz,** a law professor at the University of South Carolina) reflect the vintage quality and the wine's readiness to drink. We exclude the 1987, 1991–1993 vintages because they are not that good. A dash indicates the wine is either past its peak or too young to rate.

Whites	86	88	89	90	94	95	96	97	98	99	00	01	02	03	04	05
French:																
Alsace	–	–	26	26	25	24	24	23	26	24	26	27	25	22	24	25
Burgundy	25	–	23	22	–	28	27	24	23	26	25	24	27	23	25	26
Loire Valley	–	–	–	–	–	–	–	–	–	–	24	25	26	23	24	25
Champagne	25	24	26	29	–	26	27	24	23	24	24	22	26	–	–	–
Sauternes	28	29	25	28	–	21	23	25	23	24	24	28	25	26	21	26
California:																
Chardonnay	–	–	–	–	–	–	–	–	–	24	23	26	26	27	28	29
Sauvignon Blanc	–	–	–	–	–	–	–	–	–	–	–	27	28	26	27	26
Austrian:																
Grüner Velt./Riesling	–	–	–	–	–	25	21	28	28	27	22	23	24	26	26	26
German:	–	25	26	27	24	23	26	25	26	23	21	29	27	25	26	26

Reds	86	88	89	90	94	95	96	97	98	99	00	01	02	03	04	05
French:																
Bordeaux	25	23	25	29	22	26	25	23	25	24	29	26	24	25	23	27
Burgundy	–	–	24	26	–	26	27	26	22	27	22	24	27	24	24	25
Rhône	–	26	28	28	24	26	22	24	27	26	27	26	–	25	24	–
Beaujolais	–	–	–	–	–	–	–	–	–	–	24	–	23	27	23	28
California:																
Cab./Merlot	–	–	–	28	29	27	25	28	23	26	22	27	26	25	24	24
Pinot Noir	–	–	–	–	–	–	–	24	23	24	23	27	28	26	23	–
Zinfandel	–	–	–	–	–	–	–	–	–	–	–	25	23	27	22	–
Oregon:																
Pinot Noir	–	–	–	–	–	–	–	–	–	–	–	26	27	24	25	–
Italian:																
Tuscany	–	–	–	25	22	24	20	29	24	27	24	26	20	–	–	–
Piedmont	–	–	27	27	–	23	26	27	26	25	28	27	20	–	–	–
Spanish:																
Rioja	–	–	–	–	26	26	24	25	22	25	24	27	20	24	25	–
Ribera del Duero/Priorat	–	–	–	–	26	26	27	25	24	25	24	27	20	24	26	–
Australian:																
Shiraz/Cab.	–	–	–	–	24	26	23	26	28	24	24	27	27	25	26	–

subscribe to zagat.com

ON THE GO.
IN THE KNOW.

ZAGAT TO GO℠

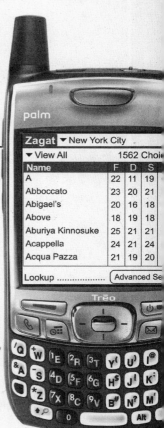

Unlimited access
to Zagat dining &
travel content
in 65 major cities.

Search and browse
by ratings, cuisines,
special features
and Top Lists.

For BlackBerry,® Palm,®
Windows Mobile®
and mobile phones.

Get it now at **mobile.zagat.com**
or text* **ZAGAT** to **78247**